[SOLDIER DEAD]

Soldier Dead

[HOW WE RECOVER, IDENTIFY, BURY,
AND HONOR OUR MILITARY FALLEN]

MICHAEL SLEDGE

COLUMBIA UNIVERSITY PRESS   NEW YORK

Columbia University Press

Publishers Since 1893

New York   Chichester, West Sussex

Copyright © 2005 Michael Sledge

Library of Congress Cataloging-in-Publication Data
Sledge, Michael.
Soldier dead : how we recover, identify, bury, and honor our
military fallen / Michael Sledge.
    p.   cm.
Includes bibliographical references and index.
ISBN 0–231–13514–9 (cloth) — ISBN 0–231–50937–5 (electronic)
1. Military funerals—United States—History. 2. War
casualties—United States—History. 3. Dead—Identification—
History. 4. Repatriation of war dead—United States—
History. 5. Burial—United States—History. I. Title.
U353.S58 2004
355.6'99'0973—dc22   2004055272

Columbia University Press books are printed on permanent and
durable acid-free paper.

Printed in the United States of America

c 10 9 8 7 6 5 4 3 2
Designed by Chang Jae Lee

This book is dedicated to the memory of Col. R. P. Harbold of the U.S. Army Quartermaster Corps, whose efforts in both World War I and World War II helped to ensure that the remains of deceased U.S. servicepersons were treated in a manner befitting their sacrifices, assuring their families that their loved ones had been found, identified, returned, and buried in a manner of which they and our nation can be proud.

Soldier Dead is also dedicated to the men and women of all the military branches who, though they probably are unaware of Colonel Harbold's actions, continue to accord our military fallen the honor, respect, and duty that he would have expected and demanded.

The final dedication is to our servicemen and -women—past, present, and future—who knowingly and willingly risk their lives for the values and safety of our nation-state. They ask to die (if they must) for a good cause if possible, but in any event, only to be remembered.

[*Contents*]

[*Acknowledgments*]

I T   I S   I M P O S S I B L E to list everyone who has rendered aid to me in writing this book, and no matter how long my acknowledgments are, they will be inadequate, for I have received far more assistance than I had ever thought possible.

Among military personnel, Larry Greer, Public Affairs Officer for the Defense POW/Missing Personnel Office (DPMO), took my first phone calls as I began my research and was a continual source of aid. Larry's photo of the remains of Lt. Michael J. Blassie, which graces the cover, is poignant for both its beauty and its representation of the "live, dead and unidentified, and finally identified" process that is detailed extensively in *Soldier Dead*. Doug Howard, Deputy Director of the U.S. Army Mortuary Affairs Center (MAC), provided assistance throughout the research and writing period. David Roath, Director of the U.S. Army Memorial Affairs Activity–Europe (USAMAA–E), dedicated large blocks of his time to me both during and after my trip to his facility. Johnie Webb, Senior Advisor to the Command-ing General, Joint POW/MIA Accounting Command (JPAC), and Col. Paul Bethke, former Commander, U.S. Army Central Identification Laboratory–Hawaii (CILHI), met with me and later kept me informed about current efforts to recover and identify our missing. Dr. Steve Anders, Historian for the U.S. Army Quartermaster Corps, guided me through the voluminous archives in his keep and researched material that called for his expertise.

Among civilians, Peter Maguire, author of *Law and War: An American Story* and *Facing Death in Cambodia*, whom I met during my first trip to the National Archives in College Park, Maryland, contributed valuable in-formation as well as his friendship and support. Mitch Yockelson, Histo-rian at the National Archives, patiently taught me to find my way through the overwhelming amount of material stored under his care. Paul Sledzik, Anthropologist and Curator of the National Museum of Health and Medi-cine at the Armed Forces Institute of Pathology (AFIP), guided me through many of the technical forensic aspects of this book. Andi Wolos is founder of a POW advocacy Web site (www.aiipowmia.com), contributed immensely to my knowledge of how the personnel reporting and recovery apparatus works within the government and military. Her experience and insights have helped me to understand not only what has happened since World War II but also how the past has influenced subsequent events. Terry Buege, whose husband was shot down during the Gulf War, shared her fears and tears with me. She made the World War I and II letters from parents and wives I had read even more heart-rending.

Among those who no longer stand on the same side of the grave as I, James (Jim) Shenton, noted scholar of American history who taught at Columbia University for more than fifty years, recalled his days as an army medic in World War II and recounted details of how he carefully tended to the dead. Jim died on July 25, 2003, before I could arrange a face-to-face meeting, but his words of encouragement have strengthened and live on in the pages of this book.

On the business side, my agent, Laurie Harper, never doubted that this was a powerful story worth the telling and the reading. Her indefatigable efforts to find a publisher who understood *Soldier Dead* reflect the dedication and perseverance of the men and women who always somehow find a way to take care of our fallen, despite seemingly insurmountable obstacles. Also, Peter Dimock and Leslie Kriesel and the staff at Columbia University Press provided invaluable editorial insight and copyediting.

And finally, friends and family were always there when I called upon them. Jim Montgomery and Stella Chapman nurtured me in my formative writing years. My breakfast buddies never once let on if they were tired of me talking about the book. Bobby, Logan, and Jessica, my three children, were always supportive, even when my path led to danger. And, finally, I cannot adequately express my appreciation to Cathy Sledge and Cathy Amy for their extensive editing and reorganizing. To all, I can only say, "Thank you."

[SOLDIER DEAD]

[*Introduction*]

It is the dead who make the longest demands on the living.
—SOPHOCLES, *Antigone*

PRIVATE 1ST CLASS FRED FORY studied the map in his hand, trying to match the contour lines with the terrain in front of him. Once oriented, he and his squad lined up one or two arm's lengths apart and began walking across the grassy field, keeping a careful eye out for trip wires and unexploded ordnance.

Fory had grown up hunting and fishing in Louisiana, and his woods experience proved invaluable in his assignment with the Army Graves Registration Service. His duty, and that of his squad and many other units that were fanned out across South Korea, was to find and retrieve the remains of U.S. servicemen who had given their lives for their country. During three years of fighting the North Koreans and Chinese, thousands had fallen, and many lay in foxholes, in bunkers, in fields, and on mountainsides. Their buddies, hard pressed to save their own lives, had been forced to leave them behind, but they had made a promise to come back someday, find them, identify them, reunite them with their families, and give them a proper burial with all due honors. And while the fallen slept, their bodies returned to the soil.

Looking for a depression in the ground, an elongated patch of grass that grew taller and greener than the rest, old military equipment, or defense fortifications, Fory and the others continued their search. From after-battle reports they knew that the remains of a soldier were somewhere in the 1,000-meter-square grid marked on the map. Eventually, their search line moved over and down three small knolls and, some hundred or so yards farther, came to the base of a cliff. There, against the cliff face, they saw that someone had built a semicircular rock wall that offered a small area of protection. They carefully climbed over the makeshift fort wall and found hundreds of machine gun and M-1 Grand shell casings, and a score or more of grenade pins and handles scattered about. In the middle of this detritus of war, they also found the bones and gear webbing of a solitary U.S. soldier.

Fory and his men knew that a furious battle had taken place at the rock fortification. In front of the rough-hewn fort and on the facing ground of the knolls lay the remains of more than 300 Chinese soldiers. What they couldn't comprehend, at first, was the large number of spent rounds behind the fort wall: one man didn't carry that much ammunition, and certainly not both a machine gun and a rifle. Adding to the mystery was a weather-beaten rope that hung down from the cliff above and behind the remains.

As they continued to canvass the site, clearing away debris from the American's remains, carefully checking for live grenades or other explosives, the searchers concluded that there had to have been several men fighting from behind the rock wall. But what had prevented the recovery of the sole U.S. serviceman? Were there possibly more remains? They continued their investigation and finally were left with a single, inescapable conclusion: one soldier had stayed behind so the rest could escape to safety up the cliff.

"There wasn't a dry eye in the squad by the time we finished recovering his remains," Fory told me one night in Princeton, Louisiana, the story still fresh in his mind and his emotions resonating in his words forty years later.

When I repeated Fory's story to Capt. Robert Sullivan (U.S. Marines-Ret.), who had served in the Pacific in World War II, he commented that the U.S. troops had probably used that cliff as a launching point for patrols, leaving one or more men in the rock fort to cover a retreat under fire, if necessary. Hearing Sullivan's analysis, I was struck with the similarity to Hemingway's Robert Jordan in *For Whom the Bell Tolls*, who, wounded, stays behind to hold off the enemy while his comrades make their escape, and wondered if this soldier had made the same fateful decision.

I believe I was chosen to do this book. I didn't write it because it would be a good item on a resume, enrich me, or get my face before the public: I already had a great career in another field. Writing these words now, I know that it was no accident that led me to Fory's small trailer house that night ten years ago. I had gone there for a reason entirely unrelated to his military duty, and his telling me the story was completely serendipitous. I did not begin work on this book at that time. Then, seven years after Fory related to me the account of his duty in Korea, and in particular the recovery of the still unnamed hero, I woke in the middle of the night and found myself sitting bolt upright in bed. I had not been dreaming. Rather, my movement had dragged me from my slumber. The room was completely dark, yet before me in my mind's eye was a blazing vision of a single, solitary soldier lying dead in a foxhole. His last moments—like those of how many others before and after him?—must have been filled with more terror, anger, hope, and dread than most people will feel in a lifetime. And, I wondered, what about those who went back to find him? What did they think? What did they feel? Was their search for the missing the exception or the rule? At such moments, when our minds are not bridled by the limits and habits of everyday waking consciousness, a desire and curiosity were planted in me that I knew would change me forever. The next day I began searching for an answer to the question, What happens to members of the Armed Forces when they die?

When I asked my friends what they knew about those killed in service, they paused and said, "Well, you know, I'm not exactly sure—I haven't thought about it." We all had some vague recollection of Dover Air Force Base, a good image of a military funeral—complete with grieving widow accepting a folded flag—and most of us had visited the Tomb of the Unknowns at Arlington. We had some ideas about how the wounded were looked after, but next to nothing about what happens after the accounts in war movies and military history books end. Who, if anybody, looks after the dead?

As I began my search for answers, I realized that I didn't even know what I didn't know. And, not having been in the military, I was faced with learning the language and the structure of an organization I had only read about. In one of my first interviews, with the Director and Deputy Director of Mortuary Affairs in Fort Lee, Virginia, Tom Bourlier and Doug Howard, the Public Affairs Officer who was also present asked if I had some more "specific" questions. I was embarrassed that I didn't know what else to ask, but I felt forces that operated with the strength of the tides motivating my search, and I trusted them to carry me where I needed to go. I was, to a certain extent, like people in times past who had no knowledge of the moon and its gravitational pull, yet observed and rode the rise and fall of the coastal waters. Slowly but steadily, I have discovered what happens to our military fallen, the extraordinary lengths to which we go to care for them—and why we do so—in much the same manner as scientists have learned to apply equations to the sublimely powerful pull between heavenly bodies.

Finally, after trusting that the tide that carried me would lift me up and leave me on a beach that held some measure of understanding, and after bouts of cynicism, doubt, incredulity, frustration, and exhaustion—highlighted by some important discoveries along the way—my view of the men and women in our armed services who live, who die, and who live to serve the dead has been radically altered. Examining the efforts made to retrieve and identify servicepersons who have died fighting for our country and freedoms has given me a new perspective on life. The sacrifices made by those who have given their lives and by those who attempt to bring them home and identify them dwarf such quotidian problems as burned bacon, stock market fluctuations, road construction, and flight delays.

My search has taken me to parts of the world I had not visited before, carried me into the past, and afforded me a glimpse of the future. I have learned that "Soldier Dead" is a phrase that, before World War II, was used to refer collectively to military personnel in all branches who perished while in the Armed Forces.

I have met simply wonderful individuals who opened doors for me without proof of any real experience or credentials beyond a burning desire. I can only imagine that in some little understood manner, their conviction connected with mine and prompted them to take extraordinary steps to help.

I have read of and spoken with those who have risked and will risk their lives to recover the remains of their comrades; those who did and do hold their political careers to be more important than the duties of their office; and those who have fought and continue to fight for the rights of the dead and their families. Finally, I have learned what happens not just to American but also to enemy Soldier Dead.

Sadly, the story is not always so clean and pressed as the guards' uniforms at Arlington. My search has been excruciatingly poignant and painful; at times I have not known whether to rejoice or to cry. At one point I developed a cynical attitude, wondering to what extent our "devotion" to the fallen was merely a societal contrivance—"conspiracy" may be a better word—to guarantee a supply of young men and women who would, in blind loyalty, lay down their lives so we could assure ourselves an ample supply of petrochemicals. At another point, when telling my breakfast buddies how much money our government spent finding, identifying, and returning the remains of servicemen, we commented together—wisely so over cups of coffee—that there had to be an "end" somewhere to the search for the fallen. And in those times when I shared my research and thoughts with friends of a more gentle persuasion, often the mother of a young man or woman, I observed the faraway look that came over the face of a parent envisioning, if for only a moment, the horror of losing a child and, even worse, not even having a body to grieve over and lay to rest.

I was carried into military circles—to the Pentagon, Dover Air Force Base, the U.S. Army Identification Lab in Hawaii, U.S. Army bases in Germany and Baghdad, Iraq. I spoke to people who played active roles in establishing military doctrine and setting policy, those who implemented them, and those who stood guard "on the walls" to preserve our way of life. I learned of the petty politics that could hamper execution of a sacred duty. I came face to face with a knee-jerk defensive stance that I call a "Penrosian attitude," explained in chapter 5, "The Return of the Dead." I spoke with those who volunteered for difficult assignments, knowing that there was no way they could please all of the people all of the time.

And I heard stories from grieving families about how their needs were left unsatisfied and how they longed for some "truth" upon which to base a belief that their missing loved one was actually dead and not languishing in a prison somewhere across the world, believing himself forgotten.

The support from my family was invaluable. Before going to Baghdad at a time when helicopters and planes were being hit by missiles, Humvees blown up, and civilian and military sites targeted by suicide bombers, I had a talk with my two sons and daughter and explained that this was something I had to do and that, even if the worst happened, what else could they wish for me to be doing other than continuing my quest? They were gravely concerned for my safety but offered only support.

At the morgue in Baghdad International Airport, where remains in that part of the country are prepared for the journey home, I spent time with an amazing group of men and women, and not just the mortuary workers. I saw twenty-year-olds troop into barracks and halls, drop their battle gear, and fall instantly asleep, even in the most uncomfortable positions. This is nothing new. We've all seen the training films on the Discovery Channel and The History Channel where enlistees are driven to their physical and mental limits and beyond. But to see these men and women saddle up and go back out into the dark, cold, hostile night *and never complain* is something else again. It bears repeating: they never complain. They may grouse, just blowing off steam, but they get up and get the job done, knowing the dangers.

After my safe return to the States, my children expressed how worried they had been. In response, I said that whatever sacrifice they and I made would be infinitely small in the grand scheme of things, particularly compared to sacrifices involved in military duty—past, present, and future. Iif I didn't come home in a body bag, it was a good day no matter what else might have happened.

The issue of learning and speaking about the dead, especially those killed in military service, is extremely multifaceted. It can be a minefield in which you don't know where to step because the experiences of those involved are so emotional, the grief so palpable, and the desire to assuage grief so strong. Yet, in this world at least, practical considerations must be taken into account, the same as in welfare, medical care, and environmental concerns.

While following press articles about how the return of remains is no longer open to the media, I realized that the main point was being missed. The real debate was not about whether we should be allowed to view the dead upon arrival but about how we, as a nation, note and commemorate the deaths of those killed in military service. When they come back in ones and twos, we are not able to avail ourselves, as a nation, of a funeral in the way that individual families do: we have an unsatisfied need to mourn. Our national commemoration, Memorial Day, has been hijacked, as have other holidays, not only by commercial interests but also by our personal desire for time off and three-day weekends. As have most issues regarding our Soldier Dead, this debate has come up before, although in a somewhat different vein.

Surprisingly, my search for information about American military fallen led me to the subject of enemy dead. Some may believe that the solution to the horns of a dilemma—achieving victory by using force without losing American lives—is to kill by remote control, where the enemy only registers as heat signatures on a display or becomes a set of coordinates punched into a computer at 30,000 feet. But it is here that I feel we need to take the next step. We must answer not only to our own dead but also to those people we kill by whatever means, because the two are ultimately and intimately intertwined.

What happens to those who die in military service is not a subject easily contemplated, much less discussed, for who wants to think of themselves or someone close to them as a disfigured pile of flesh on a cold, metal table, or worse? Yet, at times, this is the result of military duty. My enthusiasm and what I have learned have made many uncomfortable. Restaurant patrons at adjoining tables have stared in horror as I recounted some particularly poignant story or discussed grisly details over dinner, and God only knows what some of my companions thought. Business meetings have been ended somewhat abruptly when conversation turned to my book. But many listeners have borne with me—their wish to learn overcoming their resistance or reluctance—and offered encouragement and assistance.

As I acquired information about the processes and parties involved in the recovery, identification, and return of Soldier Dead and began to understand the motivations of those who choose to work in this field and those who, because of a death, are involuntarily and intimately caught up in the issue, I had to decide how to present this subject to the reader. This decision had three facets: organization, voice, and winnowing.

First, I found that my account was clearest with the chapters organized by topic, and then by timeline within each chapter to show how the subject matter evolved. To present all the topics at once, strictly chronologically, would have been to focus on the wars themselves instead of Soldier Dead issues.

Second, I had to compartmentalize myself and create some space between my thoughts and feelings and the job I was doing, much like the surgeon preparing to penetrate a patient's brain with scalpel, rods, and fingers. Ultimately, this surgeon cannot help envisioning himself or one of his family members on a table, undergoing a similar procedure. Yet he must shift into his professional role to complete the procedure successfully. Only afterward can he drop his mask and relate to the patient and the patient's family. I have had to maintain a duality that is at times maddening, and that has at other times failed. I've striven to keep my observations, feelings, and emotions secondary to those clearly evident in the facts presented and in the voices recorded and documented here.

Lastly, I've had to function as a big funnel through which facts, experiences, complaints, wishes, dreams, and nightmares have been narrowed down to the critical, essential elements. There is so much that I want to say, more than there is space available. In an attempt to take readers through some doors partially opened in the main text that is presented in a more formal manner, I conclude each chapter with an "Author's Notes" section in which I use my own voice. I hope these notes will provide additional insight and help to relate the text material to current events.

Ultimately, this is not the book that many imagined and expected, but it aims to open and improve dialogue among the public, the media, the military, the government, and the United States and hostile forces. Bullets fly both ways, and if there is ever a unifying element among the people of the world, it is the grief experienced over the loss of a son or daughter, husband or wife, father or mother. The deeds and actions of the men and women who have died in service to our country, and those of their comrades who have served the dead, have touched us all, though perhaps we do not acknowledge it or even have any awareness of their efforts. This book presents a story that I have discovered belongs to us all—that of Soldier Dead.

[1. Why It Matters]

If anything is sacred, the human body is sacred. . . .
—WALT WHITMAN, "I Sing the Body Electric"

WHEN THE ENGINES of Mars leave the battlefield, they leave behind vivid reminders of the struggle that took place: scarred land, destroyed and discarded equipment, and the corpses of those who fought and died—millions in the wars of the twentieth century alone.

During the 1900s, more than 600,000 Americans died in military service. If broadcast one portrait per second on TV, they would run for 7 complete days. The number of dead for some other countries is much greater. In World War I, Russia lost 1.7 million men, Germany 1.8 million, Britain almost 1 million, and France 1.4 million. In World War II, the Soviet Union lost 11 million military men and women, Germany 3.2 million, Britain 264,000, and France 213,000.

These numbers are overwhelming. In the best of times, armies are able to claim their dead and bury them in military cemeteries near the battle sites or eventually transport them home to their families. At the other extreme, when fighting surges back and forth across the battlefield and extends for protracted periods, the combatants have no choice but to live among the unburied dead, often keeping such close company with corpses as civilians could never envision, even in their worst nightmares.

As England's King George V stated eloquently in 1922 at Flanders, "We can truly say that the whole circuit of the earth is girdled with the graves of our dead." In simple physical terms, these dead are nothing more than a mixture of commonly found chemicals and minerals, organic and inorganic. Left to decompose, a body soon returns to the soil, leaving little trace of its physical existence. But the body of a slain soldier holds significance beyond its corporeal properties. Men who refuse to jeopardize their safety for inanimate objects willingly do so to retrieve their fallen comrades, and our government, which performs cost-benefit studies on medical care for the living, makes extraordinary efforts to retrieve, identify, and bury the remains of members of its Armed Forces.

Why do we spend enormous resources and even incur additional deaths to recover the bodies of our military fallen? Off-the-shelf explanations that we do so to give bereaved family members closure or that we have a duty to the dead to bury them at home do little justice to the complex issues underlying this process, and even less to those who shoulder the responsibility of carrying it out. To assess why and how we undertake the mission of retrieving soldiers' remains, even while battle continues, it is necessary to consider not only practical reasons but also those that lie at deeper levels.

Forensic Reasons

Morticians use thread to seal the lips of a corpse. Yet, even with sealed lips, the dead can speak, for their bodies bear evidence available to those who know how to read the signs. Military persons do not usually die in their sleep; they die horribly, violently, and their remains provide important information about the nature and circumstances of their end. Hallam, Hockey, and Howarth, in *Beyond the Body: Death and Social Identity*, state: "The knowledge ceded by the dead body may not only explain the death and the final stages of the deceased person's life, it may also contain signs of, and clues to another act."[1] Forensic investigation can reveal if the soldier died from outlawed weapons such as biological or chemical agents, torture, or friendly fire; was executed; or died from malnutrition and/or disease.

During World War II, the Surgeon General, obviously interested in the mechanistic effects of weapons of war on soldiers, said, "the Medical Department is especially interested in ascertaining . . . the type and character of the fatal wound."[2]

The desire for battlefield forensic evidence was conveyed to the soldiers in the field. Sgt. Charles D. Butte (now Lt. Col.-Retired) served with the 603rd Quartermaster Graves Registration Company in Europe. He wrote:

> The Medics first had to ensure the individual was indeed deceased, then determine the type of wound that killed him. We were told, this was important for history in determining the tactics, type of weapons, and armament which were most lethal in battle.[3]

In the aftermath of the war, the American Graves Registration Command sent personnel to "a highly specialized course designed to train identification

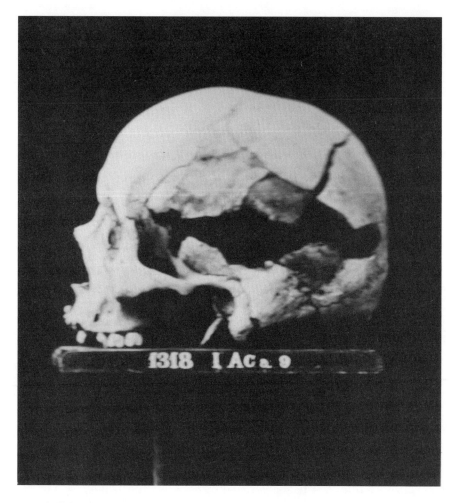

1.1   Skull from a Confederate soldier showing a fatal bullet hole. *Photograph by the Army Medical Museum, Army Medical Museum, Armed Forces Institute of Pathology*

technicians in detecting evidence of criminal violence left behind on skeletal parts." If the Graves Registration workers examined remains that bore such marks, they were to forward them to the War Crimes Commission.[4]

Perhaps the best-known use of forensics during World War II occurred during the investigation of the Malmedy Massacre. On December 17, 1944, during the Battle of the Bulge, the Army's Battery B of the 285th Field Artillery Observation Battalion encountered the German 1st SS Panzer Division at the Baugnez crossroads. The fight was brief and one-sided, and approximately 100 men—the actual number is unknown—of Battery B laid down their rifles and surrendered.

The SS troops herded the Americans into a field and guarded them with armored vehicles and foot soldiers. Stories differ as to what triggered the massacre, but there is no doubt that the GIs were gunned down by automatic weapon and small arms fire. After the initial fusillade, German troopers roamed through the field, shooting or bludgeoning all who showed any signs of life.

A few captives bolted when the shooting started, but most were cut down as they ran. Those who made it to nearby buildings fared little better: the Germans set fire to the shelters and shot the Americans as they fled the flames. The only survivors were those who made it to the woods beyond the field, a few who were shot and feigned death, and two who had not surrendered after the initial firefight.

U.S. leaders suspected before the day was out that the Germans had committed an atrocity, but it was not until almost a month later, on January 13, 1945, that the area was recaptured. The 3060th Quartermaster Graves Registration Service (GRS) Company was given the assignment of recovering, identifying, and processing the remains. The company began on January 14 and finished its initial recovery operation by late January 15. Enemy artillery fire, which had mangled some remains, complicated their efforts, as did heavy snowfall. A platoon from the 291st Engineer Battalion assisted in the search by using mine detectors to locate the metal gear on soldiers buried in the snow. Eventually, over the next four months, twelve more remains were found in the immediate vicinity.

Once the bodies were recovered, they were moved to a railway building several hundred yards from the massacre site. There, they were identified and autopsied to determine the cause of death, in order to rule out the possibility that the soldiers had died from normal combat injuries. The 72 autopsies revealed that at least 20 men had been shot in the head at close range and had associated powder burns, 20 had small-caliber bullet wounds to the head without powder burns, and another 10 had "fatal crushing or blunt trauma injuries, most likely from a German rifle butt."[5]

In a more recent example of the need to recover bodies to determine if the servicepersons were killed in a manner that could have been the result of torture or an execution, the Criminal Investigation Division (CID) of the Armed Forces Institute of Pathology (AFIP) opened an investigation into the deaths of Sgt. George Buggs and PFC Edward Anguiano, both of whom died during the 507th Maintenance Company's ill-fated journey through An

1.2   Remains of World War II U.S. bomber crewmember are examined; bullet hole in head is noted. Reports were that the crew was executed. *Pvt. J. Keen. U.S. Army Signal Corps, National Archives & Records Administration*

Nasiriyah, Iraq, on March 23, 2003, during Operation Iraqi Freedom. The 507th is undoubtedly better known for being Private Jessica Lynch's unit than for two of its members dying in suspicious circumstances.

In an act considered by many to be contrary to Geneva Convention rules for prisoners of war, the bodies of five dead members of the 507th were shown on Iraqi television, and MSNBC reported, "Defense Officials who have viewed the tape [of 507th dead] have said privately that several of the bodies had execution-style gunshot wounds to their heads."[6] Buggs's remains were found at the site of Jessica Lynch's rescue; Anguiano's remains were found nearly a month later near his stripped and abandoned truck.[7]

Other investigations into the attack on and later treatment of members of the 507th led to the determination that Sgt. Donald Walters had been captured alive and "was held separately from his fellow soldiers and killed while in custody." Walters, who was posthumously awarded the Silver Star for gallantry, the POW medal, the Bronze Star, and a Purple Heart, died from two gunshot wounds to the back.[8] (While further war crimes investigation continues, it is interesting to note that it took more than a year for the Army to release the manner of Walters's death, though the forensic results must have been known almost immediately after the autopsy and examination of the site where Walters was held.)

Without a system in place to recover bodies, identify them, and examine them, it is possible that the Malmedy Massacre and any potential mistreatment of U.S. POWs during Operation Iraqi Freedom—and subsequent occupation activity—would have been overlooked during the normal course of battle.

The use of forensic science to provide information about military deaths is important enough to warrant inclusion in the U.S. Code Title 10. Subtitle A—General Military Law, Part II—Personnel, Chapter 75—Deceased Personnel, Subchapter I—Death Investigations, Sec. 1471—Forensic Pathology Investigations. This law authorizes the Armed Forces Medical Examiner and commanders to "conduct a forensic pathology investigation to determine the cause or manner of death of a deceased person."

1.3 U.S. soldier executed during the Korean War. *Sgt. Wyatt. U.S. Army Photo: National Archives & Records Administration*

Health Reasons

Soldiers live and fight in an environment that is not only deadly but also filthy. They go weeks without bathing; bathroom sanitation is accomplished by shoveling feces out of foxholes; food is cold; clean water is often scarce; protection from the weather is scant; and sleep is sketchy—all conditions that are inimical to good health. It is like living in the middle of a garbage dump, and attempting to survive constant enemy attacks. Improving a soldier's fighting conditions cannot be thought of as making the environment healthy and pleasant. Rather, it often simply makes the situation more tolerable. Knowing that battles are often won by the army that stays healthy, or at least is less sick than the enemy, commanders want the dead removed from the battlefield for sanitation purposes. This has been achieved with more or less success, depending in large part upon circumstances peculiar to specific battles.

During World War I, the lines of trenches were relatively static and stretched from Switzerland to the English Channel. Soldiers struggled to survive in unimaginable conditions, severely exacerbated by the presence of

1.4   A U.S. soldier stands duty next to a dead Japanese counterpart. *Cpl. Schwartz. National Archives & Records Administration*

perhaps one million unburied soldiers, friend and foe, in No Man's Land. During artillery barrages, the ground would be churned and the dead would be buried, disinterred, and reburied, with bodies torn to pieces and mixed together as though run through a giant blender.[9]

Given the stationary lines, the inability to retrieve remains, and the ever-growing casualties from the senseless charges directly into withering fire, soldiers lived with the "persistent presence of the dead."[10] A French soldier who fought at Verdun said, "We all had on us the stench of dead bodies. The bread we ate, the stagnant water we drank, everything we touched had a rotten smell, owing to the fact that the earth around us was literally stuffed with corpses."[11]

Morale

To fight effectively, soldiers must have leadership, supplies, and *esprit de corps*. Morale is difficult to measure, yet is an indisputably necessary component in any successful endeavor. It is maintained, in part, by providing soldiers with as many amenities as the situation allows, even if nothing more than hot coffee and a hot meal once every two or three weeks. Morale is one product of the passionate bond that soldiers form with their fellows, a bond rarely experienced in civilian life. Combining the camaraderie of a football team, the dedication to task accomplishment of a dot-com startup workgroup, the sense of separation of a cult, the unit preservation of a police department, and the love of a family will yield a cohesive force that still falls short of the ties that bind military members together.

It is difficult for civilians to understand this connection in which a man's life depends on his buddy and vice versa. Imagine sharing a muddy hole with someone who also has been deprived of sleep, food, and water. Your buddy may be suffering from intestinal diseases, infected feet, and skin ulcers. He is as exhausted as you are. Now imagine going to sleep, entrusting your life to that person, who stays awake to watch for the enemy creeping through the darkness. You could only do that if there were a bond of blood between you. E. B. Sledge, a Marine mortarman who fought in World War II, said, "I reached the state where I would awake abruptly from my semi-sleep, and if the area was lit up, note with confidence my buddy scanning the terrain for any hostile sign."[12]

Considering the horrid conditions of war, one wonders why soldiers stay and fight at all. One reason is that they have pledged themselves to their comrades-in-arms. Johnie Webb, Deputy Director at the U.S. Army Central Identification Laboratory Hawaii (CILHI), said, "When you look at why soldiers fight, it's not necessarily for the nation, but it's for that buddy of theirs that's standing next to them in that fighting position."[13]

Marine Lt. Philip Caputo, author of *A Rumor of War*, said that the sense of brotherhood was the one honorable aspect of a "monstrous" conflict. He described his experience in Vietnam thus: "I have also attempted to describe the intimacy of life in the infantry battalions, where the communion between men is as profound as any between lovers. Actually, it is more so."[14]

Wilfred Owen, serving with the British in World War I, expressed the same sentiment in his poem "Apologia pro Poemate Meo":

> I have made fellowships—
> Untold of happy lovers in old song.
> For love is not the binding of fair lips
> With the soft silk eyes that look and long,
> By Joy, whose ribbons slips,—
> But wound with war's hard wire whose stakes
>   are strong;
> Bound with the bandage of the arm that drips;
> Knit in the webbing of the rifle-thong.

Understanding of the closeness that builds between soldiers from the very first day of training makes clear why they will risk it all to recover the bodies of their comrades, even losing the gamble at times. Caputo said, "Two friends of mine died trying to save the corpses of their men from the battlefield."[15]

Often, recovery proves to be impossible. Sledge described the Verdun-like conditions of the fighting at Half Moon Hill in southern Okinawa during World War II. Half Moon Hill was a ridgeline near the Japanese defense fortifications of Shuri Ridge, and it was littered with Marine and Japanese dead. Since the area was contested and subject to constant enemy fire, it was impossible to remove the bodies. The ground was soaked from rain and the footing treacherous. Sledge said:

> If a Marine slipped and slid down the back slope of the muddy ridge, he was apt to reach the bottom vomiting. I saw more than one man lose his footing and slip and slide all the way to the bottom only to stand up horror-stricken as he watched in disbelief while fat maggots tumbled out of his muddy dungaree pockets, cartridge belt, legging lacings, and the like.[16]

Sledge, like millions of other soldiers who have fought in hellish conditions, could only endure. Yet, even though he was in daily combat, he felt the need to attend to the bodies of his comrades. At night, the Marines would fire star shells and flares, which cast a ghoulish pall over an already ghastly scene. One man in the foxhole would keep watch while the other tried to get whatever little sleep was possible. Sledge wrote about waking during the night and looking across the surreal landscape:

> I imagined Marine dead had risen up and were moving silently about the area. . . . The pattern was always the same. The dead got up slowly out of their waterlogged craters or off the mud and, with stooped shoulders and dragging feet, wandered around aimlessly, their lips moving as though trying to tell me something. . . . They seemed agonized by pain and despair. I felt they were asking me for help. The most horrible thing was that I felt unable to aid them.[17]

When conditions allow and recovery is merely dangerous, instead of suicidal as at Half Moon Hill, soldiers take care of their dead. In the titanic struggle for Iwo Jima, though under constant attack, "In the midst of the battle the Marines buried their dead."[18]

Soldiers have a compelling need to address the concerns of their fallen comrades. If they have to bury them on or near the battlefield, they do so with much care and compassion. Richard Holmes, in *Acts of War: The Behavior of Men in Battle*, described it well: "Proper burial of the dead, accompanied by a degree of formalised mourning, is as necessary for those who die in battle as it is for those who perish in more peaceful circumstances. Having some sort of focus for mourning is useful for the dead soldier's comrades."[19]

While it is doubtful that proper burial is necessary for the dead themselves, abundant evidence demonstrates its importance to the living. The funeral, however simple, helps to dispel the wanton randomness of death in battle, and the performance of even simple rites helps the soldiers make contact with a reality they have left behind and hope to regain.[20] In somewhat more sociologically defined terms, the "unfinished bodies"—the dead for whom bereaved/survivors have not been able to provide customary rites— "haunt the imaginations of survivors . . . family and friends may be dogged by a fear that the dead and decomposing body will return, uninvited."[21]

Soldiers take particular pains to provide whatever dignity they can for their dead. During the World War II fighting in Italy, casualties were sometimes brought down from the mountains on mules and laid out in front of headquarters. One of the dead was Capt. Henry T. Waskow, from Belton, Texas. He was well liked and respected, a valuable combination for an officer, and his death greatly saddened his men. Slowly they filed by his body to pay their respects. One infantryman said, "I sure am sorry, sir." Another said nothing but held Waskow's hand for five minutes; then: "He reached up and gently straightened the points of the captain's shirt collar, and then he sort of rearranged the tattered edges of his uniform around the wound."[22]

Holmes offers several accounts of the care given to burial of fellow soldiers. Lance-Corporal Harold Chapin sent a letter to his wife detailing how they buried two men in May 1915. He described the graves as "level," "rectangular," and "parallel." Another war later, Brigadier Lord Lovat was touched by a burial in a Normandy orchard: "There was a tenderness under the apple trees as powder-grimed officers and men brought in the dead; a tenderness for lost comrades, who had fought together so often and so well, that went beyond reverence and compassion."[23]

James Patrick Shenton, medic in World War II, had the duty of cleaning, dressing, and otherwise preparing remains for transfer out of field hospitals. "We cleaned them, put on new uniforms, and tried to make them look as normal as possible."[24]

1.5   Marines soldier on past the grave of a comrade who died at Iwo Jima. *Pfc. Charlie Jones. National Archives & Records Administration*

1.6   Simple grave side services being held by two soldiers, World War I. *Lt. Wm. Fox, S.C., National Archives & Records Administration*

Because soldiers feel honor bound to take care of the bodies of their bud-dies by recovering, cleaning, restoring some semblance of order to, and then burying them, a corollary is that they do not want the bodies to fall into the hands of the enemy. The duty to care for fallen comrades is not a military tradition that has passed into the annals of history books; it is still very much a force that motivates soldiers today. During the ill-fated raid on General Adid's headquarters in Mogadishu, Somalia on October 3, 1993, U.S. Army Rangers and Delta Force operators became engaged in a fierce firefight in which 18 were killed and more than 70 injured. The mission went wrong early on and took a decided turn for the worst when a Blackhawk helicopter was shot down. A rescue force was sent in after the pilots, with the result that an increasing number of men were pinned down, injured, and killed, resulting in the commitment of even more men. At one point, Specialist Phil Lepre and others dragged the body of Private James Martin into an alley and then took cover in a building. Lepre noticed that Martin's genitals were exposed—because of the heat, few soldiers wore underwear. With bullets striking all around, Lepre ran into the alley and tried to tug Martin's pants up.[25]

After the battle, Marine General William F. Garrison sent a handwritten letter to President Clinton, listing in outline form points about what went

1.7   Marine Colonel Francis I. Fenton prays at the foot of his son's grave on Okinawa. Pfc. Mike Fenton, 19, was killed during a Japanese counterattack on the road to Shuri. *T.Sgt. Glenn A. Fitzgerald. National Archives & Records Administration*

wrong during the raid. Point 10 was: "Rangers on 1st crash site were not pinned down. They could have fought their way out. Our creed would not allow us to leave the body of the pilot pinned in the wreckage."[26]

There are many controversial issues about this battle and General Garrison's letter. Did the soldiers know the pilot of the helicopter was dead or not? Could they have fought their way out had they attempted to do so without trying to rescue/recover the pilot? In discussing morale, bonding, and recovery, these questions are irrelevant; what is important is that the commanding general wrote of a "creed" of not leaving a fellow soldier's body in enemy hands.

This bond among a "Band of Brothers"[27] is not unique to our time or culture, or even to actual events. The strong desire to retain possession of the remains of dead comrades is reflected in classical mythology. In *The Iliad*, Patroclus kills Hector's chariot driver, Cebriones, and the two of them fight over the body "like a couple of lions on the mountain heights, each as

hungry and high-mettled as the other, disputing the dead body of a stag."
In the end, after many men on both sides have died, the Achaeans prevail
and "dragged the noble Cebriones from among the weapons and the yelling
Trojans, and they stripped the armour from his back."[28]

And, later, when Patroclus is killed, Menelaus says:

> Come forward, each of you, without being named.
>   And think it infamy
> that the dogs of Ilium [Troy] should have Patroclus
>   for a toy.[29]

Family

While the soldiers who die have brothers-in-arms who look after them, back
home are brothers and sisters, uncles and aunts, nephews, nieces, cousins,
wives, sons, daughters, fathers, and mothers who may have nothing at all.
It is difficult for families to cope with the death of a loved one in any circumstance; it is more difficult when the death is premature and violent, and
it is most difficult if they have no body to mourn and bury.[30] Soldiers who
die are usually young men in the prime of physical life; they are not octo-
genarians for whom death may be a form of release or awaited transition,
and their deaths, because of how, where, and when they die, present special
problems.

John D. Canine likens the death of a member of society to the action of
a mobile: "When one part of the mobile is moved, all the other parts move
in response." The death creates an imbalance that begs for resolution. One
obvious reason is that the duties previously performed by the dead must be
reassigned among the survivors.[31] However, there are more obscure forces
behind the creation and nature of this imbalance.

When a person is alive, his physical self and his social self proceed on
parallel, if not identical, tracks, and the two are often viewed as one. However, at death the tracks begin to diverge, for the body, if not embalmed, will
rapidly decay. The social status of the deceased, however, tends to remain
with the living for a more extended period of time. Hallam, Hockey, and
Howarth describe this state as "socially alive but biologically dead."[32] This
duality of identity creates a dissonance in the minds of the living, who, in
order to achieve "closure," must recognize and accept that the new physical
status is irreversible; hence, they must establish a new social identity for the
dead that is harmonious with it. To put it another way, thinking of the social

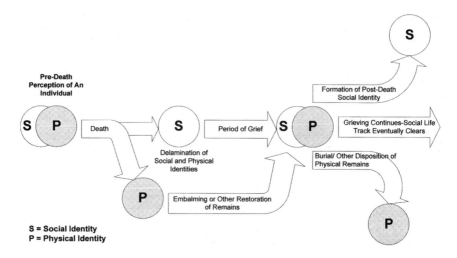

1.8   How social and physical identities are viewed during life, separated upon death, and then temporarily reunited to aid grieving process. *Graphic by Cathy Amy*

and physical selves as occupying the rails of a train track, at death the body is shunted off onto a siding, the grave, while the social self continues to move down the line until it, too, is eventually switched aside. Without this process of resolution, the social self of the dead continues to occupy space on the track that is normally assigned to the living.

Interestingly, the formation of this new social identity is a process that lends itself to considerable interpretation or even outright manipulation. The new identity that survivors create for the dead is not necessarily a fair representation of the former living person. A martyr is remembered for his ultimate sacrifice, not for his misdeeds. A leader is praised for a few notable accomplishments, not condemned for his inefficacy in reaching a broader range of goals. The eulogy of a man who lived a mean-spirited life may contain references to his ability to provide physical sustenance for his children and his dedication as a worker, while leaving unmentioned his constant infidelity, physical abuse of children, and workaholic lifestyle.

Second Lt. Paul Fussell, serving in Europe in World War II, became an unintended casualty of the creation of a postdeath social identity. Fussell had been severely injured by a shell blast that also killed his sergeant, Edward Hudson. After recovering from his wounds, he was reassigned to his unit but found that he was no longer a member of the close-knit fraternity. He later wrote, "I was obviously not welcome. No one was friendly or comical, and I seemed excluded from intimate group conversations. I had become a pariah, and it hurt."

For nearly fifty years Fussell was puzzled by his expulsion, until a friend doing archival research in military records came across a document awarding Hudson a posthumous Silver Star. Hudson had performed admirably, as did the others who served the country during that time, but the award cited him for meritorious actions far beyond the norm that he had not done. The men of Fussell's company had perjured themselves to create this fiction, and they knew that Fussell would have objected and exposed their crime; thus, they sentenced him to exile.[33]

Pericles, speaking to the assembled mourners at a public funeral during the Peloponnesian War, said, "Turning to the sons or brothers of the dead, I see an arduous struggle before you. When a man is gone, all are wont to praise him, and should your merit be ever so transcendent, you will still find it difficult not merely to overtake, but even to approach their renown."[34]

It takes time for the bereaved to form a new social identity for their loved ones and to work through their grief. The formal funeral and burial ceremonies that have evolved attempt to remedy the disjunction between the new physical state and the changing social self and provide the survivors with a process to help them grieve. Jessica Mitford, in *The American Way of Death*, puts forth quite specific criticism of funeral and burial practices in the United States, but formalized funerals do have a place. The Wyoming Funeral Directors Association states that the funeral helps the living by confirming the reality of death, providing an occasion for mourning, giving the community an opportunity to express its respect for the dead, creating a mechanism for the many to share the sorrows of a few, and encouraging the affirmation of faith.[35]

The process of grieving is highly culturally specific, and in the United States there is a general consensus about the steps required to work toward resolution of the death of a loved one. The first is the acceptance of the reality of death. Obviously, the presence of a properly identified set of remains is final proof.[36] J. W. Worden, quoted in *Beyond the Body*, says, "Seeing the body of the deceased helps to bring home the reality and finality of death."[37] For those who have lost family members in military service, the recovery and return of the body confirms the death of their loved one. Sgt. Lemuel Herbert of Scranton, Pennsylvania, was taken prisoner during World War II and, according to witnesses, executed. Based on this information, the Army reclassified his status from missing in action (MIA) to killed in action (KIA). In 1988, a farmer near Kommerscheid, Germany was plowing a field and disinterred Herbert's remains. After recovery and subsequent identification, the remains were buried at Arlington Cemetery. A niece, Mae Miller, said,

"My grandmother was always hoping and praying that he would be found. Even though he was listed as being killed, without his remains we were always hoping."[38]

That Herbert's relatives held out hope of his being alive for decades after he was declared KIA is evidence that, without strong proof of death, families almost never give up believing that maybe their missing and presumed dead soldier is still alive. Herbert's case was resolved, in part, because he had died in Europe during World War II, which the United States and its allies won and after which they occupied much of the territory of the defeated powers. In Korea and Southeast Asia, and even in the Gulf War in Iraq, the United States lost control of most of the land, and this set the stage for much of the conflict that has ensued regarding the status of missing U.S. servicemen.

For some survivors, the performance of rituals provides a sense of peace. The *Times-Journal*, Fort Payne, Alabama, carried a particularly poignant story about a family finding the lost grave of a brother killed in World War II. Charles L. Wooten accompanied his mother and her three sisters to France to pay respects to their brother, Charley Edgar "Tont" Summerfield, whose grave had been located after the family had made repeated inquiries to U.S. government offices. "My mother carried a small amount of soil from their homeplace, the farm where the family lived when Tont went off to war in 1943." Wooten described how they mixed the soil in with the "French turf that held her brother in its eternal grip" and then scooped up some French soil to take back home and mix with the earth covering the graves of his mother and father.[39]

When Creon, King of Thebes, forbade the burial of Polyneices, leaving his corpse to rot upon the battlefield, Antigone, sister to Polyneices, felt so strongly about giving him some semblance of a burial that she risked her life to do so. Her sister was not willing to help perform the sacred task, prompting Antigone to say, "If thus thou speakest, thou wilt have hatred from me, and will justly be subject to the lasting hatred of the dead." While performing a simple ceremony of sprinkling the body with dust and pouring wine three times on its head, Antigone was observed violating the king's decree and was captured and condemned to death. When confronted by Creon, she said, "If I had suffered my mother's son to lie in death an unburied corpse, that would have grieved me; for this, I am not grieved." As in much history and classical literature, Antigone's words about grief ring as true today as they did when written.

Sometimes, the family is prevented from carrying out the wishes of the deceased soldier, which may be for them an essential part of the grieving process. Staff Sgt. Kenneth Hobson II, one of a dozen Americans killed by a terrorist's bomb at the U.S. embassy in Nairobi, Kenya, told his wife, Debbie, that if he were to die, he wanted his ashes scattered off the coast of Big Sur, near where they had met. California law prohibited the spreading of crematorium remains on land or within three miles of shore, so Debbie reluctantly made alternate plans. "Personally, this is a matter of closure," she said. "Granting his wish is how I can bring some peace to my shattered life. Knowing that I cannot do this in a personal way without much red tape and expense is agonizing."[40]

√War, unfortunately, is about breaking things and killing people, and the killing often does terrible damage to bodies. Yet, even in the most violent deaths, some elements of the body often remain. As long as there is credible knowledge of the death of a soldier, and especially if it is accompanied by some sort of physical evidence, be it partial remains or personal effects, funeral rites and burial can still be satisfying to the bereaved family. Body parts, even ashes, can substitute for the complete corpse in fulfilling the role assigned to it in our formal social process regarding death: certification, preparation, eulogy, burial, all of which are designed to give the dead a new social presence.[41] And when remains are nonexistent, cannot be found, or have deteriorated, personal effects can stand in their place and be returned to family members.

Rayford "Scotty" Scott of Oceanside, California was cleaning out his attic with his son, Bryan, when they came across a rubber container that Scott had brought home from the Pacific during World War II. The container held the personal effects of a Japanese lieutenant, Matsubara. Bryan turned the effects over to a fellow teacher and Japanese native, Rie Tsuboi. Tsuboi forwarded the contents to her father in Japan, who, in turn, contacted an agency whose purpose was to find relatives of deceased Japanese soldiers. In time, Scott received a letter from the soldier's family, who expressed gratitude for the return of Matsubara's effects and asked for additional details of his death. The return of his personal items and the opportunity to receive more information about his death gave them closure. They asked for the precise location of Matsubara's burial site, but all Bryan could offer was a map with notations indicating where the battle had occurred.[42]

More recently, families have been reluctantly accepting symbols in place of the bodies of deceased loved ones. For some, the symbol is actually preferable to remains. A. R. Torres, whose husband died in the World Trade Center attack on September 11, 2001, said, "Having something of my husband's is even bigger than having body parts, because it's something you can see when the remains are unviewable."[43]

September 11 has, to a certain degree, brought family members into the fraternity that unites soldiers, firemen, and policemen, all of whom view the physical and social body as one. The body is still the person and is important to the eventual formation of a new social identity for the dead.

✦ Political Reasons

Closure is also important for governments. Complex political reasons motivate the federal government's interest in the return of our Soldier Dead. At a surface level, a soldier's body is the physical representative of a specific former living person and of all members of the Armed Forces. At a symbolic level, a soldier's body is the physical representative, or envoy, of his nation and, as such, embodies its ideology, political beliefs, and culture. Anthropologist Mary Douglas (not to be confused with archaeologist and paleontologist Mary Douglas Leakey) "argued that the human body is the most readily available image of a social system."[44] How a government views the corpses of its soldiers is indicative of how it views its citizens, and how a government views the corpses of its enemies is likewise a reflection of its attitudes toward the enemy's social and cultural system.

Soldiers do not want their dead comrades to fall into the hands of the enemy. Nor does our government, although for different reasons. A country may win a battle or even a war, but if the adversary possesses its soldiers' remains, it is a constant reminder and certain acknowledgment that, at some point, the enemy controlled not only the field of battle but also some of the victor's might.

A perfect example of the power of possession is the footage of dead American soldiers being dragged through the streets of Mogadishu by jeering crowds of Somalians in 1993. While the common military response to the scene was outrage, it is quite likely that most civilians, not experienced or trained in violent affairs, were simply horrified. It is difficult for politicians to make controversial military decisions when the results might create fear and shock among the governed.

More important, though, is that a government desires to keep peace and favor with its citizens, and the days when bodies would remain overseas for years because it was militarily inconvenient to return them are gone. Our efforts to recover and return soldiers who have died indicate that the nation's leaders expend political capital on matters of significance to its people.

Moral Reasons

There is another reason, perhaps the most important one, for the recovery and return of our Soldier Dead. During battle, with all of its grotesque and horrifying aspects, soldiers fight for their lives and for those of their comrades—they do not fight for causes. But it must be remembered that they find themselves in battle conditions because they are serving their country. The cause for which they are sent to fight must be a just and vital one. Recovering the remains of our fallen measures the political and human costs of that cause, creating a ledger against which accounts must be balanced. We must take to heart the words of the soldier, Michael Williams, in Shakespeare's *Henry V*:

> But if the cause be not good, the king
> himself hath a heavy reckoning to make, when all
> those legs and arms and heads, chopped off in
>   a battle,
> shall join together at the latter day and cry all, "We
> died at such a place," some swearing, some crying for
> a surgeon, some upon their wives left poor behind
> them, some upon the debts they owe, some
>   upon their
> children rawly left. I am afeard there are few die well
> that die in a battle; for how can they charitably
>   dispose
> of anything when blood is their argument? Now, if
> these men do not die well, it will be a black matter for
> the king that led them to it. (IV.1.134–145)

Author's Notes

"When I saw the images of the dead Americans, whose charred, lifeless bodies were being dragged through the streets of Fallujah, Iraq, and then hung on a bridge, my mind went back to 1993 [about the mutilations in Somalia]." John Figel's comments, appearing in the April 2, 2004 issue of *USA TODAY*, reminded me again of the usually undetected layering of physical and social identity, for his words, to be grammatically and technically correct, should have been, "When I saw the images of the charred, lifeless *bodies* of the dead Americans. . . ." Figel's thoughts were probably shared by many, with few detecting the subtle yet significant implications of his phrasing.

Any attempt to explain why it is important to expend resources on the dead involves the living, for surely the dead care not, and one of my first challenges in writing this book was to try to understand the "whys" of grief recovery and the importance of actual human remains in that process. Omitting the obvious physical/forensic reasons for recovering the dead, we are left with social and religious issues. Our understanding of the workings of the mind and heart has moved from very primitive to very complex theories and practices to help those in mental anguish find some relief. But, despite an ever-improving lexicon and delineation of issues, humans are not inherently any wiser or smarter than 10,000 years ago, and it is possible that what are generally considered to be advances in some fields may hinder our emotional recovery in times of grief.

Therefore, I found myself reaching back in time to find out what has been done with remains in general, and the remains of servicepersons in particular. Then, I had to try to relate these historical elements to recent events to determine if current policies exist simply because they are the most efficient and/or expedient, or because they result from a realization that there was a better way to handle the dead and, had we known and/or been able, we would have instituted these processes earlier.

It is almost a modified "Which came first, the chicken or the egg?" dilemma. A good example is the current funerary practice of third-party undertaking, which often involves embalming, canned music, and a garden-like cemetery. Has this practice evolved because of consumer demand, or because improvements and the availability of chemicals, refrigeration, and transportation have enabled third parties to "sell" these services, pushing them in the role of supplier?

Clearly, this is a rhetorical question; we can't go back and figure out what would have happened under different circumstances, and the answer is likely not an all-or-nothing proposition. In the interactive and changing relationship among the living, the dead, and the body handlers, there is seldom a one-size-fits-all solution—some families need more "proof" than others; some families have different religious beliefs and burial practices. Studying this relationship, I realized that many of our problems stem from the failure to recognize and acknowledge these differences.

But there does seem to be a universal theme that reverberates through the centuries: humans want to see their dead, if at all possible. Only then is the passing of a loved one real. Only then can we say our good-byes and begin to form a new social consciousness for those who have moved to another sphere of existence, or nonexistence, depending upon one's belief (or lack of belief) in a spiritual afterlife. While Americans have become accustomed to having remains of servicemen killed in action upon which to base an acceptance of the finality of death, other cultures make do with much less physical proof. Andi Wolos, who maintains a POW advocacy Web site, remarked that some of the Vietnamese with whom she had spoken knew their missing father, brother, or husband was dead only because if he were alive, he surely would have returned to their village.

But for someone living in Vietnam, where the fighting took place and which the foreign forces left, it is easy to base an evaluation of life or death on such simple questions. For us, the foreign forces, knowing the status of the missing, especially in the face of evidence of detainment of live and dead U.S. servicepersons, is a problem (covered at length later in this work).

Investigating the ownership of the details of death, I gained a sense of the importance of "ownership" of the bodies of the dead. Different parties at different times exercise power and control over remains, and these parties can and do put their own interests first. I realized that the remains of the dead carry "weight" with the living and that the dead mean different things to different people.

This issue led me to ask, to whom do the dead belong? I found that ownership applied not only to physical remains but also to information about the dead and to their memory. Understanding that there are different types of possession has provided insight into social discourses regarding the dead. Often taking place in a national forum, these discussions assume many shapes, some verbal, many visual. They are ways to acknowledge emotionally that, while you can rebuild a bridge, you can never replace a life.

[2. Combat Recoveries]

Friends . . . if we let the horse-taming Trojans
Drag this body off in triumph to their town,
The best thing that could happen would be
That the black earth should swallow us. . . .
—HOMER, *The Iliad*

A DEATH IS THE END of life for that particular person, but the beginning of a complicated social process founded on a belief system that accords value and allocates resources to the dead. In large part, the dead are of value as long as the living have not been able to perform their accepted and accustomed rites of separation of the social and physical self. These rites help to remove the tension experienced when someone dies. The death of a soldier is of significance on a local level because of the bond among warriors and on a higher, societal level because the soldier represents his or her country. Thus, both soldiers and governmental leaders will want to retrieve the bodies of the fallen. The interest of the family, who are not present to actively conduct retrievals but can only influence policy, must be represented by soldiers in the field who come from families themselves and by political and military leaders who make and enforce policies regarding the dead. American policy, while not unique, has been supported by a large moral authority, often commanding significantly more resources than other countries have been able or willing to devote.

In order to put that policy into effect, the military has devised and instituted recovery systems. These systems, like many technical operations, have slowly evolved from the simple to the complex. Instructions and field manuals, scant or nonexistent at first, have grown to the point where they occupy large paper and data files.

Once in place, recovery operations are constantly evaluated in terms of the application of theory to practice, and appropriate changes are made when necessary. And, since recovery operations initiate and are critical to the identification process, they include very specific and detailed operational and record-keeping procedures. Consequently, after more than 125 years of planning, trial and error, and technical advances, we are now able to recover all but a small percentage of our Soldier Dead, and we have developed scientific methods to the point where we can identify almost all recovered remains.

Definitions

The recovery of military fatalities can be divided into several categories: combat recovery, postcombat recovery, area clearance recovery, historical recovery, and noncombat recovery. These divisions are somewhat broad and there is not always a clear demarcation between one and the next. Also, phrasing differs slightly, with "retrieval" used at times and "recovery" used at other times.

The personnel who carry out recovery operations vary considerably, depending on the nature of the battles fought, their historical time period, and the type of recovery operation conducted. Obviously, noncombat personnel are not the best choice for combat recovery, and recovery operations after cessation of hostilities do not require combat skills; in fact, soldiers trained and experienced in combat often do not possess the specialized skills required for recovery efforts years later. However, personnel experienced in ordnance disposal have often been a vital part of recovery teams regardless of time proximity to combat.

Combat recovery is the most heroic and dangerous of the five categories. It is conducted under fire by those bonded to the dead. To them, the soldier's body is still the soldier they knew; they have not yet disassociated the man from the corpse and feel bound by honor and creed to care for the dead just as they would the living. Recovering bodies under combat conditions poses some of the most challenging questions about American policies, both written and unwritten, because soldiers are often wounded and killed bringing back the dead.

Postcombat recovery is also fraught with danger: unexploded ordnance, booby-trapped bodies, snipers, and the chance that retrieval teams will inadvertently stumble into enemy forces. While combat-experienced troops often assist postcombat recovery, their role is usually limited to bringing the dead to collection points where specially trained personnel assume responsibility.

Area clearance recovery occurs some time after a battle and involves searching for those remains that have not been recovered in previous operations, and may also involve disinterring bodies from temporary gravesites established when it was impossible or impractical to remove them to major cemeteries. Area clearance still poses hazards to recovery teams—primarily from field conditions, live ammunition, and booby traps—even though it usually takes place days, weeks, months, or even years after combat.

Historical recovery currently receives a great deal of attention and, accordingly, receives much support and funding. Teams of specialists, after detailed research, conduct search missions throughout the world, but particularly in Southeast Asia. These teams are composed of highly trained and qualified civilians and service personnel from all branches of the military.

Noncombat recovery occurs when soldiers die in circumstances not involving direct contact with the enemy or threat of attack. Deaths in these noncombat cases still require recovery, as the remains may be in remote locations or otherwise be difficult to extract from the site. Some death incidents are classified as "mass fatalities," and special procedures apply in such cases. Noncombat recovery generally poses less threat to those involved than the other types, but is far from risk free.

These divisions in recovery operations are not as distinct as chapters in a book; they have overlapping boundaries. For the purposes of this study, an overview of all recovery methods and history is provided in this chapter, but a more detailed analysis of area clearance, historical, and noncombat recoveries is reserved for later.

History

Our formal policy of recovering soldiers' remains for a recognized and permanent burial had its earliest origins in the Seminole Indian Wars of Florida in the early 1800s. Then, relatives could have the remains of an officer returned to them if they provided a leaded coffin to a "designated Quartermaster at a port, [and] the Department would have it forwarded free of charge to a quartermaster operating in the field closest to the area of burial." The body would be disinterred and then shipped home to the relative who had made the application for return. But, since the laws provided no funding for the government to pay expenses, the relatives bore all costs. The return of these officers' remains was an exception, as most, and all enlisted men, were buried in the field with few records kept about location.[1]

The next step came during the Mexican-American War of 1846–47. In this conflict, the U.S. Army buried its soldiers where they fell; there was little else they could do. In 1847, Kentucky authorized the return of its dead, at state expense, to a cemetery dedicated to that war.[2] Since more than 13,000 died and only 750—none of whom were identified—were recovered for final burial in an official cemetery, it is apparent that the procedures extant at that time were rudimentary and mostly ineffectual.

As a nation, the United States made its first large-scale efforts to recover, and subsequently identify and bury, military fatalities during the Civil War. Recognizing its obligation to the fallen and their families, the War Department issued General Orders No. 75 on September 11, 1861, that directed the Quartermaster General to supply hospitals with a formal paperwork system designed to keep accurate mortuary records. The General Orders also required that a registered headboard be placed over each grave.

General Orders 75 was a good start, but it was lacking in scope and depth. It did not provide for burial sites or for the disposition of those who died on campaign. In other words, it envisioned a system for the dead inside what is called the Zone of the Interior but did not offer directives for fatalities that occurred in areas of conflict.[3]

Recognizing the shortcomings of these orders, the War Department issued General Orders No. 33 on April 3, 1862. Section II established two precedents: that the primary responsibility for retrieval of combat fatalities rested with the commanders in the field, and that the commanders had the duty to identify and bury the dead:

> In order to secure, as far as possible, the decent interment of those who have fallen, or may fall, in battle, it is made the duty of Commanding Generals to lay off lots of ground in some suitable spot near every battlefield, so soon as it may be in their power, and to cause the remains of those killed to be interred, with headboards to the graves bearing numbers, and when practicable [sic], the names of the persons buried in them. A register of each burial ground will be preserved, in which will be noted the marks corresponding with the headboards.[4]

While General Orders 33 instructed commanders on what to do, it offered little guidance on how to carry out their responsibilities. Short on men and engaged in a protracted struggle, military commanders were reluctant to divert precious resources to noncombat activities. The words "as far as possible," "as it may be in their power," and "when practicable" provided a convenient excuse for those who chose to give recovery, identification, and burial lower priority than winning battles. However, as the war progressed, an excellent example of adhering to both the spirit and letter of General Orders 33 occurred during a battle near Washington, DC.

In July 1864, General Lee's forces threatened to invade Washington. Faced with a shortage of combat troops, Brigadier General Rucker quickly formed a brigade with 1,500 quartermaster employees, placed Captain James Moore in charge, and assigned the newly formed unit to Fort Stevens on the north edge of the city. Once reinforced by this hastily thrown together brigade and other troops, a Union division attacked the Confederates to drive them from positions near the fort. The Confederates retreated without offering fierce resistance, leaving Fort Stevens, and Washington, secure.

General Montgomery C. Meigs selected a site for a battlefield cemetery and ordered Moore to recover the dead and bury them. Moore and his men then not only evacuated all the dead but also were able to identify every one of them. This novel feat was accomplished because several favorable factors converged at just the right time: the quartermaster personnel, trained in logistics and record keeping, were readily available; emphasis was placed on retrieval and burial; the fight was brief and relatively mild—if there is such a thing; and the Union Army controlled the field of battle. Unfortunately, the tactics and procedures used with such success in this engagement were not employed extensively during the Civil War, resulting in scattered graves and relatively scant record keeping.[5]

After the surrender at Appomatox, the Union forces undertook the task of exhuming their dead from burial sites and transferring them to national cemeteries. Recovery parties fanned out across the countryside, searching battlefields, roads, fields, and valleys for the graves of the fallen. From 1866 to 1870, the remains of 299,696 Union soldiers were located and buried in 73 cemeteries. Another 13,575 were buried in cemeteries by military posts or in private plots. As large as these figures seem, they are 26,125 short of the estimate made in 1866 of the total number of remains to be retrieved.[6]

Apparently, the record keeping on unrecovered remains was incorrect, or many soldiers were not found. Either way, despite valiant efforts, the discrepancy illustrates the inadequacies of that era. Yet, even taking into account the number of Soldier Dead not recovered and returned, the over 90 percent success rate in retrieval was a remarkable achievement. And, most important, the moving of the Union dead from far-flung battlefields to national cemeteries established the precedent that would be followed in future wars, even when American casualties lay in foreign soil. The Civil War marked the point at which "public opinion and the armed forces would no longer tolerate the indifference that had heretofore attended the care of the nation's dead in war."[7]

Not long afterward, the United States entered the Spanish-American War and put to good use its experience in searching for and recovering its dead from faraway battlefields. In February 1899, the Quartermaster Burial Corps began to disinter and return the remains of soldiers buried in Cuba and Puerto Rico. By June 30 of that year, 1,222 bodies had been repatriated to the United States. Quartermaster General Marshall I. Ludington spoke words that became a harbinger of U.S. retrieval efforts in major world conflicts only a few years later. He said that the efforts of the Quartermaster Corps in the Spanish-American War were most likely the first attempt of a nation to "disinter the remains of all its soldiers who, in defense of their country, had given up their lives on a foreign shore, and bring them . . . to their native land for return to their relatives and friends or their reinterment in the beautiful cemeteries which have been provided by our Government for its defenders."[8]

After completing its mission in Cuba and Puerto Rico, the Quartermaster Burial Corps moved its operation to the Philippines. At the same time,

2.1   Graves of the 1st U.S. Volunteer Cavalry (Rough Riders) killed during the advance on Santiago, Cuba, 1898. *National Archives & Records Administration*

Major General E. S. Otis, commander of the Pacific Department, ordered Chaplain Charles C. Pierce to "establish and direct the United States Army Morgue and Office of Identification," which performed duties essentially identical to those managed by the Burial Corps. The records speak very clearly of the conflict between the two organizations, with D. H. Rhodes, Chief of the Burial Corps, writing, "*Chaplain Pierce* will never be lost sight of in any work he may be in charge of," and describing Pierce's final report as "indecent in its claims . . . simply bosh." Pierce adopted a defensive stance, including letters from those in influential military positions in his report. Despite the friction between the two units, the system worked. Both made valuable contributions to the recovery effort, and innovations from each became part of official procedures.[9] In this case, competition fostered improvements.

After the Spanish-American War, the Army consolidated several departments into the Quartermaster Corps, establishing a permanent military infrastructure of logistical support for Army operations. The Quartermaster Corps, founded on June 16, 1775, is composed of soldiers who call themselves "logistics warriors." They provide "the right supplies, at the right time and place, in the right quantities." An army does not travel only on its stomach; it must also have weapons and ammunition. Broken equipment must be repaired or replaced. The mail must be delivered. Without solid logistics and support in all these areas, fighting spirit is useless and morale evaporates.

The quartermasters, proficient in handling minutiae, performed the first official recovery duties in the Civil War, assisted in repatriation efforts in the Spanish-American War, and were officially, by General Orders No. 104 issued on August 7, 1917, assigned the duties of the Graves Registration Service (GRS). Henceforth, the Quartermaster Corps could recruit and train personnel exclusively for the purpose of recovering, identifying, and burying the Army's dead.[10]

During World War I, the War Department chose Major (formerly Chaplain) Charles C. Pierce, by then retired, to recruit and train men for the GRS and to oversee its operations in Europe. The service was to perform six duties: field units along the battle lines to identify remains and mark graves immediately after fighting began; establish and maintain all temporary and permanent military cemeteries that would house the American dead; keep a record of burials; assist in identification when dead were relocated from battlefield burial sites to more permanent cemeteries; correspond with the bereaved family and friends; and coordinate mortuary affairs with foreign governments.[11]

In effect, during World War I, the GRS served as the agent carrying out the desires of the people of the United States as expressed in the General Orders issued since the Civil War: to recover, identify, and bury soldiers killed in service. Two precedents were established. First was the "appearance of a theater graves registration service, with its operating units in close support to combat, and a headquarters staff charged with the maintenance of temporary burials and semi-permanent military cemeteries." Second were innovations and improvements to the retrieval process, given the need to clear the battlefield of large numbers of corpses in order to maintain morale: "The survival of wartime political regimes, whether autocratic or democratic, depended upon the will of their respective armies and peoples to endure the ordeal of blood sacrifice. All were equally concerned in removal of the dead from the sight of the living."[12] After fifty years, the desire to take care of our Soldier Dead had produced a system capable of doing so.

Once the armistice was signed to end World War I, the Memorial Division of the Quartermaster Corps assumed the duties of the GRS, with the exception that if war erupted again, it would confine its activities to the continental United States while the GRS, under orders of the theater commander, would operate in areas of combat. Also, the Memorial Division was to maintain a central database of all mortuary records, assist in identification cases that required investigative work, and ensure that grave markers were inscribed with correct information about the deceased.[13] Of course, since the first computers were not developed until World War II, the databases were voluminous card files.

In the period between World War I and World War II, the Army considered various arrangements of personnel and duty assignments for those responsible for handling military dead. Leaders were trying to avoid fighting wars relying solely on tactics developed during a previous conflict, a disastrous mistake committed in World War I. The trouble was, the Quartermaster Corps, like combat units, didn't have a crystal ball foretelling what the next war would be like, and it was not prepared to handle deaths at the start of the next global conflict.

At that time, a military Table of Organization (T/O) described the staffing and equipping of each military unit. It listed how many men and of what rank would comprise the unit. The T/O also listed the hardware assigned to and, finally, the purpose of the unit. T/O 10–297, November 1, 1940, for Graves Registration said, "Functions: Supervision of identification and burial of dead; collection and disposal of personal effects; location and registration of battlefield graves and cemeteries." The T/O made it clear that the GRS unit would be responsible for overseeing specific activities and would not be responsible for embalming, and that non–GRS service units would provide the labor for burials. Also, the GRS was not responsible for the collection of battle dead.[14]

But not all of those in positions of command agreed on the way things should be done. Colonel John T. Harris, director of the Memorial Division of the Quartermaster Corps, stated: "It seems to me that the practical way is to require the troops to dispose of their own dead and then . . . when peace comes, plans and policies can be established and carried out by civilian organizations." He was of the opinion that the troops in the field should handle the identification and burial duties while the quartermasters maintained the central records. He recommended that soldiers' training include instruction in those activities previously performed by the GRS. How he contemplated exhausted troops being able to accomplish tasks previously done by specialized personnel is not clear. Furthermore, he did not envision the extent to which soldiers would be sent into combat with insufficient training in even basic combat tactics, let alone Graves Registration duties. Fortunately, Harris's proposals failed to win approval and the existing system of GRS personnel supervising the handling of the dead was left intact.[15]

It proved to be difficult for men who had just finished a battle to collect the remains of their friends and take them to collection points where GRS personnel picked them up in trucks and delivered them to processing stations and, eventually, temporary graveyards behind the battle lines. The soldiers were generally worn out and had not yet had time to begin to form a new social identity for the fallen. In essence, they were still too emotionally wrought over the loss of their comrades to be closely involved with gathering their bodies. Also, the soldiers in the field did not always perform identification duties adequately.

Recognizing that changes in the retrieval process were needed, the T/O was modified in November 1944 to increase the size of the GRS company from 130 to 265 men, so its personnel could perform all collection and evacuation of the dead. But the theater commanders were not given an increase in manpower with which to enact the new T/O. In other words, a new policy was put in place on paper, but those in command were not allocated the resources needed to carry it out.

Faced with the dilemma of being ordered to recover the dead with non-combat GRS troops, but not being able to free up combat troops to join the GRS units, commanders reached what can only be called a "field compromise." A business line manager, under direction from a staff manager to carry out an impractical policy, will somehow figure out a way to make things work. Combat commanders are the same. Their solution: to form collection teams from members of a combat unit to recover the remains of soldiers from other (not their own) combat units. Thus, experienced combat troops from different units performed duties for each other, all under the supervision of the GRS troops.[16]

During World War II, the GRS faced situations for which it was not prepared. Not only was this a mobile war, unlike World War I, it also was carried out on a global scale. What worked for the GRS in North Africa served as a guide for Italy and Europe, but only that—a model that had to be modified as the situation required. The Pacific Theater conditions were far different from those a hemisphere away. In fact, the activities of the GRS in World War II can be summed up in one word: improvisation. Lessons about the recovery of war dead were learned as the war progressed and changes were continually instituted.

The Korean War erupted in 1950 and the United States, as usual, was not prepared. The North Koreans overran the south, except for a small perimeter at Pusan. From there, the United States and its United Nations allies staged

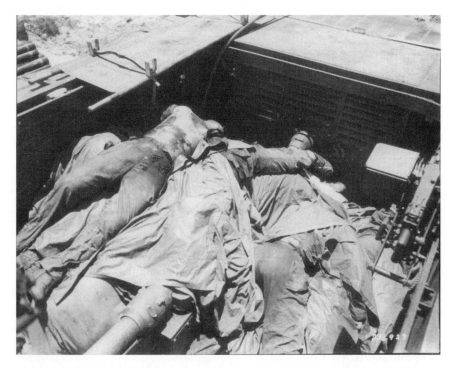

2.2   American dead piled up in a buffalo transport vehicle on Manus Island near New Guinea, World War II. *Joel Horowitz, National Archives & Records Administration*

a breakout, eventually pushing the North Koreans north of the 38th parallel, almost to the border with China. Then the Chinese threw their masses into the war, and they and North Korea forced their way back to the 38th parallel. This seesaw battle, in which territory often changed hands, prompted the United States to rethink its policy for recovering the dead.

At the beginning of the war, only one platoon of Graves Registration personnel, considerably less than 100 men, was in place. This platoon consisted of men who had been processing the usual noncombat fatalities among a large group of soldiers, and most had no combat experience. Hard pressed, GRS personnel recovered UN dead and buried them in temporary cemeteries assigned to each combat division. When the North Koreans overran the UN positions, these cemeteries fell into enemy hands, were recaptured, then were lost again. As a result, many of the temporary divisional cemeteries were evacuated—the dead exhumed for reburial at a safer location—with

2.3   Bodies of U.S. Marines, British Royal Marines, U.S. soldiers, and Republic of Korea troops are gathered for a mass burial at Koto-Ri. *Sgt. F. C. Karr, National Archives & Records Administration*

the enemy only hours away. Another tragic result of the loss and regaining of territory and the evacuations was that some dead were buried and reburied several times.

In response to the demands of the battlefield, and perhaps because it now had the capability, the United States adopted a policy that exists to this day, Concurrent Return. Generally speaking, after Christmas 1950, the day exhumations began at the Inchon cemetery, American dead were recovered from where they had been killed and taken directly to Japan. There, the bodies were embalmed and held pending disposition requests from next of kin. This procedure is still the first choice for removing dead from the battlefield.

After the Korean War, the United States mounted a sweep of accessible areas in an attempt to find the thousands of missing. It is a truth of war that control of territory translates into power, and the North Koreans, flexing their muscle, refused to allow Graves Registration personnel entry into their territory for many years.[17]

However, even with the Concurrent Return policy, the dead still had to be collected and transported to centralized sites from which to be evacuated to Japan. As it had done in World War II, the GRS set up collection points near combat units and then evacuated remains farther south. The Korean War saw the introduction of refrigerated railroad cars. The "reefers" were iced so that remains would arrive at their destination "in the best possible condition." The use of refrigeration during transportation was so successful—remains start decomposing within a very short time, especially in hot weather conditions—that the reefers were kept near airfields even after air transportation replaced the railways for remains movement.[18]

The next test of Graves Registration came in Vietnam. In this undeclared war, the United States attempted to use its military to attain limited political goals in a situation where control of land was ephemeral, the enemy was hard to differentiate from the general population, and there was no popular consensus that the war was justified. U.S. military leaders experienced the same dilemma, and frustration, as General MacArthur had in Korea—the fight was not to be to the finish, but was merely to contain the aggressors. Indeed, it could be said that the attempt was doomed to fail.

By the time of the Vietnam War, the acronym for Graves Registration Services (GRS) had been changed to GRREG, but its duties were essentially the same as in Korea, with one exception: remains, once embalmed, were sent home to the continental United States (CONUS, in military shorthand) for further preparation before being transported to the location requested by the next of kin.

In this war, as in Korea, recovery operations were somewhat compromised. Unless bodies were retrieved immediately, there was no assurance that they would ever be because control of the land in the traditional sense did not exist. If a serviceperson, alive or dead, fell into enemy hands, they had little chance of being returned because there was no front line that would eventually advance to encompass the area where they were held. They remained captive until North Vietnam decided to part with them.

In the mid- to late 1990s, the United States was able to reach an agreement with the leaders of North Korea and Vietnam to allow teams to search for the remains of its servicemen. These arrangements did not come easily and were—and still are—subject to postponement and cancellation. The difficulty in recovering the dead of these two wars is directly attributable to both the conditions under which the wars were fought and the achievement of peace by negotiation rather than by total surrender of the enemy.

Since Vietnam, the United States has found itself employing its military principally as a police force. Grenada, Panama, and the Persian Gulf are exceptions. The Gulf War and the Iraq War required the largest deployment of troops and equipment since the Vietnam War, but casualties were relatively low. In an attempt to learn from the past, the Quartermaster Corps reviewed plans made by the GRS in North Africa in World War II for guidance on how to prepare for the Gulf War.[19]

But, after repeated experiences of lack of attention to Graves Registration in peacetime leaving the system ill prepared for the next conflict, Tommy D. Bourlier, Deputy Director, Graves Registration Center, said in the September 1988 issue of the *Quartermaster Professional Bulletin*:

> Historically, Graves Registration (GRREG) is a field that has changed very little. Doctrine is much the same as during Vietnam, the Korean Conflict, and World War II. Little change has taken place because there has been little interest in graves registration during periods of peace. GRREG has been a box put on the shelf until needed [and] then taken down, dusted off, and expected to still work and fit whatever situation facing us.[20]

There are several different groups that are responsible for the recovery, identification, and return of those who die while on active duty. While it appears that their jobs overlap considerably, with the possibility of conflict, they work together quite well.

Fort Lee, Virginia is the home of the Army's U.S. Quartermaster Corps, and it trains personnel in Mortuary Affairs. While the other armed service branches have, to some degree, personnel who look after soldiers who die, the Army's forces are usually primarily responsible for the recovery of remains.

Mortuary Affairs is, essentially, the renamed Graves Registration section, and herein lies an interesting story. Prior to World War II, when there was relatively little focus on military combat casualties, there was an attempt to rename the Graves Registration Service "Mortuary Service." One reason given for the proposed change was that "mortuary service" better described the full spectrum of duties performed, while "graves registration service" described only one of the functions carried out by the quartermasters. This change was rejected, because of the expense of paperwork revision and the interests of morale. Lieutenant Colonel Harry M. Andrews, of the Memorial Division, wrote:

> It is the opinion of this office that to the public mind, the word "grave" is far less repugnant—if not [less] gruesome than the word "mortuary" and that if the designation "Graves Registration Service" is changed to "Mortuary Service" the personnel comprising same would be less favorably referred [to] in soldier parlance, and, for this reason, this office does not concur in the recommendation for the change of designation.[21]

Obviously, the eventual renaming from "graves" to "mortuary" in 1991 reflected both the Army's continuing desire to correctly label the activities of this division and the change in public usage and acceptance of terms. Of course, it is also quite possible that those in decision-making positions were only mirroring the greater societal use of euphemisms instead of previously well-understood and succinct phrasing. Jessica Mitford gives many examples of this movement:

Casket Coach	not	Hearse
Display Area	not	Casket Room
Interment Space		not Grave
Opening Interment Space	not	Digging Grave
Closing Interment Space	not	Filling Up Grave[22]

Euphemisms for negative events and objects have become almost comically commonplace. Wayward bombs cause "collateral damage." Civilians killed are "caught up in the action." Body bags are "human remains pouches."

Troops killed by their own comrades die from "friendly fire." In any event, Mortuary Affairs currently provides excellent training for the soldiers who enlist to perform the task of caring for U.S. men and women killed in military service.

The history of the efforts to recover our Soldier Dead contains stories of heroism, political machinations, confrontations, and, finally, cooperation. A more detailed look at the different recovery methods provides insight into how we approach this challenging task.

Combat Recovery

The need for recovery under combat conditions raises the troubling question of whether it is reasonable and appropriate to expose soldiers to danger for the purpose of collecting the dead. There is no easy answer because the subject changes shape depending upon what lens is used to examine it. Viewed from a political perspective, where decisions may be made at a high level to prevent foreign governments from obtaining bargaining chips, it involves the moral issue of sacrificing live men for dead and the risk of losing even more remains to enemy control. Viewed at the level of the military service unit, it involves the dilemma of a creed calling for action of a dangerous nature when there is little to be gained militarily. And on a personal level, there are two viewpoints: that of the family of the serviceperson to be recovered and that of the families of those doing the recovery.

It is a given that soldiers want to recover their fallen comrades. At the time of death, they are not thinking of identification and further handling—temporary burial or concurrent return. All they want is to bring the bodies of their friends to a safe place, and these efforts entail large risks. When Patroclus was killed in the battle for Troy, a fierce fight erupted over his body. King Menelaus, a Greek leader attempting to retrieve Patroclus's body, said, "We must do our best without him [Achilles] and see how we can manage both to bring the corpse away and save our own lives from these yelling Trojans."[23]

Admittedly, *The Iliad* is classical mythology, yet it reflects contemporary reality. Unless discretion prevails, the contested body can become a "tar baby" that requires more resources committed to retrieval, resulting in more casualties, requiring additional retrieval efforts, resulting in more casualties, in a deadly, ever-escalating cycle of death. On October 8, 1963, Air Force Captain Dean A. Wadsworth and his South Vietnamese crewman crashed as they were completing a bombing run some fifty miles southwest of Da

Nang. Another pilot on the same mission reported that Wadsworth's plane had crashed and exploded. Two Marine helicopters were dispatched on a search-and-rescue mission, only to disappear. The next day, two companies of South Vietnamese soldiers were airlifted to the general area of the crash sites and were fired upon by enemy troops. During this double rescue, three Marine crewmen were wounded and a South Vietnamese soldier killed.

As more aircraft and soldiers became involved in the recovery of the re-coverers, another fifteen men died. While there may have been some belief that Wadsworth was still alive—the crash from low altitude and the resulting explosion would have been good evidence of his death—it can be concluded that the rescuers/recoverers had been drawn into a fight because they desired to retrieve Wadsworth's remains. In all, twenty-eight men gave their lives in the futile attempt to rescue/retrieve Wadsworth and his crewman, and the bodies of two other men were never recovered.[24] Wadsworth's case is strik-ingly similar to that of Patroclus: "Over the dead man, meanwhile, those oth-ers with their pointed spears were locked in an unending struggle and killing one another."[25]

During World War I, GRS personnel repeatedly exposed themselves to enemy fire while retrieving the bodies of the dead, and their dedicated ef-forts did not go unnoticed. General Pershing, Commander-in-Chief, A.E.F., praised them:

> I have heard with great pleasure of the excellent work and fine conduct of the members of the Advance Group #1, Graves Registration Service, who are mentioned herein. The work performed by these men under heavy shellfire and gas on April 20, 1918, and the days immediately suc-ceeding, at Mandres and vicinity, is best described herein:
>
> On April 20, Lieut. McCormick and his group arrived at Mandres and began their work under heavy shell-fire and gas, and although troops were in dug-outs, these men immediately went to the cemetery and in order to preserve records and locations, repaired and erected new crosses as fast as the old ones were blown down. They also com-pleted the extension of the cemetery, this work occupying a period of one and a half hours, during which time shells were falling continu-ally and they were subject to mustard gas. They gathered many bod-ies which had first been in the hands of the Germans, and were later retaken by American counter-attacks. Identification was especially dif-ficult, all papers and tags having been removed and most of the bodies being in a terrible condition and past recognition. The Lieutenant in

command particularly mentioned Sergeant Keating and Private Larue and Murphy as having been responsible for the most gruesome part of the work of identification, regardless of the danger attendant upon their work. This group of men was in charge of everything at Mandres from the time the bodies were brought in, until they were interred and marked with crosses and proper name plates were attached.[26]

Nor were the actions at Mandres an isolated example of heroism. Charles J. Wynne, 2nd Lt. Inf. U.S.A., wrote a letter recommending giving the Distinguished Service Medal to members of a unit of the 304-Graves Registration Service for their actions in the Chateau-Thiery area. The men, "under shell fire," labored to recover, identify, and bury dead soldiers, some of whom had "been decaying for a period of two and three weeks, where the stench and rotten condition of the bodies made the work such that Burial parties feared and neglected to search these bodies even shortly after death for identification." The GRS men found it "necessary to gather various parts and limbs of bodies together before burial."[27]

Combat recovery is usually performed by experienced troops at the front, who are the best qualified to evaluate risks. These soldiers, though knowledgeable, are not immune from harm while retrieving bodies. Riley Tidwell, a private serving in Italy, was pushed to the ground during shelling by Captain Waskow, who was fatally wounded while doing so. Tidwell "laid the body along the trail on the ridge," thinking that it would be brought down the mountain on a mule later that night or the next day. After three nights, Tidwell was so fearful that his commander would be left behind when the regiment moved out that he took a mule up the trail himself to recover the remains. While performing this act of individual courage to bring back the body of a much-beloved officer, Tidwell was wounded by shrapnel, but his injuries did not deter him from his mission.[28]

A more recent example of the price paid by the living to bring back the dead is that of Kevin Crowe. Harvey Sullivan, a member of the U.S. Army's 101st Airborne Division, was reviewing The Virtual Wall[29] and found a remembrance posted by the niece of a deceased Vietnam veteran, Kevin Crowe. Sullivan sent an e-mail to Crowe's family in which he described the circumstances of his death, helpful information since they had not been informed of any details.

Sullivan described the days of fighting that he and Crowe had survived and how their units had taken heavy casualties. In one battle, two men were killed, one of whom had just been brought in by helicopter as a replacement

2.4   The body of a U.S. soldier is carried down a mountain on the back of a mule, World War II. *National Archives & Records Administration*

and was so new no one had learned his name. Sullivan, Crowe, and the others were forced to retreat, leaving one man behind. The next day an officer instructed Sullivan to set up a machine gun to offer covering fire while he took four men to recover the soldier's body. Sullivan wrote:

> "We never leave anyone behind" was an American policy, but we in the 101st made it a priority. We were told we might die, but we would never be left behind. Most of us agreed with this policy & found it very comforting in theory but in reality once a body is out of sight for any length of time the enemy will use this policy against you. They either booby trap the body, or set up an ambush around the fallen soldier.

Sullivan, knowing the dangers of a recovery effort, questioned the order, the first time he had ever done so. He wanted to attempt recovery in a manner that would minimize risk, but the lieutenant insisted on carrying out the mission as planned. Sullivan wrote: "He basically told me he was going to walk out with 4 men . . . and pick up and carry the body back." He reasoned that the lieutenant had probably raised the same objections to his commander, the company's captain, but to no avail. Despite the obvious danger, they set off on the mission.

When the recovery team bent to pick the body up, there was a large explosion, and Crowe and three others on the six-man team died instantly. One of those killed had, the previous day, enabled the unit to escape by rocketing an enemy bunker. Either the body of the unnamed soldier had been booby-trapped or a bomb placed nearby had been detonated by remote control. Whichever, the results were tragic. As it turned out, the lieutenant in charge of the recovery effort was uninjured. Sullivan and his other men immediately recovered all the bodies without further casualties.[30]

Another combat recovery effort in Vietnam fared somewhat better, but only after major efforts and extended fighting. Robert Black, a Marine decorated with the Silver Star, commanded a rifle company in the Khe Sanh area in the summer of 1968 and was responsible for combat operations and retrieval efforts. The North Vietnamese Army (NVA) had infiltrated hills surrounding the Marines' positions and ambushed a patrol. When the Marines attempted to recover their dead, they ran into a murderous crossfire and incurred more casualties. Also, in a tragic illustration of the difficulties faced by soldiers in handling tasks taken for granted by civilians, a Marine who had gone a little way down a trail to relieve himself was killed.

Black ordered his platoon leader to attempt to recover the body of the Marine who had died answering the call of nature, but told him "not to over-invest troops in the effort." Black's caution made good sense, but people not familiar with battlefield conditions can only vaguely understand the complexities of such a decision. Perhaps one of the most recent examples of the difficulties of balancing life against the value of retrieving the dead is the terrorist attacks in New York City. Immediately and for some time after the collapse of the World Trade Center towers, rescue workers continued to expose themselves to extreme hazards to find the bodies of those entombed in the rubble.

The Marines fought fiercely to retrieve their slain comrades while the NVA used the opportunity to try to kill more Americans. Eventually, after several days of combat, jet strikes, bombing runs by A-6 Intruder planes, strafing and rocketing by helicopter gunships, artillery shelling, smoke screens, and CS tear gas attacks, the regimental commander decided to use artillery barrages to form a "box of steel" to protect the recovery teams. Black wrote: "Within 30 minutes of the first round being fired, all the Marine bodies had been recovered. Later, a Force Recon recovered the body on Hill 881S."[31]

Only those closest to the dead and to the combat situation will make the choice to risk bringing back the bodies of the dead, as it is an intensely personal issue. Commanders higher up the chain of command will undoubtedly express their personal opinions, but only those who lead and participate in such missions should make the final decision.

The duties of the GRS during World War II did not usually include combat recovery, and commanding generals tended to want to maximize fighting forces and personnel in direct support of combat and to minimize nonessential personnel. General Patton said, "Nonkillers must be held to an irreducible minimum in the early echelons."[32] But when casualties were numerous, fighting soldiers at a premium, and time valuable, GRS troops were employed at the front. In particular, the landings in Sicily and Salerno had demonstrated the importance of striking a balance between "tactical and administrative requirements of an amphibious task force during the critical phase of a landing assault." The tendency to focus on fighting elements was tempered by the necessity of removing the dead from the sight of successive waves of reinforcements.[33]

After the Allies struck at the "soft underbelly" of Germany through Italy, planning began for the Normandy invasion. In view of the experiences at Sicily and Salerno, the commanders believed that the number of lives lost on the beaches of France would dwarf those killed in earlier campaigns. Also, they expected to encounter new and unexpected circumstances. Therefore, they had little confidence in predicting how proposed procedures would work.

Sergeant Elbert E. Legg, squad leader of the 603rd Quartermaster Corps, noted that the scheduled deployment time for his GRS unit was D-Day +3 and felt that three days would be "too long for mass casualties to go unprocessed on the battlefield." Since no one in his unit was parachute qualified, Legg volunteered to go in with the glider units that would deliver fighters to the front during the battle. Gliders were dangerous, even when landing in clear fields during training operations. Add inexperienced tow pilots, enemy fire, and landing fields strewn with obstacles, and the result was that many men died even before exiting the planes. Lt. Ronald A. Milton, a member of

Legg's company who later made it to Normandy, said in the 603rd *Company History*, "We cleaned out some crashed gliders. It was a mess."[34]

When Legg's glider landed, the tail section containing two officers broke away and a landing strut ripped through the main compartment, barely missing tearing off the legs of several men. Legg immediately proceeded to the assembly point and found that many men injured in landings were being carried in, including a pilot who had had both feet dragged off. Legg wrote, "I realized this was a high risk business I had gotten myself into."[35]

In the midst of fighting in nearby hedgerows, Legg selected a field to use as a temporary cemetery and began preparations for burial and record keeping. He didn't have long to wait. "As I examined the site, two jeeps with trailers loaded with bodies drove in and were directed to the corner of the field where the other bodies lay." The drivers had delivered the bodies, but they had no intention of touching them. Legg said:

> I sized up the situation and decided the time had come for me to be and to act like, the graves registration representative that I was. For the first time in my life I touched a dead man. I grabbed the leg of one of the bodies and rolled it off onto the ground. As I struggled, the drivers gave in and assisted me with the remainder of the bodies.[36]

Legg's account is an excellent example of the difficulties faced by Grave Registration. First, he was a sergeant who made a decision to put his life at risk in a novel situation, going beyond the duties he had been ordered to carry out. Also, his comment that this was the first time he had touched a body vividly illustrates one of the difficulties in training men to handle corpses: providing experience. Those in Graves Registration units had to learn on the job. Legg's actions while landing in a glider in an active combat area straddled the duties of combat and postcombat recovery, demonstrating that the difference between the two is often minor.

Postcombat Recovery

The soldiers who conduct postcombat recovery operations face difficulties almost as hazardous as those in combat recovery. In wars before the twentieth century, truces were often declared so both sides could venture out to the battlefield and tend to the dead and wounded. These truces were touchy affairs, given that the cessation of hostilities was somewhat informally arranged; there were no synchronization of watches and no guarantees that an overeager soldier wouldn't take advantage of the situation to pick off a few litter bearers.

Daniel Chisholm, fighting at Cold Harbor during the Civil War, wrote: "We sit on the works and let our legs dangle over on the front and watch the Johnnies carry off their dead comrades in silence, but in a great hurry."[37] Unfortunately, by the time Generals Grant and Lee had arranged the truce at Cold Harbor—delayed two days by communication difficulties—it was too late. Grant said, "In the meantime, all but two of the wounded had died."[38]

Calling a truce was difficult enough during the Civil War, and it is even more so now. The practice has largely been discontinued. Battles of this century employ large-scale mobility on an around-the-clock basis, a military tactic that results in the rapid mixing of friendly and enemy troops in a manner often ill defined, in which the side with the upper hand has little desire to call for a pause.

In World War II, some battles raged for days and weeks, waxing and waning; covered large expanses of ground; and mixed friendly and enemy forces in a hodgepodge. These conditions made the delineation between combat and postcombat recovery very fine, if not nonexistent. Joseph James Shomon, commanding officer of the 611th Quartermaster Graves Registration Company, wrote: "Our own lines were very indefinite. My men had to find the lines themselves. They would move in one direction, searching for bodies, until a machine gun or sniper opened fire; then they would make a hurried retreat and mark the danger zone on their maps."[39]

While there has always been a blurring between combat and postcombat recovery, during World War II there was at least a theoretically clear distinction, largely because the fighting proceeded in a methodical fashion of obtaining control over territory. Postcombat recovery actually consisted of two phases. The first was removal of the dead from where they had fallen to collection points, and the second was moving them from the collection points to areas where the next steps of disposition took place. Combat troops normally performed the first action while Graves Registration troops took responsibility for the second, and therein lay a dilemma. The general view was that it was demoralizing for soldiers to search through a battlefield and either bury or transport their dead friends to the collection points.[40] However, there were often not enough GRS troops to accomplish this and then transfer the bodies to processing areas. This problem resulted in procedures that varied depending upon the location, combat conditions, and personnel involved.

Sergeant Charles D. Butte was a member of the 603rd Quartermaster Graves Registration Company, a unit that served in Normandy from D-Day until after hostilities ceased. Afterward, he prepared a review of his experiences, in which he wrote: "The combat units were responsible for policing their area and evacuating the deceased through Battalion and Regimental Areas to the Division Collection Point." Sgt. Butte knew the rules and where responsibility lay, but he was challenged by Assistant Division Quartermaster Major John D. McLaughlin, who ordered him to go pick men up from the battlefield. Butte refused, informing the major that he should use division men to collect the remains and take them to a division collection point. In Butte's polite understatement, "The Major was not pleased to be so instructed."

After only a short time, Major McLaughlin returned to Butte with a representative of the Commanding General, with orders for Butte to do as McLaughlin requested. Butte again explained his duties to the bumptious officers and said that he did not have "sufficient personnel or transportation to do as they ordered." In addition, Butte said that he was returning to company headquarters, where he intended to report the entire incident.

Needless to say, all hell broke loose as word of these events worked its way up the chain of command. Eventually, Major General J. Lawton Collins, who outranked the Commanding General, at 2:00 a.m., "called the Commanding General of the 83rd Division and gave him direct instructions to have his people report to me (then a buck sergeant) to receive proper instructions in Graves Registration responsibilities of units in the field."[41]

Butte, a lowly sergeant who stood up to pressure from the brass, knew when to bend the rules, though. In early December 1944, a tank drove up to his position and a captain emerged from the turret. He asked for help removing the remains of a member of his unit from the inside of a destroyed tank. He explained how difficult it was for his men to handle the corpse, given the condition of the body and that the dead man was "one of the best thought of men in his unit." When Butte began to explain the rules to the tank commander as he had done many times before, Private First Class Wishart volunteered "boldly and affirmatively" to assist with the task. Though he was fired on in the process, Wishart completed his mission.[42]

The quartermaster soldiers serving in Graves Registration found that commanders in the Pacific Theater were hardly better informed than those in Europe. One company's *Unit History* says, "The average unit commander was entirely ignorant of the procedure to be taken in the event that the deceased was within his command."[43]

Knowing that GRS personnel were too few to make battlefield collection a permanent duty and that combat soldiers suffered emotional stress from handling their dead friends, military authorities reached a compromise whereby collection teams would be comprised of soldiers from different units. The personnel skilled and experienced in dangerous field condi-

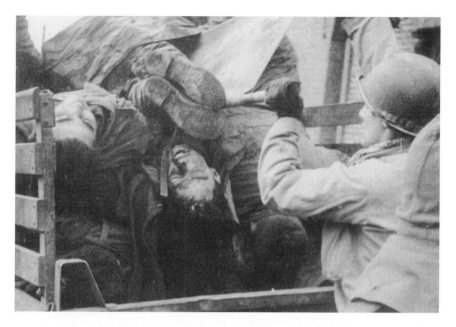

2.5   Bodies of U.S. dead are loaded on a truck at a collection point somewhere in Europe, World War II. *Retired Lt. Col. Charles D. (Bud) Butte*

tions would bring fatalities to collection points, and GRS personnel would then evacuate the dead for further processing.[44] Though this compromise improved collection, arguments calling for Graves Registration personnel to perform *all* such duties persisted until the end of the war.[45]

Once line soldiers moved the bodies of the dead to the collection points, GRS troops transported the bodies from the collection points either to cemeteries or to staging areas behind the front lines. Up to December 1950, remains were buried in temporary military cemeteries. From that time forward, they were taken to strategic locations where they would be processed for return home under the Concurrent Return Program.

The GRS personnel in World War II who staffed the cemeteries envied those who manned the collection points. In the words of Lieutenant Ronald A. Milton, "The collection points, as usual, were the glamorous and exciting part of the work."[46] To be sure, GRS people found these stations to be dangerous as well. Sgt. Harold F. Westlake, Pfc. George P. Rahrig, Pfc. Kenneth Davis, and Pfc. Clayton C. Allhouse, traveling with the 3rd Armored Division, set up a collection point at Le Sourd, France. After they had had supper, a truck loaded with Germans came down the road and stalled right in front of the collection point. The Germans restarted the motor and left

2.6   U.S. dead being unloaded from a jeep at a presumed collection point, World War II. *U.S. Army Quartermaster Museum*

the way they had come. Soon, a German motorcycle "passed up and down the road."

The next morning, Westlake, Rahrig, Davis, and Allhouse loaded their truck with casualties and retraced their route from the day before. They ran into Germans in a town that had previously been held by the Americans and were captured. When a German colonel questioned Westlake about the location of American tanks, he explained that his job was to bury the dead and he didn't know where the tanks were deployed. The Germans led the GRS unit to a World War I cemetery and instructed them to bury the dead that they were transporting. Westlake, though, was taken for further interrogation.

Soon after Rahrig, Davis, and Allhouse began digging graves, the Germans decided to move out, taking the GRS men with them. What ensued is almost comedic: the Germans and Americans wandered around, not knowing where the soldiers of either army were. Before the day was over, Rahrig and two Germans went in search of Americans to surrender to.

Westlake, meanwhile, traveled with the Germans farther and farther behind enemy lines. During the day they were strafed by P-47 Thunderbolts and
P-38 Lightning planes, and during the night the French Resistance harassed
them. They rode in a half-track that broke down, then in a truck that also
broke down, and ended up hiking. During one strafing run, Westlake made
his way to a barn, where he hid until after the Germans gave up looking for
him and moved on. Then he eventually returned to his company.[47]

While the collection points may have been centers of excitement in Europe in World War II, temporary cemeteries also saw action. It was not unusual for the GRS personnel to use open graves as ad hoc foxholes when
enemy planes strafed them.[48]

GRS personnel also retrieved the bodies of soldiers who died in Army
field medical units. James Shenton was a medic for the 106th Division, the
unfortunate unit that took the brunt of the German onslaught in the Battle
of the Bulge. The 106th, new to battle, had been thinly deployed, spread out

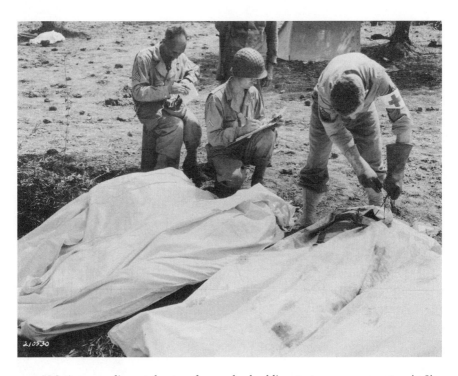

2.7   U.S. Army medics cut dog tags from a dead soldier at a temporary cemetery in Sicily, World War II. *National Archives & Records Administration*

over four times the usual space assigned to a division. Subsequently, when the Germans attacked, casualties were extremely heavy. Shenton's job at that time was to record the date and manner of death and to prepare the bodies for further processing.

Shenton and fellow medics carefully cleaned the remains and dressed them as best as they could, with the exception of their feet: boots were in such short supply that they were removed from corpses and made available for the living. Once the bodies were ready for collection, GRS personnel would pull up trucks to the field hospitals promptly at 2:00 a.m. and remove the dead. Shenton, in recounting how the dead were "spirited away," said of the GRS men, "You know, I never remember seeing any of their faces." While this may seem like something out of *The Body Snatchers*, with mysterious soldiers carrying bodies out on trucks in the darkest hours of the night, it likely was intended to maintain morale by preventing the wounded from having to observe their comrades being loaded up and driven away.[49]

2.8 A chaplain holds services while troops dig graves in Algeria, World War II. *U.S. Army Signal Corps. National Archives & Records Administration*

In the Korean War, land changed hands several times during the seesaw battles, often blurring the distinction between combat and postcombat retrieval. During the Chosin Reservoir "attack in another direction" action, Marine units were under constant assault as they withdrew from the front. A miles-long line of trucks and jeeps, crammed with wounded and dead, with thousands of foot soldiers alongside, wound along a narrow dirt road in the mountains in zero and subzero weather. All the while, the many thousands of Chinese troops who greatly outnumbered them were attacking with artillery, mortar, and small arms fire. Private First Class Doug Michaud observed: "The dead were stacked in trucks like so many cords of wood. When they ran out of truck-bed space, they laid the dead on fenders, across hoods, tied on the barrels of artillery pieces. God, there were a lot of them."[50]

The Korean War brought about two major changes in postcombat recovery. First, when possible, those killed in combat were removed before the battle was over, obviating the need for postcombat recovery. Second, after December 1950, the dead were not brought back to temporary cemeteries but were taken to staging areas and readied for shipment to Japan, in preparation for the eventual return home.

One type of postcombat recovery in Korea deserves special note. Private Robert E. Helman, of the 148th Graves Registration Company, said that the Marines were insistent about recovering their own dead after battle. While other branches expressed reluctance about handling remains, the Marines would go to great lengths to find, recover, and care for their fallen, sending out special "Rolls-Royce" patrols to bring back the dead in a first-class manner.[51]

When non-GRS personnel made recoveries in Korea, it was not unusual for them to ignore or fail to follow good procedures, particularly with regard to identification. But taking and recording critical information as soon after the time of death as possible was so important that GRS members were forbidden to accept bodies at collection points "unless certain essential information was completed." This may have seemed somewhat draconian, but it was necessary to keep the pressure on field units to properly record and preserve identification items and to secure personal effects in a personal effects pouch.[52] This scene—battle-hardened veterans bringing a corpse down from the hills only to face a thin, bespectacled clerk who refused to load the body onto a transport truck until all the paperwork "was in order"—could be scripted for a dark humor skit on *Saturday Night Live*, somewhat similar to the "Bring out your dead!" scene in *Monty Python and the Search for the Holy Grail.*

2.9   A "Rolls-Royce" Marine patrol recovered the remains of a buddy who had been re-ported as missing, Korea. *T.Sgt Frank W. Sewell. National Archives & Records Administration*

During the Vietnam War, the already vague boundary that separated postcombat retrieval from combat retrieval on the one hand and area clear-ances or sweeps on the other became even less distinct, because of the nature of the conflict and the use of the helicopter for transportation. Generally, the fighting was not about land; it was about killing those on the other side. In order to trap enemy troops, Airmobile units were deployed to attack the enemy, often in "hammer-and-anvil" stratagems. An American force would be airlifted to one area and another dropped farther away, from where they would attempt to drive the NVA up against the first force. During battle, the dead and wounded were ferried out, and once the engagement was over, the remaining forces would be flown back to base.

David Ross, medic for the 1st Infantry, was passing time in front of a hospital, watching new arrivals have their shot records processed, when "All of a sudden, four choppers came in and they didn't even touch down. They just dumped bags. One of the bags broke open and what came out was hardly recognizable as a human being." Some of the "new guys" threw up, and one "got down and started to pray." Ross said to himself, "Welcome to the war, boys."[53]

It is not exactly clear if the rough handling of remains witnessed by Ross was typical. Robert Rawls, Rifleman with the 1st Cavalry, who served in Tay Ninh from early 1969 to early 1970, observed similar actions. He said, "The way they put them [bodies] on the helicopter really just made me think about it all . . . they just threw them up on the helicopter and put all these empty supplies on top of them."[54] Were the crews of the helicopters Ross and Rawls observed callous, or just under pressure to deliver the bodies so they could continue supplying the living, who were still dependent upon them for water, food, and weapons?

An excellent example of due care given is by Ray Dussault, a "cherry" gunner on a Huey, and the rest of the plane's crew. In early 1967 they ferried soldiers into the field one morning, then returned to take the bodies of some out that afternoon. Once they reached the 93rd Evac Hospital at Long Binh, where Graves Registration was located, medics began to offload the dead. The crew chief, James C. Harton Jr., said, "The first medic reached in, gripped one of the handles on the bags, pulled it out of the aircraft, and let it fall to the ground, three feet below. I couldn't believe it; I was just stunned. I wanted to say something, but I just couldn't seem to get it out." Before the medic grabbed the next body bag, Dussault chambered a round into a rifle and pointed it at the medics. Harton then leveled his M60 machine gun on the medics also. The pilot radioed the Evac air controller that "my crew is going to shoot your medics right now."

The doors of the hospital flew open and people boiled out like ants from an anthill that has been kicked. A doctor managed to calm everybody down and the medics finished unloading the helicopter, now placing the bodies reverently on gurneys, all the while covered by the guns of the crew. While Harton had not been overly fond of Dussault up to that point, they bonded from then on.[55]

Bruce Crandell, helicopter pilot for the 229th Aviation Battalion, was witness to extreme tenderness exhibited by a ground crew. In November 1965, the 1st Battalion, 7th Cavalry became engaged in a ferocious battle with the North Vietnamese Army in the Ia Drang Valley. Crandell and the other helicopter pilots provided an airborne lifeline to the soldiers on the ground. He flew critical supplies of ammunition and water in and returned to base with the dead and wounded. On one return trip, what he saw as his helicopter was unloaded stayed with him more than "any other experience in my two tours in Vietnam":

A huge black enlisted man, clad only in G.I. shorts and boots, hands bigger than dinner plates, reached into my helicopter to pick up one of the dead white soldiers. He had tears streaming down his face and he tenderly cradled that dead soldier to his chest as he walked slowly from the aircraft to the medical station.[56]

Since the Vietnam War, actual battles have been relatively short, a matter of hours or days, and have resulted in many fewer fatalities. However, true to history, there has continued to be a lack of advance preparation for the handling of the dead. Before the Gulf War, most of the Graves Registration units consisted of reserve personnel, and most of those companies were under strength. As Operation Desert Storm readied to begin its sweep across Iraq, Graves Registration had only half the number of troops needed for the two corps stationed in the gulf. As it was, U.S. forces incurred remarkably few deaths and the planning shortcomings did not affect recovery.[57]

One Quartermaster Collection Company is assigned to approximately 179,000 soldiers and can process about 400 remains per day. Its job is to establish collection points from which evacuation is done and to perform limited search and recovery operations.[58] As such, its function is very similar

2.10   Sign at the U.S. Army Morgue in Baghdad, Iraq. *Michael Sledge*

to that of the GRS in World War II, except that instead of being interred for years, slain soldiers are now returned home in days.

There are provisions, though, for larger numbers of deaths than can be safely and logistically evacuated. During the Gulf War, the Quartermaster Corps dug large pits in the sand to be used as temporary burial sites in the event of considerable fatalities. As it turned out, these pits were used as makeshift containment areas for Iraqi prisoners of war.[59]

And, during the Iraq War, collection points moved forward with the Army and Marines traveling north. After the "end of major combat operations," field collection points continued to operate in Al Asad, Baghdad, Balad, and Tikrit. From those locations, remains where flown to Kuwait, which was a Theater Mortuary Evacuation Point (TMEP). There, remains were prepared for the flight home, usually to Dover Air Force Base in Delaware, with a few taken to the United States Army Memorial Affairs Activity in Europe (USAMAA-E).

Effect of Body Handling on Troops

Numerous studies have been conducted on the stress experienced by armed services personnel who handle remains. While it hardly needs to be stated that deployment in combat zones induces stress, Gulf War studies have found that the type of duty determines, to a large degree, the severity of post-traumatic stress disorder (PTSD) experienced. In particular, military personnel who performed grave registration duties had some of the highest rates of PTSD.[60]

Analysis has revealed three psychological components of handling remains: "the gruesomeness," "an emotional link between the viewer and the remains," and "personal threats to the remains handler." It has been suggested that future studies be conducted to determine if soldiers can be "inoculated" by a program of desensitization and taught mental techniques to prevent the formation of "gruesome thoughts." Also, according to some researchers, remains handlers should receive frequent communications from those close to them and continual reassurance that their families are safe.[61]

While the studies conducted on Gulf War veterans admittedly contain important limitations, "there is clear evidence that . . . exposure to grotesque stimuli such as human remains, mutilated bodies, and combat atrocities may result in strikingly high prevalences of psychiatric morbidity and negative psychological outcomes in exposed samples."[62]

2.11   Body of a U.S. soldier found on a hill near Sakayokal, Korea. U.S. dead were often stripped for clothing and boots. *Pfc. Robert McKinney. National Archives & Records Administration*

Author's Notes

"I will never leave a fallen comrade to fall into the hands of the enemy." This quote appears in the U.S. Army Ranger Creed, and while its original intent may have been not to leave a wounded comrade behind, there is no doubt that it has also been taken to mean that a dead comrade shall not be left behind. This statement is a promise by and an obligation of the country to the families of the fallen, and it is also a promise made between soldiers. During an interview at CILHI with Sgt. 1st Cl. Habibah Prevost, in which I asked her about the sacrifices she made in spending time away from her family to bring back the mere bone fragments of the dead, she said, "Yes, it is worth it. If it happened to me, if I were killed out on the battlefield, the guy to my left and to my right, I *know* they would come and get me; I know they would want to."

Lieutenant Colonel Gerald O'Hara of the Joint Task Force-Full Accounting (JTF-FA) phrased it differently: "If it were me, I'd sure as hell want them to bring *my* ass back!" O'Hara's unembellished comment says more that it seems because, obviously, if he were dead, how and why would he care? A pile of decaying human flesh contains much more import than its physical properties.

Yet, risking and losing lives to recover the remains of those who have already died begs critical discussion such as that in Joe Light's article, "Defending 'leave no man behind' policy: Profs examine whether soldiers should risk lives to recover bodies," in the April 5, 2002, online issue of *The Yale Herald*. This article not only lists many of the pros and cons of recovering bodies but also touches, albeit lightly, upon meaningful sociological issues.

During talks I have given to nonmilitary groups about the recovery, identification, return, and burial of Soldier Dead, I have often conducted an exercise to illustrate the many facets of recovery of the dead in situations of risk. Usually, I divided the audience into two groups, telling one to imagine that they had lost a family member in battle and the other that they had a living family member serving in the military. After a brief pause, I asked someone from the "dead soldier" side to ask someone from the "live soldier" side to send their loved one out into danger to recover remains. Immediately, the tension level in the room noticeably rose. Whereas the subject I had been talking about had been somewhat academic up to that point, when it came time to risk lives to recover the dead, matters suddenly became very real and personal and discussion began in earnest.

After a while, it became apparent that the audience had formed four groups, with each of the two original sides having further subdivided. The dead soldier side now had members who wanted a recovery attempted even with extreme risks to the living and members who did not wish to endanger others. The live soldier side also divided, some saying that if their loved one had died, they would want a recovery, and others saying that no dead person was worth someone dying for.

Usually, I just stood aside and let the four groups give and take as much as they liked. The talk often became very emotional and heated. Tears flowed—from anger, from sadness, but mostly from frustration.

Finally, I intervened and explained that I had asked them to consider questions that do not belong in a civilian setting and that can only be considered and answered by those at risk and closely associated with the dead. In essence, I had cheated, giving them a situation and question that they simply could not resolve. However, this exercise served a good purpose in that it immediately introduced the audience to the complexity of the whole subject of the recovery of the dead.

[3. Noncombat Recoveries]

But what of them buried profound,
Buried where we can no more find,
Lie dark for ever under abysmal war?
—WILFRED OWEN,
"As Bronze May Be Much Beautified"

THE UNITED STATES has dedicated enormous resources to the recovery of soldiers' remains during and shortly after battle; however, it is an unfortunate fact of war that often some are not recovered at or near the time of death. The bodies reflect the ravages of weapons and the effects of the passage of time and exposure to nature. Some of the dead lie in shallow individual graves, and many are hidden by brush or entombed in shelled bunkers and foxholes. They may not be found for years or decades, if at all. Then, too, some bodies are inaccessible—deep in the ocean—and some are simply destroyed, forever beyond any meaningful recovery.

In addition, many soldiers die in non–battle related situations. In World War II, out of 400,000 total American deaths, 100,000 were caused by transportation and training accidents, disease, suicide, and other events that also cause civilian deaths. In these cases, as in combat, soldiers die singly and in groups. And, as in combat, they often die violently and/or in locations either unknown or beyond easy access.

The servicepersons who search battlefields and remote areas for the missing do not usually engage the enemy, yet they are soldiers nonetheless. They have a quiet determination and a firm resolve to find those who have made the ultimate sacrifice, and they conduct themselves in a calm, dignified, and reverent manner. While they are usually not subject to danger from human enemies, they grapple with inhospitable geography, insensitive or self-serving political officials, and lack of information and logistical support. For them, the struggle continues long after arms have been laid down.

Sweeps

Area clearance recovery is tedious work, accompanied by mountains of paperwork and minutiae. Strenuous effort on a daily basis over a long period of time is required. While the techniques learned in area clearance in one war can be employed in the next, each conflict has unique circumstances that require different operations. The personnel involved in "sweeps" must be adaptable.

Sweeps, as we know them for the purpose of finding and recovering bodies in order to provide burial in national cemeteries or return to the next of kin, began after the Civil War. In the four-year period from 1866 to 1870, approximately 300,000 Union dead—not Confederate because the "rebels" in death had not at this point achieved the right to equal treatment—were disinterred from the battlefields and environs and reburied in national cemeteries.[1]

At the end of World War I, many of the dead had been buried in temporary cemeteries scattered throughout the war zones, but some were still

3.1   African Americans collecting bones of soldiers killed in the battle of Chancellorsville at Cold Harbor, VA. *John Reekie. Civil War Photographs, 1861–1865/compiled by Hirst D. Milhollen and Donald H. Mugridge, Washington, DC: Library of Congress, 1977, No. 0317*

3.2   Men from Labor Battalion No. 321 form a skirmish line to look for remains along the south bank of the Vesle River, near Bazoches, Seine et Oise, France, World War I. *Sgt. Carnochan. National Archives & Records Administration*

unaccounted for. Fortunately, the number of missing was not terribly large, with the eventual number of unresolved cases at 4,452.[2] The Quartermaster Graves Registration personnel were responsible for searching combat areas for the dead, and a typical mission consisted of a Graves Registration Unit and 100 laborers spread out in a "skirmish line" to comb the battlefield.[3] The men took special care, "examining every shell hole, marking graves and inspecting the very cracks in the ground, to find possible indications of a newly made tomb."[4]

When bodies were found, GRS personnel attempted to acquire as much identification information as possible: even obscure hints such as a "peculiar coin" in a pocket were useful. All of this information was recorded and forwarded to those responsible for identification.[5]

Unfortunately, soldiers' bodies were not always easy to find and recover. World War I artillery fire was so intense that men were "literally blown to atoms . . . smashed, burned, and mutilated," so that recovery was difficult, provided that remains could even be found months and years after battle.[6]

3.3   Unburied remains found along the Vesle River, near Bazoches, Seine et Oise, France. The soldier was unidentified because no papers were found and the tags were corroded by gas and body fluids. *National Archives & Records Administration*

In one example of the dedication of personnel and devotion of resources, the GRS under the command of Major Staton conducted an extensive three-week recovery operation in the forests near Parroy, France. An American officer and thirteen enlisted men had been killed in an underground bunker some seventy feet deep. This bunker was considered impervious to bombs and shells, but a "torpedo" bomb dropped by a German plane drove through the ground to a depth of approximately fifty feet and destroyed the underground shelter, burying its occupants under tons of earth and rubble.

Major Staton, his men, and 12 German prisoners sunk a shaft 30 feet square by 50 feet deep and, because of the soft soil, walled the excavation with logs. They constructed platforms at 5 different levels so that they could dig horizontal tunnels to find and recover all the bodies. In digging the shaft, the men moved more than 1,600 cubic yards of dirt, enough to fill 119 dump trucks. This Herculean effort was accomplished without the help of backhoes or other power equipment. Also, because of the soft terrain, no motor transportation could approach within 2 kilometers of the site.[7] While the German prisoners probably did most of the digging, all of those involved worked strenuously to recover the remains buried inside the bunker.

During World War II, combat fatalities were generally taken to collection points, where they were picked up and transported to temporary military cemeteries. This policy helped to keep down the number of ad hoc cemeteries and individual burials, which are hard to keep track of, and to preserve identification, so long as field personnel followed basic guidelines. However, their training was often inadequate in this regard. Also, the large number of deaths, the geographic location of areas of armed struggle, and the extensive use of airplanes and ships tended to scatter bodies in such a way that simple drop-off and pick-up plans were often not applicable.

Graves Registration was searching for a total of approximately 25,000 servicemen in Europe. They men were either Missing in Action (MIA), Killed in Action (KIA) but not recovered, or buried in isolated graves, "some lying in inaccessible places, some in recorded graves, others in burial places that might be revealed by patient and ingenious inquiry, and still others—the casualties of amphibious assaults and victims of plane crashes—that were often beyond any reasonable expectation of recovery."[8]

Western European search and recovery operations consisted of four teams: a Propaganda Team, an Investigating Team, a Disinterring Team, and an Identification Team. The Propaganda Team distributed bilingual posters throughout the countryside that explained "the methods of search and urged the inhabitants of each community to report any information they might have concerning burial places of American Dead." Newspapers and radio carried details of the missions.

After word of the recovery efforts had been disseminated, an Investigating Team visited with the leaders of each community, inspected records that had been gathered, and conducted interviews with knowledgeable people. Once information was garnered about remote gravesites and/or unburied remains, this team conducted a search, sometimes in a fashion similar to World War I skirmish lines. Unfortunately, the extensive use of land mines delayed many searches, often for years.

The Disinterring Team, composed of an investigator, an assistant who doubled as a truck driver, and laborers drawn from the locality, disinterred the body or recovered it from its surroundings and made identification on the spot if possible. If identity could not be established or was in doubt, the remains were examined carefully by the Investigating Team after being transported to a collection point.

The four teams, Propaganda, Investigating, Disinterring, and Identification, were very interdependent. While recovering remains, of course, was top priority, gathering and preserving identification material was also of paramount importance.[9]

The coordination between those at the recovery/beginning of the process and those at the identification/conclusion is very involved, and time and again untrained personnel immediately associated with handling remains have hampered identification efforts. The television and movie depiction of a soldier pulling the dog tags off a comrade and holding them in a clenched fist, promising to avenge his death, was undoubtedly based on similar ac-

3.4   A member of the Searching Team hangs a poster requesting information on American dead who were buried in the area. *U.S. Army Signal Corps. National Archives & Records Administration*

3.5   Abbe Fauchery leads a member of the Searching Team to the grave of an American unknown buried in the communal cemetery of Tholonet, France. *U.S. Army Signal Corps. National Archives & Records Administration*

tions in the field, but how was the body supposed to be identified later when Graves Registration was preparing it for burial and found the tags missing?

The search missions in liberated Europe were well under way in early 1946, and by May over 24,000 square miles in the Low Countries and almost 38,000 square miles in France—an area greater than Pennsylvania, Delaware, and Maryland combined—had been swept and 1,335 remains recovered. Further work through the summer yielded approximately another 1,000 remains, and it became clear that area sweeps had served their purpose; now "selective search" methods would be better suited to the task.[10]

When information led to a specific search area, the task was often daunting. In August 1946, a mission was launched to recover the crew of a B-17 that had crashed in Holland and sunk to a depth of 25 feet. Efforts to move a large crane to the site were unsuccessful, despite reinforcing several bridges and even building a new one. Eventually, Graves Registration used a smaller piece of equipment and, after dredging for almost 2 weeks, recovered 3 bodies. While some of the crew were still unaccounted for, the partial success was remarkable, given the marshy soil conditions and the presence of unexploded ordnance.[11] To better understand the conditions of the search, it is helpful to recall the 1996 crash of ValuJet Flight 592 in the Florida Everglades, in which 53 of the 110 victims were still unidentified at the time of burial.

The sweep of the Allied-occupied areas of Germany began in January 1946 and, for the most part, ended in Helgoland, a "grim island fortress" strategically located in the North Sea. The British had relocated Helgoland's residents to the German mainland and used the island for bombing practice. At the request of the Americans, the British not only suspended bombing operations but also "offered to put a naval craft at the disposal of the search party." While initial searches failed to make any recoveries, subsequent investigative work followed by fieldwork yielded fourteen remains.[12]

The searches in Soviet-occupied Germany were in marked contrast to those conducted in land controlled by the Allies. Soviet authorities lost no opportunity to hamstring the efforts of Graves Registration. In East Germany, "Notification of new restrictions on clearances and itineraries were repeatedly issued with no obvious purpose other than impeding freedom of movement and discouraging a systematic development of the program."[13] No deviations from submitted itineraries were permitted, meaning that Graves Registration was faced with a chicken-and-egg dilemma: they had to specify to the Soviets exactly where they wanted to search, but they didn't know where to search without interviewing local residents, and they were hampered in their interviewing efforts. Consequently, search and recovery efforts in East Germany continued until 1949, and even then there were unresolved cases begging for investigation.[14]

Soviet fears of American interference in its affairs in East Germany were not entirely baseless. Sergeant Herb Hackett, serving with the 611th Graves Registration Company, reported that some of his company members, while conducting a recovery operation for a downed air crew, hid a young woman and her mother in the cases used to carry remains and spirited them over to the American side of the border.[15] Nevertheless, any such occasional "interference" could hardly have been sufficient grounds for the Soviet obstructions.

Searches of other countries under Soviet control or influence produced varying results. In Czechoslovakia, for example, officials willingly aided the Americans. Romania conducted a public awareness program to inform its people of the U.S. search parties and provided a mortuary railroad car, no small task in a country ravaged by war. Hungary allowed the distribution of circulars, radio broadcasts, and newspaper publication, all for the purpose of aiding U.S. recovery efforts.

However, efforts in the Soviet Zone of Austria were a repeat of the East Germany experience, with impediments and lack of support, and Poland was little better. While U.S. forces worked diligently under greatly constrained conditions and performed an admirable job, they were forced to end their searches without recovering the remains of soldiers believed to be buried or lost somewhere in newly hostile territories.[16]

Search and recovery operations in the European Theater were largely concluded by September 1949, over 4 years after the German surrender on May 7, 1945. By this time, 16,649 remains had been recovered.[17] Many thousands of square miles had been covered by individual soldiers searching on foot, all following the directive that no U.S. troops would be left unaccounted for or forgotten in a foreign land against the wishes of their next of kin. It is difficult to imagine the scene in a home where a mother and father not only suffered the loss of a son but also endured the suspense of waiting for his body to be found. In one case, Oscar M. Buxton died from a heart attack just one month before his son's remains were recovered.[18] Many other parents must have gone to their graves without having the chance to give their child a burial.

The GRS initially encountered resistance from the Communist-governed countries in the Balkans, although Yugoslavia eventually relaxed its stance and offered considerable aid in an attempt "to hasten the termination of the GRS program."[19] The lesson learned from the dealings with intransigent foreign officials was that recovery soon after the time of death obviates the need for later work with possibly unknown and uncooperative political authorities.

The Mediterranean Theater consisted of the islands of Corsica and Sardinia, the Black Sea area, Sicily, and Italy up to the southern borders of Switzerland and Austria. The American Graves Registration Services (AGRS)— formed by the Quartermaster Corps after hostilities ceased, to oversee the activities formerly handled by Theater GRS units—officially created the Mediterranean Zone (MZ) in late December 1945. In a change of recovery methods, Mr. E. C. Mussatti, Chief of the Investigation and Research Branch of the AGRS-MZ, quickly established the policy that "area searching is a thing of the past." Mussatti insisted on reviewing records to determine possible individuals unrecovered in each theater of operation before mounting searches. In other words, "sweeping" the land for the missing was not done in the areas under his control.[20]

Searches for downed airmen in the mountains of Italy led the teams into pristine Alpine snow where four-wheeled vehicles could not travel, so pack animals were used to carry supplies and remains. By early 1948, the GRS had completed most of its search missions, leaving only isolated cases requiring further investigation.[21]

Efforts to recover American dead in the Africa and the Middle East Zone (AMEZ) began in May 1946, when Col. Clarence J. Blake and his two assistants, Capt. Glenn W. Rogers and 1st Lt. James R. Stirling, arrived in Cairo. They faced a daunting task of searching a large area, while having to sort through inadequate documentation, work with poorly trained troops, and contend with severe material shortages. Often the officers "thumbed" rides with other service personnel because they had no dedicated transportation.[22]

Actual searches in the AMEZ did not begin until late 1946. Most missions did not involve a skirmish line search, but instead utilized specialized searches that were launched after investigative work in individual cases. At first, efforts met with little success, and Graves Registration requested permission to "terminate future search operations." However, by March 1947, new information led officials to believe that many more recoveries were possible, and permission to end search operations was denied.[23]

Because of the need to cover large expanses of land, the GRS relied on aircraft. In one instance, there was a report of remains at Shiraz, a mountainous location in Iran, where the nomadic people were "noted for valuing a gun far above a human life." Facing an extended and hazardous journey across the Persian Gulf and then into the mountains, the GRS search team decided to reconnoiter by plane. Once over the site, they found they could land, did so, and eventually—after suffocating work in the dust—found the remains of a single U.S. soldier.[24]

The search and recovery efforts in the AMEZ culminated in an airborne circumnavigation of the African continent that began on August 24, 1946. This mission lasted over 5 weeks, extended 17,000 miles, and recovered 59 remains. Afterward, an additional 9 remains were found in Tunisia. The AGRS operations were closed in early 1948, leaving an estimated 41 remains unrecovered.[25] However, the GRS teams in both the MZ and the AMEZ had successfully located and recovered the remains of more than 3,000 American servicemen.[26]

The Pacific Theater presented a special set of difficulties that required the Graves Registration Service to be organized differently than in Europe. In North Africa and Europe, each separate Army battle group maintained its internal structure during the war, while in the Pacific, each campaign required a regrouping and reorganization of men, equipment, and channels of authority. The European command structure was like a traditional business assigning jobs to a specific division or bringing in existing divisions to work on part of a project, while the Pacific campaigns were analogous to a large company forming a task force for each major project and then disbanding it once the objective was reached. Consequently, there was little central authority over Graves Registration activities and the commander of each area of operations was responsible for locating and burying the dead. GRS personnel completed their duties in one area, then moved on to a different location.

Looking at a globe vividly illustrates the difference in geography between the Pacific and Europe. In addition to the large number of small landmasses spread across vast expanses of water, the climate and vegetation in the Pacific were much different than in Europe. As a result, remains were lost in water, scattered across the islands, and hidden by the tropical forests.

It is also important to keep in mind that the fighting in the Pacific was considerably different from combat in Europe. Much of the former involved denying the enemy the use of certain areas, not necessarily possessing them for military purposes—though of course, some locations were desirable because they could serve as bases from which to launch air strikes against Japan or as staging points for an eventual invasion of the Japanese homeland. Therefore, fighting could rage for a few days, with many casualties, and then most of the troops would pull up stakes and move on, leaving behind the dead, buried and unburied. Also, airmen went down in the vast expanses of water and jungle with few witnesses because of the sparse population. A good example of the haphazard burial of Pacific combat deaths is when the Eighth Army conducted sweep operations after the Battle of Leyte; it found that "there were many dead still unburied and many isolated burials which either had not been reported at all or incorrectly reported."[27]

All of these factors—organizational, geographic, and nature of battle—combined to delay and hinder area sweeps for remains. Finally, in late 1947, the AGRS-Pacific Zone (AGRS-PAZ) and the AGRS-Far East Zone (AGRS-FEZ) were established, and these two organizations performed the duties of Graves Registration in the most efficient manner to date.[28]

Initially, search and recovery operations in the Pacific were not as timely or organized as in Europe. Close to 80,000 servicemen had died in the Pacific during World War II, and approximately 65,000 were buried in almost 200 temporary cemeteries.[29] The rest were missing. After the Japanese surrender in Tokyo Bay, Graves Registration began the arduous process of concentrating the dead into fewer and more accessible cemeteries, pending permanent burial overseas or return home. Search and recovery operations were conducted in some zones while concentration was in process, and searches for the missing in some areas did not begin until most of the disinterring and centralization of known burials had been accomplished.[30]

The searchers put themselves at risk in boats that were not seaworthy, were swept into the sea while swimming to reach inaccessible areas, hacked their way through jungles with machetes, and scaled steep cliffs to reach remains. While searching Japan, at times they found only the ashes of the dead—unidentified and mixed with remains of soldiers of other nationalities.[31]

And as if physical hazards weren't enough, the GRS was hampered by problems originating from home. In a display of shortsighted politics, congressional inquiries "necessitated special searches," often based on "vague and inaccurate" information, that drained resources from other missions

3.6   World War II Graves Registration troops caught by the high tide at Holz Bay on Attu. *Robert Vorisek*

that were well founded. Consequently, it was recommended that search and recovery efforts "result only from directions issued through War Department channels."[32] Unfortunately, the interjection of politics into the recovery of the dead is a recurring theme in all wars.

In the Pacific Zone, search and recovery efforts began almost two years after the end of the war with Japan; the first team finally set out from Hawaii in July 1947. The lengthy delay had its roots in the same disorganization that was responsible for the "extremely muddled and fragmentary state of records pertaining to missing servicemen."[33] This mission, which combed the Marshall-Gilbert Islands, the Solomon Islands, the New Hebrides Islands, and the Loyalty and Caroline islands, revealed the weaknesses in planning and the difficulties in searching the land and water in the search area.

On June 10, 1948, the second recovery "cruise" launched from Hawaii. Using lessons learned from the first cruise, GRS personnel successfully recovered remains throughout the New Hebrides Islands, New Zealand, Australia, the Bismarck Archipelago, Guadalcanal, and the Gilbert and Ellice islands, with a final stop in the Marshall Islands. The entire search, lasting until March 1949, recovered 109 remains.[34]

Meanwhile, the searchers in China encountered a unique problem in sweep and recovery missions: the possibility that Americans were still alive in remote areas. A "ragged and almost incoherent" Chinese farmer relayed rumors to Graves Registration that American airmen were being held captive by the Lolos, a supposedly "barbarous" tribe in western China. The case was aptly named the "Lolo Case," or simply, "The Case."

Lt. Col. H. W. Wurtzler led a mission to determine if the rumors were true and, if so, to rescue the airmen. The search team encountered considerable difficulties entering the Lolo country: provincial authorities were divided by conflicting loyalties in the civil war, and Chinese support troops either refused to set foot in the area or greatly overstated the dangers when they did so. Eventually, two members of the search team posed as traders, crossed into the forbidden zone, and found that the Lolos were "quite friendly and co-operative." As it turned out, the tribe hated only the Chinese. A lengthy and extensive investigation dispelled the rumors of living Americans being held; in fact, the records do not indicate that any Americans, alive or dead, were found.[35]

By the end of 1949, Graves Registration had ceased most search and recovery missions in the Pacific and on the Asian mainland. Future historical searches were conducted decades later, but only on a case-by-case basis.

By the end of 1950, Graves Registration had ceased all active searches for World War II dead, but it began to struggle once again with a lack of resources, inadequate training, and hostile environments as the United States became involved in the Korean War. This was different from previous conflicts because it was fought in a limited manner, without the goal of unconditional surrender and control of enemy territory. During the Korean War, the United States instituted the policy of sending home the bodies of its slain soldiers as soon as possible. This was the first such action undertaken by any nation and "a departure from the long established practice of leaving remains in battlefield cemeteries or isolated locations until after the cessation of hostilities."[36]

The armistice ending the fighting on the Korean Peninsula called for the combatants to cooperate so that each side could search for and remove their dead from areas under the other's control. In practice, partly or mostly because of mutual suspicion, the opposing forces agreed to exchange the dead in Operation Glory.[37] In what turned out to be the *only* transfer of remains for decades, from July through August 1954, the United Nations delivered 13,528 remains to North Korea and received 4,023 of its missing.[38]

The United States had begun search and recovery missions in South Korea during the war and continued them into 1956.[39] These were conducted in three phases: Phase I was GRS investigation of specific leads; Phase II

3.7 A truck bearing remains repatriated from North Korea during Operation Glory drives under a welcoming sign. *Billy Maloney*

3.8   Bodies of ten American soldiers found by Korean natives and brought to the UN military cemetery in the Pyongyang area. *Pfc. Jacquet. National Archives & Records Administration*

involved detailed searches of former battle sites; and Phase III consisted of area clearances using skirmish lines, "not looking for any particular remains but for anything that [might] be there."[40]

A particularly dangerous aspect of area clearance was that unexploded ordnance lay everywhere. Private Fred Fory, whose story begins this book, encountered live mortar rounds, grenades, and booby traps. Once, when walking up a hillside that was mostly shale, he inadvertently triggered a miniature avalanche and clung to a bush to maintain his footing. He looked up and saw two Chinese potato mashers tumbling his way. In retelling this incident, he said, "I asked God to please give my feet wings," and, wings or not, he let go his handhold and, amazingly, ran up the descending pile of rocks and past the tumbling explosives. In another instance, Fory was walking down a trail when he tripped the wire attached to an artillery shell, an improvised explosive device, or IED. "Had it exploded, there would not have even been a grease spot left of me."[41]

3.9   Unexploded ordnance found at a recovery site in Southeast Asia. *Joint Task Force-Full Accounting (JTF-FA)*

Because tension, distrust, and hostility still ran high between the parties in the conflict, the Quartermaster General was not allowed to send Graves Registration teams to North Korea, and it was not until almost half a century later that an accord was reached to allow U.S. personnel north of the 38th parallel. Even after recovery efforts began in North Korea, they were and continue to be highly susceptible to local government machinations and international tensions of the moment.

The next major involvement of American soldiers was in Vietnam. Reflecting changes in battle tactics and equipment, the fallen were generally recovered soon after death. By this time, Graves Registration was called GRREG, and its duties were somewhat more limited than in previous wars; now it primarily operated mortuaries where bodies were identified, embalmed, and prepared for transportation back to families in the United States, usually within seven to ten days after death.[42]

Helicopters enabled troops to remove remains from the battlefield quickly and fly them to collection points and then to mortuaries. As a result, there was little need for area clearances. Also, since as U.S. troops withdrew and North Vietnam overran the south, there was little opportunity to perform sweeps. Those that did take place occurred soon after battles, primarily when "policing up the battlefield." After the ferocious engagement in the Ia Drang Valley in the fall of 1965, "a time when two opposing armies took the measure of each other,"[43] the survivors searched for weapons, wounded, and dead. Lt. Gen. Harold Moore (retired), then a colonel commanding the field at Landing Zone X-ray, was "determined to keep my promise that this battalion would never leave any man behind on the field of battle, that everyone would come home."[44] Colonel Moore ordered and personally supervised sweeps for his dead men and accounted for every one; he himself even pulled apart "clumps of bodies" to find and remove any Americans.[45]

Unfortunately, during the next, related battle at Landing Zone Alpha, the story was somewhat different. The fighting was even more fierce and violent than at X-ray. Lieutenant Rick Rescorla, later credited with saving hundreds, if not thousands of lives during the September 11, 2001 terrorist attack on the World Trade Center—he died while performing his duty as security chief for Morgan Stanley—called the battle "a long, bloody traffic accident in the jungle."[46] Adding further to the loss, four men were unaccounted for. Soon afterward, Captain George Forrest realized that Pfc. John R. Ackerman, one of his men in Alpha Company, was also missing, contrary to an earlier belief that he had been evacuated on a medical helicopter. Forrest did not learn of what can euphemistically be called a "procedural oversight" until he received a letter from Ackerman's mother saying that she had not heard from her son.[47]

In April of the following year, 1966, the Army returned to the Ia Drang Valley, and Colonel Moore, now the commander of the missing men's battalion, led a search at Landing Zone Alpha and the surrounding area. He said, "I decided that if we ever went back into the Ia Drang I would personally lead a thorough search for those four missing men."[48] Shortly after they began, Moore and his men found the remains of eight soldiers, some clearly identified as American by their gear, mixed together. Recognizing that they needed forensic expertise, Colonel Moore called in Graves Registration, who removed all the remains and the associated clothing and equipment. Later, four remains were definitely identified as the men who had been killed and lost five months earlier.[49]

Fortunately, Captain Forrest also found the remains of Ackerman. His work and the unceasing efforts of Colonel Moore, both immediately after the battle and in the ensuing months, are testaments to their dedication to take care of their men, alive and dead.

Since the Vietnam War, the United States has not been involved in a military engagement that has resulted in the numbers of deaths incurred in

Vietnam, Korea, World War II, and World War I. Usually the employment of American forces has been somewhat one-sided and overwhelming, at least in a military sense. Consequently, we have not needed to utilize sweeps in same way as before.

Historical Recoveries

"I am sure that isolated deceased will surface from time to time for the next 50 years." These words are from the *Personal Diary of Charles D. Butte, LTC USA QMC Ret. (then Lt.),* written during Butte's sweep of Sicily in September 1947. Lieutenant Butte knew from first-hand experience that he and others would not be able to find all the remains of missing servicemen, that sweeps would not continue indefinitely, and that remains would occasionally turn up for decades.

Sweeps after World War I ended in 1921, those for World War II dead in 1950, and those in South Korea in 1956, and the United States effectively lost control of the territory of Vietnam in 1973. But not all the missing were accounted for and search efforts have, at times, been obstructed and/or delayed. In particular, the former Soviet Union, North Korea, and North Vietnam have hindered or completely prevented area sweeps or specific investigations. At the time of his work, Butte did not envision search and recovery missions beyond a few years after the end of World War II, but after the Vietnam War, the United States eventually adopted a new approach: looking for soldiers missing from wars years and decades earlier, "historical recoveries."

A historical recovery depends on good records; a skirmish line can't walk the whole earth, and even if it could, it would still overlook remains that, over time, have been covered by forests, rice fields, roads, and railways. During the Paris Peace Accords, North Vietnam provided a list of Americans who had died in captivity. The Provisional Revolutionary Government of the Republic of South Vietnam (PRG—better known as the Viet Cong) also provided a list of American soldiers who had died while being held in South Vietnam. It proved to be highly inaccurate, and efforts from 1973 to 1975 to resolve discrepancies and to obtain remains of the men on the list met with abject failure.[50]

Knowing that they couldn't depend upon North Vietnamese authorities to provide much, if any, assistance in recovering Vietnam Soldier Dead, the Commander in Chief, Pacific (CINCPAC) headquarters in Hawaii created the Joint Casualty Resolution Center (JCRC) in Saigon in January 1973. It is the ancestor of the Joint Task Force-Full Accounting (JTF-FA) and was operational until 1992, when the two were merged. The JCRC was charged with resolving "the fate of those servicemen still missing and unaccounted for as a result of the hostilities throughout Indochina." Finding remains would be one form of resolution.[51]

The JCRC quickly began a review of available records and initiated recovery operations in areas still controlled by South Vietnam. These searches had limited success. In one case in 1973, a search conducted off the coast of Vietnam cost $830,000 and yielded only a few unidentifiable bone fragments.[52] In another case in May 1973, the JCRC removed approximately 200,000 pounds of sand—some 60,000 or 70,000 shovels full—while looking for the remains of the pilot of an observation craft that had been shot down on a beach near Tuy Hoa. Finally, a local fisherman was able to "pinpoint the exact grave location based on his personal recollection of the burial years earlier."[53]

The account of this recovery brings a picture to mind, with some comic relief. Did the fisherman go about his daily activities during the three days the JCRC dug and dug and dug, and only upon questioning come forward with the information? Was he afraid to assist? Did he even know what the Americans were doing? Did the JCRC employ a Propaganda Team, an Investigation Team, and a Disinterring Team as were used to good effect in World War II?

Overcoming suspicions and obtaining help from locals with information has greatly aided in recovering remains. During the Iraq War, an Iraqi civilian "approached a U.S. Marine patrol with the personal effects of a Marine who had been killed in a recent battle and buried by local townspeople."[54] Fortunately, the troops were on the spot soon after the loss of their comrade. After World War II, GRS officials in Iraq had little assistance from the inhabitants in finding the remains of a reported three or four isolated burials. Flash floods had washed away the mounded earth of the graves, and there were no "markers, plots, rows, nor records." Furthermore, even if the GRS men had found the graves, identification would have been highly unlikely, given that the locals typically gave away the clothing of the dead.[55]

However, sometimes efforts to get help from local residents resulted in other problems. Since the JCRC felt it lacked "vital details" concerning "loss incidents" in Southeast Asia, it designed and implemented a policy of offering financial incentives to those who came forward with information useful in finding missing soldiers and/or their remains. Obtaining permission from the American embassy in Saigon to advertise the incentive program proved difficult because embassy officials did not want to risk offending the Communist signers of the Paris Peace Accords; they felt that being cautious for the moment would result in greater gains later. Such a dilemma and gamble is part of any endeavor designed to establish better communication and relations. But this caution turned out to be pointless when three Saigon newspapers carried stories that the United States was offering money and other rewards for information regarding the remains of its military personnel.

In response, on June 14, 1973, the North Vietnamese delegate to the Four-Party Joint Military Team (FPJMT), consisting of representatives from America, South Vietnam, North Vietnam, and the Viet Cong and charged with the responsibility of resolving missing cases for all four parties, indignantly complained that the rewards program was an insult to the humanitarian policy of North Vietnam. The complaint was hypocritical, given that it was voiced after U.S. delegates had visited the Hanoi cemetery containing the remains of American POWs who had died in captivity, and it was not until the next year that these remains were returned to the United States.[56]

It was convenient for North Vietnam to claim that they delayed the delivery of remains because of what they termed the insensitive reward plan of the United States. The Soviet Union after World War II and North Korea after the Korean War also seized every opportunity to obstruct American efforts to reclaim the dead. There is little doubt that the communist countries, playing upon the United States' respect for the individual Soldier Dead, have used every means they possessed for the purpose of political or financial gain, or simply to deny the United States just because they could. North Vietnam and the Viet Cong also denied permission to search territory under their control. In addition to claiming possession of certain areas, they asserted that they controlled other areas that they actually didn't, further hindering U.S. search efforts.

Because of the uncertainty of access, the JCRC attempted only those searches that it considered reasonably safe; even so, it did not avoid hostilities. In early December 1973, a JCRC field team began to investigate a helicopter crash site in an abandoned rice paddy near Saigon. On the third day of the operation, a rocket-propelled grenade downed one helicopter, killing a Vietnamese crewman. The other two helicopters, damaged by shrapnel, managed to take off, stranding Captain Richard Reese and his men. While under heavy automatic weapons fire, Reese stood up from behind cover and yelled in Vietnamese that he and his men were unarmed. Tragically, but not surprisingly, a fusillade of bullets answered Reese's plea, and he was killed.

During the next meeting of the FPJMT, Colonel William Tombaugh threw Reese's blood-soaked shirt onto the table in front of the Viet Cong representative, accusing them of treachery in setting up an ambush to dissuade U.S. repatriation efforts (the JCRC had provided information to both North Vietnam and the Viet Cong about its impending search operations and invited them to participate). Further justifying Tombaugh's accusation was the fact that the helicopters had been painted with bright orange markers and the men in the search operation had worn bright orange bands.

In response to Tombaugh's dramatic act, the Viet Cong representative employed a tactic long used by those who have committed a wrong and wish to divert or avoid substantive discussion: he went on the offensive and "demanded that the United States desist from 'falsely accusing' them of perpetrating the fatal ambush." And in a rerun of previous experiences with hostile governments, the United States found no political support for action against North Vietnamese or the Viet Cong; there was little notice about the incident in the American press, and a public clamoring for disengagement and withdrawal did not have the stomach for further military involvement. Consequently, the JCRC turned over field operations to armed South Vietnamese troops while its specialists observed from afar. Function followed form, and the ad hoc arrangement greatly impeded the recovery and identification of remains.[57]

As North Vietnam and the Viet Cong pursued their military agenda against the south, the JCRC curtailed its already limited efforts. In any event, South Vietnamese combat troops could not be spared to conduct recovery missions. When Saigon fell on April 30, 1975, the United States made its now famous evacuation from the embassy rooftop helipad and all missions in Vietnam essentially stopped. Unfortunately, even as the curtain fell on the closing scene of our Southeast Asia involvement, American soldiers played a dramatic role: two Marines who were aiding the Saigon evacuation were killed in a rocket attack and their remains regrettably left behind in a hospital.[58]

No further actions were taken in Vietnam to recover the dead until 1985 when, following years of estrangement, Vietnam agreed to a recovery operation in which it and the United States would jointly excavate an airplane crash site at Yen Thuong. After a preliminary investigation and a review of B-52 crash records, the JCRC and the Army's Central Identification Laboratory (CIL) concluded that a Soviet aircraft or SAM missile, not a U.S. B-52, was likely the object that had crashed in the chosen location and recommended selecting another, more promising site in order to have the best chance of establishing a success record that would be the basis for future cooperation. Vietnam, though, insisted that the excavation take place as planned.

The recovery operation at Yen Thuong began in the summer of 1985 and lasted until December. The JCRC and CIL fielded a large team, including a medic, ordnance experts, and engineers. Not only did they employ earth-moving machinery, they also sifted through the claylike soil by hand. Eventually, after 2 weeks of digging and sifting, they dug a hole that measured "50 by 100 feet and nearly 40 feet deep." Yet, after moving more than 7,400 cubic yards of dirt and mud, they found no remains.[59] Though disappointing to all involved, the effort did set a precedent in that the United States and Vietnam demonstrated that they could work together. Also, it provided valuable experience in preparing for and conducting future operations.

The first historical recovery operation in which the United States participated with North Korea took place in July 1996, almost 45 years after the end of the Korean War. During this operation in Unsan County, the Central Identification Laboratory, Hawaii (CILHI) was investigating a site where an F-80 Shooting Star jet had supposedly crashed. Talking to villagers, the CILHI team learned of another location where it was believed an American had been buried. They turned to the new site and recovered the remains of a U.S. soldier from what appeared to be a foxhole burial. The remains of the Army corporal, after being identified, were returned to his family for final interment. What is telling about this historical recovery is that it proved once again the importance of contact with local inhabitants when conducting searches.[60]

Recovery efforts for those killed prior to the Korean War, on hiatus since 1950, began again in 1976 when CILHI "was established and assigned the mission to recover and identify *all* unrecovered United States service members from past wars." The laboratory's mission was to find, recover, and identify the remains of service personnel from the Korean War, Cold War battles, the Vietnam War, and "other conflicts and contingencies."[61] While CILHI's efforts to recover World War II dead have been successful, it currently works cases from that war only rarely and directs most of its energy and resources to finding those missing from the Korean and Vietnam wars. "Over 150 [World War II] sites in almost 30 countries are awaiting further investigation or evacuation."[62]

Another group, the United States Army Memorial Affairs Activity Europe (USAMAA-E) also conducts historical searches, but it is authorized to do so on a reactive rather than proactive basis. That is, USAMAA-E personnel may not mount an investigation of possible recovery sites on their own initiative, but can do so only if they receive substantial and reliable information about loss locations of U.S. servicemen. In an example of cooperation

3.10   Recovery site in Southeast Asia. *U.S. Army Central Identification Laboratory, Hawaii (CILHI)*

between former enemies, German researchers conducting independent investigations to recover remains inform USAMAA-E of their findings. Then, after a careful evaluation and approval from CILHI, USAMAA-E works with the Germans to excavate a site and recover remains.[63]

While assistance from European researchers is extremely helpful in finding recovery sites, there is a bottleneck in the process of recovering, identifying, and returning remains because any found must still be flown to CILHI for "formal" identification, even though USAMAA-E staff are sufficiently qualified to perform identification in many, if not most instances. While it is desirable that remains be identified properly—there has certainly been strong criticism of identification work in the past—it is likely that qualified personnel other than CILHI staff would be sufficiently reliable and that bypassing CILHI in select cases would return remains to the next of kin much quicker.

Interestingly, the French and German researchers who operate mostly independently and on their own money sometimes team up with Americans who do the same. Lt. Jack Curtis, a P-38 pilot for the 367th Fighter Group in France, was involved in a melee between American and German aircraft on December 24, 1944 over Trier, Germany. Curtis and 11 others found themselves facing off with 26 German planes and, after a 20-minute dogfight, all but 2 returned to base. One of the downed aviators, Lt. James Baxter, was a close friend of Curtis. After Curtis retired in 1982, he devoted time to searching for the unrecovered remains of his buddy.

Curtis began his research in Germany and eventually was directed to an association of former German pilots. As he uncovered information about Baxter's crash site, he contacted CILHI, who said they could not conduct a recovery unless someone had already found remains. Of course, that position begs the question, How would you obtain remains without undertaking a recovery? Also, many recoveries have been conducted in Southeast Asia without remains being found beforehand.

Eventually, a German group headed by Manfred Klein found a bone fragment that galvanized CILHI to send a team. Once the dig began, the investigators found "pieces of an airplane, bone fragments, and, most importantly, Baxter's dog tag." After recovery, Baxter's remains were buried beside those of his brother, who also served in World War II.[64] Curtis's efforts were recognized by Robert L. Jones, Deputy Assistant Secretary of Defense, POW/ Missing Personnel Affairs, who wrote him a letter of "esteemed gratitude" for his "unwavering efforts."[65]

Curtis's example of a recovery made long after death and by the efforts of someone other than U.S. authorities is not unique by any means. After World War I, a mother whose son was shot down while participating in the

3.11   Number plate of Lt. James Baxter's P-38 found by German researchers. *Manfred Klein*

French Flying Corps refused to accept that his remains would be lost forever. She was "a charming old lady, seemingly frail and wholly unsuited to the continued trials she made on her strength, yet one who crossed the ocean twice and walked over many miles of battle front." Through her unceasing efforts, and after encountering many obstacles, she finally obtained a statement from the German aviator who had shot down her son, and from this learned the location of the cemetery where his remains were buried.[66]

There is little doubt that, without the tireless work of Curtis and others, the remains of many Soldier Dead would simply never be recovered. To the extent that searchers other than official military groups can proceed, they should be encouraged to do so and assisted in any manner possible that protects identification material while not stifling individual initiative.

In October 2003, CILHI and JTF-FA merged into the Joint POW/MIA Accounting Command (JPAC). This merger is discussed more fully in chapter 8, "Open Wounds."

Mass Fatalities

In addition to battle deaths, U.S. servicepersons die in the same ways as civilians—vehicle accidents, sickness, suicide, and murder. And on September 11, 2001, the military and the public were bonded by the attacks on the Pentagon and the World Trade Center, classified as "mass fatality" incidents. Mass fatalities are not always from attacks; many are the correlative result of the frequency and nature of the transportation soldiers use.

On August 21, 1921, in Hull, England, a dirigible flown by British and American naval personnel exploded and fell into the Huber River. When the news reached the American Graves Registration Service (AGRS) in Paris, a team of embalmers was dispatched, along with supplies and caskets. The AGRS performed its duties so admirably that it received a commendation from the American Consul and the Commanding Officer of the U.S. Naval Rigid Airship Detachment.[67]

A more recent air disaster resulting in large numbers of deaths occurred on December 12, 1985, when a DC-8 crashed shortly after takeoff from Gander International Airport in Newfoundland, Canada. All souls died,[68] including 8 crew members, 236 soldiers from the 101st Airborne Division, and 12 other U.S. soldiers from other units. Immediately, the Army marshaled its support and recovery personnel.

Good relations were established early on with the Canadians, allowing not only for cooperation between the two countries in determining the cause of the accident but also for the timely transfer of remains to the mortuary at Dover Air Force Base. There, pathologists conducted their investigation and reported that "at least two bodies had not been recovered." Major General John S. Crosby flew to Canada to meet with members of the Canadian Aviation Safety Board and officials of the Royal Canadian Mounted Police to discuss "the feasibility of resuming search operations."

While the Canadians favored a less costly and slightly delayed option—searching after spring thaw—the United States argued for an immediate search, stating that unless quick action were taken, the Army would likely be accused of possessing an uncaring attitude that would result in unfavorable

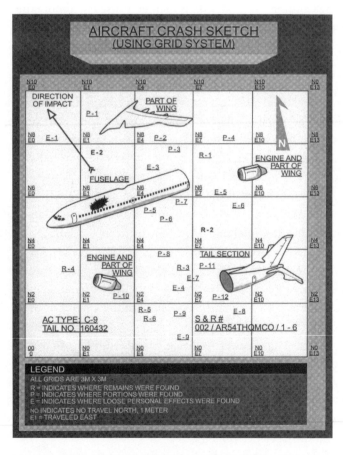

3.12 Aircraft crash sketch. *Joint Pub 4–06: Joint Tactics, Techniques, and Procedures for Mortuary Affairs*

press and, perhaps, congressional action. The U.S. position prevailed and a second recovery team was dispatched to Gander on January 8 to perform another search.

The second recovery effort, performed mainly by 6 four-man teams of Graves Registration specialists from Fort Lee and Fort Bragg, began by going over ground previously covered by the Royal Canadian Mounted Police—Graves Registration personnel had been prohibited from performing the initial search, another example of the issue of control over the bodies of the dead. While 60 days were allocated, the search was completed in only 26 after 2 more complete remains and more than 300 body parts were found. The Mounties should not be too harshly criticized for overlooking them, as

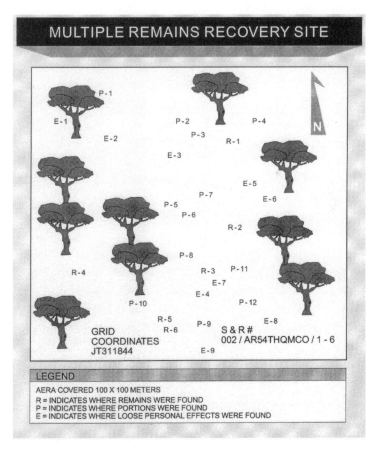

3.13 Multiple remains recovery site. *Joint Pub 4–06: Joint Tactics, Techniques, and Procedures for Mortuary Affairs*

a 6-inch snowfall had covered the crash site and rendered the discovery of remains and body parts difficult.

The Gander Tragedy proved that mass fatality recoveries may involve obtaining the cooperation, assistance, and/or permission of other governments; that these governments may have to be persuaded to allocate resources to a cause about which Americans feel more strongly than they; and that a successful recovery operation requires trained and experienced personnel both in the field and in the lab.

Partly as a result of the Gander experience, and recognizing that recovering remains in peacetime would require trained personnel who could be immediately deployed, the Quartermaster Corps activated the 54th Quartermaster Company (Mortuary Affairs) in Fort Lee, Virginia, to be ready on short notice to help with mass fatality incidents. Soon afterward, the company served in Somalia, Haiti, Bosnia, and Kosovo, and provided assistance after the Murrah Federal Building bombing in Oklahoma City.

Later, the 54th was called to the Pentagon to help with recovery efforts after the September 11 terrorist attack. Because the site was considered to be a federal crime scene, the Quartermaster Mortuary Affairs soldiers worked closely with the FBI and other state and federal agencies to recover remains and personal effects.[69] Eventually, remains of almost all of the 184 victims of the attack were recovered. Identifiable remains of 5 people—a 3-year-old on the plane, and 4 adults working in the Pentagon—could not be found despite heroic efforts under very difficult and risky conditions that included searchers working in a still smoldering building.

Author's Notes

Combat recoveries bracket one end of the recovery issue and historical recoveries the other. In combat, the factors of the risk/return equation are clear: is the risk to life worth the benefit of remains recovery? In other recoveries, though, the equation is more complex and is accompanied by corollary elements.

It was learning about noncombat recoveries that really opened up the rest of the Soldier Dead process to me. While studying combat recovery, I was too caught up in my mind's fantasy of gallant troops grabbing the dead by their legs and arms and running through a hailstorm of bullets and mortars to deliver the bodies of their buddies to safety. I would dare say that this is as far as most other people get, too, in imagining the recovery process. In recoveries where there is not the pressure of a military engagement, it is important to establish and follow a rigid and controlled procedure to allow the best opportunity for later identification, return, and burial.

I soon found that more and more of my interviews were with serviceper-sons who participated in noncombat recoveries, rather than combat recov-eries, for several reasons. First, theater personnel, who perform most combat recoveries, move around and are hard to reach, so it is difficult to find ser-vicemen who pulled their dead comrades off the battlefield while hostilities were ongoing unless you are on the spot. And even if you *are* at a combat site where U.S. servicepersons died, access is often blocked or denied—more on this will follow. For battles in earlier time periods, already existing sources on recoveries under duress proved to be very useful, while for noncombat recoveries, live interviews gave me the opportunity to obtain important de-tails not previously well described.

When researching current and archival material on noncombat recover-ies and interviewing people who plan and conduct these operations, I had my introduction to the politics associated with our Soldier Dead. The search for remains of those killed many years ago is a subject that is highly charged, both emotionally and politically, and there is a sharp division between the point of view of members of the Armed Forces and that of the public. Gener-ally, servicepersons feel that the search should continue indefinitely and that cost should be of little consideration. When I told Lt. Col. Gerald O'Hara, Public Affairs Officer for JPAC, of my calculations for the cost of histori-cal recoveries in Southeast Asia—slightly over $1.2 million per identified remains—he said, "God, what a wonderful country—that we can do that!" However, when I gave this figure to others outside of the military who had not lost someone, let alone lost someone and not been able to recover their remains, the responses ranged all the way from "You know, that's just too much money" to "Why should we care what it costs?"

When I brought up the cost with officials at the different organizations that conduct the historical recoveries, the responses were at times less direct, ranging from indifference—"Oh, I didn't know that number"—to objec-tions and challenges—"We don't like to assign a number to what it costs to recover remains." In a sense, this subject is like medical care in that no one wants to be the bad guy affixing a dollar value to something as important as health, yet no one wants to be stuck paying the bill, either.

At times, when the subject of cost is brought up, the conversation can approach comedy. A good example is the August 8, 1997, DoD News Briefing by Alan Liotta, Deputy Director, Defense Prisoner-of-War/Missing Personnel

Office (DPMO), on recoveries in North Korea. In this meeting, Liotta was asked if the United States was "greasing the skids" with money. He explained that payments—$100,000 minimum, with a $50,000 down payment at the start of an operation—made to the North Koreans were for legitimate expenses. When asked how the money was paid, he said that it was paid *in cash*, which prompted the next question, "Are you going to take a big bag?"

But ultimately, as in any endeavor and despite the statement, "No specific limitations exist on the amount that can be spent to search for, recover, and identify eligible deceased personnel," that appears in the U.S. Army Regulation 638–2, money has to be a consideration, though perhaps unmentioned, just as in medical care. No one anywhere has an unlimited budget. The finances of recoveries exist in a kind of limbo where the dollars shouldn't matter, but they do.

When I talked to the field personnel, usually lieutenants and staff sergeants and below, who are most responsible for "getting the job done," I was struck by their unlimited dedication to their task. They are mostly free from the politics of the issue and, like others before them, they find a way to carry out their mission. They work through equipment failures, logistics snafus, and language barriers. They fight poisonous snakes, hostile environments and weather, and tropical diseases. They sift through tons of soil for thumbnail-size pieces of bone that can scarcely be distinguished from the dirt. They are away from home for long periods. And they are all volunteers.

Listening to these volunteer workers, I realized that I was looking at Hemingway's definition of a "hero," for they all exhibited "grace under pressure." Without that characterization, any account of their work would be insufficient. Honor, for them, is not a word in a book or inscribed on a plaque: it's an unseen uniform that they wear constantly and proudly.

"Your children, they get angry at you. They say, 'Mom and Daddy, why are you leaving me?' I tell them all the time, this is the profession that I chose; it's for my country, but it's for you, for later on." This is what Sgt. 1st Class Habibah Prevost of CILHI told me she said to her children when I asked about the amount of time she spent away from home and the effect on her family.

Another aspect of noncombat recovery is the privacy of the dead. Soldiers in the field do not want their dead comrades to be seen by anyone on the outside. They do not want pictures taken of a corpse's arm, still sleeved in a tattered and blood-soaked uniform, hanging out of a bombed Humvee. While I was embedded with the Army's 54th Quartermaster Mortuary Affairs Company in Baghdad, the Public Affairs Officer in Kuwait gave me several pages of instructions for the media. Paragraph 8 said that news media representatives cannot disclose the names of those injured or killed until the proper military casualty section has notified the next of kin. The paragraph continued, "Service members will not prohibit news media representatives from viewing or filming casualties." But, of course, photographs containing "a recognizable face, nametag, or other identifying feature or item will not be used."

But, like other journalists who had been to Iraq, I soon learned that it didn't matter what the instructions said—it was strictly taboo to view, much less photograph, remains, and it was even forbidden to photograph a transfer case containing "HR" (human remains). I could, however, photograph stacks of empty transfer cases. Apparently, Mortuary Affairs personnel felt that the inclusion of remains changed what had previously been a utilitarian box of metal into a vault, crypt, or carrier of precious cargo. It is not the vessel, but the contents—hidden though they are—that commands the reverent treatment.

This "field prohibition" on photographing U.S. dead is not new. Susan Sontag provides an excellent discourse not only on previous attempts by governments to limit photography of images that "show how war evacuates, shatters, breaks apart, levels the built world," but also on attempts to obtain photographs that "would drum up support for soldiers' sacrifices."[70]

Our military is a jealous husband of its dead. Some of the issues about viewing them, including the ban on media access that extends beyond the battlefield to the points of loading and offloading of remains, are discussed further in the "Author's Notes" to chapter 5, "The Return of the Dead." Also, in chapter 7, "All Bodies Are Not the Same," I discuss how the standards we apply to enemy, or combatant, dead are different: we tend to display enemy remains but not ours.

Again, I found myself coming back to the same question: To whom do the dead, *all dead*, belong? The answer has its roots in what the dead mean, and to whom.

[4. Identification]

> But let my death be memoried on this disc.
> Wear it, sweet friend. Inscribe no date nor deed.
> But let thy heart-beat kiss it night and day,
> Until the name grow vague and wear away.
> —WILFRED OWEN, "With an Identity Disc"

CARRYING OUT THE PROMISE to military service personnel to find and bring them back home only partially fulfills our obligation. We must also identify their remains, for it is a name that transforms a casket full of biological material and minerals into a son, brother, husband, and father, or daughter, sister, wife, and mother. Confidence in the identification of remains helps the bereaved to face the reality that their loved one is dead. But even if the Soldier Dead had no family whatsoever to whom a name would be important, the members of the Armed Forces consider their comrades to be family and desire that they be brought home and buried with all due recognition.

Simply stated, identifying remains is done by matching information gathered from them to the known data from possible candidates and, if there is a preponderance of evidence, making a finding. The identification process is as follows:

1. taking and recording antemortem information from living service members;
2. taking and recording postmortem information from remains;
3. analyzing antemortem and postmortem information and finding possible matches;
4. making a final determination of the identification of remains, or making an exclusion of identification.

Would that it were so simple. Identification of the dead is, has been, and will always be problematic, requiring concerted efforts to look beyond the effects of violence visited upon flesh and bone and the more gentle actions of time that slowly erase evidence of mortal existence. But as our ability to destroy flesh and bone has improved, so has our ability to identify the dead. American identification specialists have made fundamental changes in two main areas: recovering remains as soon as possible after death and employing highly advanced forensic and biochemical methods.

Advances in the forensic field have created ethical problems in the same way that developments in the medical field have—just because we *can* do something, does that mean we *should*? As in medicine, the choices are not always clear-cut and often involve extremely sensitive issues. Those charged with making decisions regarding identification must learn to live with the unenviable fact that they will not be able to satisfy all people all of the time. Family members of servicepersons presumed killed must, at times, face the fact that there may be no final accounting to their full satisfaction.

Taking and Recording Antemortem Information

The oldest and most obvious method of taking and recording information from soldiers when they are alive occurs in the minds of fellow troops—they "remember" what their comrades looked like, what they wore, where they were when they were killed, and how. Of course, this method is quite fallible: the dead may have been new members of a unit little known by those who fought alongside them; soldiers may exchange clothes and personal effects; or a whole unit may be nearly wiped out, leaving few survivors with useful personal knowledge of those who perished. And memories are riddled with omissions, contradictions, and inaccuracies even when formed in the best of circumstances, let alone in life-and-death struggles.

Desiring to provide some evidence of their identity, Union soldiers in the Civil War, long before higher-ups adopted a formal policy requiring identity disks or dog tags, wrote their names on "slips of paper and pinned them to their blouses." Not wanting to miss a good business opportunity, entrepreneurs advertised "Soldier's Pins" in *Harper's Weekly Magazine* that were made from silver and gold and inscribed with name and unit designation. Other vendors also sold identification disks just prior to battle. Eventually, the U.S. military caught up with the desire of its members and their families to help reduce the number of unknowns and required, beginning in 1913, that soldiers wear identification tags. During World War I, most wore circular aluminum disks, and the well-known rectangular shape, the ubiquitous M1940 tag, came into use in 1940.[1]

Dog tags contain certain social information about the soldier, depending upon the time period issued. Currently, they list the last, first, and middle name, social security number, and religious affiliation. In earlier times, the tags were embossed with the service member's serial number and name and address of next of kin, but they have never contained much physical information beyond blood type, which is to facilitate transfusions, not necessarily to help identification. Consider the case of a plane crash in which remains and dog tags may all be mixed together. Unless other physical data is recorded on the dog tags or elsewhere that can be used to associate body parts, then recording only the names on the tags is of limited use; we can, with some certainty, know that Jones, Smith, Williams, and Dugan were on the plane when it crashed, but not whose remains are whose. Clearly, biophysical antemortem information is needed.

The obvious physical characteristics of a member of the Armed Forces are recorded at the time they enter service: age, height, weight, sex, race, blood type, scars, and tattoos. One record that is particularly helpful in identification is that of dental features, including missing teeth, fillings, crowns, and bridges, because skulls and teeth are particularly durable and likely to survive trauma that would eradicate other physical evidence. The Civil War comments of Captain Warren H. Cudworth, 1st Massachusetts Infantry, regarding a particular identification notes an early use of dental work: "Occasionally something would be found to identify the remains, but not often. One former member of the First, whose skull lay bleaching upon the top of the ground, was identified by some peculiarity connected with his teeth."[2]

Prior to and during World War I, dental characteristics were recorded either in a soldier's civilian life or upon visiting a dentist while in service, and records were kept in the form of dental charts. Once taking x-rays of teeth and mouth structures became commonplace, it was recognized that maxillofacial characteristics could be used to supplement "tooth" identification and even to analyze facial anatomical features.

Other medical information is maintained for service members and updated during visits to the doctor. If, during training, an enlistee sprains his ankle or knee and an x-ray is taken, then this record is available for future use. An x-ray for current health purposes may reveal old fractures or unique bone structures that can also be a reference if needed. The mortuary that is processing remains will request a copy of medical and dental records from the home base of each service member who may possibly be the unknown deceased.[3]

The early 1990s saw the incorporation of DNA analysis in remains identification and by 1992, trainees for the U.S. Army at Fort Knox, Kentucky, were giving blood and buccal (mouth) swabs for storage.[4] The oral swabs were discontinued in 1996 when blood specimen cards were developed. The cards took a third less storage space and cost much less: $1.00 versus $2.67. They must be kept frozen, though, and the Armed Forces Repository of Specimen Samples for the Identification of Remains (AFRSSIR) keeps more than 3 million cards at its storage facility in Gaithersburg, Maryland. The current specimen card may soon be replaced by a model that does not require freezing, but since it would take a considerable amount of time for every current and incoming service member to give a blood sample on a new card, the frozen storage facility would have to be maintained in the interim.[5] The purpose of the cards is printed on the back:

2. Principal Purpose:
  Information in this system of records will be used for the identification of human remains. The principal purpose of the information is to
identify reference specimen samples that will routinely be stored and not
analyzed until needed for remains identification program purposes.

Of course, obtaining DNA specimen reference cards from living service members cannot help identify those killed before the cards were adopted. Accordingly, the Armed Forces have begun an outreach program to obtain DNA from the maternal lines of those unaccounted for—and presumed dead—from the Korean War and, as of December 2002, had obtained 2,881 family reference samples.[6]

Taking and Recording Postmortem Information

The taking and recording of postmortem information has undergone a major transformation during the last 100 years, particularly during the last 50. Early postmortem data consisted mainly of information from social sources, while the end of the twentieth century saw the addition of substantial physical and biochemical details. And whereas at first, the information was gathered primarily in the field, now it is obtained through extensive examination of remains in white-walled laboratories.

During World War I, most identification work was done at the gravesite, either during the original burial or during the concentration and repatriation process (discussed in later chapters). "Immediately after an engagement, the burial officer of a regiment . . . took out with him into the field a detail of men, whose duty was to locate the bodies and bury them, after searching for and recording all personal articles found upon them, and by which they might be identified."[7] Later, a Graves Registration Service officer or a noncommissioned officer (appointed from among enlisted personnel) was charged with the duty of visiting gravesites and, once "reasonably satisfied" with the identity of the buried remains, "affixed a plate bearing the letters 'G.R.S.' to the cross."[8] The plate was the Good Housekeeping Seal, so to speak, of a valid identification finding. At any point when bodies were exhumed and reburied, officials searched for identification disks, "burial bottles" (glass containers in which whatever items had been used as a basis for identification were stored), and hospital tags that might have been placed with or attached to remains or clothing.[9]

World War II procedure initially followed that of World War I. And, when time allowed, specific individuals had the duty to obtain remains information. The Graves Registration *Technical Manual 10–630*, issued on September 23, 1941, charged the chaplain with searching the dead for personal effects and other identifying media. If identification was made without dog tags, then those items used were to be placed in a burial bottle, if possible, and interred with the remains or "pressed into the soft earth" at the head of the grave.[10]

However, the chaplain did not have the sole responsibility for searching remains at the time of initial burial: medical personnel assigned to Graves Registration units assisted with the identification of "portions of a body dismembered by explosion." They took fingerprints, prepared dental charts, noted anatomical characteristics, and "inspected the body for other identifying media."[11]

After the end of World War II, it was recognized that the identification methods established during the conflict were not suited to postwar work, for several reasons: manpower was wasted when teams of gravediggers stood around while identification tasks were conducted; "so-called identification analysts and their assistants were, generally speaking, deficient in the knowledge of anatomy requisite to their work"; and there was a shortage of supplies for use in the field. The Quartermaster General engaged Dr. Harry L. Shapiro, Chairman and Curator of Physical Anthropology at the American Museum of Natural History in New York City, to make recommendations to increase the effectiveness of identification efforts. Dr. Shapiro observed the fieldwork currently in progress and proposed that a central identification laboratory be established where remains and all associated "media found in or near the place of burial" would be processed by well-equipped and well-trained personnel. As a result, the Central Identification Point (CIP) was opened in Strasbourg, France in August 1946 and, for the most part, graveside identification procedures were discontinued for World War II Soldier Dead.

4.1 Information is taken from the remains of two 1st Cavalry soldiers killed in the Admiralty Group, World War II. *U.S. Army Signal Corps. National Archives & Records Administration*

Knowledgeable and experienced civilians contributed to the CIP. New York Police Detective John Aievoli assisted with creating identification techniques and procedures. He so greatly aided identification work that officials in the Memorial Division "considered his efforts among the most helpful of any individual in the entire European GRS organization." CIP's process was thorough, including a careful examination of all clothing and equipment and a painstakingly detailed search of remains for physical characteristics and embedded evidence that might provide clues to identity. In addition, anatomical and dental charts were prepared and fingerprints taken, if possible.[12]

In the Pacific, men who had been trained at the CIP in Europe established a Central Identification Laboratory (CIL) in Honolulu, Hawaii, in 1947. As in Europe, many of the personnel had to be taught from the ground up.[13] Eventually, additional CILs were set up in Japan and Saipan.[14]

The use of central laboratories to identify World War II dead proved so successful that it has continued in one form or another ever since. Shortly after the United States was embroiled in the fight between North and South

4.2   Clothing of remains being scrubbed to discover a personal identification number (PIN), which will help greatly in identification, World War II. *U.S. Army Signal Corps. National Archives & Records Administration*

Korea, a CIL was established in Kokura, Japan and operated there until 1956. During the Vietnam War, Graves Registration personnel at mortuaries at Da Nang and Tan Son Nhut made identifications and prepared bodies for return home. After the withdrawal of U.S. forces from South Vietnam, a central lab was set up in Thailand (CIL-THAI). Upon the fall of the South Vietnamese government in 1975, the lab was relocated to Hawaii (CILHI). Its mission was altered so that, in addition to extracting information from remains brought to the lab, it also became responsible for conducting field missions—using highly trained personnel to plan and conduct recoveries improves the chances of finding remains and identity information. The scientists moved from the lab to the field and now play a very active role in both choosing sites and conducting recovery operations.[15]

It is important to note that CILHI's mission is to find and identify remains from previous wars; identifying those from current conflicts is handled differently in that Mortuary Affairs units, such as those in Landstuhl, Germany, process and identify remains if their number is not too great.

Larger numbers are flown to Dover Air Force Base in Delaware for identification and preparation for return to the next of kin.

Dr. William Belcher, a civilian anthropologist working with CILHI, has been on numerous historical recovery operations and conducts the search at each site as an archaeologist would, employing similar graphing, mapping, and marking techniques. The detailed record gives the best chance for an organized recovery of the remains being sought as well as clues about the possible presence of other, undiscovered remains.[16]

An excellent example of the need for such organization can be seen in the unilateral return of 208 remains by North Korea from 1990 to 1994. The chain of evidence associated with them was not only broken, it was hardly established in the first place. Without knowing where they had been disinterred, it was next to impossible to narrow the selection of potential unknowns. Also, the disarticulated remains of the men were mixed together, making it very difficult to separate individuals. The result was that by December 2002, only 10 of the 208 had been identified.[17]

But even though scientific processes in the lab provide ever more postmortem information, advances will still be needed in field identification because the possibility, or even likelihood, of nuclear, biological, or chemical deaths may result in remains being interred for long periods before being returned; it is even possible that they will need to be cremated if Host Nations—countries that allow U.S. troops to be stationed in their territory before and during conflicts in neighboring areas (Kuwait and Saudi Arabia were Host Nations during the Gulf War)—refuse to allow contaminated remains to be buried in their soil. Prior to the Iraq War, cremation was considered as a means of safely handling remains, but a Department of Defense press release served notice that this method was not acceptable to the U.S. public. Instead, remains were to be stored while other possibilities were explored, notably the use of special barrier containment systems.[18]

When most people think of taking information from remains, the first thing that comes to mind is dog tags. While tags do play a major role, just issuing them does not assure identification of remains because there is much room for error and mishandling. First, dog tags must be worn or be on the person of the soldier. The War Department's *Technical Manual 10–630: Graves Registration*, September 23, 1941, gave clear instructions that the tags should be "habitually kept in the possession of the owner."[19] But there were exceptions: sometimes the soldiers themselves were lackadaisical about wearing dog tags, sometimes instructions were given to remove identifying media during certain missions in order to prevent evidence of troop positions from falling into enemy hands in the case of capture or death.[20]

Also, in addition to *wearing* dog tags, service personnel need to wear the *correct* tags. During the Korean War, because some remains were found with the wrong tags, Army officials thought that soldiers, for reasons still unknown, sometimes exchanged dog tags before going on patrol. This breach of procedure was so injurious to later identification that the squad or patrol leader was automatically reduced in rank if his men "did not comply with ID tag regulations."[21] Retired Colonel Tom Rexrode of the Quartermaster Corps, when informed of the problem, speculated that the North Koreans and Chinese could have switched the tags on remains themselves out of spite.[22] His explanation makes sense in that finding the dead with switched tags would not have provided information as to *how and when* they were switched, and the records do not indicate that the problem was discovered during regular inspections of live troops or upon subsequent examination of those killed. Also, it was quite common for the Chinese and North Koreans to physically handle U.S. dead when stripping them of any usable clothing and equipment, so there was opportunity for mischief.

Even when service personnel do regularly wear their own dog tags, they must be present with remains, both when found and when processed later. Unfortunately, neither situation can be guaranteed. In some cases, the physical destruction of human flesh is such that there is little, if anything, to which a dog tag can remain attached. The Quartermaster in World War I commented that "Such occurrences were, fortunately, rare, but it was hard for relatives not conversant with these terrible happenings, to realize how easily a man might be all but annihilated."[23] In other instances, dog tags are present with the dead, but the condition of remains is such that they are found only after a thorough search. One persistent World War I GRS man "went into the interior of the body and found that a shell fragment had pushed the tag into the intestines."[24] During the identification process of Soldier Dead after World War II, the practice of fluoroscoping remains became common and was used to discover not only dog tags but also personal effects and other objects that could provide information useful in identification.[25]

Even when servicemen died with dog tags on, it was not uncommon for inexperienced personnel to remove them. In World War I, "one man collected all identification discs from a group of dead and forwarded them to Headquarters instead of burying one disc attached to the body and placing the other on the grave marker."[26] Correct procedure in *Technical Manual 10–630* was that "One of the two identification tags worn as prescribed in

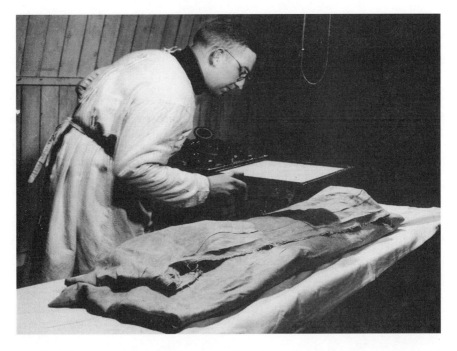

4.3   Remains are examined by fluoroscope in order to find embedded objects, World War II. *U.S. Army Quartermaster Museum*

Army Regulations will be left upon the body to be interred or shipped with the body. The duplicate tag will be removed at time of burial and securely attached to the grave marker."[27]

To a certain extent, Hollywood has contributed to myths about handling dog tags. Many movies have shown a GI or Marine pulling the dog tags from a fallen comrade, while swearing vengeance on the enemy. What then happens to the dog tags is left to the imagination, and the viewer probably does not pause to ponder how the remains could be identified once the tags were removed. A good example of such an error is a scene in *Saving Private Ryan* in which the squad members sort through bags of dog tags near a glider landing, looking for those of Ryan. Fortunately, recent movies have more accurately depicted the burial of Soldier Dead, including the handling of dog tags. In *Windtalkers*, about Navajos serving as radiomen in the Pacific during World War II, a battlefield burial site scene clearly shows a dog tag affixed to the cross at the head of each grave.

Other physical items recovered from remains and the immediate area that provide important clues are personal effects: wallets, photos, keys,

4.4   Conducting services at Saipan: dog tags on markers are clearly visible, World War II. *U.S. Army Photograph. National Archives & Records Administration*

rings, engraved pen and pencil sets, watches, identification bracelets, books. Clothing and equipment can also help, as some equipment is numbered and issued to a specific soldier, shoe sizes vary, and names are on garments.

The presence or absence of some physical items provides information that can be a part of the puzzle. For instance, Senior Master Sergeant Gina Nolan of the former Joint Task Force-Full Accounting (JTF-FA) (JTF-FA and CILHI have now merged) is a life support specialist who studies equipment recovered from airplane crash sites. Nolan's examination can lead her to make valuable assessments about who was and wasn't involved. For instance, if she finds a quantity of parachute D-rings that exceeds what a single parachute contains, it is likely that more than one person was present at the crash site. Conversely, the absence of some equipment may lead her to believe that not all those originally on the plane were there when it crashed, meaning that one or more may have left the plane in one way or another.[28]

The dog tags and other media, though, are a source of information in the social sense; service personnel can and do switch clothes and equipment, forget to carry gear or carry extra gear, exchange personal effects, or ask their comrades to "take this letter to my wife." These sources, while better than nothing, are combined with actual physical evidence obtained from remains when possible.

One of the most important pieces of physical evidence, especially when remains are thoroughly decomposed, is the skull with its accompanying jaw, because dental and facial structures yield valuable clues. In World War I, dental charts were used, but only for "corroborative evidence rather than primary evidence upon which identifications were either confirmed or denied."[29] However, during GRS work in the Pacific in the spring of 1946, dental characteristics became the primary identifying element because tropical conditions had reduced flesh to such a putrid state that little other information could be obtained. Facing a shortage of dental technicians, the Naval Dental Officer taught classes on tooth charting during the voyage of the freighter *Lawrence Phillips* to the recovery area.[30] In the Korean War, mutilated remains were treated as "search and recovery" cases and "patrol

4.5   Cpl. Russell H. Lange counts teeth and makes a dental chart of an unknown soldier exhumed near Butchers Bridge on the Munda trail, New Georgia, World War II. *Fluharty. National Archives & Records Administration*

leaders or other GRS men were required to certify . . . that [a] thorough but fruitless search had been made for the skull."[31]

Forensic dental examination was also critical for the identification of those killed on the *U.S.S. Forrestal* during the fire that ravaged the aircraft carrier on July 29, 1967, during the Vietnam War. Sergeant David Paul Gregg, an identification specialist, was serving with the 243rd Field Service Company at the Da Nang mortuary when the remains from the ship were brought in. He and others worked continually for 72 hours to make identifications. Actually, to say that "remains" were identified is particularly accurate because the intense fire had reduced the soldiers' bodies to practically nothing, leaving only skulls. Even then, the old-fashioned charts—indicating dental features, fillings, missing teeth, and bridgework on a paper schematic of the upper and lower jaw—were the main method of recording dental characteristics.[32] It was not until after Vietnam that the military began a conscious effort to gather and use dental x-rays in identification. In particular, after the 1985 crash of a planeload of 101st Airborne members in Gander, Newfoundland, in which everyone aboard was killed, copies of full mouth x-rays—panoramic x-rays, or panorex—of current service personnel began to be stored at Monterey, California.

Dental charting was only used to support other evidence of identification in World War I, but enough advances have been made in recording and comparing information that a single tooth now can provide a definitive identification.[33] With panorex, not only do the teeth of remains give clues, but the sinus passages and bones of the face provide additional evidence. Odontologists—dentists—work closely with forensic anthropologists who, though trained and experienced in full-body bone structure, often defer to the odontologists when it comes to facial structures.

Of course, as important as skulls and teeth are, much information is available from a close examination of the rest of the remains. Dr. Robert W. Mann, an anthropologist at CILHI, first lays out the bones to compile a "biological profile," which is anything that can be told about the remains: sex, age, race, manner of death. The pieces of the puzzle have to fit: if the remains are found at a supposed aircraft crash site yet the evidence indicates that the service member died from a mortar blast, then further research, archival and physical, is required to sort out and explain the discrepancies.

As Dr. Mann lays the bones out in anatomical order from head to toe, he looks for the duplication of certain bones. If he finds two right scapulas, he pulls another table over and lays the extra shoulder blade on it, for now he knows that he is dealing with two individuals. Then again, both a left and a right clavicle do not mean that only one individual is present. Dr. Mann

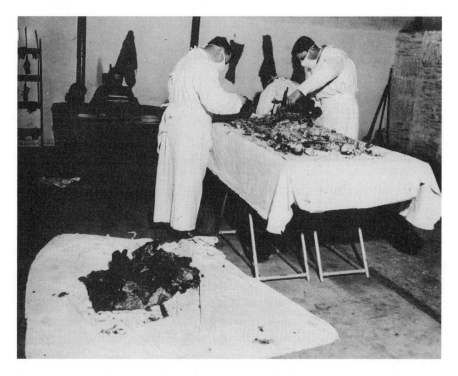

4.6 Parts of a skeleton being assembled in their respective positions, World War II. *U.S. Army Quartermaster Museum*

thinks of the human skeleton as 206 links of a chain, many of which are proportionate to each other in size, so "in the case of a missing link, you can still put the pieces together in the right order or you are able to reasonably ascertain that, because the left and right clavicle are of such different sizes, you are working with more than one individual."[34]

When those killed in military duty are quickly recovered, as is desired, they often have flesh from which fingerprints can be obtained. Fingerprinting was employed en masse in World War II and Korea, and *Technical Manual 10–630* called for medical personnel to record the thumbprints and fingerprints of the right hand, if available.[35] The current manual for identification of deceased personnel, *Field Manual No. 10–286*, also calls for fingerprinting all remains and, when the dead soldier is believed to be a member of the Air Force, obtaining footprints, because men shot down in planes were more likely to wind up scattered over great areas.[36]

However, special techniques had to be developed for taking fingerprints from corpses exposed to the elements, submerged in water, or otherwise compromised. The manual currently in use has a 36-page appendix of in-structions on fingerprinting; it explains how to "break" rigor mortis, how to remove the skin from the fingers of decomposed remains—they are then photographed, or a technician wraps the skin around his or her own finger and takes a print, and how to handle charred remains, and continues with examples of other difficult cases.[37]

While dental, anthropological, and fingerprint evidence is still part of current identification procedures, over the last ten to fifteen years, DNA analysis has also been used to help identify the dead, and technical manuals will eventually be rewritten to include DNA testing for current deaths. For deaths that occurred in years past—identification of historical recoveries—DNA sampling has given mixed results and is used as a "last resort" procedure.

Analyzing and Finding Matches

There are two main aspects of analyzing postmortem information and comparing it with antemortem data obtained from living service members: *who* does it and *how*. In its simplest form, the method mainly used until the early 1900s, matching of information from the living with that from the dead was a process of personal recognition performed by those closely associated with the soldier while alive. Recognizing the validity of such a method, a "Statement of Personal Identity," Department of Defense Form 565, is still a part of the identification process. However, Philip Caputo, who served in Vietnam, said, "The interesting thing was how the dead looked so much alike. Black men, white men, yellow men, they all looked remarkably the same."[38]

There are several potential pitfalls to relying solely on a statement of personal recognition. When the Union Army returned to Chancellorsville a year after its defeat there and combed the battlefield for its dead, those familiar with the deceased compared what they found with what they remembered: "I saw where poor Captain Kirk lay. His skull was entirely exposed, and lying on top of the grave. The fatal bullet that took his noble life was partly pushed out of the skull. We identified his remains by a peculiar mark on his shoulder-strap, one of which still adhered to his bones."[39] But what if, for some reason, another soldier had been wearing Captain Kirk's peculiar gear? Then the mistaken identity would have resulted in two errors, for the wrong soldier would have been designated as Captain Kirk and the real Captain Kirk would likely have remained an unknown.

The identification of World War I Soldier Dead was done primarily on the basis of social information: dog tags, personal effects, eyewitnesses. The

Quartermaster said, "The bodies of a vast majority of the dead possessed metal tags and no doubt to identity ever arose," and "To find a tag on the body was, of course, the most conclusive means of identification."[40] As discussed later in this chapter, there are issues associated with overreliance on social data.

After World War I, T. Wingate Todd of Case Western Reserve University in Cleveland, Ohio, collected more than 3,300 skeletons and subsequently published several articles that set forth methods for determining certain biological features: age, sex, race, stature.[41] While anthropological methods were available, they were not widely employed at the beginning of and during World War II, when identification procedures followed those of World War I—allowing that social evidence by itself could be conclusive. Regulations said: "The body will be searched and all personal property removed," and "When conclusive evidence of identity of deceased is not present, the fingerprints of both hands will be taken. If this is not possible, a tooth chart will be filled out and notation made on report of interment of anatomical characteristics."[42]

But after hostilities ceased, the American Graves Registration Service shouldered the task of identifying the thousands of unknowns. Its anthropologists at the central identification labs, looking for scientifically sound methods to assist them, began using W. M. Krogman's article, "Guide to the Identification of Human Skeletal Material," published in the *FBI Law Enforcement Bulletin* in 1939. Krogman's piece functioned as a "working manual." At the same time, Mildred Trotter, from the Department of Anatomy at Washington University, working at CILHI in 1948, prepared a new set of long-bone measurements that replaced the equations relied upon since 1899 to estimate the height of the body from which the bones came.[43]

However, the anthropologists' work after World War II mainly consisted of gathering data, not comparing it with information from antemortem records, which was a job held tightly by the Graves Registration Service. Basically, the experts obtained measurements and recorded the biological profile of the deceased while less-trained personnel did the final matching. At a minimum, this separation of duties left those doing the bone work professionally frustrated, as they were not able to gain "an awareness of positive contributions leading to the identification of any of the unknowns" or to conduct research.[44]

During the Korean War, the Quartermaster General asked Dr. T. D. Stewart of the Smithsonian Institution to continue studying the skeletal features of those killed in that conflict, and Stewart's work contributed greatly

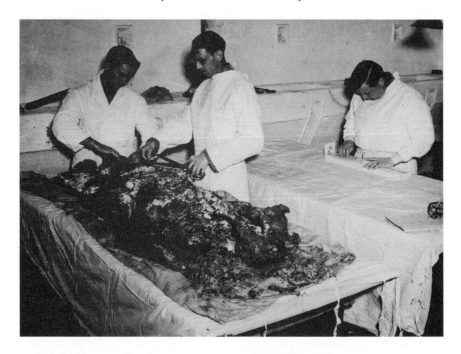

4.7   Technicians conduct bone measurements, World War II. *U.S. Army Quartermaster Museum*

to the field of age estimation of young American males.[45] However, he found that, despite a very broad job description, the central identification lab anthropologists were "almost wholly involved with the anthropological side of the identification procedure" and exercised little supervisory or advisory authority.[46] Again, the Graves Registration Record Division maintained its role as chief matchmaker.

Eventually, though, the Army accorded the anthropologists a larger role in the overall identification process at the laboratory in Kokura, Japan. This was the beginning of the development of anthropological methods to identify military remains.[47] When the identification lab moved to Thailand after the Vietnam War, the anthropologists' role expanded to include a formal report of identity finding that was "scientifically sound for presentation in a court of law." Also, in a very important development, anthropologists were engaged to conduct investigations, both in the field and in files that contained information about deaths: "after-action reports, statements of incident, aircraft manifests."[48]

Ever since, anthropologists have been recognized as a highly trained individual who can make valuable contributions beyond the postmortem study of remains. CILHI has the largest single group of forensic anthropologists in the world and the Armed Forces Institute of Pathology, home to physicians and scientists in many fields, is also called upon to assist with identification.

Since the early 1990s, the United States has adopted and well funded the policy of continuing to search for its Soldier Dead from World War II, the Korean War, the Cold War, and the Vietnam War, and the process of identifying remains has become somewhat dichotomized. The Joint POW/MIA Accounting Command (JPAC) is the newly formed (as of 2003) unit merging the former U.S. Army Central Identification Laboratory Hawaii (CILHI) and the former Joint Task Force-Full Accounting (JTF-FA). JPAC conducts recovery operations of soldiers missing from the Vietnam War and also mounts worldwide operations to find those from other time periods. The identification of current deaths, such as those from the Iraq War, is handled by the Office of the Armed Forces Medical Examiner (OAFME) and Mortuary Affairs.

Over time, the reliance on mostly social methods of identification has lessened as the role of anthropological, odontological, and biochemical methods has increased. The continually developing physical methods do not supplant previously established methods; rather, they greatly supplement them. In this manner, the identification of Soldier Dead has become increasingly successful, even given the destructive effects of ever more potent weaponry.

To reduce as much as possible the errors in identification—which has occurred—the matching of information from remains with the records of those presumed killed has evolved over time to incorporate data from as many sources as possible, and identification is based upon the preponderance of evidence.[49] Also, the personnel doing the actual comparisons have become highly trained and specialized.

A new tool used for identification of both historical and current deaths is molecular DNA analysis. The Armed Forces DNA Identification Laboratory (AFDIL), located in Rockville, Maryland, performs both nuclear and mitochondrial analysis to determine if remains are those of a particular person. In nuclear analysis, the DNA extracted from the nucleus of the remains cell is amplified through a process called polymerase chain reaction, or PCR, that mimics the natural replication of DNA so that a sufficient quantity is available for testing. Researchers also have to subject cells from the person presumed deceased to a similar process, and then compare the results of the two tests. Of course, there must be items available from which the deceased's cells can be taken, such as baby teeth, toothbrushes, stored semen, or blood. The need for a current specimen is the reason for the DNA specimen cards now prepared from blood samples of current Armed Forces member.

In the case of historical recoveries, it is not likely that any surviving objects will yield cells from which the deceased's nuclear DNA can be extracted. In these cases, scientists fall back on another method, mitochondrial DNA (mtDNA) analysis. Two properties of mtDNA make it useful. First, the mitochondria, or powerhouses, of the cells yield hundreds and thousands of DNA molecules, whereas the nucleus contains only two copies per cell, and these large numbers of mtDNA increase the success rate of PCR amplification. Second, mtDNA is inherited through the maternal line, with few if any changes other than from random mutations. Thus, a son's mtDNA will look the same as his mother's, his sister's, and even that of his sister's children. Therefore, the maternal relative of a missing serviceperson can provide mtDNA samples for comparison to samples obtained from remains.

While mtDNA amplification is more likely to produce a sufficient sample of DNA for typing than nuclear amplification in many cases, the latter is the first choice since it provides a direct reference to the deceased. Also, since mtDNA is inherited by all maternal descendants, many individuals may share the same mtDNA. It is conceivable that missing soldiers Jim Smith and John Davis share a maternal ancestor at some point and that this association is not known. If the recovered remains undergo mtDNA testing, Smith could be identified as Davis, or vice versa. Of course, rarely is identification made solely on the basis of a mtDNA match—other evidence is considered. Yet the discrimination level of mtDNA analysis is sufficiently high to be used with confidence in the identification process.[50]

In cases when remains are badly decomposed or otherwise "insulted" by fire, fragmentation, or chemical processes, it is often not possible to obtain good nuclear DNA. Dr. Mann recounted a situation in which a plane went down in Vietnam and exhaustive digging yielded only one bone fragment. Since the D-rings for two parachutes were found, so it was assumed that two individuals had been involved in the crash. But since usable DNA could not be extracted from the burned bone fragment, there was no way to tell from which soldier it had come.[51] (What happens to unidentified "group remains" is covered in chapter 6, "Burial.")

Before the use of DNA analysis, traditional comparisons of postmortem and antemortem physical data used only fingerprints, dental, and anthropological features, and it is likely that there will always be a combined approach using all these factors to solve identity questions. The Pentagon terrorist attack caused extensive trauma to bodies, from both impact and fire, and dental features "served as the sole method of identification" of 30 percent of those killed there.[52] The DNA specimen cards were available for 50 of the military members and helped to provide a direct reference for those remains from which DNA could be extracted.[53]

Fingerprints are now taken from all remains when possible, even if there is little question about identity, such as a four-star general slumping over at his desk from a heart attack.[54] Fingerprint comparison, though, is not infallible: good-quality prints may not be obtained; only 70 percent of service member prints are on file with the FBI; and of those on file, 15 to 30 percent are not usable.[55]

The actual comparison of ante- and postmortem data presents challenges because possible matches for a recovered unknown may be very large. In the case of a recent plane crash in which it is known who the 8 crew members on board were, the comparison process to associate and identify remains is not too daunting—although it is quite possible that there may be portions of remains that can't be associated with a single individual. But if several hundred remains are disinterred from gravesites in North Korea, a distinct possibility at some point in the future, then it will be very difficult to match their anthropological and dental characteristics to information in the files of the more than 8,000 missing unless efficient means of comparison can be devised.

Computer-assisted data comparison has aided the process of matching. During the Korean War, IBM "punch cards" were introduced, containing certain identification characteristics of each service member: name, rank, serial number, race, shoe size, scars, tattoos, fractures, hair color, height, dental work, year of birth, location of death. If an investigator had an unidentified remains with no skull, he could ask for a card sort on the existing features and obtain a list of potential candidates. Ensuing work could further reduce the possibilities, or even result in positive identification.[56]

CILHI has developed advanced computer matching techniques and established a database of all available dental records of U.S. Armed Forces members whose remains have not been recovered/identified. A forensic odontologist enters data obtained from remains into a specialized computer program, the Casualty Automated Recovery and Identification System (CARIS), which then sorts out possible matches. With a narrowed list of Soldier Dead candidates, the scientist requests the original dental records from the Casualty Data Analysis section and then performs a closer comparison of the records to the remains.[57]

FAMILY REFERENCE COLLECTION FORM

Nuclear DNA Analysis   AFDIL CASE NUMBER _____

DONOR INFORMATION

LAST NAME	FIRST NAME	MIDDLE NAME

SOCIAL SECURITY NUMBER (If Applicable)	HOME TELEPHONE

HOME STREET ADDRESS

CITY	STATE	ZIP	COUNTRY

DATE OF BIRTH (Month/Day/Year)

FAMILY RELATIONSHIP

PLEASE CIRCLE YOUR KINSHIP TO THE MISSING INDIVIDUAL
* Primary Donor For A Nuclear DNA Reference (See list of Primary Donors on Page 2)

MISSING INDIVIDUAL INFORMATION

LAST NAME	FIRST NAME	MIDDLE NAME

DATE OF BIRTH (Month/Day/Year)	SOCIAL SECURITY NUMBER (If Applicable)

4.8   Flowchart of family relationship for nuclear DNA testing. *Armed Forces DNA Identification Laboratory (AFDIL)*

FAMILY REFERENCE COLLECTION FORM

Mitochondrial DNA Analysis   AFDIL Case #: _____

DONOR INFORMATION

LAST NAME	FIRST NAME	MIDDLE NAME

SOCIAL SECURITY NUMBER (If Applicable)	HOME TELEPHONE

HOME STREET ADDRESS

CITY	STATE	ZIP	COUNTRY

DATE OF BIRTH (Month/Day/Year)	ETHNIC GROUP (See Table On Page2)

FAMILY RELATIONSHIP

PLEASE CIRCLE YOUR KINSHIP TO THE MISSING INDIVIDUAL
* Primary Donor For A Mitochondrial DNA Reference

- *GRANDMOTHER — GRANDFATHER
- *AUNT — *UNCLE — *MOTHER — FATHER
- *COUSIN-Female — *COUSIN-Male — *SISTER — *BROTHER — MISSING INDIVIDUAL — SPOUSE
- *2nd COUSIN-Female — *2ND COUSIN-Male — *NIECE — *NEPHEW
- *3rd COUSIN-Male — + DAUGHTER — + SON
- *3rd COUSIN-Female — *GREAT NIECE — *GREAT NEPHEW — +Biological Children Of Missing Female Can Be Used As A Maternal MtDNA Reference

MISSING INDIVIDUAL INFORMATION

LAST NAME	FIRST NAME	MIDDLE NAME

DATE OF BIRTH (Month/Day/Year)	SOCIAL SECURITY NUMBER (If Applicable) Or SERVICE NUMBER (If Known)	CONFLICT (If Applicable)	
		BRANCH OF SERVICE (If Applicable)	REFNO (If Applicable)

4.9   Flowchart of family relationship for mtDNA testing. *Armed Forces DNA Identification Laboratory (AFDIL)*

Another form of computerized dental identification, *WinID*, was used after the Pentagon terrorist attack to compare antemortem and postmortem dental information. This method of analysis was the fortunate result of a planning meeting earlier in the year to digitize previously existing x-ray and dental chart information to enable quicker comparison in the future. Much of the equipment required to perform this upgrade had just been shipped to Dover Air Force Base and was set up to process dental identification records from the Pentagon dead.[58]

When AFDIL does a DNA analysis, a computer program compares the polymorphisms—differences—between the remains and the references. Then an analyst assigned to the case manually performs a double check.[59] Clearly, without the aid of sophisticated computers, the matching of ante- and post-mortem data would be much more time-consuming and subject to error.

But, while obtaining DNA from the remains of current service members has helped in making identifications, getting usable DNA from the remains of those killed decades ago has been difficult. Dr. Thomas D. Holland, Scientific Director at CILHI, has supervised the exhumation of unknowns from World War II and the Korean War, and says that attempts by AFDIL to extract usable DNA from them have not been very successful. Dr. Holland suspects that the use of a formaldehyde-based hardening compound and, perhaps, extensive fluoroscoping may have caused the DNA strands to cross-link and fold in on themselves, rendering the samples useless for analysis.[60] Until these problems are resolved, exhumations of other World War II and Korean remains for the purpose of DNA testing will wait. However, CILHI, in May 2003, was able through its newly updated dental analysis program to identify one of the unknowns as Private Ronald D. Lilledahl, and is hoped that the improved dental matching program will allow future identifications.[61]

There is still one problem in identifying remains: lost or nonexistent antemortem medical records. The experts were stymied in some identification efforts after World War II because there was no master file of dental records as there was for fingerprints.[62] In the years after the Korean War, personnel files were moved around a great deal, and many were burned in a 1973 fire at the National Personnel Records Center in St. Louis. There were also serious lapses in common sense with regard to medical records. For example, the Army personnel on the Gander flight were, unfortunately and in what can only be described as an extreme lack of foresight, carrying their medical and dental records.[63] The plane, fully laden with fuel, crashed on takeoff and exploded. Needless to say, the records were destroyed.

Still, twenty years later, obtaining antemortem medical records for Armed Forces personnel is not as easy as might be thought. Karen Giles, Director of Mortuary Affairs at Dover Air Force Base, said that the number one obstacle in making identification of remains was obtaining medical records of those believed to be deceased.[64] The nature and manner of death, the condition of remains, and the availability of experts are not the chief culprits; instead, obtaining, maintaining, and transferring the right paperwork is. Furthermore, an exhaustive audit of CILHI by the General Accounting Office (GAO) in 1992 said, "Our review of 113 antemortem records on file at CILHI showed that in many cases, the records did not have all of the essential information typically need to make an identification."[65]

While the GAO review applied to CILHI operations in the early 1990s— and the deficiency in antemortem information as well as the lack of physical control of remains, inadequate library, and incomplete file case management have all since been addressed—it is baffling that the problem in obtaining antemortem information has continued to this day.

Discrepancies, Errors, Issues

Given the amount of technology, time, expertise, and expense allocated to recording antemortem information, obtaining postmortem information, and then comparing the two, one might wonder how there could still be any unidentified Soldier Dead at all, or how identification might be subject to question. Unfortunately, the terrorist attacks on September 11, 2001 provided an excellent, if unwanted, education about the difficulties of identification in cases of severe trauma and fire.

In wartime conditions, it was often more difficult to establish identity, as many recoveries and burials were done under extreme stress and there were hardly enough resources to care for the living, let alone the dead. While identification is supposed to begin at recovery/burial, the old saying, "When you are up to your rear end in alligators, it's hard to remember sometimes that your initial objective was to drain the swamp," certainly applies: teams responsible for securing bodies/remains are often under pressure from enemy or environmental forces.

During World War I, soldiers killed were often hastily buried in battle-field cemeteries with little dignity and scant attention to identification.[66] There were mix-ups: at times they were buried at irregular intervals but crosses were placed with proper spacing, so that bodies were "one, two, three and four graves either to the right or left of their respective markers."[67] To help maintain a record of "burial irregularities," the GRS prepared a report showing:

(1) Where more bodies are found in a grave than the grave market specifies.

(2) Where graves opened contain no bodies.

(3) Where graves opened for a certain person are found to contain the remains of an entirely different person.

(4) Where burial is improperly made, such as buried face down, at an insufficient depth or not in coffin.

(5) Discrepancies between grave marker and tag on body.[68]

These problems manifested themselves in the next world war as well. Markers were created for graves containing no remains; grave reports sometimes listed two individuals with the same grave location. In the Pacific Ocean area, grave concentration records showed more bodies being exhumed than were listed in theater records as having been buried. Most unsettling was the realization that some Soldier Dead had become separated from their identity during concentration operations.[69]

At the beginning of the Korean War, GRS personnel were stretched too thin to perform or oversee all burials. One unfortunate result was the loss of identification information when untrained troops assumed GRS duties: "the neglect in recording all identification media when it was readily available was costly, as later events proved."[70]

In the Vietnam War, even though the time between death and arrival at the morgue had been reduced to hours, proper identification was not to be taken for granted. 1st Lieutenant William (Bill) Grafe (discharged) was Chief Mortuary Officer and Executive of the Da Nang Mortuary from 1967 to 1968. After a firefight in Quang Nam, several soldiers were killed and one body that had been taken to the Graves Registration collection point needed identification. A sergeant from the unit viewed the remains and said, "Yeah, that's Quinn." Procedure at that time required two visual identifications, and a second man from the unit said, "Oh yeah, sergeant, that's Quinn." Grafe checked the roster and found the name John Quinn. After being embalmed, the body was transported to the family of the deceased. Two days later, John Quinn "turned up very much alive," and, as Grafe said, "The shit hit the fan." He quickly reread the service unit roster and found that there was a serviceman named Quinn Tichenor. After this case of misidentification, no remains left the mortuary without fingerprints and dental charts, if they could be obtained.[71]

The Tichenor error, or one like it, was bound to happen for at least two reasons. First, social evidence—dog tags, visual identification, and personal effects—was considered sufficient to make identification. Second, as in every previous war, there were not enough trained personnel in Graves Registration Services to handle the dead. Gregg, the specialist who had worked in the Da Nang morgue prior to Grafe, felt that the replacements for him and others leaving at the same time were poorly motivated, poorly trained, and poorly supervised.[72]

Gregg also had heard of a mother insisting that a casket be opened, only to find the wrong body inside. The story goes that, even though the remains were not recognizable, the mother knew it was the wrong body because of the watch on its wrist; it was not the one her son would have been wearing. While this account is anecdotal, it well expresses the desire of the family to "view" remains. Purportedly, John Quinn's mother opened the casket too, but was not able to confirm or deny identification because of the condition of the remains.

Family members wanting to make certain that the remains are, indeed, those of their beloved is not a recent phenomenon. Amos and Sarah Colley's son died from his wounds received at the Civil War battle of Cedar Mountain, and they paid to have his body shipped home to them in Maine—at that time, families sometimes had the option of receiving remains if they were able to bear the cost of embalming and transportation. When Mr. and Mrs. Colley opened the casket to pay final respects to their son, they were shocked to find not only the wrong body, but the remains of a Confederate soldier. They buried the unknown soldier in the local cemetery and later, after finally receiving the correct remains, buried their son in the family plot.[73]

While opening the casket may seem like a very natural thing for the family to do, the stark reality is that very often what is inside bears little resemblance to the deceased, or even to a person at all. Knowing that families would likely be horrified by what they saw, the government has tried to communicate to the next of kin, or Person Authorized to Direct Disposition of remains (PADD), that such a viewing may yield little information and may result in additional emotional distress. During World War II, Senator Richard B. Russell of Georgia received a letter from Alvin R. Sammon of F. Q. Sammon Funeral Home, inquiring if there were a law against opening the casket of a returned Soldier Dead. Sammon, brother-in-law to the deceased's father, reported that the family wanted to open the casket in order to confirm identity. The soldier in question had died in a plane crash and burned along with four others on the plane.

R. P. Harbold of the Memorial Division of the Quartermaster responded to Senator Russell's question, stating that there was no such law. However, Harbold also explained that, in the case of traumatic death when remains were in a hermetically sealed casket because of circumstances that prevented embalming or were not displayable, the casket was marked "not to be opened." But, he noted, state and local laws allowing, the instruction was advisory only. In such cases, a letter was normally sent to the "receiving undertaker explaining the nature of death, condition of remains when received by the preparing undertaker, the establishment of identity of the deceased," with the goal of encouraging the family to accept the remains and identity without seeing for themselves.[74]

✓ Of course, the family's confidence in the government's identification efforts depends upon many factors, not the least of which is information about how the process works. In World War I, there was some public misunderstanding of the detail involved in identification, and the press reported concerns about accuracy. Lt. Col. Edward Comm held the belief—proven time and again to be valid, whether the subject is impending corporate restructuring or the receipt of information about terrorist threats to the United States—that the absence of information creates a vacuum that people will fill with anything, right or wrong, and that the best way to prevent misconceptions is to provide full information, from as close to the source as possible. Comm wanted stories about the identification work to "come from the field rather than from Washington."[75] Obviously, he was aware that word from what is now called a "no-spin zone" would help the government make its case in the forum of public opinion.

In World War I, a U.S. soldier killed in France was interred, and soon afterward his father came to visit the gravesite. The father wanted to bring his son back to the United States, but this was forbidden at the time. Later, the body was exhumed and its identification checked, and it was reburied in a permanent cemetery. At this time, a dental chart was prepared and, along with other evidence, sent to Washington and later forwarded to the father for his review. The father and consulting dentists felt that there was a mistake— that the body purported to be his son's was that of another serviceman. The body was disinterred again, another, more detailed dental chart was made, and the body was re-reburied. A consulting dentist again responded that the corrected chart did not show a certain type of crown that he had put in the son's upper left jaw. The body was exhumed and examined a third time, and the dental chart was amended to show the particular feature that the son's dentist had mentioned.

By this time, any family member would have reasonable cause to doubt what was being reported, and the father cabled a request "that his son's remains be not removed until his arrival in Europe." Armed with a model of the "Richmond" crown that had been installed in his son's mouth, the father attended the fourth exhumation of the remains in question. The officer in charge of the cemetery persuaded him to not watch the actual disinterment, but to wait some distance away. Then the officer extracted the particular tooth containing the unique dental work from the remains and carried it to the father for comparison.

The anticipatory tension for all involved must have been palpable. The father and other family members had, for months if not for a year or more, lived with the uncertainty of not knowing if their loved one had been found and properly buried. The cemetery in question was the site of a great deal of activity; there would have been open graves everywhere, wagons loaded with caskets, workmen with well-worn shovels, and many men in uniform hurrying to and fro. And, off to one side, two figures—one, the GRS official, representing the government's attempt to recover and identify more than 70,000 Soldier Dead, and the other, a father, emblematic of the extended families of the fallen—facing each other, both hoping for a final accounting. In this case, the father found a perfect match between the copy and the actual tooth and was satisfied with the identification.[76]

In another case, though, matters were not resolved so conclusively. An Air Force lieutenant was reportedly buried in an isolated grave in France, near Tronville. The identification evidence was "meagre," consisting of a monogrammed handkerchief and incomplete grave marker notations. The grave was opened and found to contain two bodies, both in such a state that little physical evidence could be obtained, but one wore underwear with the initials of the supposedly deceased. The family was skeptical of the findings, so the grave was reopened and a dental chart made. The family rejected both the clothing and the dental evidence, stating that the deceased had worn clothes with his full name written on them in indelible ink, that the dental chart was inconclusive, and that the parts found near the crash site were not from the type of airplane in which their son had flown. In this case, the GRS and the family were at an impasse; the government made its determination on the evidence it considered sufficient and closed the file.[77]

In an excellent example of how history can repeat itself, the same kind of disagreement between the U.S. government and a family occurred again after the Vietnam War. In this case, the Army morgue in Vietnam identified remains based on information from the medical records of the supposedly deceased. The family, though, provided medical information different from what was in the files. CILHI reexamined the remains, found them to be consistent with the existing records, and said, "the decision for a recommended identification was valid."[78] Who was right? Until and unless the remains are disinterred and a DNA test is completed, the answer can't be known for sure.

There is not much information available about identification concerns pertaining to World War II remains, but, since the dead were not returned until at least two years after the end of hostilities, it is likely that few, if any, caskets were opened because of the condition of the contents. Also, the public was probably trusting of the government's efforts to identify and return the dead and less likely to question results.

In World War II, the statement, "Thus, there is absolutely no question of the possibility of the positive identification of remains"[79] appeared in a publication directed to the families of those killed. This was a highly propagandized claim that, although desirable, was patently false. However, it was consistent with the other politically influenced statements of that period. But even if not 100 percent true, the statement does not mean that the identification efforts were riddled with errors. The government did, and still does, despite occasional exceptions, work diligently to ensure accuracy.

While the interval between death and return of remains was less during the Korean War than World War II, it is still likely that few caskets were opened. Yet even though the public had not yet become as suspicious and jaded as after the Vietnam War, the Korean War marked the beginning of general disillusionment with both the war cause and the government's efforts to fully account for its military personnel. This loss of innocence, so to speak, was one of many factors that laid the groundwork for the establishment of family "activist" groups that protested the government's similar lack of accounting for Vietnam servicemen.

A great deal of controversy surrounds the identification of Soldier Dead recovered from the Vietnam War. Sergeant 1st Class Frank Parrish, a Special Forces advisor to the South Vietnamese, was on a mission on January 16, 1968, near My Tho when he and his group were ambushed. Parrish and a fellow Special Forces member, Early Biggs, were reportedly captured and summarily executed. Five years later, in June 1973, remains were found, identified, and returned to the Parrish family for burial. Johnnie Parrish, Frank's older brother, had doubts about the identification and was, as he recollects, told that he "could accept or reject the findings," but that they were final.

However, in late December 1989, Johnnie and other family members were told that remains recently turned over to U.S. authorities by the Vietnamese had been identified as Frank Parrish and that an exchange with those previously interred would follow. But because of botched communications, the disinterment and exchange of the now unknown remains and the preparations for the burial of Frank Parrish were undertaken without the family being informed.[80]

As important as, and perhaps more important than, the failure to communicate is the fact that any misidentification can result in multiple other problems. First, if the remains buried were not those of Frank Parrish, whose were they? Was there a missing service member on the books who could have been accounted for had the identification been done correctly? The remains originally identified as those of Frank Parrish were, 14 years later, found to be those of Army Spc. 4th Class Carl Wadleigh. For 36 years, the Army and Wadleigh's family believed that Carl had gone AWOL, based in part on records indicating that he had not shown up for a medical procedure in 1968. Then, in November 2001, Army officials asked for blood samples from two of Carl's siblings. After conducting tests comparing the DNA from the remains to those from the siblings, officials concluded that Carl Wadleigh had, indeed, died fighting for his country, and he was given a full military funeral. Unfortunately, Wadleigh's parents had died before his honor was restored.[81]

And, on the flip side, if a Missing in Action (MIA) case is closed by the misidentification of remains, there is the real and distinct possibility, if this person is actually being held as a prisoner of war (POW), that he or she might be overlooked during settlement talks with opposing countries. Frank Parrish could conceivably have been held as a POW and the United States would have been none the wiser.

Many of the problems with identification technical work can be directly attributed to lack of support—both in resources and in properly trained personnel—but it is hardly fair to say that there was a conspiracy to perpetrate fraud upon the American public. CILHI, in particular, has come under fire in the past for shoddy work. At one point its operations were overseen by a technician, Tadao Furue, who had learned anthropology in the lab and had no formal schooling. Furue's methodology, "morphological approximation," "has not been accepted as having sound scientific basis for utilization as a method of identification."[82]

In morphological approximation, Furue claimed to be able to estimate, within a relatively small range, the stature of individuals from only partial sections of long bones. While there has been much credible science on height estimation from complete long bone measurement, it is quite a stretch to calculate usable estimates from only a section of a long bone because the range of possible heights is so great as to include most, if not all, service personnel. In particular, anthropologist Dr. Steven Byers prepared a paper for Dr. Michael Charney, a noted anthropologist, who was reviewing CILHI's forensic findings. Dr. Byers calculated that, at best, there was a 15-inch range in possible height using the method of estimation from a section of a humerus, or upper arm bone.[83]

When Dr. William R. Maples, another prominent anthropologist, participated in a review of CILHI, he and the other investigators were "pushed inexorably toward a painful conclusion: some of Furue's identifications of the Pakse remains simply would not hold water," and "many of the identifications were made on distressingly little evidence indeed, based on an examination of the scantiest of remains." (The Pakse case involved remains from an AC-130A gunship that had been shot down over Laos on December 21, 1972.) But no one accused Furue of evil duplicity—only of trying too hard to make identifications to offer families some relief. Indeed, during his tenure, Furue bought equipment and reference materials using his own funds.[84] But his desire to try to bring closure to families actually compounded their grief in some cases.

Fortunately, though, at or about the time of Tadao Furue's death in 1987, a "nationally prominent senior forensic anthropologist," Dr. Ellis Kerley, was hired as Scientific Director at CILHI. However, Dr. Madeleine Hinkes described, the staff still worked out of a "horrible little building" on a dockside pier where import cars were unloaded.[85] According to Dr. Holland, current Scientific Director, the lab in Hawaii labored under a shortage of personnel, money, and recognition from 1976 to 1991, and it wasn't until 1992 that it was given the resources necessary to adequately carry out its duties and responsibilities.[86]

Since there have always been difficulties in making some identifications, some form of review is necessary. After World War I, a Board of Review was established and assigned cases in which there were irregularities or uncertainties. By August 1922, it had reviewed 1,746 cases, identified 1,061, and referred 685 to Washington for further investigation.[87] Another Board of Review was established after World War II, in the spring of 1947, and was staffed with three or more commissioned officers. The board had the duties of deciding upon cases of identification referred to it and evaluating the "nonrecoverability of remains." In making identification, the board followed instructions that laid down the rules, as it were, indicating when identification would be conclusive unless conflicting evidence existed. For instance, if an isolated remains had a dog tag on the neck or directly nearby, such as in a pocket, the remains would be associated with the identity on the tag. A paybook or paycard would be conclusive evidence only if found in the clothing of the slain soldier. If all but one of a group of remains could be identified and the names of all group members could be ascertained with relative certainty, then the unidentified remains would be identified by the process of elimination. The board, once it reached its decision, forwarded its findings to the Memorial Division for subsequent approval.[88]

Currently, the Casualty and Memorial Affairs Board of Officers will "assist . . . in the resolution of special cases that involve the identification, non-identifiability, or nonrecoverability of the remains" other than those from the Vietnam War, which are handled by the Armed Forces Identification Review Board.[89]

There is perhaps no better example of discrepancies, errors, and issues in identification than the case of the Vietnam unknown. Congress, enacting Public Law 93–43, decreed that the remains of one member of the U.S. Armed Forces whose identity was not established be interred in the Tomb of the Unknowns. During 1981–82, the Reagan administration, in an honorable attempt to pay due respect to the Vietnam veterans and to those killed and to form a collective remembrance of the faceless soldier who served our country, began pushing for this grave to be filled. However, because of advanced recovery/identification methods and the fact that many deaths were from gunfire rather than the more destructive forces of artillery, there were few unknown candidates, and most were quickly eliminated, leaving two remains as, supposedly, truly unidentifiable. But one had a full upper dental structure that would likely provide enough postmortem information for identification, should antemortem dental records be located, so the other remains labeled X-26 were chosen by the process of elimination.

That process diverged from previous unknown identification methods, in which a decorated serviceman, guided by his own internal compass, made a choice from several available candidates. Also, Public Law 93–43 called for remains that were mostly complete, but X-26 consisted of only fragmentary portions. Tradition was followed, though, when the records, or most of them, in the file of X-26 were destroyed and, following a solemn ceremony, the remains were buried at Arlington on Memorial Day 1984. But it is not fair to say that the Unknown Soldier was laid to rest, for an intense struggle over his burial later ensued.

After suspecting for years that the Vietnam unknown at Arlington was her son, Mrs. George C. Blassie became aware of evidence recovered at the site where the X-26 remains were found and learned of advances in DNA profiling that could be useful in establishing identification. She began urging the Pentagon to disinter the remains and to run tests. Finally, on May 14, 1998, the Vietnam unknown was exhumed; a biological profile was prepared by CILHI anthropologists and an mtDNA test conducted by AFDIL. On June 30, 1998, the then Secretary of Defense, William S. Cohen, announced that the tests did, in fact, confirm the identity of the remains to be that of First Lieutenant Michael J. Blassie of the Air Force.[90]

The disinterment of the Vietnam unknown encapsulated several competing issues. First was the desire to maintain the sanctity of the tomb—not to disturb the remains. Second was the desire to satisfy the need for a full accounting when possible. Third, opening the tomb would, in effect, open Pandora's box in that the government might then be faced with requests for reinvestigation of other unknowns. Fourth was the matter of legal precedence—according to 24 U.S.C. 295(a), the Secretary of Defense was "required to obtain congressional authorization to *entomb* remains in the Arlington Memorial Amphitheater. There [were] no statutes governing the *disinterment* of remains from the Tomb of the Unknowns."[91] But last and most important, the disinterment of Michael Blassie was the correction of action taken in haste: there had been sufficient cause to keep the remains of X-26 at CILHI, pending the receipt of further information or development of new techniques.

Blassie was making a low-level attack run in an A-37 on May 11, 1972, when he was hit by antiaircraft fire and crashed in a near inverted attitude; no parachutes were observed and an explosion followed immediately after impact. Because of enemy activity, it was five months before South Vietnamese troops recovered four ribs, part of a pelvis, and a right humerus near an ejection seat found close to the plane wreckage. Also, personal effects, including money, Blassie's military ID card, dog tags, and other identifying items were recovered, but lost somewhere on the way to the mortuary.

Despite the existence of records showing that Blassie's personal effects had been found near the bones and that, according to the South Vietnamese troops, the bones were definitely recovered near the crash site of an A-37, CILHI recommended in 1978 that the "Believed To Be" (BTB) status of Michael Blassie be removed from the remains, an action concurred with by the Chief of Air Force Mortuary in 1979 and subsequently acted on by the Armed Services Graves Registration Office in 1980.

One of the main reasons for concluding that the remains were not those of Blassie was the anthropological evaluation that deduced, from the length of the recovered humerus, that the estimated height of the deceased was too short. Yet, when considering the range of heights—that of the remains was thought to be from 5'5" to 5'11½" while Blassie's height was recorded as 5'11" to 6'¾"—the measurements seem too close to rule out Blassie. Also, the results of a blood test that was only relatively accurate in the best of circumstances indicated that the blood found on a flight suit near the remains was not Blassie's.

It is one thing to remove a BTB status from remains, but quite another to assert that the remains are truly "unidentifiable." Also, if the logic of the analysis recommending this particular BTB removal is closely reviewed, a couple of glaring contradictions come to light. First, the Pentagon stated that finding identifying personal effects near the crash site does not mean that the remains are those of the person to whom the effects belong. Yet the results of the blood typing from the flight suit *were* accepted as part of the evidence that the remains *were not* Blassie's. Second, the forensic exam by CILHI in the late 1970s indicated that the remains were hardly likely to be Blassie's, but the one conducted after disinterment did not reach a similar conclusion.[92]

Supposedly, even Tadao Furue felt that the remains of X-26 "had been wrested prematurely from his care."[93] Basically, despite official protests to the contrary, it is clear that a combination of bad science and political pressure to entomb an unknown resulted in the improper interment of remains that were later identified.

Given the problems with Blassie and other cases from Vietnam—in handling, in identification, and in subsequent case review—one has to wonder about the identifications made by the U.S. military. While there can be little doubt about accuracy now, even when working with small pieces of remains, such a confident statement cannot be made about the past. The GAO audit of CILHI in 1992 addressed the question of whether or not the 223 Southeast Asia remains identifications made prior to 1987, when CILHI was under the direction of Tadao Furue, were valid. The GAO did not itself review prior cases, but did consider the reviews, conducted by consultants hired by the Army, of a substantial number of previously closed identifications. These consultants concluded that "most of the cases were good, strong, or positive identifications." The GAO felt that any analysis it did "would add little, if any, insight to what had already been disclosed"—basically, that too much time had gone by, too many people who had worked the cases were no longer available, and it was obvious that problems had existed in previously closed cases.[94]

There are unresolved identification issues from World War I and World War II—not missing servicemen, but soldiers who died in close proximity and in situations that not only caused their remains to be commingled but

4.10 Cross marking the grave of two unknown men whose remains are commingled. *National Archives & Records Administration*

also resulted in neither of their names being known. These men were buried together as "unknowns," and there is very little that is currently being done to sort them out and determine who they are.

Author's Notes

"What have I gotten into, what sort of business have I gotten into?"

Dr. Thomas D. Holland, who was the Scientific Director of CILHI at the time I interviewed him in November 2002, spoke of his initial doubts as he sat behind his desk and reminisced about his first days at the Army lab in Hawaii. He had agreed to relocate from Missouri to Hawaii, leaving his wife—with a small child and a newborn—to sell their house and follow him later. Just before his move in spring 1992, Holland watched President Bush respond to heckling by a family POW activist group by telling them to "Sit down and shut up!" This prompted even more consternation about his decision.

Dr. Holland is a dedicated professional with a calm demeanor, and Bush's harsh words no doubt grated on his sensitivities. Yet, ten years later he was still in Honolulu, continuing to bring scientific expertise to a field that badly needed it and granting me a thorough interview.

This chapter concludes the first half of *Soldier Dead* and lays the foundation for accounts of repatriation, burial, and offering tribute, the most visible stages in the treatment of deceased military personnel. These processes couldn't take place without the little understood and more obscure—"obscured" would be a fit description at times—processes of recovery and identification.

Since we struggle with the creation of a postdeath identity of those killed in military service and wish to determine whether or not the loss of life has been for a worthwhile cause, it is necessary to develop a reliable process by which remains are recovered and identified. Once we have retrieved and identified bodies, they can be returned to the next of kin, who can then proceed with their individual good-byes and mourning. Also, the families and the nation can then begin to balance the scales as they assess the results of the armed conflict, with the dead on one side and the benefits to the living on the other.

As in any foundation where construction faults are carried forward to the more visible structure, errors in identification create doubts in the minds and anguish in the hearts of the living. What is the error rate now in identification? What was the rate in previous wars? In asking these questions, one must understand that the definition of "error" as the mistake of one body being tagged with the name of another is a gross oversimplification. While this is certainly the most obvious form of misidentification—and it has happened—the issue is much more complicated because of the manner in which bodies are mangled and commingled in modern warfare. It is probably accurate to say that it is "not an error" if most of the remains one buries are those of the deceased. That is, a family member would likely be satisfied burying or otherwise providing a final disposition for remains so long as the majority represented their loved one; the presence of some amount of the remains of others would be of little consequence, to them at least.

The military does not like to talk in detail about problems identifying the pieces of bodies that often wind up on the sterile tables at Dover; they would much prefer discussion in general, euphemistic terms. Interviewees have taken a very cautious and defensive tone, waiting to see if I was simply a voyeur roaming among them, looking for an arm, foot, or other piece of flesh to seize upon and morbidly examine. To the extent that I have been curious about the details of identification, I believe I have asked many of the questions that lurk in the minds of many people: Why is the casket closed? How did he/she die? What, exactly, am I burying? How do I know I'm burying who you say I am? These, and more, are all questions that exist even if not asked outright.

Once interviewees were reassured that I was not writing to titillate—usually only after a discussion in which I expressed some working knowledge of forensics and an appreciation for the sensitivity of the subject by describing my research into earlier time periods—the atmosphere relaxed somewhat. Yet at times when talking to body handlers, I could glimpse the information I wanted, but saw that it was surrounded by sensitive nerves and required very careful extraction. I was, of course, an outsider, while they wore the garments of a secret order.

With personnel having a forensic background, the identification issue was discussed in a nonemotional, almost clinical manner. But with Public Affairs Officers, Commanders, and Directors, the conversation at times took a decidedly defensive tone, and when I brought up the problems of identification in the past, I sometimes sensed a tacit reluctance to acknowledge them as the officials quickly returned to the excellent job currently being done. Also, I could sense trip wires that, if triggered, would have abbreviated the interview.

The Quartermaster's World War II statement in the brochure, "Tell Me About My Boy," that "there is absolutely no question of the possibility [of error] of the positive identification of remains" is a goal, not a guarantee. Yet time and again, the military has shot itself in the foot by asserting something that later proved not to be the case. This is not to say that the intentions were evil, only that to profess perfection in a very complicated task riddled with potential for error is asking for trouble. And the military seems at times doomed to repeat the errors of the past.

One of my observations while doing research and conducting interviews was how many of the relatively current problems that I read about or learned about through interviews had appeared before in historical records. Besides examples mentioned previously and those that follow in later chapters, the Air Force seems to be cursed with repeated identification problems with its gunship crews. During the Vietnam War, on December 21, 1972, an AC-130

Spectre was shot down over Pakse, Laos. Thirteen years later, thousands of commingled bone fragments were recovered. From them, CILHI made a positive identification of 13 of the 14 missing crew members (2 others had bailed out and been rescued). Later, "scientists determined that identification for 11 of the crew were impossible to make scientifically. The Army later admitted that it had erred by making individual identifications rather than designating the remains for a group burial."[95] Of course there was pressure to make individual identifications—who wants a group burial?—but errors like this erode confidence in other cases. Later, during the Gulf War, another gunship, the Spirit '03, was shot down, and the manner of handling the unidentified group remains led to a firestorm. This story will be covered fully in chapter 8; in a nutshell, both the Pakse case and the Spirit '03 case were complicated by poor communication with the families.

In my research, I was also struck by the presence of statements *predicting* identification problems. Many Armed Forces personnel had made pointed observations about shortcomings in the design or implementation of identification procedures. In July 2001, J. Jarrett Clinton, M.D., M.P.H., Acting Assistant Secretary for Health Affairs for the Department of Defense, prepared a memo for the Army, Navy, and Air Force in which he pointed out that the goal to have reference specimens on file for all service members by December 2002 would likely be missed because of errors and failure to enforce compliance with existing policies regarding collection. Dr. Clinton's words in his final paragraph, "The critical importance of an accurate specimen sample, available for casualty identification, cannot be overstated," proved only too prophetic.[96] Despite the fact that collection of DNA samples from active and reserved military members had begun in the early 1990s, there were only 50 reference specimens on file at AFRSSIR for the Pentagon terrorist attack victims. While certainly identification efforts were almost completely successful for these fallen, having DNA samples on hand would undoubtedly have made the job easier.

[5. The Return of the Dead]

Refrain your voice from the weeping,
And your eyes from tears;
For your work shall be rewarded,
And they shall come back from the land of the enemy.
There is hope in your future;
That your children shall come back,
To their own border.
—JEREMIAH 31:16–17

WHEN A FAMILY SAYS "Good-bye" to a loved one leaving to serve in the military, it is understood that they are also saying, "Maybe I'll never see you alive again." Most families, though, do not readily acknowledge a deeper level of the parting that also says, "Maybe I'll never even see your body again." Yet, the risk of serving in a far-off land populated by enemy forces intent on wreaking havoc by the use of physics, chemical reactions, and machines entails the very real possibility of permanent loss of the physical self and the accompanying loss of social identity.

Because most of our country's wars have been fought on foreign soil, the return of our war dead is complicated by factors related to distance: intransigence of other governments, extended supply and command chains, lack of preparation, and hostile geographic and climatic conditions. Yet the United States has continued to maintain its policy of returning its fallen soldiers, a precedent that other governments have only recently begun to emulate.

In the past, when the living were struggling with the battles of the moment, Soldier Dead and their families had to wait. When hostilities ended, we searched for the dead who had been unaccounted for and buried them together. Still, this was not their final resting place. Governmental officials, military leaders, and families asked themselves, What next? This was not a rhetorical question, for the U.S. policy of providing a final disposition for the dead has been at variance with other countries' policies regarding their fallen, and even within the United States the policy of final disposition has varied according to the historical time period and geographic location of the conflict, as well as postwar economic conditions. Perhaps most important, carrying it out depended not only upon the ability of the public to make its desires known but also upon its power to enforce the enactment of those desires.

The treatment of war dead can be divided into several distinct areas: who has the right to control remains, how the disposition of those remains is accomplished, how related decisions and actions are carried out, and how those decisions and actions are perceived. One recurring theme throughout is the delicate interplay between the families of service personnel and the government; the families do not have any direct say in the disposition other than what the military grants and/or Congress legislates. Of course, those officials prefer to avoid risking the ire of bereaved family members because the government has little control of the agenda in a public debate, but sometimes circumstances are such that a choice has to be made among options that are all undesirable.

Who Decides

The first serious effort to repatriate American dead from foreign war zones took place when the United States brought back the remains of several thousand servicemen who died during the Spanish-American War and Philippine Insurrection.[1] These returns, from relatively small military engagements, established the default policy that the bodies of those who died in service would eventually be returned home, particularly if their families so desired.

In World War I, the United States made its first major commitment of Armed Forces overseas. Hundreds of thousands of young soldiers walked the gangplanks onto transports that would take them across the Atlantic and into battle, and scores of thousands were killed and buried where they lay, if they were buried at all. While the United States entered the war with the policy of bringing home its Soldier Dead, there was no thought of doing so immediately; wartime conditions did not allow for collecting and transporting the dead, only for establishing and maintaining their identities and providing them, at best, a decent burial, hopefully temporary.

However, the logistical problem of handling large numbers of decayed remains and the questionable acceptance of the return policy by allied countries prompted the War Department to "secure some method of finding out the body of opinion as to the return of dead from the relatives themselves." A questionnaire was sent to each party named on the emergency address supplied by the deceased soldier, and a sizable majority expressed their desire to have the remains brought home.[2]

The War Department also attempted to interpret public opinion by reviewing "statements of public men, both in Congress and in the press." Former President Theodore Roosevelt asked that his son, Quentin, be buried where he fell. A group named the Philadelphia Public Ledger took the same position, but another, the Bring Home the Dead League, advocated a repatriation policy.[3] *The Casket*, a trade magazine for undertakers, carried an editorial that called for the return of the dead because American undertakers would be assured considerable "new business."[4] Even Colonel Pierce, the father of Graves Registration, weighed in with his opinion that it was "only right that the bodies of our heroes should remain in the vicinity of the place where their lives were sacrificed for the United States."[5] The public's desire was best encapsulated by the words a mother "bluntly told" Secretary of State Robert Lansing: "You took my son from me and sent him to war . . . my son sacrificed his life to America's call, and now you *must* as a duty of yours bring my son back to me."[6]

The debate about whether or not to repatriate the remains of those killed was not protracted. Reflecting public sentiment, Secretary of War Newton D. Baker said in 1919:

> The War Department wishes to reiterate its pledge to parents and relatives, that no body will remain abroad which is desired in this country and that no effort will be spared to accord fitting and tender care to those which, by request of the families concerned, will remain overseas in the Field of Honor.[7]

Accordingly, recognizing the desire, or more precisely, the *necessity* to offer a return of the dead, Congress passed Public Law No. 389 on March 4, 1921, authorizing funding for the recovery of World War I Soldier Dead. Baker's explicit statement of the government's contract with its citizens and the ensuing passage of related legislation have echoed through the years and have had far-reaching effects that could not easily have been predicted.

Baker's words would seem to have resolved any question about the return of remains, but once the repatriation process began, there were still people who thought the dead should be left buried overseas. Owen Wister, author of *The Virginian*, the basis for the movie with the same name, and Thomas Nelson Page, author and ambassador to Italy, jointly wrote an article that appeared on the front page of the April 15, 1921 issue of *The New York Times*. The article, a reprint of Wister's letter to the American Legion and Page's letter to the *Times*, both addressed to *The New York Times* Paris Bureau, was titled, "Plead For Our Dead In France." Wister and Page tried to make a case for not disturbing the graves of American soldiers in France. Wister said:

> The other day on my way to visit Quentin Roosevelt's grave I stopped at the American Cemetery near Nesles. In smooth turf and among white crosses gaped ugly holes. Out of these holes were being dragged—what? Boys whom their mothers would recognize? No! Things without shape, at which mothers would collapse.[8]

Page's remarks were slightly more oblique:

> We were told that the bodies are to be exhumed. Standing there it seemed incredible. It seemed desecration to dig them up. It would be impossible could those who loved them best see their present resting place. When General Lee was asked to lend his name to a plan to re-move the Confederate dead from Gettysburg, he replied that he had always felt that the fittest resting place for a soldier was the field of honor on which he had nobly laid down his life. We knew as we stood there that he was right.

Wister and Page's polemic "plea" brought immediate protests from House Representative C. C. Dickinson from Clinton, Missouri, and William Henry Dennis, a Certified Public Accountant from New York City. Both Dickinson and Dennis had lost a son, and their letters are poignant testimonials to the need for preserving the right of next of kin to make the final call regarding their loved one. Dickinson's letter, addressed to Secretary of War John W. Weeks, told how he, his wife, and his son's widow anxiously awaited the re-turn of "the body of the husband and son," and reminded Weeks that Con-gress had approved and funded the repatriation program.[9]

Dennis's reply to Wister's "disgusting appeal" was a strongly worded and well-thought-out blend of logic and emotion that is worth reading in full. In a few pages, Dennis eloquently addressed the political, economic, historical, and human rights issues concerning the repatriation of Soldier Dead, and also offered his personal perspective as a bereaved parent. He said that mili-tary cemeteries are "a beautiful inspiring sight"; that pacifists would "admire the cemetery close by while calmly eating their luncheons and declare, with pride, their Americanism"; that many relatives would be prevented from visiting the graves of their loved ones because of travel expenses; and that France would certainly take care of the graves of American dead, "but only until the next war, which will undoubtedly be more devastating than the last." Furthermore, the rights of the next of kin had been recognized by the U.S. government; Generals Pershing and O'Ryan had the right to be proud of their men but not the moral authority as to final burial, as neither bore the grief of the loss of a son; and the Graves Registration Service had "gone far beyond the call of duty in carrying out the monumental task assigned them."[10]

Needless to say, Weeks promptly replied to the criticism of Wister and Page and gave his reassurance that the policy of the United States regarding repatriation by next of kin, if so desired, would not change.[11]

Twenty years later, William Dennis's prophetic statements were realized when Europe and much of the rest of the world went to war again and the United States, despite efforts to avoid it, again committed its servicemen and women to defend its principles. The attack on Pearl Harbor brought the war home, and America responded as before: late, unprepared, but willing to shoulder its responsibility as a guardian of the free world. This defense did not come cheaply, costing over 400,000 American lives from battle and related military activities.

On December 9, 1941, just two days after Pearl Harbor, C. C. Reynolds, Colonel, Quartermaster Corps, advised the War Department to add the following sentence to the Adjutant General's condolence telegram to the relatives of those who died: "No remains can be transported to the United States until after termination of hostilities, when the Quartermaster General, Washington, D.C., will, if possible, and upon written request of the next of kin, bring the remains to the United States for final interment."[12]

Emory S. Adams, Major General, The Adjutant General, followed the Quartermaster's recommendation and issued instructions to all commanding generals that "During the period that the United States is at war, the shipment home of remains from foreign possessions and other stations outside the continental limits of the United States is suspended."[13] The Secretary of the Navy issued similar instructions. Also, the Navy's Bureau of Medicine and Surgery said that "burials, whenever possible, should be made ashore in selected sites and that 'the marking, identification, and preservation of graves should conform to detailed procedures which had been set up by the War Department in its Graves Registration Service.'"[14]

The reasons for not returning remains were that shipping space was needed to support the war effort, there were not sufficient resources, and there was no military structure in place to accomplish these returns. Strict interpretation of the no-return policy, though, had a major fault in that it was "possible for a soldier to die in Canada or Mexico, within sight of his home in the United States, and yet his remains must be left at the place of death until some future ideterminate [sic] date."[15] Such was the case of Lt. John C. Clack, killed in Canada. Clack's father had requested that his son's remains be returned and, upon initial rejection, wrote to Congressman Estes Kefauver, Representative from Tennessee, providing information about the location of the burial site and asking if an exception could be made, given that his "only child" had died in Canada.[16]

Kefauver followed up by writing the War Department, presenting the argument for return, and asking for further consideration.[17] The War Department acted quickly: it rescinded the original return policy and replaced it with a revised statement that allowed the current return of remains "from points on the North American Continent by commercial carrier transportation other than air or ocean or coastwise vessels."[18]

As World War II progressed, with deaths mounting and many more expected, Col. R. P. Harbold, at the request of the Armed Service Forces Headquarters, submitted Policy Study No. 34 on August 14, 1943. It recommended that "should the requests for return of the dead buried in any Allied country attain or exceed 70 per cent of the total known American burials therein, all dead will be returned."[19] At the time of this analysis, the United States and its allies were committing all available resources to the war, and any slackening of the effort for any reason would only lengthen the conflict and result in even more deaths. Harbold undoubtedly knew, despite the difficulties and costs involved, that adopting a policy different from that in World War I would cause a public uproar, perhaps even a violent protest. His initial plan, though, contained a time bomb: it called for the return of the dead only if 70 percent or more next of kin requested it. While it is easy to see where this number came from—it is very close to the return request in World War I—it doesn't take much of a visionary to foresee the revolt that would ensue if only 60 percent requested return, or 50 percent, or even 1 percent. Conversely, there was also potential for strife should a sizable minority of families wish for remains to be buried overseas, because of the desire either to disturb the dead as little as possible or to transform a place of battle into a remembered hallowed ground.

Addressing the vote-counting section of Policy Study No. 34, the Navy's Bureau of Medicine and Surgery, responsible for Navy and Marine dead, asked what would happen if the majority of next of kin favored "permanent burial in the area where the dead had fallen." Colonel Harbold assured the Navy that it was highly unlikely that more than half of families would want their dead to remain overseas and that, should this be the case, "the matter will be taken up for a determination as to the establishment of American cemeteries abroad." In fact, after an initial review of next-of-kin letters, it was felt that the World War I ratio of 4 returns to 3 overseas burials would shift to 4 to 1 after World War II.[20]

Harbold's answer was a defense of the position stated in Policy Study No. 34, but it also contained an admission that it would be difficult to refuse the request of "any considerable minority favoring burial of the dead wherever they fell."[21] Again, the question of who controls the bodies of the dead was a fundamental issue during the interlude between when they were temporarily interred and the cessation of hostilities, at which time final disposition was to be undertaken.

Eventually, and wisely, the Armed Service Forces Headquarters questioned the return program posited in Policy Study No. 34 and suggested that "every desire of the next of kin should be fulfilled."[22] Incorporating this recommendation, the final policy regarding the return of the dead was that the next of kin could request return or burial in the American military cemetery closest to the late soldier's temporary burial site.[23] The military policy was codified by Congress in Public Law No. 383, passed on May 16, 1946, which stated:

> That the Congress hereby declares it to be in the public interest to provide for the evacuation and return of the remains of certain persons who have died since September 3, 1939, and whose remains are buried in places located outside the continental limits of the United States and could not be returned to their homeland for burial due to wartime shipping restrictions.

The bodies of those who died in World War II had scarcely been either buried in overseas cemeteries or returned home when the Korean War erupted. At first, those killed were handled in the same way as in World War II: temporary cemeteries were established with the understanding that, when circumstances permitted, a repatriation program would be instituted. This policy was quickly altered to a Concurrent Return program when it became apparent that land was not going to be taken and held as in the previous two wars; many killed in battle would be unburied, and temporary military cemeteries would fall into enemy hands. Another reason for the policy was that the people of the United States did not have the same affinity for South Korea—or practically any Pacific or Asian country, for that matter—as they did for European countries, to which most citizens owed their heritage. A further, immediate reason was that when it became known that the body of Lt. General Walton Walker was returned to the United States soon after his death in a jeep accident, there was "public clamor to 'send my boy home, too.'"[24]

Concurrent return of remains also obviated a lengthy and burdensome process of checking with the next of kin and establishing and maintaining foreign cemeteries. Undoubtedly, the policy reflected popular sentiment that had probably always preferred immediate return, something that could not be accomplished previously given the large numbers of deaths and lack of transportation.

The Concurrent Return policy has been in effect since December 1950, and the amount of time between death and return to the family has continually decreased. In the Vietnam War, the bodies of soldiers were delivered to the family members approximately seven days after death.[25] Today, according to the Joint Pub 4–06: *Joint Tactics, Techniques, and Procedures for Mortuary Affairs*, concurrent return is still the "preferred method of handling during periods of conflict."[26] It is unlikely that this will change, unless a future conflict results in large numbers of dead, there is a strong sentiment for the country where the deaths occur, or remains are contaminated.

Along with the World War I and World War II policy that the next of kin (NOK) had, within certain parameters, final authority as to the disposition of remains, came questions about who *was* the family, or NOK, and what happened in conflicts among them. During World War I, the NOK designation followed a ranking order. A soldier's widow had the highest priority in determining disposition of remains. After her, the choice fell to the children, oldest son first. If there were no widow or children, the soldier's father had the right to decide. If he were deceased, then the mother could decide. Following her were all brothers, oldest first, then all sisters, oldest first. If the deceased had no surviving father, mother, or siblings, uncles and then aunts decided.[27]

At times, divorced parents were the nearest relatives of the deceased, and difficulties experienced in marriage continued into the contest for possession of the dead. Colonel Pierce reviewed the matter and "recommended, that, neither widow nor children appearing where conflicting claims are made by divorced parents, the one designated by the deceased soldier in his emergency address be held entitled to direct disposition of his remains."[28] This policy was unimpeachable in that it assigned NOK designation to soldier and removed the government from the unenviable position of arbitrating between contentious parties. In a slightly modified form, this policy stands today in that the Person Authorized to Direct Disposition of Remains (PADD), defined in Army Regulation 638–2 and as designated by the military service member, makes the decision about where remains should be delivered.[29]

In World War II, it was also necessary when sending out letters to the next of kin to make clear who would have the right to decide:

> If the deceased were married: The surviving spouse has the first and final right. However, he or she must not have been divorced or separated at the time of death, or since remarried.
>
> If the husband or wife has remarried, or the parties were divorced or separated, prior to his death, then the preference passes to sons who are over 21 years of age.
>
> If there is no son over 21 years of age, the preference passes to the daughters who are over 21 years of age.
>
> If there are children under age, or no children at all, then the right to dispose of remains passes to surviving relatives in the order of their relationship to the deceased.
>
> If the deceased were not married at the time of death, then the decision rests first with the father. The mother has next rights in the matter.
>
> After the father and mother, brothers over 21 years of age, in the order of their seniority, and sisters over 21 years of age, in the order of their seniority, may make the decision.
>
> If there are brothers and sisters under age, or no brothers or sisters at all, the right to dispose of remains passes to other relatives of the deceased in the order of their relationship.[30]

It is interesting that during World War I and World War II, short of a married survivor, the NOK designation accorded preference to men, whether a father, son, or brother. It is even more interesting that during World War II the Army's Memorial Division asked for clarification about who had the right of possession of remains, and the General Counsel noted that "There is no Federal law or universal rule as to the particular person who has the legal right to the possession of a dead body for purposes of burial." In its reply to the Memorial Division, it attached "suggested wording" for a brochure—presumably "Tell Me About My Boy"—that would explain the transfer of the dead to the next of kin; this wording "differentiates between sons and daughters, and brothers and sisters." The General Counsel admitted that "the law does not, generally speaking, make any distinction as to sex in determining the relative interests of the next of kin to the remains" and that a gender preference was chosen because it was "expedient" to do so.[31]

The World War II policy with regard to a remarried widow(er) was different from that in World War I in that the widow no longer had authority to provide instructions as to the disposition of remains "unless the next nearest relative should claim the right to disposition on the ground of her remarriage." The Quartermaster did not assume the responsibility of finding the next-nearest next of kin.[32]

In World War I, the situation also arose where relatives with preferential rights lived in Europe, not the United States. The Quartermaster recommended that, in cases where the closest relatives lived in those European countries still in "considerable distress," such as Poland and Russia in particular, the wishes of the relatives residing in the United States would take precedence.[33] Upon consideration, Colonel Pierce left the decision to the relative with preferential rights, with the exception that if the request to return the remains to the foreign country could not currently be complied with because of "distress," then they would be interred in France until such time as the transfer could be effected. If the relative wished the body to be returned to the United States, "the case will then be handled in the ordinary way."[34]

With regard to a repatriation policy, the U.S. government and families have reached a general agreement concerning the return of the dead, but there are other factors that play a role in deciding what happens. The manner and timing of return depends in large part upon the circumstances and location of death. While the government has been quite successful in returning its Soldier Dead to their families, primarily because the public has steadfastly insisted on repatriation, not all other countries have willingly acquiesced. Indeed, some have gone out of their way to frustrate American efforts.

It is very significant that we have adopted the term "repatriate" in reference to the return of soldiers killed in service. While "return" has appeared frequently in government documents and policy statements, "repatriation" was also used quite often, particularly when referring to the large numbers of dead buried overseas during World War I and World War II. "Return" has more of the connotation of getting back that which was lent, while "repatriate" conveys the meaning that the desired object is subject to another's control and must be "freed" in order to be returned.

At the start of the overseas repatriation program, a total of 1,880 bodies were returned from the Spanish-American War, with little objection from military authorities in the Philippines.[35] During World War I, when 70,000 soldiers were buried in England and Europe, matters were not quite so simple. At that time, no European nation had adopted a policy for return of its dead, and U.S. officials had difficulty explaining to them that American policy reflected the wishes of the families back home.[36]

Great Britain had "always refused the return of English dead except in spectacular cases of individual national heroes"—the body of Lord Nelson, hero of Trafalgar, was reportedly stored in a keg of rum for the return to England—and France and Belgium, while not specifically objecting, initially resisted our efforts on the grounds that transportation diverted to return U.S. dead would "so derange the reconstruction as to endanger the rights of the living."[37]

Negotiations between the Americans and the French began in earnest on March 20, 1920. M. Maginot, the French representative, stated that his country did not object in principle to the removal of American dead, but there was insufficient support available for the Americans and the French would oppose favor shown to them, since more than 1.5 million French dead still lay in the Zone of the Armies.[38] The Americans responded that "public feeling in the United States would be satisfied if it could be published that the French Government had removed its previous objections to removal operations in the Zone of Battle." The American representatives assured the French that the date by which they would be ready to bring home the bodies of soldiers whose families had asked for them would probably be very close to the date that the French had suggested they could begin. Also, the removal of the dead would result in very little disruption of French efforts to rebuild. The point was that the U.S. government rightfully wanted to address the sentiment of its grieving citizens by demonstrating that it was not being prevented from carrying out its promise to bring home remains for families who wanted to provide a final burial.[39]

However, the Americans and the French did not see eye-to-eye on a particular detail, sanitation. Specifically, the French were worried about flies. Whether they were using this supposed health menace as a cover for other unstated objections is not exactly clear, especially given that there were previous agreements on the movement of bodies *within* the Zone of Armies and that more bodies were being disinterred and reburied during negotiations in spring 1920 than were actually anticipated to be removed. Eventually, the United States acquiesced to the date posited by the French, "any time after September 15, 1920."[40]

The French postponement was, in part, understandable. The infrastructure, one of the casualties of war, was insufficient for the needs of the living, let alone the dead. Americans, whose cities, roads, bridges, water mains, power lines, sewer lines, hospitals, schools, and churches had not been damaged, let alone totally destroyed, had no real grasp of the devastation that had been visited upon France.

With Great Britain, matters related to the repatriation of World War I Soldier Dead proceeded relatively smoothly, but not always without complications. The British at first offered to forever maintain the cemeteries in which American graves were located. Secretary of State Robert Lansing conveyed the appreciation of the United States to British officials, but stated that "the privilege is reserved of bringing to the United States . . . the remains of such of our soldiers and sailors whose final interment in the United States may be desired by their relatives."[41] Consequently, "major exhumation activities" began in Devonshire on February 3, 1920, and the first shipment of 18 bodies left England on the *S.S. Northern Pacific* on February 23, 1920.[42]

A particularly thorny issue arose, though. In the fall of 1920, the United States wanted to return "certain bodies of deceased American soldiers to the parents or relatives of such soldiers who reside in Great Britain." Colonel Brown of the British Imperial War Graves Commission was quite concerned that if this were allowed, the press might take up the cause, and "an agitation [be] started which might result in the British Government being forced to remove a large number of their dead from France to the British Isles." The British were reluctant to refuse the American request outright and sought a way "to stop this movement gracefully."[43] The commission's desire for the two nations to reach an understanding on this delicate subject, while avoiding press scrutiny, illustrates some of the complexity of resolving control of the bodies of the dead, both between and within countries.

Great Britain finally waived its objection to the return of bodies to relatives in the British Isles, but asked that the United States follow its own policy, with no "display of any kind" when the caskets were transported. This meant no flags draped over them, no accompaniment by uniformed soldiers, and shipping crates constructed of ordinary wood "marked according to the usual instructions."[44]

In Europe, requests had to be made to each country to approve the removal of American Soldier Dead, and the United States found it somewhat difficult to secure permission because each country was determined not to grant privileges greater than those offered by others. Also, Americans were not the only soldiers buried in Europe; the dead of Great Britain, France, and Belgium also lay in graves beyond their homelands, and if a country granted the United States permission to remove its dead, relatively minor in number only by comparison to the losses of others, other countries might demand the same.[45]

The War Department decided to exhume all the American remains in Germany, Luxembourg, and Poland, return them to those families who desired them, and inter the rest in permanent cemeteries in France. Germany, though, had other ideas and, in July 1920, refused "to allow the disinterment of American soldiers buried in the interior of Germany." Subsequent and intensive negotiations followed, resulting in approval for the repatriation effort, provided the Americans bore all costs and supplied the transportation. While it is not exactly clear why Germany at first refused, resentment about the terms of the Treaty of Versailles, lack of financial ability, and lack of infrastructure may all have contributed. In fact, other countries had made similar requests and had likewise been denied, but it appears that they had planned on Germany's providing assistance "in the matter of costs, of material, and of rail transportation."[46]

While there was initially some resistance on the part of foreign governments after World War I to America's policy of repatriation, there was no great political impediment (with the exception of a delayed return of the dead from the ill-fated Russian Expedition that is covered in chapter 8, "Open Wounds"). Unfortunately, the same cannot be said about World War II. After hostilities had ceased, the Quartermaster was faced with a set of new problems. World War II was a worldwide conflagration, so remains of service personnel were scattered not only throughout both hemispheres but also in territories controlled by unsympathetic nations. In particular, the United States experienced a severe lack of cooperation from the Soviet Union. Of course, officials did not say, "You can't take the bodies of your soldiers home." Rather, they stymied search efforts by throwing up a series of obstacles: failing to provide information, establishing onerous policies and rules about how search operations could be conducted, and denying entry into certain areas. (Fortunately, relations with Russia improved dramatically during the 1990s, and we now have much better access and more cooperation in our repatriation efforts.) Such difficulties, stemming in large part from the fact that we did not control the territory where remains were located, were repeated in the Korean and Vietnam wars.

Interestingly, many countries, including those that have previously hindered American repatriation efforts, have begun to institute their own programs for the return of war dead. The British, for instance, adopted their first return policy after the Falklands War, leaving only 23 bodies to be buried at the "Blue Beach" Military Cemetery.[47] Officials of countries that are, or have been, in conflict with the United States have said that they will help recover our few thousand if we help them recover their hundreds of thousands. While such a policy of "cooperation" is to some degree a diversionary ploy, any action to account for and return their own dead helps to focus attention on the high price of armed conflict in human lives and suffering. Perhaps the cooperation between countries to find, recover, and bury their fallen may lessen the desire to wage war in the future.

Politics

The return of American dead requires extensive advance planning, and support and approval from nations in whose soil the soldiers are buried. Once the United States receives permission to cross borders and conduct exhumation activities, the Graves Registration Service teams cannot just run around digging up graves and carting off remains—national and local ordinances and customs must be obeyed and observed. At times, American officials have to carefully court local authorities who have the final say in matters of graveyard operations.

Britain, after World War I, required a license for each exhumation and would not allow one within three months in cases of death caused by infectious disease. Certain "specially malignant diseases" required that a skilled pathologist be present when the remains were disinterred.[48] Similarly, every exhumation in Italy had to be attended by an Officer of Hygiene who, in order to comply with the Sanitary Law of Italy, had to certify that the death was not the result of a contagious disease.[49]

In France, the GRS also encountered health concerns that became ensnarled with local politics. While it was disinterring remains in Kerfautras Cemetery in Brest, France, city officials complained that the public health was endangered. The cemetery was small and bordered by residences, and it was impossible to "avoid the spreading of the odor of disinterred bodies and of disinfectants." Also, smoke from the burning of coffins added to local citizens' distress. At one point, a physician alleged that he had two patients who had "already suffered contamination."[50] Officials were "particularly unwilling to obey the French Government's instructions issued from Paris" and were suspicious that Brest would not receive the "usual fee for the disinterment of the bodies." While there is some question as to whether the Americans sufficiently cultivated relationships with local government staff, the city was also said to harbor "bolshevik tendencies."

The dissent that began in Brest spread to a neighboring town, Lambezellec, and on April 17, 1920, a meeting was held of town representatives, Graves Registration officials, and the Chief of Hygiene of the Department of Finistere. The former mayor of Brest, who had been "removed from office by the National Government because of his radicalism," was "especially antagonistic," and charges were again leveled that the exhumations had infected the local populace, even causing a death. Also, the Acting Mayor of Brest stated that French laborers who carried old caskets to be burned were exposed to the unsanitary habits of the men who handled remains.

In response, the GRS Liaison Agent explained that if the coffins were not burned then the same French laborers would "carry them off for use as fire-wood, or to make cupboards and shelves." Subsequently, exhumation operations were suspended for two weeks while Paris conducted an investigation, the result of which cleared the Graves Registration Service and authorized it to resume operation.[51]

It is possible that Great Britain and the rest of Europe were cautious about disinterring remains and the need for sanitation because of the virulent flu pandemic that had swept through those countries only a few years previously, exacting a toll in human life that was greater than the already staggering losses from war. However, it is very clear that the United States continually encountered foreign apparatchiks offering resistance disguised as concern, often for the purpose of personal gain.

It is a truism of war that men are not always buried in neat, individual graves like those in the typical urban cemetery; they are often thrown together, locked in death as in battle, into mass graves. During the process of exhuming the dead in Germany in 1921 for return home or final burial in France, the Graves Registration Service encountered such a mass grave in Worms, Hochheim, Germany. According to records, only one American soldier's remains were interred with those of 137 soldiers from several other countries. It took months of negotiation for the GRS to obtain permission from the respective governments to open the grave; Great Britain was the most reluctant to approve the project. Eventually, the British Imperial War Graves Commission granted permission, but only if its representative was present. Luckily, the American, identified by his Army identification tags, was the thirty-third body exhumed. The first thirty-two were reinterred in individual graves and the American remains forwarded to a morgue for further disposition.[52]

Repatriation efforts for World War II Soldier Dead were also affected by national and local interests. In the Pacific, planes had often been flown with combined Australian and American crews. When these crashed, remains of individuals often could not be separated, and Australians War Graves officials "were unwilling to release them to the American Graves Registration Service, even though most of the dead might be Americans."[53]

The Scandinavian countries firmly voiced "refusal to permit disturbance of the dead until their kin folk had spoken." Hence the problem was how the GRS was to notify the NOK if it did not know who was buried. In Denmark, the GRS worked through political channels and obtained permission to disinter American remains in order to establish identity, but "Reburial in the same grave was mandatory." Sweden required the United States to suspend exhumation operations at Malmö until the next of kin expressed their wishes. It was two years before families could be polled, and all remains but two were later evacuated.[54] In the meantime, the cemetery was classified as a temporary Military Cemetery. During the repatriation process, remains were located, recovered, and temporarily interred in such designated places until the NOK had decided on final disposition, either burial in a permanent overseas Military Cemetery or return to the United States.

The resistance to repatriation efforts for American dead intensified during the Korean War and the Vietnam War, for several possible reasons: the United States did not control the territory, totalitarian countries had possession of the remains, and North Korea and North Vietnam insisted on trading bodies for economic assets in a ghoulish form of ransoming.

It was not until 1993 and 1994 that North Korea unilaterally returned 162 sets of remains, but it wanted $4 million compensation, a figure that U.S. officials considered unreasonable and finally reduced to $2 million by 1996. While negotiations went on regarding adequate and due compensation, all further repatriations were halted.

Unfortunately but not unexpectedly, the experience with North Vietnam was hardly any better. During negotiations in Paris, North Vietnam "had provided a list . . . of those who had died while held in captivity, and had even permitted a visit to the grave sites near Hanoi by U.S. delegates in May of 1973." But it was not until early March 1974 that these 23 remains were released to American authorities. And in a vivid example of political intransigence and refusal to cooperate in the spirit of agreements, North Vietnam withheld the remains of one aviator that had been "buried alongside those of the other 23" because he had not died in captivity, but when he was shot down. Finally, as a footnote, the remains of the twenty-fourth soldier, 1st Lt. Fryer, were not turned over until September 30, 1977, 3 years after his cemetery comrades had been disinterred and flown home.[55]

Planning and Organization

Once the U.S. government and the public had worked out an agreement about the return of Soldier Dead and effectively communicated this policy to foreign governments, there still remained the daunting task of exhuming, preparing, and returning tens and hundreds of thousands of remains. The most significant repatriation programs took place after World War I and World War II, because those wars resulted in the most deaths and because remains were not returned during hostilities but buried in temporary cemeteries pending final disposition. Return programs that began in the Korean War were based on the newly adopted Concurrent Return policy and thus did not involve a postwar undertaking to handle large numbers of remains within a short time period.

After World War I and World War II, families had to wait two, three, four, or five years and longer before being able to bury their loved ones. This delay had many perfectly logical reasons, but logic plays little part in the normal range of human emotions, let alone at the extreme edge of grief that accompanies death. The wait undoubtedly hampered the ability of the next of kin to form a new social identity for the dead. Yet, in reviewing the logistics, it is difficult to see how the situation could have been handled otherwise. Given the relatively small number of military casualties in recent years and the current policy of returning them within days, the concept of returning many tens of thousands (or hundreds of thousands) of bodies to the United States is difficult to grasp. Despite the government's best intentions, it was simply overwhelmed.

The first problem the United States faced, beyond that of locating and identifying its dead, was determining the desires of their families. Shortly after the armistice was signed on November 11, 1918, the War Department sent the deceased soldiers' next of kin "a communication requesting their desire as to the disposal of the bodies of the deceased." A total of 74,770 cards were sent to families, of which 63,708 replied; 43,909 "requested the return of bodies to the United States" while 19,499 requested that the bodies remain in Europe.[56] Thus, the initial expected rate of return was approximately 69 percent.

When preparing for the World War II repatriation program, the government expected that the return request would be at least 80 percent, for several reasons. First, in World War II many bodies were located in the Pacific and Asian mainland, areas where it was believed that families were less comfortable leaving their loved ones than in Europe. This opinion was supported in part when 75 percent of the next of kin of those killed in this the-ater favored return.[57] Another reason was that even when deaths occurred in Europe, where families might have accepted final burial as in World War I, the public was concerned that the new military cemeteries would fall under enemy control, as all World War I cemeteries, save Brookwood Cemetery in England, had been overrun by Germany.[58]

The original expectation of a substantially larger World War II return rate turned out to be unfounded: only 171,000 of the more than 280,000 re-covered remains from all over the world were eventually repatriated.[59] This return rate of 61 percent was virtually identical to that of World War I. But even though the NOK requested remains at the same rate, the number of deaths in World War II were much greater and presented logistical chal-lenges not previously encountered.

As difficult as it was to poll World War I families, doing so after World War II was even more problematic because of the larger number of deaths. The War Department contacted the next of kin of those 280,000 whose re-mains had been found and for whom positive identification had been estab-lished. In a time before computerized databases and laser printers, obtaining and maintaining correct information regarding the location of temporary burial sites and next-of-kin addresses, and preparing such a large volume of paperwork, required extensive organization and support.

It is sometimes hard for people to make up their minds about the most trivial quotidian concerns. The angst involved in signing a statement as to the final disposition of a family member must have been tremendous. Un-doubtedly, while some felt at ease with their decisions, there were others who agonized, delayed, and finally responded, only to change their minds later. When ascertaining the desires of the next of kin, the World War I Cemeterial Division sometimes received the original request and then as many as five changes. And at times, the request to return the remains of a soldier was not received until after they had been disinterred from the original burial site and concentrated in a permanent cemetery.[60] For example, Mrs. Elsie Mi-chael of Bethlehem, Pennsylvania, first asked that the body of her brother, Private Stanley E. Mitman, be interred in France, but later wished for his remains to be sent to her so she could bury him.[61]

The GRS could not continually exhume and bury soldiers multiple times—although they were often buried three, four, five, or six times as it was—and finally adopted a policy in 1921 that "after a body had once been disinterred and the cemetery evacuated, the last reported request must be considered final, and no further changes of decision could be considered."[62]

5.1   A soldier places flags by the graves of remains that are to be repatriated. *S.Sgt. Parker.*
U.S. Army Signal Corps. National Archives & Records Administration

After World War II, families were again asked to choose either final
burial overseas or the return of remains, and the Quartermaster was again
put in the undesirable position of having to set "a fixed date after which
requested disposition of remains will be irrevocable."[63] Anticipating action
by Congress to pass legislation containing a timetable for the return of the
dead, the Army Service Forces, on December 14, 1945, instructed the Quartermaster General to prepare a schedule that would govern the operations of
the Graves Registration Service. By December 29, the Quartermaster replied
with a detailed illustration of 37 separate activities, divided into 9 operational cycles. The first action would be creation of a Master Control Graves
Location Card File and the last would be "preparation of delivery papers
which would accompany remains to their final destination."[64]

Many of the cycles in the master plan were to run concurrently, while
some were to follow once earlier cycles were complete. Adding to the complexity was that the Quartermaster could not authorize certain work to be
done until appropriations had been made, and even if funds were released

for the return program, postwar conditions could still throw the return program off schedule.

The military is similar to any large organization, public or private, in that one of the toughest questions that has to be answered is how to structure authority. In many organizations, some personnel have a dual reporting relationship in which they owe operational allegiance to a local general manager and functional allegiance to someone higher up. For example, the human resources manager of a manufacturing plant may be responsible for hiring and training on the local level and under the day-to-day control of the plant manager, but must perform those duties according to corporate guidelines created at a divisional or national level. Obviously, for the system to work, the local plant manager and local human resources manager must feel that the policies laid down at a higher level are applicable to immediate matters at hand. In the case of Graves Registration duties with regard to repatriation, the question was whether the commanders in the field or high-level Quartermaster officers would be responsible for conducting operations, and to whom field personnel would directly report.

After World War I, "it was realized that a special organization was needed to handle the specific problems of exhumation, shipment and concentration of the remaining bodies," and Major General H. L. Rogers recommended that Colonel Harry F. Rethers of the Quartermaster Corps be given authority over all mortuary operations in Europe. However, Rethers was to consult with Commanding Officers when conducting operations in areas under the command of U.S. troops.[65] After the end of World War II, the original plan was to establish an overseas American Graves Registration Command (AGRC) whose geographic divisions would be different from those created for Army Theater Commanders conducting wartime operations. There would then be a central overseas command for repatriation similar to that in World War I.

But World War II was different than World War I, and the organization was modified accordingly. During hostilities in World War II, the GRS operated under Theater Commanders, and its troop numbers were counted against the theater troop ceiling. In other words, the generals, Patton, Bradley, and MacArthur, were in charge of taking care of their dead. While combat conditions may have required such decentralized control over GRS activities, Policy Study No. 34 recommended that the Return of the Dead Program, as it was called in World War II, could best be accomplished by establishing an overseas command of Quartermaster units that would report not to Theater Commanders but to higher-level Quartermaster commanders.

However, after aborted and delayed organization attempts, the War Department issued General Order 125 on December 29, 1945; it was sufficiently ambiguous to allow modification of the different geographic areas. Basically, the order established separate zones of command for the AGRC, but for the most part subordinated those zones to Theater Commanders so long as their positions existed. Afterward, the AGRC had final responsibility for repatriation of the dead since their duties continued past the point at which combat commands were needed.[66]

Repatriation efforts had to be coordinated not only within the Army but also among the major branches of the Armed Forces. During World War I and World War II, the Army included the Air Corps, and the Marines were—and still are—part of the Navy. By agreement during World War I, the return of Navy and Marine dead was handled by the Army, a sensible arrangement given that the Army Graves Registration Service had been responsible in large part for the burial of Navy and Marine casualties and was well staffed because of the large numbers of Army dead.

But, as in any bureaucracy, often what is planned is executed in such a manner as to cause confusion, not only among those responsible for carrying out their duties but also for family members. In particular, the Cemeterial Division of the Quartermaster Corps sent correspondence to some relatives of deceased Marines asking them about their desires for disposition of remains when those relatives had already received the bodies from the Navy.[67] Such mishandling, as understandable as it may seem, created doubt in the families' eyes that they had actually received the correct remains. And even if they were convinced that they had, the reopening of a wound that had barely begun to close was painful and harmful to the grief resolution process. Eventually, the Cemeterial Division adopted the policy that the Marine Corps Headquarters was the "next of kin" and that it "would accept without question" instructions from the Marines as to disposition of remains.[68]

In World War II, as in World War I, the Navy was provided information regarding exhumations and identifications, and it was then responsible for contacting the next of kin to determine if the remains were to be returned or interred in a national cemetery.[69] Thus, only the Navy had direct communication with the NOK, and the Army followed its instructions regarding their desires.

Logistical Difficulties

As organizational issues were somewhat more complicated after World War II than World War I, so were logistics. Common elements, though, were inadequate staffing; dearth of material, supplies, and transportation; and the geographical and climatic conditions of areas of search and recovery. But the return of weapons of war, ammunition, and food stocks was one thing; the return of human remains was another matter entirely.

In World War I, disinterment work was supervised by an embalmer, who had a technical assistant and checker who kept all necessary records. A squad of laborers was employed to actually open the graves and move the remains to the processing area, where they would be sprayed with a disinfectant and searched for identification tags or marks, then placed upon a clean blanket and wrapped in such a way "that the remains should appear in the most presentable condition." The aluminum strip and identification disk that had been attached to the cross marking the temporary grave were removed and "pinned to the blanket over the chest of the remains." Muslin excelsior pads were put in place to support the body and prevent movement during transportation.[70]

After World War I, the Graves Registration Service initially "was absolutely dependent upon the United States for the delivery of caskets, blankets, sheets, embalming fluid, disinfectants, deodorants, preservatives, aluminum stripping, stencil machines, stencil paper, rubber gloves and other items."[71] It was not until early summer 1920 that supplies began to arrive in sufficient quantities, and not until late summer that they could be purchased in Europe.[72]

Perhaps the most obvious necessity was caskets. In World War I, metal caskets were employed. They were inspected for any defects and subjected to air and water tests to assure that there was no leakage of any kind, always a concern when working with biological material; no remains were to be transported home without a perfect container. The United States tried to procure them overseas, but after several attempts resulted in receiving products that did not meet quality standards, contracts were made at home.[73]

In European repatriation operations after World War II, the Quartermaster General knew by the middle of May 1946 that a delay in casket production would force a drastic revision in the planned schedule of returns.[74] And once production and shipment of caskets was ramped up, a steel strike in the United States during the summer of 1947 resulted in the delay of 58,000 caskets earmarked for the Pacific. The Quartermaster General desired to postpone the first returns scheduled for the fall, but the War Department, seeking to "maintain public confidence in the [return] program," denied the request.[75] The GRS would simply have to do the best it could.

The United States no longer embalms its dead overseas and returns them in caskets. Instead, remains are placed inside stainless steel "transfer cases" that are flown to a U.S. base, usually Dover Air Force Base in Delaware, where they are processed for return to the next of kin.[76] These transfer cases are often mistakenly referred to as "caskets" or "coffins" in the media. It is easy to see how reporters working only occasionally with the movement of Soldier Dead can make this error, given that the cases bear a passing resemblance to caskets. However, as discussed in chapter 6, "Burial," there is a great deal more work to do after remains in transfer cases have arrived at a military morgue.

In addition to materials and supplies, the Quartermaster Corps found itself short of staff, especially trained personnel to find, identify, and prepare remains for burial or return. After the fighting is over, servicepersons wish to go home as soon as possible and their families desire their immediate return. But for the families of those killed, the war is not over until all the missing have been accounted for and buried, either overseas or at home, and this requires considerable manpower. Thus, the U.S. government was trying to serve two masters, the families of the living and those of the dead.

Generally, to combat the shortage of troops, the GRS adopted the policy that trained personnel would be used to supervise the critical aspects of exhumation, preparation, and transportation, and local labor hired when possible. After World War I, the Graves Registration Service had difficulty hiring workmen to perform most of the less-skilled tasks. Even though France had lost 1.4 million men in the war, labor was plentiful since those who survived could not begin immediately to restore their country because the funds to pay for rebuilding were to come from German reparations, yet to be collected. The French government did not want the AGRS to bring in outside workers to a particular site; it required instead that help be hired from the local labor pool. The United States was eager to employ this workforce, but faced a myriad of French laws regarding wages and employer liability. Also, French law required employers facing liability issues to appear in a French court, an action the United States had rejected for many years. A solution was reached by signing agreements with French contractors who assumed all financial and legal responsibility for the workers.[77] In essence, the French companies became subcontractors for the AGRS, a business tactic that was and is commonly used by employers to avoid liability.

When possible, systems were designed to obviate problems stemming from language barriers—French laborers could not speak English and Army personnel were not conversant in French. In the port of St. Nazaire, for example, where caskets were tested and repaired, supplies were organized according to task in numbered bins so that a workman who was ready for the

5.2   Empty remains transfer cases stacked up outside the U.S. Army Mortuary in Da Nang. *Sgt. Donald Mitchell (discharged)*

5.3   Empty remains transfer cases stacked up outside the U.S. Army Mortuary in Baghdad: little has changed since Vietnam. *Michael Sledge*

necessary materials to furnish the interior of a casket had only to point to a number on an index on the counter; he would be given a "bundle containing the blanket, sheet, pillow, etc., which were put in the interior of the casket before dispatch to the field forces."[78]

The shortage of trained and experienced GRS personnel and available labor was much the same after World War II. The Army found that many of its seasoned Graves Registration companies were redeployed away from areas in which "two-thirds of the dead were buried" and that the organization responsible for the final disposition of the dead existed on paper only.[79] The lack of foresight—even reluctance—to plan for the management of Soldier Dead may have reflected a refusal to consider the consequences of violent conflict, a preference to allocate resources to the most immediate tasks at hand, or a paucity of trained field and staff officers who could envision a complete circle of enlistment, training, battle, death, and return. Regardless, the United States once again had to play catch-up.

While most deaths in World War I occurred in Great Britain and Europe, in World War II U.S. service personnel fell in practically every longitude and latitude. The Pacific area was particularly inhospitable and reluctant to give up its dead, nor did it hold particular appeal to U.S. units charged with the responsibility of working little-known islands, lagoons, and jungles. The 9105th Technical Service Unit (TSU) was established in spring 1947 to conduct disinterment operations in Hawaii and the Pacific Zone. When officers assigned to Hawaii in July discovered that their duties would take them to the remote areas of the Pacific, many applied for either a transfer or a discharge.[80]

Embalmers and trained assistants were in very short supply, so unlicensed embalmers were employed. And the shortage was even more acute in the Pacific, an area that had trouble attracting and keeping qualified personnel.[81] Fortunately, in a purely pragmatic sense, there was no shortage of bodies to use for training. Knowing they would soon be handling many thousands, the Americans perfected techniques in the "mass handling of remains" when they moved almost 5,000 German dead from Epinal, France, to Andilly, Germany, during the period from late September to mid-December 1946. Even though the exercise involved the disinterment and reburial of former enemy casualties, respect was shown during the process with privacy fences erected around the grave sites and honor guards keeping watch at night over the casketed remains. In addition, care was given to preserving identification.[82]

Another critical logistical detail of returning the dead was transportation, or rather, the lack of it. In spring 1920, repatriation operations began first in Great Britain; the United States initially attempted to hire motor transport, but could not obtain sufficient numbers of carriers and had to wait until the summer for a shipment of cars and trucks from the U.S. mainland.

The GRS officials elsewhere in Europe did not have much better luck and were continually forced to improvise. It was almost impossible to hire local motor transports, and work was delayed until vehicles and spare parts were shipped from the United States. The GRS sought to repurchase cars that had formerly been sold to the Ukrainian government and, after having made all required arrangements and performed overhauls necessary "before the cars were finally fit to move," was served an injunction by Ukrainian representatives that prevented "removing them from the place of storage."[83] The Ukrainians likely could have pressed their legal case before the vehicles were repaired; their waiting until after the United States had invested a sizable amount of time and money to recondition the transports is a good example of the extent to which some foreign countries have attempted to extract resources from U.S. repatriation efforts.

The GRS also had to obtain marine transportation. While the main cause of death in England in World War I was the flu, there were two notable shipwrecks that caused a large loss of life, eventually requiring the GRS to charter the S.S. Groningen to carry caskets, trucks, motorcycles, tents, and other supplies to Islay, "one of the bleak and desolate islands off the west coast of Scotland and north of Ireland." The island contained the graves of American soldiers killed when their transport, the Tuscania, was torpedoed on February 5, 1918. Many American troops were rescued by the valiant efforts of British sailors and island inhabitants before the ship sank, but more than 100 perished and their bodies washed up on the shores over the next 2 days. Eight months later, the transport Otranto collided with another ship, lost its steerage, and eventually foundered along the rocky coast, resulting in more than 300 deaths. Removing the American Soldier Dead during the summer of 1920 required enormous effort: laborers, trucks, fuel, supplies, and tools all had to be brought in, and the weather can be pictured from the words of the Commanding Officer: "They tell me here this is the best season of the year,—if it is the best, Lord deliver me from the worst." Tents were blown down, roads were "almost impassable," the field kitchen broke down, and the laborers wanted to quit. Since some cemeteries were located close to where large groups of bodies had washed ashore, removing them for shipment home meant digging through water-filled trenches and carrying stretchers bearing remains up treacherous cliffside trails.[84]

The first repatriation effort to employ an airlift occurred in Norway when 42 of 44 deceased World War II personnel were recovered. The remaining two, by wishes of their NOK, were reburied in the graves where they had been temporarily interred.[85] Late in the Korean War, an exercise was conducted in which the Air Force flew remains to Japan, and during the Vietnam War, air transport was established as the main means for the return of Soldier Dead, even to the point where large cargo jets will make worldwide trips with but a few remains. In Baghdad during the Iraq War, troops waited for available aircraft to carry them to Kuwait while a Hercules C-130 was utilized to carry a single set of remains to the same location. Certainly, the living wait on the dead in more than one manner.

In those rare cases where the bodies were to be delivered to relatives overseas, the Quartermaster encountered extreme difficulties due to primitive transportation methods. The extent to which the United States was willing to go to fulfill its promise is illustrated by a particularly difficult return case in World War I. The officer in charge of a convoy to the Greek island of Icaria wrote in June 1922:

> I was informed that the village to which the remains were to be delivered was some 10 or 12 kilometers distance over the mountains. I was also informed that there was not a road to this village, and that it would be necessary to transport the remains by hand. Two long poles were securely fastened to the casket, and twelve men employed to convoy the remains by hand to its destination.[86]

High summer temperatures undoubtedly exacerbated the already trying environmental conditions of this return.

In addition to supplies, staffing, and transportation, the European communication infrastructure was another casualty of war. In one World War I example, there was a major mix-up between the Paris and the Washington, DC offices of the GRS, with the usual accusations and counteraccusations that the field office (Paris) "did not know its own business" and that the home office (DC) "was not functioning properly." The misunderstanding was due to a series of errors, electronic garbling of cables, mistranslation by clerks, and the use of singular and plural forms of "cemetery," which when reviewed in retrospect seem almost comedic. However, a series of letters cleared up the misunderstanding "by explaining their origin as being beyond anyone's control."[87]

Certainly, finding, identifying, moving, and reburying—sometimes several times—thousands of bodies is a logistical undertaking that at times yields imperfect results, however honorable and noble the attitude of those involved.

Reverence

Once plans for repatriation had been established, logistics dealt with, resources put in place, the next of kin polled, and remains located and exhumed and prepared for return, the dead were removed from the country in which they had lain and returned home. Initial reluctance notwithstanding, the nations for whom our men and women had fought were thankful for the assistance and expressed their gratitude with due respect and honor. Arrival home has frequently, but not always, been noted with outpourings of warmth, support, and recognition.

The respect accorded to remains began with recovery, and extended to initial burial, exhumation, and further handling. On April 15, 1921, the Quartermaster issued a "Manual of Regulations and Tables of Organization of the American Graves Registration Service, Q.M.C. In Europe" that provided detailed instructions as to how American dead were to be exhumed, prepared, and transported. The manual stated that cemeteries were "consecrated ground" and that "Careful and reverent handling of remains is the duty of each person connected with the operations and all Officers will be held responsible that these instructions are always complied with." In order to thwart morbid curiosity seekers, screens were placed around cemeteries to conceal workmen opening graves and removing remains.[88]

But the screening policy sometimes was not enough to provide privacy. As the GRS began to conduct exhumation operations in the Halawa Naval Cemetery on Oahu, it found that the traditional screens could not be employed with sufficient effect because the cemetery was located in a valley and could easily be viewed from a heavily traveled highway. To avoid public display of its activities, GRS officials asked the military and civilian police to prevent "loitering by outsiders and the use of cameras."[89]

Once the remains were disinterred, prepared, and placed in caskets, they were stored in temporary morgues to await transportation to either permanent Military Cemeteries or ports for future shipment home. In World War I, during the concentration process prior to the return of remains, the morgues were guarded around the clock and fine sand was poured on the walkways so it would be readily apparent if trespassers gained access. American flags, long used to bestow honor upon American dead, draped the interior of the buildings and covered each casket.[90]

If the next of kin had made a final disposition decision requesting return, those remains were moved to ports of embarkation and loaded onto transports for the voyage back to the United States. When the American Soldier

Dead were moved within other countries or from one country to another, their former host nations performed solemn farewell ceremonies. During the spring of 1921, a group of bodies were to be transported to the port city of Antwerp; while remains were usually moved by train or truck, these were carried by barges on canals that ran through France, Belgium, and Holland. The decision to utilize canals was based on economics—water routing was less expensive than rail—but it also brought an unexpected benefit in that this method of transportation provided an opportunity for local populations to pay their respects. The Europeans had been witness to American soldiers arriving from the west and then fighting their way east. Now, those who had lost their lives were slowly and serenely being borne back toward the setting sun, and their passing was noted with proper regard.

In Belgium, a farmer ceased his field work and stood upon a cliff with the others from his village to watch the procession of dead below and, when "the convoys had passed, the man remained for a few seconds, with head raised and arms outstretched as if in reverent prayer." As the Soldier Dead made their solemn journey through the serene canals, honor guards fired volleys of three, cannons boomed in salute, and men, women, and children lined the banks and bridges and strewed fresh flowers on the barges. All commercial traffic was halted, and "mounted lancers rode along the canal banks." Hats were doffed, heads bowed, and many tears fell into the waterway. In all, the journey through the canals took two weeks, providing ample time for schedules to be posted and ceremonies held.[91]

While no allied countries were openly antagonistic toward the return of American dead, some were not overly helpful, either because they felt that showing strong support would elicit feelings among their citizens for a similar policy or because they were reluctant to disturb the dead unless the next of kin specifically requested it. After World War II, the citizens of Spain and Portugal, however, were especially sympathetic to the Americans reclaiming their dead, and "the piety of peasant communities gave an emotional touch that was not so apparent in Protestant countries of northern Europe." Indeed, throughout the Iberian Peninsula, the removal of American dead was accompanied by religious ceremonies, "often with entire villages in attendance," kneeling as the flag-draped coffins passed by, and "Every cortege was accompanied by the local mayor and parish priest."[92]

Once remains slated for return reached ports for the voyage home, the port countries conducted ceremonies honoring the young men who had come to their defense. The first group of World War II remains from Europe to be returned were loaded onto the *U.S.A.T.* (United States Army Trans-

5.4   Barge carrying disinterred remains of American World War II dead up the Meuse River en route to Antwerp for eventual repatriation. *S.Sgt. Parker. U.S. Army Signal Corps. National Archives & Records Administration*

port) *Connolly* in Antwerp, and the Belgians hosted a moving ceremony. U.S. General Lucius D. Clay, the person most responsible for the Berlin Air-lift, spoke simply and eloquently, offering both hope and a warning that are still relevant today, as he stood by the casket of a fallen soldier:

> We have not yet found the lasting peace for which these men died in their youth. We must determine that free men everywhere should stand together in solid front to ensure a world in which there is ever-lasting peace, in which the dignity of the individual is recognized and maintained.[93]

In an interesting combination of reverence and the formation of a new social identity for the dead, the World War II Soldier Dead on the ships re-turning to the United States were listed on a passenger list with their name followed by "Deceased": "James William Brown—Deceased," for example.[94] The preparation of such a list emphasized that those handling the remains were responsible for looking after the dead as they would the living. Also, listing the dead as "passengers" partially forestalled the splitting of their physical and social identity, saving that task for the next of kin to handle individually.

When the casketed remains arrived—World War I dead in Hoboken, New Jersey and World War II dead in New York City and San Francisco— they were protected during unloading by netting strung between the ship and the water.[95] Once safely ashore, they were stored until they could be transported to distribution points throughout the country. Similar in fashion to mortuary warehouses in Europe, the storage facilities were refinished in "a manner befitting the memory of the deceased."[96]

But the voyage home was not always so reverent. During the return program after World War I, there was a major flap about alleged careless handling of remains. In April 1920, at the French port of Brest, the *U.S.A.T. Mercury* took on approximately 200 cases containing casketed remains. Paul H. Hershey, Supervisory Embalmer for the AGRS, boarded the *Mercury* the day after the cases were loaded and, according to his report, noticed that the shipping case of the remains of a nurse was standing head down and that "the remainder of the bodies were in about five feet of water." Hershey also stated that during the loading of shipping cases he

5.5   Flag-covered caskets in a temporary warehouse, probably World War II. *U.S. Army Quartermaster Museum*

observed that "about four men would get hold of the box and roll it over three or four times in order to get it in proper position, and then they were lowered down in the water."[97]

Hershey's statement was received by R. P. Harbold, Lt. Col., Infantry— the same Harbold who would play such an instrumental role in taking care of the dead in World War II—who requested that an investigation be held upon arrival of the *Mercury* at Hoboken. Harbold was indignant that remains that had been so carefully tended to by field personnel were subjected to such callous handling by those transporting them:

> If American boats with American crews can not accord a certain amount of respect to our dead to such a small degree as to handle them properly and guard them against such accidents as the flooding of compartments it would be much better to send these bodies home on War Vessels or in Foreign Bottoms.[98]

Upon arrival, the shipping cases were examined and all necessary repairs made. Also, Col. H. K. Taylor conducted a hearing in which he took sworn statements from the crew of the *Mercury*. All swore that the bodies had not been turned end over end, that none had been turned on its head, and that although water had accidentally gotten into the hold, they had promptly pumped it dry before any serious damage was done to the shipping cases and caskets. However, Mr. F. S. McMurray, Master of the *Mercury*, did testify that he observed French stevedores carelessly handling some cases, either because they were incompetent or because "evidently some of them were under the influence of liquor."[99]

Colonel Taylor concluded his investigation, stating that he did not find any evidence of rough handling of the cases contained the caskets and that he did not "believe there was any truth in the statement made by Mr. Hershey."[100] But Taylor was a little too quick in his dismissal of Harbold's concern about the insensitive treatment of remains as reported by Hershey. In fact, a careful reading of Taylor's questions to those who gave statements leaves two impressions. One, he generally asked questions in such a way that the respondent could reply with what seemed to be known answers—a tactic that recalls the adage that an attorney should never ask a question to which he doesn't already know the answer. Two, Taylor apparently overlooked, either intentionally or otherwise, an alternative interpretation of some of Hershey's comments. Instead, he took Hershey's words verbatim without analyzing their context, and this literal rendering allowed him to cast some disrepute upon the embalmer's testimony.

Specifically, Hershey stated that the shipping cases were lowered down into the water. It is clear that the cases were not lowered into water and that the hold accidentally partially filled with water later that night. Hershey, observing it the next day and then later making his statement, may have assumed that the water he saw had been present the day before when the loading was done. Also, Hershey stated, "They had the body of this nurse, Miss Cairns, standing head down, and the remainder of the bodies were in about five feet of water." Colonel Taylor solicited statements from *Mercury* crewmen that the case containing the remains of Cairns was in an entirely different hold from the one that had inadvertently been flooded. Again, a careful study of Hershey's words (Hershey was not present during Taylor's hearings) would make a thorough investigator want to ask him, "Did you observe the Miss Cairns's case in the same or in a different hold as those that were in water?"

It was clear that water did leak into the hold and that some cases were damaged. It was also clear that there was rough handling of some cases. Furthermore, it was found that some of the caskets themselves were not thoroughly cleaned of mud before being sealed in shipping cases. And it seems that there was corroborating evidence of a shipping case, but not necessarily that of Miss Cairns, standing on end.[101] Regardless of what may have actually happened, there was a renewed emphasis placed on the reverent handling and transportation of remains.

Two important conclusions can be drawn from this case. The first is that many people come into contact with remains and it is likely that not all of them will be as caring as is desired. The second is that officials will sometimes take an approach that appears to be thorough and competent and correct, but is actually little more than a disguised attempt to do away with, not solve, what is to them perhaps nothing more than a paperwork problem or a nuisance.

While there may have been some controversy about what, exactly, transpired with the remains shipped home on the *Mercury*, there is no argument about what Staff Sergeant Emmitt S. "Bud" Minor encountered in February 1965 while supervising the unloading of Vietnam dead from a C-135 that had been flown to Travis Air Force Base near San Francisco. Minor noticed a camera case on top of one of the stainless steel remains transfer cases in the hold—photographers had been allowed into the plane. He picked it up and asked, "Who belongs to this case?" When a photographer answered, Minor told him that *nothing* was to ever be placed on top of remains except a flag. While remains have, out of necessity at times, been loaded on top of one another during transportation, they are unstacked at the first opportunity and covered with a flag.

Minor went back to his duties, and when he returned to that section of the hold a few minutes later, he found the same photographer standing on top of the remains transfer cases, snapping pictures. Minor said, "I put my hands on the man and physically removed him from the airplane." While there was no harm done to the photographer, he subsequently filed a complaint and Minor narrowly avoided a court-martial.[102]

Regardless of their sometimes questionable handling, homecoming for the remains provided an opportunity for the public and their representatives to acknowledge the country's debt to those who had died. Unfortunately, it also provided an opportunity for politicians to draw attention to themselves. On October 10, 1947, the first group of World War II dead returned to the United States at San Francisco, and the reception was "simple but impressively dignified." But the next shipload of remains that arrived at New York was received in a manner that can best be described as mixed. The long parade of

5.6 A caisson bearing the remains of a soldier awarded the Congressional Medal of Honor proceeds past solemn onlookers on the way to memorial services held in Central Park, New York City. *S.Sgt. G. Scott. National Archives & Records Administration*

a single representative Soldier Dead through Manhattan streets seemed more fitting for the return of heroes than for the dead, and the ceremony at Central Park was marred by long speeches. The services at the actual pier where the remains were unloaded were more subdued and reverent.[103] New York seems to have learned from the World War II repatriation ceremonies in that the observance at the removal of the last steel beam at the World Trade Center site in 2002 was without speeches or other needless pomp.

Once the shipping cases of the dead were received at port, they were transported to distribution centers throughout the country and either delivered to or picked up by the next of kin or their representatives. As in ocean transport, there were variances in care. In August 1921, Frank Mitchell, an American Legion member in Bridgeport, Connecticut, read a newspaper account that the casketed body of a deceased serviceman had been irreverently left on the doorstep of a residence. Mitchell wrote to the Adjutant General of the U.S. Army in reference to this article, saying that any such callous act should be duly punished. Col. George H. Penrose, Chief of the Cemeterial Division, wrote to Mitchell in response and explained the circumstances:

5.7   First delivery of American World War II dead to the next of kin at a San Francisco funeral parlor. *U.S. Army Signal Corps. National Archives & Records Administration*

the casket would not fit the stairway and was, by request of the father of the deceased, placed on the porch.

But instead of only dealing with the facts, Colonel Penrose's response contained a mildly disguised attempt to shame Mitchell. The opening paragraph said:

> I cannot conceive how a post of the American Legion would, for one moment, believe that such neglect would be possible; that this Division would, for one moment, permit of such an occurrence, as the remains of the deceased soldiers are as sacred to us as they can possibly be even to the families, and all due respect has ever been shown.

It is quite possible, despite the best intentions and efforts of higher command and despite Colonel Penrose's statement, that an occasional error could occur or a disrespectful delivery take place. Mitchell later wrote back to Penrose, saying that, "it [making the complaint in his original letter] was not done with the intent of geting [sic] your Dep't in DUTCH." Penrose, in his reply to this apologia, said that he was "satisfied" with Mitchell's explanation for his actions.[104]

In another incident soon after, Mr. Harry B. Reid wrote to the Secretary of War, informing him of what he considered to be irreverent care of the dead while the remains were being driven through the streets of New York. Reid stated that the truck drivers smoked, "gaily going to their various destinations, as if they were transporting coal or some like matter." Reid also complained that the trucks were driven at high speed and with no mufflers.[105]

Colonel Penrose, to whom the letter was referred by the Secretary of War, responded to Reid within the week. Penrose's brief letter, less than one page, not only missed the point, it contained another cloaked attempt to shame, similar to that in his earlier letter to Frank Mitchell.[106] However, Reid was not so easily intimidated and replied, stating that "the War Department [Reid assumed Penrose was with the War Department] has not read my letter carefully" and that "The tone of your letter . . . is particularly rasping to me, as it seems that you are not looking to remedy fault, but setting the matter to your own satisfaction before my complaint is verified or not."[107]

What happened next was that Reid's letter to Colonel Penrose ended up on the desk of John Weeks, Secretary of War, who took action and then responded appropriately to Reid. Weeks did not, however, just tell Reid what he thought the New Yorker wanted to hear; rather, he repeated the War Department's intention to provide reverent treatment to the dead and stated that "Commanding officers have been particularly cautioned to select suitable men for escort duty." Weeks also reminded Reid that many families anxiously awaited the delivery of caskets containing the remains of their loved ones and that prompt delivery often "necessitates a degree of haste in transporting caskets from docks to railway stations."[108]

Colonel Penrose's attempts to gloss over the actual facts and to cast aspersions upon the person making an inquiry were not unique to his time; others through the years have exhibited the same "Penrosian Attitude" that has caused much unnecessary distrust on the part of families of the dead. Weeks's letter is an excellent example of the need to counteract the attitude's effects. He first had to remove frustration and distrust created by a lower official before addressing the original topic brought up by the member of the public. Unfortunately, often when trust is lost, it can never be completely restored.

A uniformed escort of the same rank as or higher rank than the Soldier Dead accompanied each casket from the port to the point of final distribution. They were to render emotional support to the family, staying to attend the funeral if requested. Escorts, in their representative capacity for the government, were often the only personal contact the family had with the military. There was some fear that the family might resent the appearance of a healthy young man alongside the casket of their loved one, but such was not the case. At first, the policy was that the escorts could not accept any gifts, but the Quartermaster soon learned that many families considered it an honor to bestow a gift upon the person who had rendered such dedicated service to their dead member.[109]

Amazingly, uniformed escorts did encounter problems, but not from family members. In New York, a Marine honor guard in full dress uniform was preparing to carry remains to a cemetery when the Pallbearers' Union "intervened, causing a distressing and embarrassing disturbance." The Marines respectfully stepped aside and avoided making a disgraceful situation even worse. Wisely, Colonel Bare of the Quartermaster Corps informed the press of the incident, and the resulting negative publicity raised the public's ire against the union's actions.[110]

From New York City and San Francisco, under uniformed escort, the bodies moved throughout the United States, back to their families. Years ago, these same families had seen their men off to war, anticipating an eventual homecoming. Now, there was a homecoming, but one quite different from the ticker-tape parades that accompanied the return of the living. This homecoming was triumphant only in that it was the beginning of the end for the bereaved. One of the most heartbreaking returns was that of the four Borgstrom brothers from Tremonton, Utah. Within six months during 1944—the year in which the majority of U.S. servicemen lost their lives—the brothers Clyde, Elmer LeRoy, Rolon, and Rulon (Rolon's twin) were all killed, though each served in a different branch of the military and in a different theater. Only the deaths of the five Sullivan brothers "constituted a greater loss to any family." In recognition of the sacrifices of the four brothers and their family, a two-day tribute was conducted. The caskets arrived home in Tremonton on July 25, 1948, four years after their deaths, and the bodies "lay in state" during the afternoon, accompanied by sentries from the Army, Navy, Air Force, and Marines. The elaborate yet dignified ceremony began the next day in the Mormon Church at Garland, Utah, and ended with simple graveside rites and burial.[111]

It is impossible to imagine how any family could deal with the tragedy of such a loss. It is even more difficult to envision the pain of losing four children to violent, premature, and sudden deaths and then having to wait four years to bury them. For the Borgstroms, the government got it right. In other situations, the government's actions set the stage for a protracted struggle regarding the return of the dead.

Suspicion and Distrust

A recurring theme in the history of Soldier Dead is family dissatisfaction with the military's efforts to account for and care for the dead. At a minimum, this dissatisfaction is expressed over delay or irreverent handling. At the other end of the spectrum, families feel that the government has created a myth, or even perpetrated a hoax, about its concern for those who have died. Many believe in a vast conspiracy to hide instances of large numbers of remains left unrecovered, sometimes under control of the enemy. Certainly, the Penrosian Attitude of some officials has hindered relations with its citizens regarding Soldier Dead. An increasingly sophisticated, informed, and unapologetic public has demanded that the government be more forthcoming about those killed and those still unaccounted for, and the government has made great strides in providing information and involving family members, particularly since the Vietnam War. But the natural tension that exists between those who hold knowledge and power and those who consign their loved ones to them creates a situation where suspicion and doubt can easily breed. Much of the public dissatisfaction is focused on four areas: the fact that the government has de facto control of the whole process, the delay in returns, identification issues, and accounting for the missing.

First, it has clearly been established that the military can exercise its authority, at least to a large degree, over its soldiers even after they are killed. The Graves Registration Technical Instruction pamphlet, prepared by the Quartermaster Corps in 1918, stated that:

> It is contemplated in cabled instructions from the War Department that all officers, enlisted men, and civilian employees of the Army, Navy and Marine Corps, who may die within the Field of Operations of the A.E.F., shall remain buried and in the absolute custody of the G.R.S. until the end of the war.

With regard to delivery of remains, the Technical Instructions said, "In no case, therefore, will bodies be delivered into the custody of relatives until the war is ended."[112]

After World War I, repatriation of the dead did not begin in earnest until 1921, even though the armistice was signed in November 1918. This delay, which the public understandably considered protracted, had several causes: reticent foreign governments, lack of planning, insufficient infrastructure, shortage of supplies and personnel, and difficulty in locating and identifying remains. But to a grieving family longing to provide final services no excuse is totally sufficient, and there are many people eager to take advantage of the situation. Playing upon the raw emotions of bereaved families, a Paris undertaker disseminated a circular in which "he declared he had commissions to return the bodies of various dead soldiers and in which he claimed to have the assistance of the 'Purple Cross.'" The scam artist promised to quickly return the remains of those buried outside the Zone of the Armies for "an average cost, delivery New York, of $605.00."

The bogus offer angered Americans who had lost loved ones, prompting the rhetorical statement, "'It looks like, if the French can get them out for money, the United States could get them out for loyalty to its citizens.'" This incident eventually required intervention by the Secretary of War, with the result that the Quartermaster General initiated diplomatic efforts to "impress upon this man [the Paris undertaker] the unwisdom of circularizing American families who were in sorrow" and to prevent the "premature removal of American dead by private firms."[113]

Despite U.S. efforts to repatriate Soldier Dead as quickly as possible, some relatives displayed great impatience and tried to make private arrangements to retrieve the bodies of their loved ones. The Cemeterial Division rejected all attempts by these "well-to-do" people to go around the system, because allowing them to create a privileged class of Soldier Dead would embitter the great majority of survivors who were of "modest means." Even then, families less well-off still made frequent accusations that the government was granting favors to the wealthy and returning remains to them faster than to ordinary citizens.[114]

Unfortunately, and much to the government's chagrin, some families were successful in personal endeavors to secure remains. In April 1920, Col. Charles C. Pierce was contacted by James H. Durbin of the Office of the Secretary of War, who wanted to know if there was any exception to the War Department's general policy of repatriation. Mr. Durbin had been contacted by Congressman John W. Rainey of Illinois on behalf of a constituent who wanted to go to France to retrieve the body of his son. Congressman Rainey told Durbin that he had been informed that the remains of Lieutenant Edward Hines of Chicago had been returned by his family.[115]

Colonel Pierce promptly responded that there was no exception to the policy of the U.S. government being responsible for the recovery, identification, and removal of remains and that:

> The body of Lieut. Edward Hines of Chicago . . . is in a class by itself. No permit was given for the removal this body. Its removal was effected surreptitiously and in violation of all regulations. The newspapers hinted at the collusion of French Municipal authorities and the use of money in connection therewith. The removal took place without American sanction or knowledge and in utter violation of all our regulations.[116]

After World War II, the dissatisfaction was even more widespread. The public who had accepted the exigent actions of a draft, rationing, price controls, and casualty lists to win the war was suspicious of the government's efforts to return the dead. Any error in handling World War II remains was "construed as conclusive evidence of ineptitude and indifference in the discharge of a sacred trust." The "Top Brass" were viewed with suspicion and distrust and the "Caste System" had "managed to imbed its pernicious tentacles in the officers' corps of the armed services."[117] It is not clear what agenda the higher levels of military officers were alleged to be pursuing, but the lack of a specific motive did not deter critics.

The first returns of World War II dead outside of the continental United States did not take place until fall 1947, more than two years after the end of the war. This meant that some families received news of their loved one's death several years before they received the remains. The body of Private Louis Schleifer, who died during the attack on Pearl Harbor on December

7, 1941, was not returned home to Newark, New Jersey until October 1947, almost six years after his death.[118]

As mentioned earlier, the remains of those who died within North America could, in limited cases, be returned for burial provided they were not transported by "air or ocean or coastwise vessels." This modification, slight as it was, to the War Department's directive on December 13, 1941 prohibiting the shipment of *any* remains was made over the objection of the Quartermaster General—the originator of the no-return directive—who stated that the public had become "more or less educated on this subject and has generally accepted the views and decisions of the War Department." There is some doubt that the public had unquestioningly "generally accepted" the official position, especially when it was clear that airplanes "in a large number of cases" and ocean transports were returning empty from the Alaska Command, where deaths had occurred. The Quartermaster General, Gen. Edmund Gregory, was, by all accounts, more concerned with "the embarrassments that would be visited upon the War Department if the original policy . . . underwent the slightest modification" than he was with the needs of the bereaved.[119] General Gregory's objection did little to foster trust or faith and is an excellent example of a stick-with-what-was-first-said attitude that has continually plagued relations between the military and families.

During World War I, the next of kin received notice of the death of their soldier and, if available, information about where the remains were buried. All too frequently, though, conflicting information was supplied, resulting in considerable anxiety. In order to assure that only correct information was disseminated, the Quartermaster centralized reporting of burial locations and processed all requests for details of graves through its U.S. and Paris offices.[120]

After World War I, the U.S. government desired that its dead be repatriated in a "dignified and reverent manner, expeditiously, and with as little publicity as possible." To this end, GRS personnel "were cautioned against making any statements, verbal or written, pertaining to the operations other than those made through the regular official channels."[121] Doubtless, this policy was put in place in part because interviews of GRS personnel revealing internal administration problems "of no concern to the public whatsoever" had upset "Americans relatives reading the account."[122]

And after World War II, the government was very sensitive about information supplied to the public. The Quartermaster General, under the Supervisor of the War Department Public Relations Division, printed a pamphlet, "Tell Me About My Boy," prepared in response to the most frequently asked questions posed by the families of those killed overseas. The introduction contained the statement: "Seeking information from unauthorized persons is inadvisable. Official sources alone should be sought to avoid the dissemination of erroneous information and the disappointment which a wrong answer might bring."[123]

But what happens when the official source of information is felt to be either inaccurate or not fully forthcoming? And what happens in cases where the information regarding the dead is tied up with facts of such a sensitive nature that its disclosure would compromise the safety of current and future operations? These are difficult questions, as it is quite possible—some would say probable—for the government to hide details of missions gone awry, gross incompetence, or unauthorized operations in the name of national security. Family members find themselves wondering whom they can trust.

Many areas of conflict with families have been obviated by the policy of Concurrent Return. However, the removal of the issue of delay has done little to resolve a more fundamental area of conflict, ascertaining that soldiers are actually dead. If you don't have possession of remains, then how do you actually know who is dead and who isn't? This question has plagued the families who never receive any remains.

As in any potential conflict, how a respondent answers a question is often as important as the information conveyed. When none is given or available, a vacuum exists, and it will inexorably be filled, either with correct or incorrect information. And if military leaders prevaricate or make dissembling statements that are later found out, a white-hot fire is kindled in the hearts of the surviving family members that will burn long past the later provision of correct information.

Families know that service personnel are sometimes killed in a manner or location that renders obtaining remains for return difficult, if not impossible. However, the government has lost a great deal of credibility because of its failure, in some cases, to follow through on information regarding missing persons or remains, or its efforts to cloak oversights in misstatements, deceptions, and claims of national security.

Since its formative stage at the beginning of the twentieth century, the U.S. policy of repatriation of its Soldier Dead has solidified into the position that all dead are returned home, immediately if possible, save those that are contaminated. The policy change to bringing all the dead back instead of giving the next of kin the choice of return or burial overseas has come about because of several factors. First, we now have the physical/technological/logistical ability to return remains immediately.And since the end of World War II, our wars have been conducted in far-flung corners of the world with allies for whom we felt little affinity—only national concern. There is scant desire for U.S. dead to lie in Somalia, Afghanistan, Kuwait, or Iraq, and often the countries where they die have little love for America, either. It is interesting that giving the next of kin the choice of letting their dead loved ones repose in the land in which they fought and died is no longer a consideration. Furthermore, it is difficult to envision a situation where the next of kin would even want this choice.

However, when conditions have not allowed for concurrent return, our Soldier Dead have been buried as best could be accomplished under the circumstances, with the promise that we would return for them. Despite delays and complications, repatriation efforts were eventually conducted and, to some degree, are ongoing. These efforts have not come cheaply. By the end of 1922, 45,588 World War I Soldier Dead had been repatriated at a cost of $396.04 each, for a total cost of just over $18 million.[124] By the conclusion of the Return of the Dead Program on December 31, 1951, 280,994 remains had been recovered and only 10,011, or less than 3½ percent, were unidentified.[125] Of those killed, 171,000 were repatriated at a cost of $564.50 each, for a total cost of $96.5 million.[126] As significant as these figures are, they do not include the cost of burial overseas at the end of either world war or the current costs of continuing to recover, repatriate, and identify remains—estimated to be $100 million annually.[127]

In acknowledging the first time it was assigned the duty of repatriation in World War I, the Office of the Quartermaster General stated:

> For the activities of this Service have been, and always will be, in a peculiar sense, the carrying out of a sacred obligation, the fulfilling of a pledge made by the War Department to the people of the United States, that the graves of American dead should be perpetually honored and cared for, and that those men who fell should be returned to their homes, should their kin so desire.[128]

Acknowledging the difficulties in carrying out the pledge, the Quartermaster said:

> Its accomplishment involved an undertaking so comprehensive in its scope, so replete with the unexpected, the pathetic and the heroic, that, to follow its development and the conscientious, sympathetic and

diligent concern of the officers and personnel associated in the work, would be to recognize an achievement which will stand forth in world relief a credit to American reverence and patriotism.[129]

Author's Notes

"Once you've stood next to body bags containing the dead and flown in planes that somebody is trying to shoot down, everything else gets put in perspective."

This was my answer to the question, "What was it like in Baghdad?" posed by my civilian friends upon my return to the States after being embedded with the Army's 54th Mortuary Affairs Company. Military friends didn't ask, but simply nodded their heads when they heard of my trip.

Baghdad was my introduction to the "real world" of repatriating our Soldier Dead from the Iraq War. I attended the funeral of Sgt. Charles Poole, whose B-52 had been shot down over North Vietnam and whose remains were recovered in 1995, and I have talked to many, many people closely involved with bringing military dead back from all over the world. But watching the Mortuary Affairs and Air Force personnel performing their solemn duty was an unforgettable experience that needs to be shared with others.

There is another story associated with my trip to Iraq that bears mentioning, that of media access to the dead. During World War I and World War II, the press was allowed to photograph remains as they were removed from the war theaters and upon their arrival home. In fact, elaborate ceremonies were held when the dead returned to the United States. During the Korean War, remains were photographed as they were loaded onto transport ships in Japan, but their arrival home was not recognized or commemorated as in previous wars. Remains were flown to the United States from Vietnam by the tens and scores at a time and, as illustrated by the flap over Bud Minor's supposed manhandling of a photographer, media photographs were allowed. There was, however, no national day of mourning or recognition of the return. After 1991, even taking pictures was prohibited.

Previously, bodies arriving at Dover Air Force Base and other return locations were met by a "Fallen Soldier" detail, and the receiving ceremony was open to the media. This event, while seemingly offering the dead due respect and recognition, provided the opportunity for multiple news photographs and stories. There might be an article and accompanying photo of transfer cases being loaded onto aircraft overseas, another story on their arrival at Dover, and another story, along with photos of the grieving widow, at the time of final burial; the same dead were portrayed before the public possibly three times or more. As an unnamed military figure told me, "We kept getting hit over the head with these images."

Just before the Iraq War, the media ban at Dover was extended to all bases where remains are handled, meaning that transfer cases containing remains were not to be viewed or photographed anywhere along the chain of custody. I may have been one of the few, if not the only media person allowed to witness the movement of remains, but even this access was tightly controlled. In fact, my first moments in Baghdad were spent negotiating about what I could and could not photograph.

What does the media blackout mean? What is its impact? Why was it put in force? The answers depend on whom you ask.

From military members' comments and from the well-known aversion to losing American lives in wars considered by many to be of questionable value, I believe that the 1991 ban on press access to the return of the dead is grounded in the desire to minimize the public outcry over body bags. The military will vehemently tell you that the media strictures are to "protect the privacy of the families," but I can't help believing that they are also trying to carry out our national agenda with the use of military force while de-emphasizing the persistent corollary that the use of force results in the loss of life.

The media are quick to point out that they are not only allowed but actually encouraged to attend repatriation ceremonies for the dead brought back from historical recoveries. This apparent contradiction in policy suggests darker motives on the part of those in charge: the overwhelming desire to avoid hammering the U.S. public with images of the dead, out of fear that public ire may rise even further against U.S. participation in war. To be sure, talk of needing 20,000 body bags for the Gulf War did not make for pleasant dinner conversation.

What is most striking about the continuing debate onkeeping the dead from view is that no one is asking the right questions. One that we wrestle with is: To whom do the dead belong? The media are allowed reasonable access to incidents involving death. Recently, in my hometown there were some rather grisly pictures of a body being dragged from the Red River in Shreveport, Louisiana, and I thought the local TV station was overreaching.

On March 30, 2004, the Supreme Court ruled on a case brought by Allan Favish, a Los Angeles attorney who filed a Freedom of Information Act request for the pictures of the body of former Clinton aide, Vincent Foster.

Favish alleged that the government's investigation into the circumstances of Foster's death had been conducted in an incompetent manner and that photos might sustain his claim. The case ended up in the Supreme Court, which unanimously decided against Favish, saying that the family's privacy interest trumped the public's interest. In arguing its case, the government said that if Foster's photos were released, then photos of dead soldiers might also have to be released.

Obviously, there is an ongoing struggle between private and public interests, but the question that comes to my mind is how a picture of a flag-shrouded transfer case being loaded onto or unloaded from an airplane can be considered a breach of family privacy. This question is not quite as simple as it seems. Contrast the event of a single soldier being killed and returned versus scores and hundreds. If many deaths occur in a short time period, there is no "linkage" of repatriation coverage to the specific names of those actually killed. If there is only a single death over many days or weeks, then it would be easy to associate repatriation with that deceased serviceperson.

There is also the danger that if the government takes the "family privacy" position to its logical conclusion, it will no longer announce the names of those killed, only the numbers. And if the logic is followed further, the government could, theoretically, refuse to announce even the number of dead.

Another question that is not asked is how we, as a nation, note the sacrifices of those killed and their families who are left behind. It is fortunate that our dead are brought home soon after death instead of months and years later as in World War I, World War II, and the Korean War. (While Korea did bring about the policy of Concurrent Return, remains were still returned via slow boat.) Yet the prompt return of remains means that there is no occasion to receive, en masse, our Soldier Dead in a fitting ceremony, and this diminishes the collective recognition of the lives lost in military duty.

Military officials to whom I have spoken say that they cannot envision a situation in which the media would, once again, be allowed to attend the return of the dead. And the large majority support keeping the dead shrouded from public view at all times and letting only the family make the choice to allow media representatives or not.

Now, with the loss of media coverage, what little national recognition there was is reduced even further. While some have tried to provide a visual image of the dead—the display of 500 pairs of empty Army boots in Chicago's Federal Building Plaza in January 2004 is good example—we still lack a poignant reminder of the national loss of American lives in Iraq.

[6. Burial]

The grass is waking in the ground,
Soon it will rise and blow in waves—
How can it have the heart to sway
Over the graves,
New graves?
—SARA TEASDALE, "Spring in War Time"

NORMAN WARREN BIRCHER, Harry Warner Jr., and Glendon Place all have one thing in common: they died during the Normandy Invasion and are 3 of the more than 9,000 who now lie buried in the American cemetery overlooking the beaches where they spilled their blood. This graveyard (it *is* a graveyard, despite the prevalence of euphemisms) is a beautiful sight, as are Arlington National Cemetery in Virginia, the Punchbowl National Cemetery in Honolulu, Hawaii, Meuse-Argonne Cemetery near Verdun, France, and the other cemeteries that hold the remains of our military fallen.

The "Fields of Honor" which American servicemen and -women have fought, died, and been buried have claimed their share of emotional real estate, and the sites help to both form and preserve an image that reminds citizens collectively that someone else paid the price for their well-being. Few of those who walk through the rows and rows of white crosses and stars are not viscerally overwhelmed by the sheer numbers of bodies that lie beneath them. And few of those visitors realize the efforts extended by the living to provide a final resting place for those who made the supreme sacrifice. If they did, their gratitude would extend also to these unnamed heroes who had to care for the dead on the difficult journey from battlefields to temporary graves to permanent cemeteries.

Battlefield/Isolated Burials

Our history of warfare is replete with instances of burying the dead where fighting occurred, because there was little else that could be done. When possible, we have used cemeteries, both temporary and permanent. As in combat and postcombat recovery operations, the distinction between "battlefield burials" and "temporary cemeteries" is one of degree rather than of class, and all of the former from the early 1900s forward have been considered "temporary." Battlefield burials were done during active conflict and in the immediate vicinity of where death occurred. The fallen were buried in haste, with minimum attention paid to the removal of personal effects and equipment. However, identification has almost always been a primary concern.

Temporary cemeteries were located relatively near battlefields, but typically differed from battlefield burial sites in that they held more bodies, were more adequately staffed, and were often planned in advance. Also, temporary cemeteries were used to concentrate the dead so that it was possible to keep better records, maintain the grounds, and organize remains for either eventual return home or permanent interment.

Some cemeteries started as groups of battlefield burials, only to later become temporary cemeteries and then permanent ones. An excellent example is the World War II permanent cemetery at St. Laurent, located on a bluff that commands a view of the Omaha Beach landing area of Normandy. St. Laurent was established twenty-four hours after D-Day, and the soldiers who died in the landing were the first buried there. Later, because of its proximity to the invasion area, its graceful surroundings, and the availability of transportation and nearby lodging, it was chosen as a permanent cemetery.[1]

It was during the Civil War that orders were first issued to Commanding Generals to provide burial sites near battlefields. Prior to that time, the burial of soldiers was haphazard and poorly organized, with grave locations and identities often lost. Since then, recovery and identification of the dead have steadily improved, thanks in large part to the reduction in battlefield burials.

During World War I, 15,000 of the 75,000 combat fatalities in Europe were buried during the stress of battle in isolated graves.[2] Since the "War to End All Wars" was marked by long periods in which the armies were positioned along nearly static fronts, with neither side able to claim the field or to perform burials in conditions of relative peace, interment of the dead was risky at best. The U.S. Quartermaster said:

6.1   Burying the dead at Fredericksburg, VA, after the Wilderness Campaign, May 1864. *Timothy O'Sullivan. National Archives & Records Administration*

6.2   Civil War graves near City Point, VA. *Mathew Brady. National Archives & Records Administration*

Battle conditions make it impossible to bury men either decently or with any surety that their identity will be preserved. Those who have seen these temporary hasty inhumations made by devoted friends or by soldiers in the line of their duty, with chaplains endeavoring to give the last rites of religion wherever possible, and to keep a record for the future, while perhaps high explosives undo the work just finished and leave new dead to be dealt with, can realize without words what was the situation in the battle area of France after the armistice. Temporary burials were sometimes marked by a rifle, by a rude improvised cross, by a stick in the ground, with the identity indicated as well as possible at the time: the grave might vary from six feet to six inches in depth, and many were the cases in which bodies were hardly buried at all. There were also, of course, trench burials of many bodies together and such, if not separated, soon became like charnel houses; so it was the duty of the Graves Registration Service to follow these temporary in- humations as they were reported and, as conditions made it possible to approach these areas, to re-mark the grave with a wooden "V" shaped peg on which was a stamped metal plate indicating the soldier's iden- tity, and to improve the situation of the grave when necessary.[3]

At the beginning of World War I, Capt. H. R. Lemly of the Cemeterial Branch of the War Department asked the British how they handled their dead. Lieutenant Colonel W. V. L. Applin replied that they considered it "impracticable to embalm bodies of soldiers killed in battle, and we have never attempted to do so," and that it was not "practicable to bury dead sol- diers in coffins or caskets." "Where the dead are thick they are collected and buried in a common grave," Applin wrote, and "where the bodies are more scattered and in all cases of dismemberment by high explosive the bodies are buried where found."

Applin's letter to Captain Lemly also contained an account of the recov- ery of the body of a British officer in which those who performed the task were greatly endangered. As a result of this experience, "a general order was issued from the [British] Commander-in-Chief that under no circumstances was the body of an officer or man to be brought back for burial."[4] However, these British guidelines were unacceptable to American ideals and only em- phasized that the United States would have to make its own way without the benefit of others' experience.

After the war, on February 1, 1924, the U.S. Army issued the "AR [Army Regulation] 30-series" that reflected its experience gained during World

War I and formalized the duties of those connected with the retrieval and burial of war dead. It "prescribed both methods of burial in active theaters of war and procedures for reporting such burials." AR 30–1810 of the series specified "detailed procedures and responsibilities as to burials on the battlefield." It also provided a plethora of other rules regarding registration of unmarked graves, handling of unburied remains, burial of enemy dead and "outlaws," maintenance of morale and proper hygiene, processing of identification tags, making and preserving identification, and the prohibition of monuments in temporary military cemeteries.

The 1924 AR 30-series established several precedents. The Quartermaster General, during wartime, was to oversee a Graves Registration Service that would be activated by the War Department. The GRS, while owing allegiance to higher-level quartermaster authorities with regard to objectives to be achieved and general guidelines, was under the day-to-day supervision of Theater Commanders. Finally, the detailed regulations made it clear that Graves Registration was "here to stay" as a technical function and that it required planning, support, and integration with the overall operations of soldiering.[5]

But during the years following 1924, there was still insufficient emphasis on the need to handle the dead in a specific, organized way. Three months before the attack on Pearl Harbor, the Quartermaster of the I Army Corps in Columbia, South Carolina made a request for "'any instructional data governing graves registration; field burials and the safeguarding and recording the effects of deceased personnel." His request, eerily clairvoyant, was met with the Quartermaster General's reply to use the aforementioned AR 30-series issued seventeen years earlier.[6]

Even with these regulations in force, there were still differences concerning how to handle combat deaths, as some believed that burial should be performed by troops in the field rather than by a specialized unit. In particular, on the eve of World War II, Colonel John T. Harris, director of the Memorial Division, felt that the Quartermaster Corps would be overtaxed by burial duties, and he questioned "the wisdom of establishing any temporary military cemetery during the conduct of active operations." Harris thought it would be best for combat troops "to dispose of their own dead and then . . . when peace comes, plans and policies can be established and carried out by civilian organizations."[7]

Colonel Harris's plan would have resulted in burial operations similar to those used during World War I, at best, and perhaps even more comparable to the burial practices followed during the Civil War. It is likely that the much larger numbers of deaths in World War II, combined with the world-wide extent of military operations, would have meant fewer recoveries and an identification rate much lower than what was actually achieved, perhaps as low as the Civil War rate of only 58 percent. Fortunately, Harris was not able to muster much support for his position.

However, General J. Lawton Collins, commander of the 25th Division at Guadalcanal, used battlefield burial as the most militarily efficient method rather than pursuing other choices. To justify burying the dead where they fell, he "insisted that undue concern for the dead at [the] expense of succor to the wounded was an expression of false sentiment that had no place in war."[8] Though Collins's either-or attitude may certainly have been appropriate in some situations, it is almost equally certain that other options were available at times.

Technically, the obligation to bury the dead fell upon the quartermaster troops. However, when staffing was inadequate, as it was for much of the initial stage of the war, "combat elements of the various task forces were expected to look after their own. Furthermore, this obligation was stated in terms so vague as to be all but incomprehensible to the untrained personnel of organic burial units established for the emergency."[9]

The first burials of any magnitude in World War II occurred in the Pacific Theater when the Japanese attacked the Philippines. The Army was forced to cobble together such assets as it could find or make available in order to perform burials, make identifications, and keep records. American forces were ill prepared not only for the attack by the Imperial Army of Japan but also for handling the large numbers of deaths that ensued. At Quinauan Point, bodies lay in the tropical sun for fourteen days before GRS troops were given the task of burying them.

Captain S. J. Gladys headed up much of the GRS activities in the Philippines and worked diligently to execute his duty. Knowing that the Army could not hold its positions, he hid burial records behind the walls of the Malinta Tunnel, but they were nonetheless discovered by the Japanese who, by all accounts, "willfully destroyed" them in an Orwellian gesture of altering history. The loss of these records, along with the obliteration of graves by indiscriminate bombing, greatly hampered and even rendered impossible the later recovery of many remains. As noted in the next chapter, "All Bodies Are Not the Same," defeating the enemy means gaining superiority over not only living combatants but also the dead.

After the fall of the island of Corregidor, in Manila Bay, General Wainwright, Commanding General, United States Forces in the Philippines, in charge of operations in the Pacific Theater, appealed to the Japanese head-quarters for permission to bury the Americans and Filipinos who were killed. The Japanese denied Wainwright's request because giving him access to the battlefield would have provided information about their casualties, since Japanese, American, and Filipino bodies were all in close proximity. Conse-quently, all the bodies were "heaped in huge funeral pyres and cremated."

When the Japanese achieved victory and Americans were interned in prison camps, "Under intolerable conditions of physical hardship and men-tal torture they persisted in their efforts to realize the ideal that no American soldier shall be buried without identification or in an unregistered grave." Captain Gladys, even while imprisoned at Cabanatuan, Philippines, contin-ued his duties as a Graves Registration officer, burying the dead and main-taining records.[10]

As the war progressed and the U.S. forces began to mount offenses, Pa-cific burials were conducted differently than those in North Africa or Eu-rope. Marines, leading the assault on Japanese forces, "called for a graves registration platoon of combat personnel which was to follow the landing force ashore and make proper disposition of all fatalities." While the Army preferred to concentrate burials in temporary military cemeteries, utilizing collection points to gather and forward the dead, the Marines did not have the luxury of time, space, or men to do the same. Instead, they were forced to bury those killed pretty much where they died. Later, when conditions permitted, they went back over the battlegrounds—which often consisted of entire islands—and concentrated the dead into temporary cemeteries. How-ever, even this process was delayed at times to allow bodies to decompose more completely first—it was easier and more sanitary to move skeletons or remains that had lost most of their fluids.[11]

The battle for Okinawa was marked by the death and battlefield burial of well-known and well-liked syndicated newspaper columnist Ernie Pyle, who was covering combat activities on Ie Shima, a small neighboring island. Pyle had taken cover in a foxhole and was killed by a sniper's bullet through the head. Corporal Stanley Entman, a member of the 3063rd Graves Registration Com-pany who helped bury him, said, "Pyle was the only person buried in a wooden casket instead of being wrapped in a poncho." When questioned about where the casket came from, given that such containers were not normally used, Ent-man replied that someone probably had made it for Pyle out of respect, using whatever material was on hand.[12] As will be seen later, the use of caskets, while seemingly reverent, actually often hindered later disinterment efforts.

6.3   Group of graves at a water point in New Georgia showing how hastily dug graves are sometimes surrounded later by Army installations. *U.S. Army Signal Corps. National Archives & Records Administration*

Pyle's burial, at the end of the war when resources were more available, was not representative. Partly because of the lack of space but certainly because of the lack of time and manpower, the trench burial method was commonly employed in the Pacific.[13] Using earth-moving equipment to excavate large trenches allowed large numbers of remains to be buried in short order—an important consideration given the tropical heat. In fact, trench burial is now the preferred method, should unusual circumstances make immediate interment necessary.[14]

Plans for the invasion of France called for avoiding the proliferation of battlefield burials during World War I, in which "2,240 temporary sites were used." The same plans provided GRS support for the landing at Normandy, but difficulties encountered in breaking through on some beaches necessitated establishing battlefield graves, since the dead could not be evacuated either to ships or to planned temporary cemeteries in areas still under German control.[15]

6.4   U.S. Marines pay their final respects to Ernie Pyle, who was killed at Ie Shima. (Note: This burial is a classic, by the book trench burial, with individual graves counter-sunk in the trench.) *National Archives & Records Administration*

However, soon after the beginning of World War II, during the invasion of Sicily in July 1943, support for Graves Registration had been nonexistent. While losses on the beach were nominal, it was still difficult to locate and bury the dead because GRS troops had no transportation. A division officer wrote, "Being on foot, the graves registration officers had to hitch hike, find picks and shovels, and had difficulty in locating men to dig graves." The result was that "attached graves registration units were immobile and the division commander instructed each regiment to bury its own dead."[16] The exigent action of troops burying their own often led to difficulties in making identification and retaining grave locations, as combat troops were not technically trained in establishing ID, burying, and recording grave sites.

Two months later, when Allied troops landed in Italy, U.S. Armed Forces began to understand not only the importance of removing the dead from the battlefield as quickly as possible but also how to do so efficiently and how to make better use of temporary cemeteries.[17] From that point forward, at least in the European Theater, the focus moved from battlefield burials to collec-

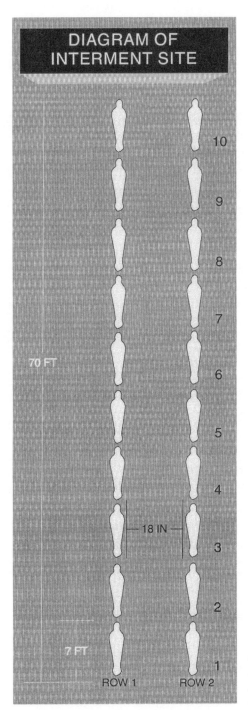

DIAGRAM OF
INTERMENT SITE

10

9

8

7

70 FT

6

5

4

— 18 IN —

3

2

7 FT

1

ROW 1   ROW 2

6.5   The current trench burial system, in which remains are laid head to toe. *Joint Pub 4–06: Joint Tactics, Techniques, and Procedures for Mortuary Affairs*

tion points, with eventual transportation to more official temporary cemeteries. Of course, isolated burials still took place, particularly when planes crashed far from friendly forces, but were reduced considerably once GRS units began to accompany combat troops on landings.

During the initial phase of the Korean War, in the last half of 1950, as the North Koreans pushed U.S. forces back down the peninsula, many of the dead were left unburied on the battlefield or in isolated graves. When the United States broke out of the Pusan Perimeter and began reclaiming land it had lost, GRS personnel, often assisted by organic units, began to recover these remains. Then, at the end of 1950 and the beginning of 1951, the United States adopted the policy of Concurrent Return, thus mostly obviating the need for battlefield and temporary burials unless circumstances were extremely dire. This happened not long afterward. When the North Koreans began to be pinned against their northern border, China entered the war, sending human waves against the UN lines. The 2nd Army Division was "trapped and partially overrun by enemy [Chinese] enveloping movements" and had to leave many of its dead behind during its retreat, some "without even hasty burial." The 8th Cavalry Regiment, after relieving the Republic of Korea (ROK) 11th Regiment, was attacked and cut off, with hundreds of its cavalrymen killed and buried in the hills of Unsan.[18] These soldiers, for the most part, remained where they fell or were buried, as the United States was not able to reclaim this territory or to mount recovery missions.

The current policy of the U. S. Armed Forces still calls for no temporary burying of remains unless circumstances require it: if the number of dead overwhelm Mortuary Affairs resources or there are "extreme situations when the tactical and logistical situation leave no alternatives." Temporary interment may be necessary when remains cannot be decontaminated of nuclear, chemical, or biological elements, even after several attempts.[19]

One thing is certain: if U.S. troops are called upon to perform even hasty, temporary burials on or near the battlefield, they will do so in a manner that reflects the heart and soul of the act. Although Walt Whitman, the "poet of the body," did not serve on the front line, he nursed the wounded during the Civil War and must have heard their nightmares. He well described battlefield burials in "Vigil Strange I Kept on the Field One Night":

> My comrade I wrapt in his blanket, envelop'd well his
> form,
> Folded the blanket well, tucking it carefully over head
> and carefully under feet . . .

I rose from the chill ground and folded my soldier
    well in his blanket,
And buried him where he fell.

Temporary Cemeteries—Concentration

Temporary cemeteries are those established to serve as an initial burial
site for those killed in combat or as a concentration burial site to which
remains are moved from battlefield or isolated burials. Some temporary
cemeteries were eventually closed when all the remains were removed, and
others were later converted into permanent cemeteries. Also, as previously mentioned, there was not a clear distinction between battlefield burial
sites and temporary cemeteries. Thus, by the end of World War II, Colonel R. L. Talbot, Chief, Cemetery Plant Division, divided the European
cemeteries into categories I, II, and III. Category I were those likely to
become permanent military cemeteries. Category II were those that were
conveniently located and to be maintained until the repatriation of the
dead had been completed. Category III were small cemeteries from which
remains were to be evacuated as soon as possible and moved to a Category
I or II cemetery.[20] During World War I, the cemeteries did not carry a
Category I, II, or III designation, but were merely defined as "temporary"
or "permanent."

During World War I, after burials during battle:

> Graves Registration Service workers went into the field and located the
> graves as soon as possible. These they opened, confirmed the identifi-
> cation, placed the bodies in boxes and reburied them in a local cem-
> etery, if there were one nearby, or, if there were not, they laid out a
> little concentration cemetery of their own in which were buried those
> found in the immediate vicinity.[21]

After the armistice, the concentration of remains became the first task in
preparing them for repatriation or final burial. As in any organization and any
major project, it was necessary to clarify lines of reporting and responsibility,
and it was affirmed that troops employed by the GRS took their orders from
the Chief, Graves Registration Service, but that Army commanders would still
"exercise disciplinary and sanitary control over all troops within their jurisdic-
tion."[22] The GRS troops, as do their modern equivalents, provided a specialty
service and have traditionally worked under this dual authority.

6.6   Temporary cemetery at Aisne, France containing the remains of 78 American dead, World War I. *Sgt. Carnochan. National Archives & Records Administration*

Starting in March 1919, a second phase of concentration began in which remains were moved to larger concentration cemeteries, usually extensions of previously existing French military cemeteries. The idea was to continue to reduce the number of cemeteries, a desirable goal given that at one time there were 1,836 locations on file in Washington.[23] During this process, the GRS had four primary concerns. The first was to establish and preserve the identity of remains. An officer was responsible for identification work performed on all remains under his control and was to be present in cases of exhumation when caskets were broken or collapsed.

The second concern was that rules of hygiene be established and followed to protect those conducting exhumations and those living or working in the immediate vicinity. This required, for one thing, sufficient caskets of proper quality, and metal caskets with rubber gaskets were employed. "As soon as the casket [if any had been used] was opened and the remains uncovered, they were liberally treated with disinfectant fluid." Remains were examined for items that would help establish identification, placed on a clean blanket, and then "wrapped so that the remains should appear in the most presentable condition, according to the best undertaking practice." They were also treated with a fluid containing creosote and necrosan in order to prevent the release of fluids and odors.

The third concern was safe transportation. The casketed remains were enclosed in a wooden shipping case, and the total package weighed between 500 and 700 pounds. Rules of conveyance were established that called for careful handling, and morgues were located close to shipping facilities so as to minimize the number of times the case had to be physically manipulated.

Finally, the fourth concern was the respectful treatment of bodies. Military escorts accompanied remains when they were being transported, storage facilities were properly cleaned and decorated, and "employees were forbidden to ride upon or lean against the shipping cases."[24] Despite the goal that remains be respectfully treated at all times, there were exceptions, as the example of the *Mercury*, described in the previous chapter, indicates.

A different type of problem arose in what became known as "Do Not Disturb" cases. In World War I, many relatives desired that the bodies of their fallen be touched or moved as little as possible—left where they were and not moved to a permanent military cemetery. This sentiment may have originated either in the romantic notion that sons, husbands, and fathers were merely "asleep" in a protected pocket in the soil or in the superstitious notion that graves are taboo. After all, the dead were certainly much more "disturbed" by the event that had killed them than by the act of moving them from one grave to another. Whatever the basis, though, the Graves Registration Service attempted to honor these wishes as much as possible.

Still, Do Not Disturb cases presented special problems. For one, many battlefield and temporary cemeteries were scheduled to be abandoned after the transfer of remains. Who was to have responsibility for maintaining the graves of those not moved? What if the grave was in the middle of a farmer's field? Generally, for practical reasons, it was necessary to move the dead at least once, since many were scattered throughout France and other parts of Europe. In doing so, the U.S. government had to follow the lead of the country where they were buried. In Britain, the government was willing to provide care for graves that were to remain undisturbed. France, however, required the relatives to purchase the plot of land where the body lay and obtain approval from the mayor of the commune. Also, the relatives were responsible for the upkeep of the graves. It is easy to understand France's position, since many thousands more graves were on its territory than were in British lands.

Even when Do Not Disturb graves were originally located in what was to become a permanent cemetery, there were complications because, after repatriation of the dead, most if not all remains had to be disinterred and reburied in a uniform manner; the original burial might not have been in accordance with later adopted standards, and it was also the policy that all burials in permanent cemeteries be in a reburial casket, thus necessitating the "disturbance" of remains.

If a Do Not Disturb burial had occurred in a "purely American cemetery that was to be abandoned," the policy was to coordinate matters between the family and the French government as to a future burial site, in either a community or a military cemetery. But, as in the case of isolated burials, the family was responsible for all upkeep.[25] However, for Do Not Disturb graves located in French or British cemeteries, the United States did not take the position that it needed to rebury the remains in a reburial casket or place graves according to a standard formula. In this case, the only reason for disturbing remains was to resolve questions of identification. Ultimately, the next of kin chose the Do Not Disturb option in 161 cases.[26]

Some World War II next of kin also desired that the remains of their loved ones be disturbed as little as possible. In honoring this request, the War Department "canceled plans for the evacuation of Category III cemeteries" to Category II cemeteries, with the result that these remains were only moved once—from the small, temporary cemetery to the final and permanent Category I military cemetery.[27]

Respecting a Do Not Disturb request took an unusual turn in Anchorage, Alaska, when Sergeant Robert Vorisek was assigned to the 9108th AGRS company. During his duty in Alaska and the Aleutian Islands, he helped build the military cemetery at Fort Richardson. Vorisek said, "There was one grave we weren't allowed to touch; we couldn't exhume the body and move it. We had to build the cemetery around the grave. That was the grave of Kermit Roosevelt, President Teddy Roosevelt's son."[28] Kermit had committed suicide during his duty in Alaska and, in keeping with the wishes of his late father, was buried where he died, so the cemetery had to be constructed without disturbing his remains.

It wasn't only Americans who desired that some graves be left as they were. The French sentiment and care for the dead were depicted by an elderly peasant woman in Bazoches, France, after World War I:

> [She] had for a considerable time tended the grave of a young American soldier who had been buried in her little garden. She had rounded

it off trimly, planted it with geranium and sweet herbs and watered it every day. It was lovely, that little mound, and she was always thinking how happy his poor mother would be to come one day and see it.

But, just before Memorial Day, the remains were disinterred and moved to a military cemetery. The volunteer caretaker "was desolated; her American comrade that she dreamed of by night and whose grave she tended by day was gone!" And she asked, "Is it, Monsieur, that by some chance you may know where they have taken him?"[29] This example further illustrates the impact of the dead upon the living, and how the dead retain, or in this case actually obtain, a social presence.

The concentration of remains in World War I was hindered by the difficulty of finding graves in the first place. The French army reportedly lost 50,000 graves—completely understandable, though regrettable, given the mass artillery barrages and close-quarters fighting that often raged for long periods within a small area. The struggle was so intense that "it was not infrequent for graves to be opened by shell fire and for burial parties to be stricken down in the process of their duty."[30]

Graves Registration, while performing concentrations of graves, also recorded information for its own use and for giving to the next of kin. Knowing that it faced a shortage of resources, the Cemeterial Division accepted assistance from the Red Cross, whose personnel prepared Search Reports with information obtained from company records and statements from fellow combatants of the deceased or those who worked to bury them. These reports and statements were helpful in locating graves and establishing identities. The Search Reports also contained "a brief account of any worthy or heroic actions attending the death of the soldiers, and by interviews with their comrades, they often learned of their last words, or of the expressed desires of the dying men." Additionally, the reports "were recorded, not only for their historical significance, but as a consolation to their bereaved families."[31]

However, these efforts were met with mixed emotions by families of those killed who perhaps did not understand the difficulties involved. In March 1919, C. W. Bailey wrote Lieutenant Colonel Pierce a letter expressing his gratitude for finally being informed of the burial place of his son. Bailey, while praising Pierce's efforts, was critical that it had taken so long—the armistice was signed on November 11, 1918, so his son was undoubtedly killed no later, and probably earlier, than that date. He said, "the delay in receiving information as to the death of our boys has been inexcusable."[32]

World War II presented its own set of difficulties in the burial of remains. In the Pacific, the distinction between battlefield and temporary cemeteries was vague because during the island-hopping campaign complete islands were often battlefields. On Iwo Jima and Okinawa, would a burial site be a battlefield burial or a temporary cemetery? Okinawa also presented the GRS with a unique problem: the large numbers of dead on naval crafts from ka-mikaze attacks. In order to offer an alternative to burial at sea,

> A beach was designated as a sort of central collection point, where the charred and mutilated remains form the stricken ships were received by a special Army detail and evacuated in motor trucks to the Island Cemetery.[33]

This example of the Navy taking its dead to shore to be buried when possible illustrates the point that the Navy uses burial at sea only as a least favored, rather than preferred, option.

Another recurrent problem in the Pacific Theater, because of inad-equate initial high-level support, was that of "small cemeteries and iso-lated burials," which Army headquarters wished to avoid, given the dif-ficulties in maintaining large numbers of small burial sites, consolidating graves, and identifying remains. Just one example was Hollandia, Dutch New Guinea, where there were multiple cemeteries that the Commanding General was ordered to consolidate. That a central cemetery had not been established soon after landing and that separate cemeteries had not been combined into one some five months later indicated a "collapse of com-mand responsibility,"[34] directly attributed to previous deficient training of GRS personnel, failure to adequately staff and equip GRS units, and a lack of emphasis by commanders on any function that did not directly support defeating the enemy.

Even after land was captured in the Pacific, little importance was placed on the concentration of cemeteries, and it was not until December 1944 that Admiral E. J. King, Commander in Chief, United States Fleet, recommended to the Joint Chiefs of Staff that, while Admiral Nimitz's earlier statement that there was no "expressed or implied" policy for disinterring and reinter-ring soldiers' remains was technically correct, "such a policy [of exhumation and reburial] will be needed."[35]

The Joint Chiefs of Staff studied the matter of concentration and, on February 17, 1945, issued Policy Memorandum No. 12, making the Army Graves Registration Service responsible for the exhumation of remains from isolated graves and small, remote cemeteries and their subsequent reburial

6.7   Sgt. Jack Congrove of Brooklyn, New York, checks dog tags on a grave where a bivouac area is now located. *U.S. Army Signal Corps. National Archives & Records Administration*

in larger, more conveniently located cemeteries. Such activities, though, were not to interfere with military operations or transportation.[36]

But the Army still did not sufficiently address the structure, training, and logistics needed to handle deaths. By March 1946, burial records showed that 65,487 remains were located in 201 cemeteries in the Pacific and Asiatic mainland, and concentration efforts had immediately run into trouble. For one thing, even in relatively small battle areas, graves were scattered all over islands and atolls. For another, the memorial markers that Marines often constructed "above a body or group of remains" impeded recovery efforts because sometimes there were no bodies beneath them and other times the names on the markers were associated with remains found elsewhere. And, all too often, the dead were buried with live grenades still attached on their webbing; the handles had rusted and would come off during disinterment.[37]

Eventually, though, the dead were concentrated into ever fewer cemeteries, involving several moves at times. Approximately 73,252 remains were gathered in Manila, Saipan, Honolulu, Yokohama, and Calcutta. The largest concentration was in an aboveground mausoleum at Manila that held more than 30,000 remains.[38]

6.8 Gravestone for a fallen comrade at Iwo Jima. *Pfc. E. D. Drdek.*
National Archives & Records Administration

As the U.S. Armed Forces fought their way to the homelands of their enemies, the question of whether to bury American soldiers in enemy soil arose. There was initial reluctance to do so, as though German or Japanese dirt would somehow "contaminate" them. Also, objections were voiced that any remains buried in those countries would have to eventually be disinterred, "disturbing" the dead. Obviously, the soil in Germany or Japan is inanimate, soulless, and indifferent to whose remains it holds, and remains certainly do not care where they are buried—or if they are even buried at all. The objection to leaving American bodies in enemy soil had to do with the feelings of the living and the generalized enmity felt toward a warring nation and its people. In essence, the issue was the association of the social identity of the dead with the location of remains in a land from which "evil" had sprung. But practical considerations overruled emotional arguments, and a temporary cemetery was established at Hardt, Germany, once the Allied forces crossed the Rhine.[39]

Even after experiencing the results of poor preparation in previous wars, at the start of the Korean War the United States was woefully unprepared to handle its battlefield dead. The 8th Army Quartermaster had two existing directives that set policy, AR 30–1805 and FM 10–63, but the "extremely fluid tactical situation called for deviations" and the GRS was forced, as it has often been, to improvise.

Consequently, the Army resorted to establishing temporary cemeteries, with each division "opening and closing them as they fell back to the final perimeter lines." This was a reversal of the policy established in World War II, in which temporary cemeteries were established at central locations for several divisions. Also, the abandonment of cemeteries to an approaching enemy was, for the most part, a first. By August 1950—North Korea launched its attack on June 26—there were eleven temporary cemeteries, some containing as few as three remains.[40]

As the United States and its UN allies fought their way out of the Pusan Perimeter and began to push the North Koreans back to the 38th Parallel, temporary cemeteries came once again under U.S. control. And, as the North Koreans were pushed above the 38th Parallel, more temporary cemeteries were established along the battle route, including in Pyongyang, the capital of North Korea, and Kaesong. When the masses of Chinese troops forced the U.S. soldiers back south, the Pyongyang temporary cemetery was abandoned without evacuating remains interred there.

Remains buried at the temporary cemetery at Kaesong were exhumed and taken to Inchon for reburial, but the Chinese and North Koreans continued their relentless drive south. In late December 1950, during the withdrawal from Inchon, the cemetery was evacuated, an arduous feat given the frozen ground. The GRS required assistance and recruited local laborers "with the cooperation of the local police." The 114th GRS Company, commanded by 1st Lt. Elmer C. Norum, completed the evacuation "in the face of an enemy advance," a singular moment and a precedent in U.S. history. The remains were taken to Japan and eventually repatriated to Hawaii and the mainland.[41]

Final Resting Place

The whole objective of retrieving, recovering, and identifying our Soldier Dead is to give them a final burial, with honors, where the family desires.

The honor guard, sounding of "Taps," and folding and presenting of the burial flag to the family are all part of the solemn ceremony. The ritual is especially poignant because the dead are mostly young; their photographs emanate freshness and vitality, and are vivid reminders that the dead gave up not only their lives but also their futures.

In 1850, Congress approved funds to establish a permanent cemetery in Mexico City for the soldiers who died in the Mexican-American War. Unfortunately, because of the crude techniques involved, when the remains of 750 American dead were exhumed from their graves along the road to Mexico City to be transferred to the cemetery, none could be identified. This is, perhaps, the first official Tomb of the Unknowns for the United States.[42]

The first large-scale burials in national military cemeteries began shortly after the end of the Civil War. But before these remains could be moved to a final resting place, they had to be found. General Meigs of the Quartermaster Corps issued General Orders No. 40, QMGO, July 3, 1865, which read:

> Officers of the Quartermaster's Department on duty in charge of the several principal posts, will report to this office, without delay, the number of interments registered during the war, white and black, loyal and disloyal, to be separately enumerated.
>
> All offices of the Quartermaster's Department who have made interments on battlefields during the war, will report the number of the same, giving the localities, dates of battles, and dates of interment.[43]

Captain James M. Moore, who had supervised perhaps the first recovery mission conducted by the Quartermaster Corps, led a recovery/burial team to Andersonville Prison in Georgia. There, he and his men reburied 12,912 Union dead and placed headboards containing the name, rank, regiment, state of service, and date of birth of those who had been identified. The headboards of 461 received an "Unknown U.S. Soldier" inscription.[44]

Later operations conducted by newly promoted Lieutenant Colonel Moore were not as successful— not because of lack of concern on his part, but because many grave markers were plowed under and graves were overgrown or otherwise destroyed. The major reasons for the loss of grave site locations were that military operations had first claim to resources or no permanent cemetery had been established immediately after a battle. When cemeteries were built soon after a battle, both recovery and identification rates were much higher; 82 percent of the dead buried in Gettysburg shortly after the Union victory there were identified.[45]

James Russell, in an 1866 issue of *Harper's New Monthly Magazine*, discussed the need for Congress to pass legislation to provide permanent burial sites and recognition for the common soldier. Russell didn't want the states to assume control of remains, as was done initially at Gettysburg, and he "applauded the decision of a Union general at Chattanooga to bury soldiers in a way that minimized state affiliation." The major general had "explained his decision by declaring that there had been 'quite enough of *State Rights*; that these soldiers had died fighting *for* the Union, *against* rebellious States, and now we had better mix them up and *nationalize* them a little,'"[46] emphasizing the importance and presence of the social identity of the dead.

By 1870, almost 300,000 Union soldiers had been found, disinterred, and reburied in 73 cemeteries. Established originally for Union dead, these followed the trend that had begun in civilian cemeteries in that they were "more elaborate and [took] on the characteristics of gardens."[47] Military cemeteries have continued to reflect further development of the theme of a well-landscaped garden.

The hatred felt between the North and the South did not immediately dissolve with Lee's surrender at Appomattox. Either fearing that Union graves would be "desecrated by Southerners" or perhaps experiencing it, the U.S. Army moved bodies from small burial sites or isolated locations and, in possibly the first concentration process of any size, reburied them in larger cemeteries surrounded by stone walls. To further protect the graves, Congress made it a federal crime to vandalize a national cemetery.[48]

Reflecting both lack of concern for Rebel dead and lack of compassion for the bereaved families—and perhaps in an effort to prevent the formation and preservation of a collective memory of the Confederate Army—it was not until the early twentieth century that Congress authorized furnishing headstones for the unmarked graves of Confederate soldiers. Even this gesture, though, was without conviction. The act of March 9, 1906 (34 Stat., 56) that called for the Secretary of War to erect the headstones was construed to mean that only graves in "national cemeteries, Confederate burial plots or other military reservations under its [national government] control" were qualified to receive markers.[49]

By 1927, more than 60 years had passed since the end of the Civil War—time enough, hopefully, for wounds to heal from the war between the states—and the United States had become involved, as one nation, in the Spanish-American War and World War I. Now it was time to mark *all* Confederate graves, wherever they were, and legislation—Bill 10304—was introduced to do just that. However, some still harbored animosity. The Sedgwick Women's Relief Corps No. 17 of Santa Ana, California, wrote to W. F. Kellogg, Secretary of State, that they disapproved of the bill and wished for it to be defeated.[50] Fortunately, the 70th Congress felt otherwise, passed H.R. 10304, and thus authorized the Secretary of War to "erect headstones over the graves of soldiers who served in the Confederate Army and who have been buried in national, city, town, or village cemeteries or in *any other places* [italics added]."[51]

However long it took to settle some accounts, the Civil War marked the beginning of honoring the death of the common soldier. Kurt Piehler, in *Remembering War the American Way*, notes that before this war, great leaders received accolades while the everyday man passed into obscurity.[52] There can be no more honor paid to Soldier Dead than to find them, identify them when possible, and then set aside land for a graveyard in which they are buried. Regardless of the size of the tombstone or monument, or their title or accomplishments while living, in death all bodies occupy the same amount of space in the earth.

After the Spanish-American War, many of the dead were returned to the United States while others were interred in a permanent military cemetery in the Philippines in order to demonstrate America's commitment to that country.[53] The offering, as it were, of American dead as a symbol of care and concern for others was the topic of much debate after World War I; many felt that our dead, all of them, should serve as silent emissaries to our allies, while others wanted their return. Supporters of not repatriating World War I remains predicated their view, in part, on the proposition that the war dead could still be of service for "their country and for Western civilization" and that "Each individual soldier's grave would serve as an enduring monument to the cause of freedom for which they bled and died."[54] This "extended duty" position illustrates the significance of the postdeath social identity assigned to soldiers.

Marshal Petain, on behalf of his country, said, "France would be happy and proud to retain the bodies of American victims who have fallen on her soil." General Pershing accepted this offer, but with the understanding that the American people would have the final word. When a party in the Chambre des Députés attempted to pass legislation in February 1919 "forbidding the exhumation and transport of bodies for three years," Pershing notified the State Department. Doubtless, if we had had 75,000 live soldiers instead of remains on French soil, France might have felt very differently. But the dead can be made to mean what we wish, and control over them translates into influence over the living. Thomas Mann's words, "A man's dying is more the survivor's affair than his own," continue to ring true. An alarm was raised, but the issue was resolved, giving the next of kin final say about where remains should be buried. The United States was able to enact its program of repatriation for those families who desired it.[55]

As the concentration operation wound down in Europe during 1920, the Graves Registration Service headquarters was moved to the United States and renamed the Cemeterial Division, a designation more reflective of the future focus of activity, providing a permanent burial site for the dead. Colonel Charles C. Pierce, Chief of the former Graves Registration Service, was named Chief of the Cemeterial Division.

During the final burial process, the Cemeterial Division adopted the sensible policy that remains that were to stay in France were to be buried in the permanent cemetery closest to the concentration site, but some families often wanted relatives buried next to each other. This request presented problems because the individual graves might have been a considerable distance apart and in sites that were evacuated at different times. However, recognizing that family desires were of extreme importance, the policy was modified so that "Upon request of the nearest of kin, remains of blood relatives will be concentrated in one cemetery, the cemetery selected to be the one which will require the least disturbing of remains."[56]

The honoring of such family requests took an unusual turn in World War II when Theodore Roosevelt Jr., son of President Roosevelt and brother of Quentin, who was killed in World War I, died of a heart attack during the Normandy invasion. Theodore's wife and brother wanted his remains to be interred in a permanent U.S. military cemetery near where he had fallen. Soon after the end of the war, Roosevelt's family asked that Quentin's body be moved from "its isolated location and buried next to that of his brother." The request to bury brothers side by side was usually honored, but only when their deaths occurred in the same war. However, an exception was granted and "these two sons of Theodore Roosevelt lie today [next to] each other at the Normandy cemetery."[57]

There were other requests by family members for World War I remains to be buried in a permanent cemetery other than the closest, and to honor each one would have vastly increased costs and delayed completion of the cemeteries. However, the Quartermaster General, in a display of sensitivity, heard and decided each case on its own merits, and "those presenting some special and important reason" were granted an exception.[58]

As permanent cemeteries were being established after World War I, the question arose whether any scheme of segregation should be used: should officers be separated from enlisted personnel, aviators be buried in a separate section. It was decided to follow the original policy established in November 1920 and make no distinction by rank or military division; only the unknown dead would be interred in a separate plot so as to aid identification efforts.[59]

At first, five permanent World War I cemeteries were chosen: four in France at Suresnes, Romagne, Belleau Woods, and Bony; one in England at Brookwood. Soon there was doubt that five would be enough, but there was also the desire to avoid creating too many cemeteries—the British government "had decided that no bodies of British soldiers would be returned home" and maintained all cemeteries that contained 40 or more of their Soldier Dead, an expensive policy because there were more than 3,000 separate burial places. In August 1921, the U. S. War Department authorized three more cemeteries: Fere-en-Tardenois, Thiaucourt, and Waereghem. Each European site was chosen for its historical significance and proximity to an area of fighting. These cemeteries were eventually renamed as follows:

OLD NAME	NEW NAME	NUMBER OF GRAVES
Romagne	Meuse-Argonne	13,938
Belleau Woods	Aisne-Marne	2,220
Bony	Somme	1,830
Fere-en-Tardenois	Oise-Aisne	6,071
Thiaucourt	St. Mihiel	4,231
Suresnes	Suresnes	1,497
Brookwood	Brookwood	435
Waereghem	Flanders Field	365
Total number of burials		30,587[60]

After the repatriation of the World War I dead, the United States turned its attention to furnishing grave markers for overseas permanent cemeteries. The precedent for using stone markers was established after the Civil War when General J. J. Dana, of the Quartermaster Corps, said:

Public opinion seems to be turning to a more permanent mode of marking the graves than by wooden head-boards, and I would respect-

6.9   Panorama of cemetery at Romagne (Meuse-Argonne). *Pvt. H. W. Pagchen. National Archives & Records Administration*

fully give it as my opinion that the sentiment of the nation will not only sustain the expense of marble or other permanent memorial, but, moreover, that it will be likely to demand it in a few years, if not now established.[61]

The decision to use stone markers for World War I graves had some unexpected consequences. First, John W. Weeks, Secretary of War, became aware that the design that had been approved for crosses was similar to the iron cross of the German army, prompting a change to the Roman cross.[62] Second, in November 1925, Mrs. Frederic W. Bentley, member of the American Battle Monuments Commission (ABMC), wrote Dwight F. Davis, Secretary of War, that the ABMC had learned that, while Orthodox Jews desired that the Star of David mark the graves of their dead, some Reformed Jews desired "that no distinction be made between them and their Christian comrades."[63]

Third, when the previously existing wooden crosses were slated to be replaced with the permanent marble markers, there was some consideration

6.10   Labor troops cover caskets in trench burial at Romagne (Meuse-Argonne). *Pvt. H. W. Pagchen. National Archives & Records Administration*

about converting them to salvage, and thus recouping monetary outlays. But R. P. Harbold sent a memo to the Quartermaster General that to do so would be "repugnant to this [Cemeterial] Division. They have been dedicated to a sacred purpose and it is recommended that after their use as grave markers is accomplished, they be treated the same as unserviceable flags—burned, in order to avoid misuse or desecration."[64]

Many of the same processes took place after the end of World War II. There were 36 temporary cemeteries holding approximately 140,000 American deceased: 24 in France, 4 in Belgium, 3 in Holland, 2 in England, 1 in Ireland, 1 in Luxembourg, and 1 in Switzerland. In planning for the permanent interment of Soldier Dead, the War Department, on September 8, 1945, issued a report, "Plan for Repatriation of the Dead of World War II and Establishment of Permanent United States Military Cemeteries at Home and Abroad." In it the War Department called for 9 permanent overseas cemeteries in the European Theater of Operations. Major General Robert M. Littlejohn, Commanding General, American Graves Registration Company, noted that the selection of cemeteries was

based on technical factors only, "with no consideration for the sentimen-
tal or historic aspect of the war." He prepared his own list of 6 proposed
sites, chosen with more insight into the significance of where Soldier Dead
reposed. It included:

> St. Laurent in France, because of its proximity to Omaha Beach;
> Cambridge Cemetery in England, which held the remains of casual-
> ties of the Eighth Air Force and Army units;
> Margraten in Holland, home to the bodies of those who died in the
> drive to the Roer [Rohr] River and those killed in Germany;
> Neuville in Belgium, where those killed around Aachen and during
> the drive into the Siegfried Line were buried;
> Hamm Cemetery in Luxembourg, for those who died in the Battle
> of the Bulge;
> Epinal in France, contained the remains of those who died on the
> drive through the Vosges Mountains and the battle for the Colmar
> Pocket.[65]

Another party making recommendations about permanent cemeteries
was the American Battle Monuments Commission (ABMC), mentioned
above. It came into being with Public Law 534, enacted by the 67th Congress, and was charged to "erect suitable memorials commemorating the
services of the American soldier in Europe, and for other purposes." In
1934, the Quartermaster Corps transferred responsibility for World War
I cemeteries to the ABMC, and it was initially envisioned that the same
process would apply after World War II: that the commission would take
charge only after repatriation and the establishment of overseas cemeteries. Knowing that the ABMC would have eventual responsibility for the
cemeteries, the Quartermaster General proposed that it participate in their
selection.

Besides soil conditions and proximity to major battle sites, a major factor
in the evaluation of a potential cemetery site was its ability to hold sufficient
graves—a number with a wide range of estimates because at the time the
sites were being considered, there had been no final disposition of the dead
and the number of remains that were to rest permanently in European soil
was unknown.

Eventually, the ABMC, the Office of the Quartermaster General, and the
American Graves Registration Company in Europe settled on Cambridge,
Margraten, Henri-Chapelle, Neuville-en-Condroz, Hamm, St. Laurent, and

Epinal; later, Draguignan, St. James, and St. Avold were added to the list, for a total of ten permanent cemeteries in the European area.[66]

The selection of World War II permanent cemeteries elsewhere required that differences between the ABMC and the Office of the Quartermaster General (OQMG) be resolved. The ABMC envisioned a larger number of cemeteries than did the OQMG. Like others after World War I, the commission felt that overseas cemeteries—more accurately, the bodies of American soldiers in graves—would be tangible representatives of the United States and its willingness to fight for the cause of freedom and democracy. The OQMG, while certainly not making cost considerations a primary factor, did attach a great deal of weight to economic matters and argued that fewer cemeteries would be more easily established and maintained.

In the Mediterranean area, the ABMC called for five permanent cemeteries while the Quartermaster General felt that two, one at Nettuno near Anzio and one at Florence, would be most appropriate. The ABMC and OQMG met in April 1947 and agreed on those two sites.[67]

North Africa required only one permanent cemetery, located at Carthage, Tunisia, but its selection was unexpectedly compromised after permission to use the first-preferred location was denied by the French Antiquities Service because "excavation had revealed that it contained ancient ruins." Despite this, some officials of the Quartermaster's office wished to persist in efforts to obtain "Site A," but Col. L. R. Talbot wisely pointed out that continuing to make this request "would only antagonize the French." Eventually, in accordance with Talbot's recommendation, the OQMG withdrew its plan for "Site A," and "Site B" was approved and final burials begun on September 14, 1948.[68]

In the Pacific, the ABMC and the Quartermaster General again had different plans for permanent American cemeteries, but they did agree on Hawaii and the Philippines. The creation of the cemetery in Hawaii, in the Punchbowl—a hollowed-out volcano top overlooking Honolulu—did not go as smoothly as might have been expected; much local opposition arose, based on three objections. First, the site would be too small for the number of future burials of veterans. Second, the graveyard would contaminate water supplies. Third, and perhaps the most honest complaint, was that "We don't want a city of the dead overlooking a city of the living."

While the arguments for and against Punchbowl splashed back and forth, the Army, trying to execute its solemn charge to repatriate those re-

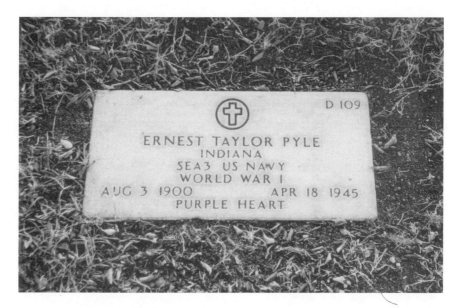

6.11   Grave marker for Ernie Pyle at his final burial site in Punchbowl, Hawaii. *Michael Sledge*

mains slated for return, had little choice but to employ aboveground storage. Finally, the path was cleared for construction to begin in August 1948, three years after the end of the war in the Pacific. It wasn't until July 1, 1949 that the first public burials took place, when the remains of Ernie Pyle and four others were finally laid to rest.[69] Pyle had originally been buried at Ie Shima over four years earlier, and the journey of his remains from first burial to last is very typical of the length of time that often transpired between a soldier's death and his final interment. It does seem fitting that Punchbowl in Hawaii was chosen, as it is lofty and, figuratively at least, close to heaven; also, the Hawaiian indigenous population originally called the volcano top *Puowaina*, or "Hill of Sacrifice."[70]

Construction of the other permanent Pacific cemetery at Manila did not begin until January 1949, but it went relatively quickly and most interments were done by the end of the year. The Manila cemetery was also designated to be the final resting place for war dead "for whom no specific instructions had been received, and all recovered unknowns."[71]

Currently, the American Battle Monuments Commission oversees the operations of our overseas military cemeteries. Punchbowl, since Hawaii was admitted to statehood, is no longer under its supervision. The final World War II cemeteries and the number of burials are detailed below:

Old Name	New Name	Number of Burials
Neuville-en-Condroz	Ardennes	5,328
St. James	Brittany	4,410
Cambridge	Cambridge	3,812
Epinal	Epinal	5,255
Henri-Chapelle	Henri-Chapelle	7,989
St. Avold	Lorraine	10,489
Hamm	Luxembourg	5,076
Margraten	Netherlands	8,302
St. Laurent	Normandy	9,387
Draguignan	Rhone	861
Florence	Florence	4,402
Nettuno	Sicily-Rome	7,861
Carthage	North Africa	2,841
Manila	Manila	17,206
Punchbowl	Punchbowl	13,854[72]
Total number of burials		107,073

Families had the option of burying repatriated remains in private plots or state and national military cemeteries. Of course, the most well-known national cemetery is Arlington, home to many military service personnel, including the unknowns from World War I, World War II, the Korean War, and, for fourteen years, the Vietnam War. The selection and burial of the Vietnam Unknown was considered by many to be politically opportunistic and was marked by controversy. The selection and burial of the unknowns from the previous wars, though, did not involve the same issues and directly expressed the nation's gratitude to all soldiers killed in those wars.

On October 24, 1921, in Chalons-sur-Marne, Sergeant Edward F. Younger, awarded for valor and a Distinguished Service Medal recipient, walked into a chamber at the Hotel de Ville and solemnly contemplated four flag-draped caskets. It was only appropriate that a soldier who had similarly faced the horrors of World War I be given the responsibility to decide who among the dead would be the nation's representative.

Each of the caskets contained the remains of an unidentified American soldier, each disinterred from a different cemetery. Prior to the arrival of the four at the Hotel de Ville, Major Harbold and Colonel G. V. S. Quackenbush, both of the Quartermaster Corps, burned the four burial forms that had accompanied the remains. Also, all related records containing additional information about where the remains had first been found were destroyed. Earlier on the morning of the 24th, Major Harbold had "re-arranged the caskets by placing them on different [shipping] cases other than the ones on which they reposed during the night." The goal was to completely destroy all documentation and remove any possibility of knowing from which cemetery each remains had come.[73]

Sergeant Younger indicated his choice by laying a spray of white roses on the casket, then stood at attention and saluted. In choosing one of the four, Younger said, "I went into the room and walked past the caskets. I walked around them three times. Suddenly, I stopped. It was as though something had pulled me. A voice seemed to say: 'This is a pal of yours.'"[74]

The chosen unknown, after being showered with honors, ceremonies, and outpourings of sympathy and gratitude, was transferred to the cruiser *Olympia* for transportation home to the United States.[75] The *Olympia* arrived at the Navy yard in Washington, DC on November 9, and the Unknown Soldier was taken to the rotunda of the Capitol, where he lay in state. On the morning of November 11, 1921, exactly three years after the signing of the armistice, the World War I unknown—with a full military escort and accompanied by President Warren Harding, Vice President Calvin Coolidge, members of Congress, generals, Medal of Honor recipients, and a large number of other dignitaries—was carried to Arlington Cemetery. Many thousands more lined the streets that the cortege followed. At Arlington, the soldier was interred under a simple white marble monument. It was not until December 1929 that a contract was let for the building of the official Tomb of the Unknown Soldier.[76]

After the World War I unknown was buried, the American Legion "complained that many visitors had failed to show proper respect at the grave, and in some cases they [had] dishonored it by using it as a bench, or picnic table." The result was that soldiers from Fort Myer began guarding the tomb, maintaining a silent vigil twenty-four hours a day, regardless of weather, and they still do so today. Many hundreds of thousands, if not millions, have witnessed the changing of the guard, but what is little known is that the Army, short of funds, resisted the idea of mounting it. However, under pressure from the White House and Congress, the Army assigned a detail to stand watch.[77]

The process for selecting the World War II and Korean War unknowns was a bit more complicated. Initially, under Public Law 429, the 79th Congress called for the Secretary of War to arrange for choosing, returning, and providing final burial for an unknown from World War II, and plans were drawn up to select five unknowns, one from each different wartime theater, and to inter the remains with honors on Memorial Day 1951. But, upon the outbreak of the Korean War, President Truman accepted the Secretary of Defense's recommendation that the matter be deferred, and it was not until 1956 that Public Law 975, passed by the 84th Congress, called for the burial of unknowns from World War II and the Korean War on Memorial Day 1958.

Choosing the World War II unknown was done in two steps. Instead of having a representative from each of the five different combat theaters, as originally suggested, one was chosen from the transpacific area and one from the transatlantic area. These two candidates were transferred to the *U.S.S. Canberra*, pending final selection, the second step.

The Korean War unknown had been chosen from the unknowns at Punchbowl and transferred to the *Canberra* in advance of the two World War II candidates. Once all three were on board ship, Hospitalman 1st Class William R. Charette, "the Navy's only active enlisted holder of the Medal of Honor," faced the caskets of the two World War II unknowns and made his choice by laying a wreath of carnations on one. The World War II and the Korean War unknowns were transferred from the *Canberra* to the *Blandy*, which then proceeded up the Potomac to Washington. The *Canberra*, still bearing the remains of one World War II unknown, sailed farther out from the coast and committed its precious cargo to the deep.[78]

Burial at sea begins with the command, "All hands bury the dead." After a prayer, the remains, enclosed in either a casket or an urn, are "committed" to the sea, a benediction is given, three volleys are fired, "Taps" is sounded, and the burial flag is encased and stored for future use. Unlike in land burials, the flag is not returned to the Person Authorized to Direct Disposition of remains (PADD) unless they supplied it with delivery of the remains.[79]

Currently, burial at sea "is permissible only when refrigerated storage facilities cannot be made available aboard ship and transfer to shore cannot be accomplished within a reasonable time or is operationally inadvisable."[80] However, the PADD may contact Navy Mortuary Affairs to request burial at sea for the remains of active duty members of the Armed Forces, honorably discharged veterans and retirees, dependent family members of those just listed, and certain U.S. civilian personnel.[81]

Then, there are unintended burials at sea. The battleship *Arizona* became an unplanned burial site during the attack on Pearl Harbor, but was not officially designated as a grave memorial until Public Law 87–201 was enacted

6.12   A chaplain reads burial services for Marines who died on Saipan and were buried at sea from a troop transport. (Note: Apparently, these Marines had died while en route to medical care and there were no facilities to keep their remains on board ship.) *Pfc. George Mattson. National Archives & Records Administration*

and funds were allocated for this purpose in 1961.[82] Fittingly and touching, those *Arizona* crewmen who survived the attack may direct that their cremated remains be placed inside the water-filled No. 4 gun turret.

Inhumation-Exhumation-Preparation

The burial process today is very sanitized, and funeral homes go to great lengths to "shelter" family members from the grim reality of putting a body in the ground. The deceased is embalmed, casketed, and then buried, often within a concrete vault. Due respects are paid, in a simple or elaborate ceremony. All the while, any necessary equipment is kept out of sight and the earth—dirt—is carefully covered up. Final burials of military personnel have many of the same characteristics of civilian burials—with the addition of certain military honor rites. However, final burials of soldiers killed in past wars were often the last, and most polished, of several interments, and

6.13   Gun turret #4 of the battleship *Arizona,* where incinerated remains of the ship's former crew are buried, should the next of kin so desire. *Michael Sledge*

many dedicated people had to do a great deal of unpleasant work so that the dead could be laid to rest to the satisfaction of the living.

Before the early 1950s, it was not unusual for a serviceperson's remains to be buried three or more times before final burial, which meant that there were also several accompanying exhumations. The 300,000 Union soldiers who were reburied in national cemeteries had to be removed from their previous graves. The 78,000 World War I dead were buried, disinterred, and reburied several times. Many more died in World War II than in World War I—but still less than the Civil War—and they also were often buried several times. Those killed at the beginning of the Korean War were buried in temporary cemeteries and later disinterred for return home or burial in the Punchbowl. Then, from the spring of 1951 forward, there were few burials and subsequent disinterments, at least by American forces. In Vietnam, many of our Soldier Dead were buried by the North Vietnamese and by opposing forces in South Vietnam; later they were disinterred for return home.

Obviously, there has been a great deal of movement of remains about which the general public has little knowledge. And when they did think about exhumation and reburial, many felt strongly that the dead should not be disturbed or that the work was so grisly that it was better to leave the remains as they were.

As bad as the images of disinterring are, those of actually *handling* the decayed and often mutilated remains of military personnel are beyond the imagination of most people. Frequently it is said, "You want to remember him as he was," and the picture of a fully intact soldier in a clean uniform reposing gracefully in a hollowed-out pocket beneath the ground comes to mind. The reality is radically different, and those who have worked diligently, perhaps with little training or preparation, so that remains will have a dignified final burial *do* remember him as he was: lying in pieces at the bottom of a rotten casket, or mostly bones covered by a combination of earth and mere remembrance of flesh. After all, that is where the term "remains" comes from.

The men and women who handled remains were many times repulsed by their job at first, seeing the disfigured doppelgangers of previously living young men, but later coming to consider the work an almost sacred obligation. Nobody looked forward to exhumations, but most discharged their duties in a professional and respectful manner. To them, the "Things without shape, at which mothers would collapse," as described by Owen Wister in his letter to the American Legion, were the bodies of comrades still in need of care and concern; with few exceptions, they were willing to do their part. Wister's abhorrence, though, was shared by many.

6.14   Remains of GIs disinterred from cemeteries in Germany that were brought to Margraten, Holland for reburial. *Retired Lt. Col. Charles D. (Bud) Butte*

From an anthropological viewpoint, the "disgust" associated with handling remains has been observed to be universal. Darwin considered disgust "one of the six basic emotions." A study in Africa, India, the Netherlands, the United Kingdom, and an international airport found that people were disgusted by corpses and body parts, among other objects. The basis for this reaction is likely to be part cultural and part genetic; people refine an inborn desire to avoid things that can either pose a potential threat to their own health or represent that threat. Decaying flesh can pose a health risk, and body parts and gaping wounds vividly depict a failure to protect the body envelope as a barrier against infectious agents and harmful objects.[83]

From a cultural perspective, the very idea of "digging up the dead" conjures up images of clandestine, midnight graveyard visitations by those with less than honorable intentions, bent on trespassing into that mystical/spiritual, taboo land of the dead. Or, in less superstitious but more euphemistic terms, we feel that the dead are sleeping and should not be "wakened." The origin of the word "cemetery" is in the Greek word for "dormitory," meaning to sleep, and, according to the *Dictionary of Word Origins*, by John Ayto, early Christian Greek writers first applied the term to burial grounds, likely because of the Christian concept of the resurrection of the body from its "sleep." John 11:11 says, "Our friend Lazarus has fallen asleep, but I'm on My way to wake him up."

In another example connected to Christianity, the Bible, notwithstanding some beautiful imagery of flesh becoming grass or flowers and the flesh of Christ as communion, contains many metaphors of flesh as sin, and rotting flesh as the very embodiment of ultimate corruption. This link between putrescent flesh and ungodliness serves to reinforce the reluctance to touch the remains of anyone, soldiers included.

Another reason for difficulty in viewing a decaying or decayed corpse is that it makes the living acutely aware that their own hold on life is much more tenuous than they would like to believe. Ultimately, we are all food for worms. And, finally, as flesh decomposes, regardless of its origin, be it people or animals, it is just plain unpleasant. There are fluids, maggots, fecal matter, and, of course, the overpowering smell. These are the realities associated with inhumation and exhumation.

Of course, those in favor of "leaving the dead as they are" are not likely to be performing a careful and cognitive analysis of the matter—they are reacting on deeply held belief systems that are autonomous. To a certain extent, the Do Not Disturb cases stem from the families' desire to not even think about the condition of their loved one.

Yet the flesh and bones of Soldier Dead were the former homes of whatever spirit may have inhabited them, and we retain a residual appreciation
of their social identity and treat the remains with dignity and respect, even
while performing the unpleasant and disagreeable task of physically handling them. After World War I, a Special Commission from the State of
Massachusetts

> visited Europe for the purpose of viewing the activities of this [Graves
> Registration] Service, rendered a very complete report giving the de-
> tails of the field operations and in conclusion made the following
> statement: 'Massachusetts has, up to this time, been the only State to
> make an independent and thorough examination of the unattractive,
> but very necessary, work of the Graves Registration Department, to
> ascertain if their findings are to be given full faith and credit by our
> people. Our inquiry and investigation appear to justify the claims of
> the Department that every effort has been made to do the business part
> accurately, decently and with all respect, and after that to bestow the
> honors due to the heroic dead.[84]

6.15   Company A 322 Labor Battalion removes remains from a temporary cemetery for relo-
cation to Romagne (Meuse-Argonne). *Sgt. Ryden. National Archives & Records Administration*

Because of the sensitive nature of the proceedings, World War I visitors, including "interested relatives and friends," who wished to witness exhumations had to apply for written permission from the Graves Registration Headquarters in Europe.[85] Photographs of graves and of cemeteries were allowed, but only under control and supervision of the Graves Registration Service.[86] In World War II, however, photographs of graves were not to be sent to the family because many burial sites were of a temporary nature and would later be relocated. Also, "The newness of the graves and cemeteries, in many cases, would not give suitable and satisfying background and general appearance for a picture."[87]

In addition to providing for reverent care, it was important to address health issues during exhumation and inhumation. To allay fears of the spread of disease, Dr. H. Fettes, the Chief Medical Adviser to the City of Luxembourg, prepared the following statement after observing GRS exhumation operations after World War I:

> The undersigned certifies that he was present during the exhumation of the American soldiers who fell on the field of honor, and were buried in the Grand Duchy of Luxembourg at Walferdange, Hollerich, Luxembourg, Roeser and Oettange, and that the process of exhumation, disinfection and the new method of putting bodies in the coffins has been so up-to-date that it was admired by the Medical and Sanitary Corps and that it will be an improvement of the present sanitary laws of the Grand Duchy.

Dr. Fettes's statement also contained reassurance that the American operations did not have any adverse affect on the health of the local population.[88]

During World War II, on an average daily basis, the United States lost service personnel equal to the number killed in the crash of a Boeing 747 with a full complement of passengers. During the period of the most intense fighting in 1944 and 1945, it was as though several jumbo jetloads of men and women went down daily. Knowing that the United States would soon be faced with the daunting task of handling large numbers of dead in a short time, and recognizing that these remains would need to be disinterred for repatriation or final burial in an overseas military cemetery, Col. R. P. Harbold and Col. Thomas R. Howard, both of the Quartermaster Corps, prepared a letter on uniform burial practices, to be signed by the Quartermaster General and distributed to all military commanders.

Harbold, experienced from his Graves Registration duties in World War I, and Howard said that "economy in the exhumation of remains and restoration of the burial sites to owners in their former usable condition were the primary purposes which all temporary cemeteries in the theaters were intended to serve," and that these goals were endangered by the "extravagant methods of burial and cemeterial construction." Their letter was released to all commanders on August 13, 1944. It noted that there was much "competition" in burying the dead and in cemetery construction, and that this would only delay and increase the cost of eventual disinterment.

Also, Harbold and Howard debunked the belief that it was better to embalm and then bury soldiers in caskets or metal liners. First, field embalming only temporarily delayed decomposition; after two years, the condition of remains treated this way was essentially the same as those given a "simple soldier's burial." Second, when remains were casketed without proper venting, the anaerobic action of bacteria during the decomposition process often destroyed identification clues that might have been preserved had the body not been buried in a container. Finally, all remains, regardless of how buried, were to be disinterred at a later date and placed in uniformly manufactured caskets for return home or burial overseas. The letter recommended that they be buried in either shelter-halves—half of a pup tent—or wrapped in a blanket, as doing so allowed for quick decomposition with the "body liquids and results of decomposition . . . absorbed by the earth."[89] This was in contrast to World War I policy, in which burial and reburial caskets were frequently used if available.

While embalming was not done to any significant degree in World War I and World War II, it was employed during the Civil War, but by opportunistic civilians, not the military. Thomas Holmes, generally called "The Father of Embalming," was a registered physician who concluded that poisonous embalming compounds in use at that time were injurious—had even caused death—to medical students performing dissection during their training, and developed a safer alternative that he marketed. By luck, if you want to call it that, Colonel Elmer Ellsworth, President Lincoln's former clerk at his Springfield, Illinois law office, was killed while removing a Confederate flag from an inn. Lincoln desired to hold services for Ellsworth at the White House, and Holmes obtained permission to embalm the body.

Apparently, Holmes did an excellent job, as his work was praised in Washington newspapers, and as the number of deaths climbed, his services were much sought after. In fact, the market for embalming dead soldiers was so great that undertakers competed for corpses on the field of battle; officers were a prized find, as their $80 fee was substantially greater than the $30 charge for enlisted men. Eventually, the business attracted many unscrupulous operators and, in March 1865, the War Department put out General

6.16 Embalming surgeon at work on a soldier's body. *Civil War Photographs, 1861–1865/ compiled by Hirst D. Milhollen and Donald H. Mugridge, Washington, DC: Library of Congress*

Order No. 39, "Order Concerning Embalmers," to ensure that only properly qualified embalmers were licensed. To prevent grieving families from being unfairly taken advantage of, the Provost Marshal of the Army issued a price schedule for services.[90]

Of course, establishing and maintaining the identity of remains during the process of inhumation and exhumation was of paramount importance. As a precaution against somehow losing identification information, the use of the "burial bottle" was advocated by D. H. Rhodes of the Burial Corps, who, in 1899, worked to recover American dead from the Philippines.[91] A "piece of script, bearing the name, rank and organization of the deceased, with the date of reburial, will be placed in a small bottle, which after being tightly corked, will be inserted in the blanket." The "Manual of Regulations and Tables of Organization of the American Graves Registration Service, Q.M.C. In Europe," issued April 15, 1921, required the field forces to take "every possible precaution" in finding and preserving identification during exhumation and inhumation.[92]

With World War II came the extensive use of high-speed aircraft laden with fuel and explosives. Crashes would mingle and burn remains to the extent that it was difficult to separate them. Often, no single individual body or body part could be identified and all were buried together. At other times, skulls could be identified and were buried as separate individuals while the rest of the remains were buried together. When the Army transport *Joseph V. Connolly* made port in New York with the first shipment of Soldier Dead from World War II, it carried 6,348 caskets containing 6,251 remains. One casket contained the remains of four men who had died in an airplane crash.[93]

Now, because of the ability to recover and identify ever smaller remains, the situation occasionally arises in which additional remains are found after a burial. In this case, the PADD has several options:

1. Disinter the interred remains, place the additional portions in the casket with the principal remains, and re-inter
2. Place the portions in an appropriate container and inter in the same grave site above the casket with the principal remains
3. The Army will dispose of the portions by complete incineration.[94]

The advent of DNA analysis has led to another twist in the final disposition of remains: the question of how small a portion should be tested and what should be done with unidentified remains, if there are any. There have been and can be cases in which thousands of remains portions are found and recovered. While all, regardless of how small, now are candidates for DNA testing, Dr. Craig Mallak, Commander, Medical Corps, United States Navy, and Chairperson of the Office of the Armed Forces Medical Examiner (OAFME), said that deciding how far to carry out expensive genetic testing is his responsibility.

Once remains associated with all people involved in a death circumstance have been identified *and* all "major portions" have been identified, Dr. Mallak may cease DNA testing on smaller portions of remains. Just *how* small is a judgment call and depends upon the situation. At this point, the Casualty Affairs Officer will talk to the family members, tell them that all soldiers have been identified and that they will have remains returned to them, and ask if they want the unidentified remains buried in a group or destroyed. Only if

6.17   Arlington marker for grave of commingled remains. *Michael Sledge*

all families agree will remains portions be treated the same as medical waste, such as an appendix or gall bladder that has been removed: incinerated. If any family members do not agree, a group burial is performed.[95]

The Korean War was a period of transition from "how it was" to "how it is." At the beginning, the dead were buried in the traditional manner, albeit under pressure and in land that later changed hands. By early 1951 the bodies of those killed were transported to Kokura, Japan for processing and return home without temporary burial. The Concurrent Return program, desirable as it was, presented new problems because handling remains that had not fully decomposed was most unpleasant, to put it mildly. A whole new system of handling remains "on the move" had to be created, implemented, and fine-tuned, and it was not without defects—some ships arrived at Kokura "shoe-top deep in maggots."

Also, Korea reintroduced the embalming of remains. While during the Civil War, at least a small percentage of total dead were chemically treated, it was necessary to embalm practically all of the Concurrent Return fatalities; however, delays in processing made it somewhat difficult to do so efficiently. The GRS wished for remains to be flown from Korea to Japan, a job the Air Force would have liked to avoid. However, the GRS convinced Air Force officials that remains would not contaminate aircraft and that the reduced number of deaths during the current stalemated positions and armistice talks would not tax airlift capacity. Exercise GRALEX (Graves Registration Air Lift) was employed from April 5 to 16, 1952.[96] Since then, air routing has been the first choice for evacuation and transportation of remains.

The whole process of burying and disinterring our military fallen is such a sensitive subject that much of it shielded from public view. Doubtless, there are those who would just as soon not know the details. And there are certainly those who think it best that family members not have too much information, even if they request it. Whatever the different perceptions, beliefs, and benefits and detriments of burial and subsequent exhumation, one thing is certain: there has been a prodigious amount of effort dedicated solely to putting our military fallen into the ground—and removing them from it again. Estimated somewhat conservatively, the amount of dirt excavated to bury, often several times, the dead from the Civil War forward has been enough to fill the Great Pyramid of Cheops almost three times over. This figure is even more significant when it is realized that not only was three pyramids' worth of dirt dug *out* of graves, the same amount had to be put back *in*.

The actual hands-on work of burying and digging up the dead was done mostly by men who in their ordinary lives before service would never have imagined themselves performing such activities. The wherewithal to accomplish this task came from a variety of sources: feelings of care, commitment to duty, ability to obtain emotional distance, and threat of force.

Tom Dowling served in World War II and buried the dead from Omaha Beach. He said:

> We picked them up, began our burial details and vomited our insides out at times. It was the faces of the dead GIs. . . . Some stared wide-eyed; others had died in the middle of a scream, and their mouths hung open. Others had no face at all. After a while, I heard a noise breaking the heavy silence hanging around me as I went about recording. To my left, Coogan was doing his job, but from deep inside him someplace came low guttural groans as from a man in pain. He was a man in pain, as we all were.[97]

Other men felt pushed beyond their limits. George Clampa was burying the "bodies . . . stacked like cordwood" from the Battle of the Bulge and felt like he "was having a nervous breakdown"; he said, "I felt like I couldn't take it anymore, the green bodies, the grotesqueness of death. I wanted no more of it." A lieutenant put a .45 semiautomatic to Clampa's head and said, "Get to work, soldier." Clampa reluctantly returned to his duties.[98]

After the cessation of hostilities in World War I, it appears that African American labor battalions performed much of the disinterring and reburying, and the Quartermaster did make at least one statement to this effect: "The handling of the bodies was entirely new work to the colored man, but, after witnessing the manner in which the white personnel performed the various operations, they prove to be efficient in the disagreeable task."[99] While there is little other written evidence regarding the use of black labor, there is ample photographic evidence showing the racial composition of the men doing the shovel work.

When it came to burying remains in the United States, there were objections to government participation in an activity that some felt could best be handled by private enterprise. During World War II, Senator Henrick Shipstead asked the War Department to explain the government's position of according veterans free burial in national cemeteries. Shipstead had received a letter from Russell Egner, Sales Manager of Acacia Memorial Park, a cemetery, in which he expressed concern that the government's policy of paying for the interment of its service personnel "interferes with organized business and free enterprise." Egner suggested that the government provide a cash bonus to the families of the deceased rather than burial at government expense.

Egner's request, via Senator Shipstead, wound up on the desk of R. P. Harbold of the Memorial Division of the Quartermaster Corps, who responded diplomatically that the veterans who died constituted less than 3.5 percent of total deaths a year in the United States, and that this should not "be considered as menacing, impairing or restricting trade possibilities of any industry or enterprise associated with burial of the dead." Harbold then contrasted the desire for economic incentive with the desire of the dead "to be committed to a final resting place under the care and maintenance of their Government, and as long as that Government survives, they will sleep amidst thousands of their comrades." He continued:

> The flag for which they fought will wave majestically and protectingly over their graves each day from dawn till dusk. Now unborn generations of descendants will pass into obscurity but the names of these veterans will be perpetuated, their graves will be carefully maintained and their military service will be enscrolled upon the simple, but dignified grave marker, by that Government under which they lived and for which they fought.

Harbold's letter was addressed to the Congressional Section, G.A.S. Division, which relayed his response to the Under Secretary of War, Robert

Patterson. Patterson's response to Senator Shipstead followed the theme of Harbold's explanation but omitted his eloquent, chastising comments.[100] Harbold, once again, had been a champion for the dead.

Finally, after remains are recovered, returned, identified, and prepared for burial, the casket is delivered to the address specified by the Person Authorized to Direct Disposition (PADD). When possible, remains are prepared so that they are presentable. When they are not considered "viewable" by the military authorities who did whatever embalming could be done, the remains are wrapped very carefully in plastic sheets, covered by a muslin cloth, and then wrapped in a green wool blanket. Then, a uniform decorated with all appropriate medals and designations is pinned to the blanket.[101] The placing of the uniform in this manner raises an interesting question: For whom is it intended? While the next of kin is informed of the condition of the remains and has the right to open the casket, it is expected that they will not do so. Obviously, then, the uniform must be meant for someone other than the family, and certainly not for the deceased. The process of elimination leaves only the military brothers and sisters of the dead who cared for and prepared the remains. Of course, it is possible that the family has some peace of mind knowing that the "unviewable" is buried with a uniform, the same as a mostly intact body would be, but the desires of the extended family, the military, certainly must play a role. The existence of this symbol—a full dress uniform—as a display of living servicepersons' affection for the dead sometimes has unexpected consequences for the family of the deceased, and is discussed further in chapter 8, "Open Wounds."

Personal Effects

During World War I and World War II, the personal effects of the dead were sent to their families as soon as possible. The prompt and complete return of the few items a soldier had on his person or in his quarters "became a token of good faith" that the government would return the remains after the cessation of hostilities.[102]

For the family members, personal effects are the last tangible evidence of their loved one and a mouthpiece for those in the grave, saying, "The rip in this wallet was from the mortar blast that took my life at Bastogne," or, "This is the letter I wrote to you in the plane before the drop—I was going to mail it at the first opportunity," or, more recently, from the Pentagon attack, "This is the grocery list you gave me this morning—I would have stopped by the store on the way home." These items not only affirm the existence of the

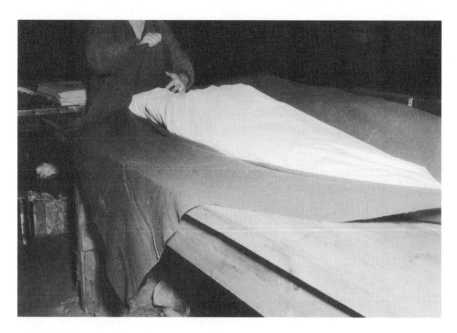

6.18　A War Department civilian wraps the remains of a World War II soldier in a sheet in preparation for shipment back to the United States or final burial overseas. *S.Sgt. Parker. National Archives & Records Administration*

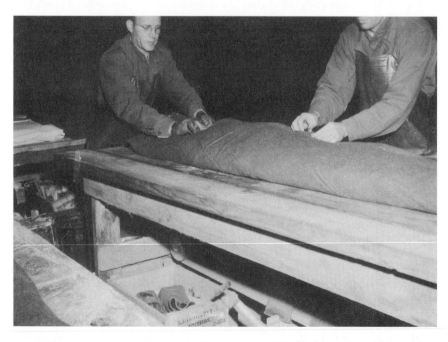

6.19　War Department civilians pin a blanket around remains in preparation for shipment back to the United States or final burial overseas. *S.Sgt. Parker. National Archives & Records Administration*

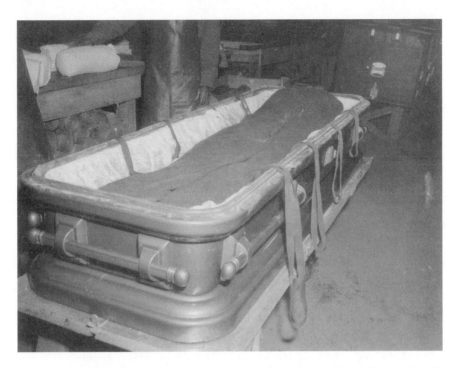

6.20   War Department civilians place prepared remains in a casket and secure it with straps and muslin pillows. *S.Sgt. Parker. National Archives & Records Administration*

6.21   Staff Sergeant Daniel Geoffroy of Dover Air Force Base Mortuary simulates the meticulous preparation of a uniform for remains. *Michael Sledge*

deceased, they also mark the point in time when they were killed: a stopped watch, a faded newspaper, or a ripped daily organizer.

Those who handle remains can easily adopt a remote and rather abstract view of the deceased, especially if they are working with bones or bone fragments. However, Graves Registration—or current Mortuary Affairs—personnel say that handling a soldier's personal effects is more emotionally wrenching than touching their bones or decayed flesh. Sergeant Herbert E. Hackett, who served in the 611th Quartermaster Graves Registration Company in Europe during World War II, was disinterring remains and removing personal effects when he came across a packet of photographs in a soldier's pocket. The pictures were of the dead man's wedding a few months earlier.[103]

The current Director of U.S. Army Mortuary Affairs, Tom Bourlier, describing his experiences in Vietnam, said, "The most difficult thing I had to do was to handle the personal effects of those who died."[104] Douglas (Doug) L. Howard, Deputy Directory of the U.S. Army Mortuary Affairs, voiced similar sentiments when speaking of his Vietnam service. As a young father himself, he was particularly disturbed by reading letters to and from the children of deceased service personnel.[105]

The handling of personal effects begins when the deceased soldier is first found, and ends when the appropriate military authorities are notified that the proper person has received the items. In between, there is a great deal of room for mishandling, either intentional or unintentional.

Army regulations clearly establish the responsibility for handling personal effects. Article XXII, paragraph 163 of the 1913 *Regulations for The Army Of The United States* called for the "care and custody of the effects of deceased persons" to be safeguarded and delivered to the legal representative or widow of the deceased, and a receipt to be sent to the Adjutant General of the Army. Paragraph 8 of the Army Regulation No. 30–1810—from the AR-30 series of 1924—called for the collection, inventorying, and distribution of personal effects. Its few lines there have now been expanded to eleven pages in the *Joint Tactics, Techniques, and Procedures for Mortuary Affairs in Joint Operations (Joint Pub 4–06,* 1996). The process of handling personal effects breaks down into a few basic steps: obtain possession, inventory, and deliver. But, of course, the devil is in the details.

In World War II, Lieutenant General Edmund B. Gregory, the Quartermaster General, wanted to avoid the confusion associated with handling personal effects in World War I by establishing a single, central point from which items belonging to the deceased would be sent back to the United States, to be forwarded to family members.[106] However, being human, the

personnel processing effects are not impervious to humor. Harry Mullendore, who served with the 607th Graves Registration Company in World
War II, remembered a particular personal item that was not returned with
the body of its owner: an address book. The book had been divided into
sections, with some unusual labeling: "Married," "Single," "Brunettes,"
"Blondes," "Redhead," "Thin," "Plump," "Motherly," and "Surplus." Mullendore and his fellows passed the address book around and entertainingly
speculated about the necessary characteristics that a woman would have to
possess to be classified as "Surplus."[107]

An ironic and bitter example of the unique nature of personal effects is
the case of an American who was killed, buried in Holland, and disinterred
by Robert Gibson, who served with the 3059th Graves Registration Company. Gibson noted that, "The left hand of another exhumed airman still
clutched a lucky rabbit's foot."[108]

Not all personal effects are returned to the family, or Person Authorized
to Receive Effects (PARE). Regulation No. 30–1810 gave instructions that
these objects "be screened to remove those which by their presence may
cause embarrassment if forwarded to the next of kin." Current instructions
in *Joint Pub 4–06* also call for the removal of embarrassing items, but with
added emphasis on "pornographic material or letters." *Joint Pub 4–06* also
requires the removal of items than may disturb the recipient, such as those
"that are contaminated, mutilated, burned, blood stained, damaged beyond
repair, or unsanitary."[109] But, good intentions aside, removing items that
might upset family members sometimes has the opposite result.

Some personal effects are not returned because they are stolen, either off
the body of the dead or somewhere along the way home. When possessions
are not controlled and returned to the family, the result is often heartbreaking. Paul Weiss of Hayfield, Minnesota, wrote to the Chief of Army Chaplains to ask about his son, Wilfred, who was wounded in action at Cam-
pabasso, Italy, on November 1, 1944, and died three days later.

> He was 27 years old at the time of his death and if at all conscious at
> any time during these three days he yet lived, he surely would have
> something to say or a last message to convey to us, his father, sisters
> and brother or someone. . . . Also, did he receive a proper Christian
> burial? I am sure he did, but we'd like to hear and be assured. What
> came of his personal belongings outside of the few things we received
> by the Effects bureau which consisted of but an old leather wallet, a
> pocket knife and a cigarette lighter? . . . Did he suffer greatly and did he

realize he had to make the supreme sacrifice and was his End a peaceful one in his Lord and Savior Jesus Christ? This means much to us, his father, sisters and brother.[110]

While there is no evidence to indicate that the son's personal effects were stolen or that they were not later returned, it is obvious from Weiss's letter how important having "his personal belongings" was.

To prevent theft, there are elaborate safeguards built into the process of handling personal effects, but it does not take much imagination to envision how the system could break down. In the Korean War, when remains were transported from the front to areas behind the lines, the "personal effects pouch" was tied to the body, secured with a numbered seal, and opened only by authorized personnel to perform inventory or to process the contents for return to family members. Other personal effects were placed into a safe box that was firmly affixed to the refrigerator-car wall; the box was locked in the presence of the escort, who then took possession of the key.[111] In earlier wars, when the dead were buried on the battlefield, in isolated graves, or in temporary cemeteries, a search for personal effects was made upon exhumation and any recovered were forwarded to Graves Registration. At times, when the inside of the coffin contained decayed remains, rotting clothing, and soil, it was necessary to sift the contents through a screen to find personal effects.[112]

There is another reason for searching remains for personal effects that is as important as, and perhaps more important than, providing the family with the belongings of their loved one. It is that the items often give clues to the identity of the remains. While there has been some confusion caused by unique objects found, such as an engraved cigarette case won in a card game, items such as class rings, wedding rings, and wallets are examples of personal effects that can be very helpful in identifying the fallen.

Record Keeping

The Armed Forces do not end record keeping with the death of a service member; in fact, death begins a whole new process of accounting. Someone has to know where the remains are, who has requested their return, and where and when they are to be transported; personal effects have to be collected, cleaned, stored, and forwarded to the proper people.

In World War I, the deceased's "name, number, rank, organization, place of death, location of burial and the name of the next of kin" were written on

6.22   Bags containing personal effects of U.S. servicemen killed in Vietnam await shipment from Da Nang. *Sgt. Donald Mitchell (discharged)*

one side of a 5" x 9" note card; the other side listed if the body was sent to
the United States, the date of arrival, the foreign port it was shipped from,
the American receiving port, whether shipment was to the home or to the
National Cemetery, the bill or lading number, and the "location of the final
resting place of the body."[113]

In World War II, the responsibility for keeping records of death and burials fell to the Quartermaster Corps, which, in March 1941, had moved the
Memorial Division down the chain of organization to branch level. Whereas
the chief of the Memorial Division had reported directly to the Quartermaster General, the chief of the Memorial Branch now reported to the director
of the Service Installations Division. What this meant was that eight months
before the entry of the United States into World War II a critical part of the
Quartermaster Corps had been not only deemphasized but also moved into
a division that had little understanding of the duties required to maintain
records of the dead.

Colonel R. P. Harbold, who had played an important role in the Graves
Registration Service in World War I and had, during the return of the dead
from that war, filed a report on the questionable treatment of the dead on

the *Mercury*, was named head of the Memorial Branch, and he led a vigorous fight against manpower shortages, pressure to standardize correspondence to the next of kin, and efforts to delay the statistical reports concerning the burials of Soldier Dead. He felt that "letters to relatives and next of kin of the dead demanded the utmost of care in composition; they must be tactful and sympathetic in expression and avoid any suggestion of stereotyped phraseology." Possessing first-hand experience of the difficulties in locating, identifying, and returning World War I dead, he also had a keen awareness that delays in gathering and compiling data would carry a heavy price. He stated that

> requirements for recording burial data were determined by rows of the dead lying in hundreds of military cemeteries beyond the seas—not by conclusion based on a folio of tentative organization charts and procedural diagrams in the Office of The Quartermaster General.[114]

Harbold and his staff were engaged in a struggle against recommendations made by "outside practitioners" hired by Brigadier General H. A. Barnes, Director, Organization Planning and Control Division. General Barnes felt that "a fresh viewpoint" was needed and had called in contract consultants, who viewed the duties of the Memorial Branch as a mechanical process—disseminating information—not dispensing care and concern. The so-called "efficiency experts" had little appreciation of the need and responsibility to tenderly handle the worst possible communication that a family could ever receive.

Colonel Harbold eventually prepared Policy Study No. 34, a comprehensive and visionary paper concerning the administration of Soldier Dead duties, dated August 14, 1943, in which he advocated moving the Memorial Branch from under Service Installations and combining it with Graves Registration, a division that reported directly to the Quartermaster General. This study included a lengthy and detailed exhibit listing the difficulties presented by the current arrangement of the Memorial Branch. It was titled "Barnacles," an obvious slight to General Barnes. Harbold must have retained, and probably honed, some of his World War I wit and sarcasm— recall his statement that if American ships with American crews couldn't transport the dead respectfully, then war vessels or foreign carriers should be used. Wit and sarcasm aside, nine months later, Harbold's recommendation concerning elevating the status of the Memorial Branch was implemented when, in May 1944, the Memorial Branch was reinstated to division level and combined with the Graves Registration Service.[115]

The main impetus for this move was the increasing number of deaths: it was clear that the reporting of fatalities and record keeping for burials would overwhelm the small staff that existed up to that point. In essence, the elevation to division level was similar to the establishment of a cabinet-level position such as the Department of Energy, Department of Transportation, or Department of Homeland Security—all organizational units created after a crisis of some sort had occurred. Unfortunately, though, hindsight indicates that had the Memorial Division retained its status at the beginning of the war and been adequately supported, there would not have been a two-year delay in the "completion and verification of burial records."[116]

Another problem with record keeping was that during World War II, reporting information to families was initially a shared responsibility. The Adjutant General distributed reports of death, while the Office of The Quartermaster General was responsible for disseminating information regarding the dates and locations of the burials. When the Adjutant General supplied burial information, it was often out of date, as the Graves Registration Service frequently moved and reburied bodies, usually in an effort to concentrate graves. The conflicting information created doubt in the families' minds "'when bodies are returned as to whether or not the bodies are those of their loved ones.'"

In order to spare next of kin the pain and uncertainty that accompanied errors of the dual reporting system, the Adjutant General "ceased the practice of giving any burial information" and joined with the Quartermaster General and the War Department to review the existing policy and placement of responsibilities. Eventually, on September 11, 1943, the Secretary of War approved a directive that clarified the conveyance of burial information to the family. The Adjutant General, in its initial disclosure, was to state that a follow-up letter would be issued by the office of the Quartermaster General containing burial information.[117]

Burying military dead with honors is not a recent practice. Thucydides' account of the funerary rites of warriors who died in the Peloponnesian War reads as though it could have appeared in *The New York Times*.

> In the same winter the Athenians gave a funeral at the public cost to those who had fallen in this war. It was a custom of their ancestors, and the manner of it is as follows. Three days before the ceremony, the bones of the dead are laid out in a tent which has been erected; and their friends bring to their relatives such offerings as they please. In

the funeral procession cypress coffins are borne in cars, one for each tribe; the bones of the deceased being placed in the coffin of their tribe. Among these is carried an empty bier decked for the missing, that is, for those whose bodies could not be recovered. Any citizen or stranger who pleases, joins in the procession: and the females relatives are there to wail at the burial. The dead are laid in the public sepulcher in the most beautiful suburb of the city, in which those who fall in war are always buried; with the exception of those slain at Marathon, who for their singular and extraordinary valour were interred on the spot where they fell. After the bodies have been laid in the earth, a man chosen by the state . . . pronounces over them an appropriate panegyric. . . . Pericles, son of Xanthippus, was chosen to pronounce their eulogium.[118]

Apparently, the Greeks had less trepidation about seeing the bones of their slain warriors than we do today; it would be hard to imagine the bones of unidentified Soldier Dead "laid out in a tent" for all to honor. Of course, the Greeks did what their technology allowed them to do; our level of advancement provides us with different choices.

The public is called to honor the fallen. Theodore Roosevelt, in a 1907 Arlington National Cemetery dedication to the dead of his regiment, said, "a few had the 'supreme good fortune of dying honorably on a well-fought field for their country's flag.'"[119] During World War I and World War II, two of Roosevelt's own sons had this "good fortune" and another, Kermit, killed himself while stationed at a military base. Ultimately, the final resting place for fallen military is but a marker of our debt to them and their families. No ceremony can do much to assuage the loss borne by the living.

Author's Notes

"But in a larger sense, we cannot dedicate, we cannot consecrate, we cannot hallow this ground. The brave men, living and dead, who struggled here have consecrated it far above our power to add or detract."

Lincoln's words are as meaningful now as they were when spoken in the Gettysburg Address. There is no "fixing" the bereaved of someone killed in service. There is only the offering of some form of recognition of their sacrifice, such as is as reflected in the words of Pericles, speaking to those who gathered at a public funeral for Peloponnesian dead: "Comfort, therefore not condolence, is what I have to offer to the parents of the dead who may be here."

The reader may note that I have not dedicated much space to the details of a formal military funeral. In writing this book, I found that deciding which facts, stories, and information to present was a challenging task: there is so much to tell. I had intended to give a detailed description of the full military escort, firing of guns, and sounding of "Taps," but I felt that this was a familiar enough scene and that I should devote more time to less well-known and little-understood burial topics.

But I will mention one aspect of military burial that is perhaps not easily imagined: the respectful and reverent relationship between the comrades of the deceased and the grieving family. The funeral of a soldier is very similar to that of a law enforcement officer or firefighter. Those who served with the dead convey their personal wishes to the bereaved; also, they stand as representatives for the larger community that is not present but is served by those on both sides of the soil.

While researching this book, I toured several great military cemeteries. Arlington, of course, but also Verdun, Punchbowl in Hawaii, Normandy, and the U.S. Soldiers' and Airmen's Home National Cemetery in Washington, DC. Some of these locations are frequently visited, some are more solitary, and each has its own special spirit.

At Arlington, the chatty, touristy environment offended me at first, but I reminded myself that the crowds did not have the benefit of my research or experiences and that many of the hyperactive children and teenagers around me would, in a few years, be wearing a uniform.

The changing of the guard at the Tomb of the Unknowns silenced the crowds. I looked at the faces of the people watching the solemn ritual and tried to fathom what they were thinking, what they knew about what they were seeing. I alternated between wanting to gather them around and tell them a story, much as a worn and weathered traveler would share his experiences with his friends during a slow evening by a warm fire, and, on the other hand, wanting to get a megaphone and bellow out that what they were witnessing was not even the beginning of the beginning of a story.

I wandered up and down the hills and through the lanes where few others ventured, and even those who did usually rode the tour shuttle. Arlington is a wonderful cemetery, but my real sense of the dead came more strongly to me at other burial grounds.

At the Punchbowl in Honolulu, doves filled the hollowed-out basin with a diminutive and plaintive cry: a single bird might not be noticed, but the sounds of hundreds joined together in an unorchestrated chorus that formed a soundtrack for the visual beauty of the cemetery. While walking among the headstones, I came across an elderly man with a small electric grass cutter in his hand; he was kneeling by a grave and slowly, carefully trimming the already well-tended grass around a grave. I wanted to ask him who was buried there, but left him alone with his thoughts and memories.

The U.S. Soldiers' and Airmen's Home National Cemetery is like an old veteran: he doesn't stand as straight as he used to, but he still stands tall under the spreading branches of the trees that shade the graves.

The Verdun cemetery is located in rolling farmland that also houses French, German, and English cemeteries. The song, "Where Have All the Soldiers Gone?" seems to float through the hills and valleys, wrapping its theme and lines around the multitudinous rows of crosses. There are so many dead soldiers. When I tried to contemplate the grief of the family members, I found myself incapable of doing so, stymied, as though I were trying to understand the Theory of Relativity. I walked among the hoar-covered marble tombstones and found myself viewing the cemetery as a single unit instead of as individual graves, much like single soldiers are lost in a division of troops standing in formation.

Verdun is old history. To a certain extent, even with my research background, I can distance myself from World War I with its millions of dead. But Normandy has the names of men who might still have been alive, had they not been killed in action. I stood in the cemetery on a cold February day, one of few visitors, and as I walked between the tombstones the names of the dead kept coming up before my eyes. The thought that for every grave I was looking at there were two others back in the States made me even more aware of the price paid in World War II. And to top it off, I was looking at just *one* cemetery of *one* country.

It was while wandering through the many graves, away from noise and distracting thoughts, that I began to really sense the dead. They spoke in a soft, almost undetectable manner, like gentle ocean swells that pass beneath a vessel at sea. Whenever I ran into any of the numerous difficulties in creating this book and needed support, I went to the cemeteries in my mind and listened again to the voices of the dead, because I knew that whatever sacrifice I might be making was trivial compared to the price paid by those whose remains lay beneath the ground.

And it was among the white markers that I began to realize that we no longer have a postdeath national commemoration of fallen soldiers. I feel that we have lost a singular, commemorative, and group remembrance. We have the overseas cemeteries for World War I and II. For Korea, we have the hundreds of unknowns buried at Punchbowl, all in one section, and thus have a sense of the group participation and ensuing death. But what do we have for Vietnam and Iraq? We struggle to find something that can adequately serve as a reminder of the price of war.

Memorial Day 1920 was a pivotal event in the healing process following World War I. Prior to that time, the aftermath of the monumental struggle consisted of rebuilding infrastructure and just "getting by." The Graves Registration Service planned and coordinated the ceremonies in every European country where American Soldier Dead had been buried; every grave was decorated with a flag, and cemeteries were adorned with flowers and wreaths. Clergy presided over the solemn ceremonies. In England, similar care was given to the 108 cemeteries containing American dead. Colonel Rethers of the GRS "issued orders that civilian employees be sent to every locality to purchase flowers, which they placed, together with a flag, upon every grave."

And when it came to the expression of feelings, quartermaster personnel penned the following:

> As for the spirit of the French people on this occasion, it is almost impossible to draw a picture that would convey the desired impression of their friendly attitude, and of their pathetic and most touching expression of respect for our dead. While the American people have undoubtedly a very genuine sentiment regarding the more sacred and emotional phases of life, they not infrequently lack the power of expressing their real feelings, or they are prevented from the same by a hesitancy to appear, as they think, sentimental. But the French people have no such scruples. They feel deeply and have a trained ability of expression.[120]

Now, Memorial Day is a commercialized event, and the papers devote much more space to advertising than to the memories of those whose deaths make such ads possible. It seems that there is no matter of the heart or spirit that is beyond trespass for the purpose of making a buck, and I'm ashamed for our country when May rolls around. For my part, I celebrate Memorial Day on its original date, May 30, and resist the urge to take advantage of a three-day weekend with the "new and improved" date of the fourth Monday in May.

Fortunately, there have been efforts to educate the public about the existence of Soldier Dead as a group, rather than as lost individual lives scattered throughout America. The Vietnam Wall memorial is an excellent substitute for a common cemetery because it provides, in one place, a visual image of the dead. The previously mentioned 500 pairs of boots displayed in Chicago is another example, but it is far too ephemeral; something else of a more permanent nature will eventually have to be designed and constructed for the dead of the Gulf War and the more recent Iraq War.

I predict that, some years hence, Americans will need to create a fitting memorial for the fallen from the Gulf, or else we will continue to be haunted by the memories of those who died for us.

[7. All Bodies Are Not the Same]

I am the enemy you killed, my friend.
I knew you in this dark: for so you frowned
Yesterday through me as you jabbed and killed.
I parried; but my hands were loath and cold.
Let us sleep now . . .
—WILFRED OWEN, "Strange Meeting"

·

A DRILL INSTRUCTOR in Robert Heinlein's book *Starship Troopers* tells a batch of new recruits, "War is not violence and killing, pure and simple; war is controlled violence, for a purpose. The purpose of war is to support your government's decisions by force."

If it were possible to render a country incapable of pursuing aggression or offering resistance by means other than the use of violence, war would not necessarily mean taking lives. However, as it has in the past and will likely continue to in the future, armed conflict involves death. And where there is death, there are bodies, both our own and those of the enemy.

The official position of the United States is to provide enemy dead much the same treatment that is given to our own fallen. This position is codified in several forms. Chapter II, Article 16 of the Geneva Convention I states:

> Parties to the conflict shall record as soon as possible, in respect of each wounded, sick or dead person of the adverse Party falling into their hands, any particulars which may assist in his identification.

The "particulars" include the cause of death. Also, the identity disks and personal effects of the dead are to be forwarded to the proper Information Bureau.

Chapter II, Article 17, of the Geneva Convention I states:

> Parties to the conflict shall ensure that burial or cremation of the dead, carried out individually as far as circumstances permit, is preceded by a

careful examination, if possible by a medical examination, of the bodies, with a view to confirming death, establishing identity and enabling a report to be made. . . .

They shall further ensure that the dead are honourably interred, if possible according to the rites of the religion to which they belonged, that their graves are respected, grouped if possible according to the nationality of the deceased, properly maintained and marked so that they may always be found.

Our military's *Joint Tactics, Techniques, and Procedure for Mortuary Affairs in Joint Operations (Joint Pub 4–06,* 1996) says that combat commanders are in charge of mortuary affairs in their area of operations and that, "The responsibility extends not only to deceased personnel of U.S. forces but also to friendly, third country, and enemy dead."[1]

Yet, even with these strictures for handling enemy dead, the remains of Uday and Qusay Hussein, sons of Iraqi dictator Saddam Hussein, both killed in an American attack on July 22, 2003, were not turned over to relatives for burial until August 2, ten days later. This delay, while seemingly justified to allow time to prove their deaths to unbelieving Iraqis, also undoubtedly angered and antagonized many others who, though they had no love for the Husseins, desired for the sons to be buried in accordance with their religion—by sundown on the day of death. That the United States took ten days to do what should have taken much less time and that the remains were displayed revealing the now-infamous autopsy "Y" incisions served only to create more danger for U.S. troops.

The Graves Registration Service *Technical Instructions (Revised to include Nov. 11, 1918)* used by the American Expeditionary Forces in World War I stated that enemy dead should be buried in separate plots, that identification efforts should be made, that records should be kept, and that enemy personal effects should be sent to the Prisoners of War Information Bureau.

The Graves Registration Technical Manual, TM 10–630, in existence at the start of World War II said:

Robbery and maltreatment of the wounded or dead on a battlefield are outrageous offenses against the law of war. It is the duty of the commanders to see that such offenders, whether members of the armed forces or civilians, are promptly apprehended and brought to trial before competent military tribunals. Like other serious offenders against the law of war they may be sentenced to death or such other punishment as the trial tribunal may be legally authorized to impose. Any indication of maltreatment of the dead should be reported to the commanding officers of the sector where it has been discovered.[2]

The manual also stated that, "*Records of the burial of enemy dead will be made as complete as for American Dead* [italics in the original]."[3]

Interestingly, the U.S. Army regulations evolved somewhat during World War II so as to place less emphasis on the handling of enemy dead. By 1945, the updated field Graves Registration manual, FM 10–63, devoted much less space to the subject and discussed it in more general terms. While FM 10–63 did require Graves Registration to "maintain the same records on the enemy dead as on our troops," gone were all references to the mutilation or other mistreatment of enemy dead.[4]

These agreements and policies are well and fine, and it is better to have them than to have none, but in the real world American actions have frequently deviated from official positions. The moment one of our soldiers dies, a support system goes to work to record his death, retrieve his remains, make and preserve identification, and provide for temporary interment or return home. When an enemy soldier dies, though, we often ignore or horribly mistreat, even mutilate them. U.S. history, old and relatively new, contains many examples of our failure to honor the humanity and religion of our slain enemies.

Edgar L. Jones, veteran of World War II, wrote in "One War is Enough," in the February 1946 issue of *The Atlantic Monthly,* that soldiers in the Pacific "boiled the flesh off enemy skulls to make table ornaments for sweethearts, or carved their bones into letter openers."[5] Roscoe C. Blunt Jr., infantryman in World War II, played soccer with the head of a dead German soldier. Blunt also pulled the head off of a decaying German corpse while attempting to retrieve souvenirs.[6] In preparation for Operation Glory, the negotiated return of the dead of both sides in the Korean War, Private Fred Fory said that when it came to the UN troops, "We were very respectful, very careful to keep the remains separated. When we were retrieving the Chinese remains, we just threw the bones into a burlap bag any way we could and brought them down the mountain."[7]

During his tour of duty in Vietnam, Marine Lieutenant Philip Caputo was present when the bodies of four Viet Cong were brought into headquarters on a trailer. The Marines were going to bury the remains in a cemetery that was hardly more than a body dump, but were ordered to leave them out in the sun so American soldiers could "get used to the sight of blood." Eventually, the dead rebels were buried near Da Nang, only to be disinterred

7.1   Bodies of dead Chinese troops are dragged into a mass grave. *Cpt. Valle. National Archives & Records Administration*

for the benefit of a visiting general. Caputo reflected, "What kind of men were we, and what kind of army was it that made exhibitions of the human beings it had butchered?"[8]

The Gulf War, fought by a highly trained volunteer army, saw its share of atrocities perpetrated on Iraqi dead. Anthony Swofford, a Marine sniper, and others in his unit were ordered to do the "cleanup" of enemy positions that had been destroyed. This cleanup was similar to the Vietnam-era "policing up" the battlefield in that weapons were to be removed, intelligence gathered, and enemy dead buried. One of Swofford's buddies, Crockett, "found a corpse he particularly disagree[d] with." During the next several days, the Marine went "to the corpse again and again, day after day, and with his E-tool [an entrenching tool used to dig foxholes] he puncture[d] the skull and with his fixed bayonet he hack[ed] into the torso."

Swofford eventually buried the dead Iraqi, but Crockett said, "Look around, the dead motherfuckers are everywhere. I'll find another one." Sadly, Swofford noted that Crockett was not unique in his attitude or actions.[9] Nor was Swofford himself entirely innocent. He did not mutilate bodies, but he was guilty of another crime: stealing the enemy's identities when he pilfered the dog tags from three dead Iraqi soldiers. Realizing the gravity of his crime, he said, "Maybe I am responsible for three Iraqi families living the horror of not knowing what happened to their sons and fathers."[10] To be certain, the United States does not have a monopoly on mistreatment of the vanquished dead, nor is such mistreatment a recent or unusual occurrence. Old Testament history contains many examples of the victor flaunting success. For instance, when Saul was killed and the Philistines—who were stripping the slain—found his remains, they cut off his head and fastened his body to the wall of Bethsan, where all who passed in and out would view it.

Also, for every American failure to honor the remains of its enemy, there is a similar example of the enemy doing the same to American dead. Nevertheless, we have been quick to deplore our enemies for their behavior, while using Orwellian arguments to justify ours, in effect saying that "all bodies are equal, but some bodies are more equal than others."

Obviously, there is a vast gap between the fine oak tables upon which politicians wearing clean and freshly pressed suits lay out and sign agreements printed on white, pristine paper and the smoke, chaos, grime, and blood of the battlefield where fighting actually takes place. The disparity between theory and practice is well understood by those who actually wage war. General William Tecumseh Sherman, most remembered for his scorched-earth, "March to the Sea" campaign in Georgia during the Civil War and less well known for his subjugation of the Plains Indians afterward, commented about war without euphemisms or attempts to depict it as anything less than what it actually was. In a letter to James M. Calhoun, mayor of Atlanta, September 12, 1864, he said, "You cannot qualify war in harsher terms than I will. War is cruelty, and you cannot refine it."[11]

Once it is understood that the nature of armed struggle involves not only killing but also hunting, trapping, maiming, and slaughtering human beings, it becomes clear that instead of asking why all bodies aren't treated the same, we should wonder how we could expect them all to be treated the same. Given the training, racial prejudices, combat stress, taunting, and desire for battlefield justice that the soldier experiences in combat, the mistreatment of enemy dead, though not desired, should come as no surprise. The abuse of Iraqi prisoners during the occupation period after the Iraq War was no surprise to many students of the military who understand that service in *any* country's armed forces entails exposure to dehumanizing experiences.

Training

Citizens go through a radical transformation to become soldiers. Our society's mores, and often our own morals and ethics, forbid us to kill—except in certain closely limited situations. Eighteen-plus years of training must quickly be counteracted so that *some* killing is not only allowed but encouraged. Dave Grossman, retired lieutenant colonel, said, "From a psychological perspective, the history of warfare can be viewed as a series of successively more effective tactical and mechanical mechanisms to enable or force combatants to overcome their resistance to killing."[12]

Eventually, the killing can become a spree, as described by Wilfred Owen in "Apologia pro Poemate Meo":

> Merry it was to laugh there—
> Where dead becomes absurd and life absurder.
> For Power was on us as we slashed bones bare
> Not to feel sickness or remorse of murder.

And, with enough training and exposure to combat and death, a soldier will not only kill his enemy during battle, he will also do so when it is not required.

Second Lieutenant Paul Fussell served with F Company in World War II and gave a graphic description of a slaughter perpetrated by American soldiers. A group of fifteen to twenty German troops were surrounded in a large crater and wanted to surrender. Fussell wrote:

> Their visible wish to surrender—most were in tears of terror and despair—was ignored by our men lining the rim. Perhaps some of our prisoners had recently been shot by the Germans. Perhaps some Germans hadn't surrendered fast enough and with suitable signs of contrition. (We were very hard on snotty Nazi adolescents.) Whatever the reason, the Great Turkey Shoot resulted. Laughing and howling, hoo-ha-ing and cowboy and good-old-boy yelling, our men exultantly shot into the crater until every single man down there was dead.[13]

Heinlein's phrase, "controlled violence," is an oxymoron. The violence employed by warriors cannot be turned on or off at will; it is the product of a deliberate and extensive program of training, conditioning, and refinement. It is carefully nurtured, whipped to a crescendo, and released at the time of battle. And upon achieving victory—defined as winning control over the battlefield or killing the enemy, or both—the genie does not go willingly back into the bottle. It is little wonder that the enemy is often shot while surrendering and their dead, who can offer no resistance, are subject to extreme abuse. Apparently, Fussell and his fellow GIs had come a long way from the reticent recruits who began basic training.

During training—"conditioning" might better describe the process—a soldier loses much of his individual identity, learns to follow orders, and bonds with his fellow soldiers. Philip Caputo likened the process to "intense indoctrination, which seemed to borrow from Communist brainwashing techniques." He and the others in his company "had been transformed from a group of individuals into one thing: a machine of which [they] were merely parts."[14]

Eventually, the soldier-to-be learns to handle weapons, which are for dispensing force. Therefore, the soldier learns to handle deadly force. The soldier trains with weapons by attacking other soldiers in a sophisticated form of laser tag and by live-fire exercises at simulated enemy targets. These targets can range from paper, usually used at the beginning, to full-size, human-form imitations. The progression from a paper target to one more lifelike is a form of behavior shaping, or "systematic desensitization," a phrase coined by behaviorist Joseph Wolpe.

In drill, soldiers practice bayoneting dummies that are often constructed to look like the enemy. In World War I, the British War Office revised its training principles. No longer was trying to kill or cripple the enemy sufficient; now, instead of just learning new behavior as a tool necessary to be victorious, soldiers were conditioned by the equivalent of George Orwell's Two Minutes Hate program, described in *1984*. Robert Graves wrote:

> Troops learned instead that they must HATE the Germans, and KILL as many of them as possible. In bayonet-practice the men had to make horrible grimaces and utter blood-curdling yells as they charged. The instructors' faces were set in a permanent grin. "Hurt him, now! In at the belly! Tear his guts out!" . . . "Now that upper swing at his privates with the butt. Ruin his chances for life! No more little Fritzes!"[15]

The British instructors were well aware that a man can be trained to handle a weapon, but he has to *want* to use it. He has to have the willingness to plunge the bayonet, pull the trigger, or drop the bomb. There are two ways to develop this: make the act of killing antiseptic and distant, such as killing by remote control; or make the soldier hate the enemy so much that killing becomes an act of mere extermination of lesser beings.

Captain Norman Allen served in Korea with the I Company/5th Cavalry. They witnessed another company attack a hill with disastrous results:

> Just short of the objective they [U.S. troops] were turned back and left five dead under the brow of the hill. For the next three days we had to stare at these five bodies, arms outspread, stranded against the rocky crest. A terrible sight, but there was nothing to do but look. At this point I believe the men in I Company learned to hate. It is very important for infantrymen to hate; it's easier to meet the enemy when you do, when you're at the end of the rope—hungry, desperate, sleepless, mean, angry. . . . If you can't hate, you might hesitate before pulling the trigger and hesitation could kill you.[16]

Conscious and deliberate hate training is frequently a component of military preparation. Caputo and the others in his training class were instructed to chant in unison, "Ambushes are murder and murder is fun."[17]

This type of training is not a thing of the past. At "Camp Freedom" at Tazar Air Base in Hungary, the U.S. Army trained Iraqi exiles to assist with the upcoming invasion of their former homeland. A marching drill song was:

> Yellow bird with a yellow bill
> Sitting on my window sill.
> Lured him in with a crust of bread
> And then I crushed his little head.[18]

In order to prepare and acclimate men to the gore they will encounter in battle, training has taken some unusual turns at times, such as making recruits crawl through pig guts while machine-gun fire snapped overhead.[19] The transition from citizen to soldier is neither easily made nor quickly reversed. As Ernie Pyle wrote, "Our men can't make this change from normal civilians into warriors and remain the same people."[20]

Racial/Cultural Prejudice

With proper training, a soldier can equate killing with ridding the world of a pest, threat, or disease. Can you bayonet your friend? Can you gouge out your neighbor's eyes? Hardly. Can you shoot a stray dog? Probably not. A rabid dog, though, must be eliminated by any means possible. The goal in training is to reduce the enemy to a level lower than that of a stray dog walking the street. In World War II, in which propagandists as well as armed forces fought and scored victories, references were constantly made to the Japanese "mad dogs," "yellow dogs," and "ants."[21]

The United States viewed the fight in Europe as a war to end Nazism but desired—at least as was expressed widely—the extermination of the entire Japanese people, and this difference in goals stemmed largely from racial and cultural attitudes. Our soldiers are not raised from birth, as Kurt Russell is in the movie *Soldier,* or cloned in a test tube; rather, they are civilians with a specialty—war making. As a soldier-to-be enters the training process, he brings along his cultural, racial, and religious prejudices. During training, these biases are fanned white-hot and forged into a blade as sharp as a razor to be wielded against all enemies.

John W. Dower's *War Without Mercy: Race and Power in the Pacific War* depicts the racial attitudes that permeated the ranks of those who fought and those on the home front who supported the war. While people believed in the occasional "good German" who had fallen under the influence of an evil leadership, there was no dichotomy with the Japanese: all were "Japs," corruption a part of their racial heritage, and deserved annihilation. Dower's book contains many statements by political and military leaders that the United States needed not only to destroy Japan as a military nation but also to reduce it to "a nation without cities—a nomadic people."[22]

The desire to "kill all Japs" was expressed by Paul V. McNutt, chairman of the War Manpower Commission, a federal organization created to coordinate the mobilization and organization of the nation's labor pool. He said he was in favor of "the extermination of the Japanese *in toto.*" When queried if he meant the Japanese military or the Japanese people, "he confirmed he meant the latter, 'for I know the Japanese people.'"[23] McNutt's statement is clear evidence of the leap that was made from the effort to eliminate a menace—"mad dogs"—to attempted genocide. Since how we feel about the enemy when alive is closely connected with how we treat their dead, racial prejudices play a significant role.

U.S. history contains many instances of racial prejudice played out on the battlefield. On November 27, 1864, Colonel J. M. Chivington, a Methodist minister, took command of a garrison near Sand Creek, Colorado. Chivington informed his juniors they would attack a nearby camp of Arapaho and Cheyenne Indians, who had all previously made peace with the U.S. government. When several officers protested that the attack would break their promise and amount to nothing less than murder, Chivington's response was, "I have come to kill Indians, and believe it is right and honorable to use any means under God's heavens to kill Indians."[24]

The attack was mounted and a wholesale slaughter ensued: 28 men and 105 women and children were killed. Afterward, the soldiers scalped many of the dead and even mutilated the genitals of both male and female corpses. Not only did the American soldiers attack the encampment, they did so even though the Indians were flying both the American flag and the flag of truce; furthermore, the soldiers struck when many braves were away on a hunting expedition. Genital mutilation seems to be a recurring theme in treatment of the enemy—no doubt it represents the ultimate control and invasion of another person's body.[25]

At the end of the nineteenth century, United States actions in the Philippines again illustrated the prevalence of racial prejudice in political and military matters. After the Spanish-American War, the United States refused to grant independence to the Philippines. Revolutionary leader Emilio Aguinaldo, along with a group of influential Filipinos, resisted America's rule by fiat and declared independence. Consequently, President McKinley decided to send in a 59,000-man expeditionary force to put down the so-called rebellion.[26] To political leaders, the conflict in the Philippines was little different than the war with the Plains Indians. Secretary of War Elihu Root stated that the United States would use the "methods which have proved successful in our Indian camps in the West."[27]

Root, like Colonel Chivington, drew upon his Christian upbringing, attributing crusader characteristics to the U.S. troops fighting the Filipino insurgents: "I claim for him the higher honor that while he is as stern a foe as ever a man saw on the battlefield, he brings the schoolbook, the plow, and the Bible."[28] A mostly guerrilla campaign followed, with atrocities committed by both sides, but the Americans claimed they fought the only way they could against a determined insurgency that followed no rules of combat. General "Hell Roaring" Jacob Smith, a former Indian fighter who had participated in the Wounded Knee massacre, issued orders:

> I want no prisoners. I wish you [Major Littleton Waller] to kill and burn. The more you kill and burn, the better you will please me. The interior of Samar must be a howling wilderness.[29]

Similarly, regarding the war in the Pacific during World War II, John Dower notes: "It was a common observation among Western war correspondents that the fighting in the Pacific was more savage than in the European Theater. Kill or be killed. No quarter, no surrender. Take no prisoners. Fight to the bitter end."[30]

In Vietnam, the battle was not as much to win territory as it was to kill enemy troops. The shooting of wounded was commonplace on both sides. Caputo said:

The marines in our brigade were not innately cruel, but on landing at Da Nang they learned rather quickly that Vietnam was not a place where a man could expect much mercy if, say, he was taken prisoner. And men who do not expect to receive mercy eventually lose their inclination to grant it.[31]

Another point to take from the examples of America's conduct toward enemy soldiers is that policy may be set and agreements signed in boardrooms, but implementation takes place in the field according to the desires of those closest to the action. And field soldiers take cues from their commanders. Admiral Halsey, commander in the Pacific during World War II, was "the most notorious for making outrageous and virulently racist remarks

7.2   Japanese grave marker carved by Marines at Iwo Jima. *T.Sgt.*
Kress. National Archives & Records Administration

about the Japanese enemy in public." His pet phrase for Japanese was "yel-low bastards," and he frequently spoke of them as "monkeymen" or "yellow monkeys," even stating that he was eager to get some "monkey meat."[32]

With ingrained and encouraged racism permeating the ranks of both civilians and military, treatment of the enemy dead could hardly be expected to fly very high on the radar of a soldier's conscience. After a battle at Balan-giga during the Philippine Insurrection, American troops captured a group of rebels and forced them to "remove the Filipino dead from their freshly dug mass grave and to replace their bodies with those of the Americans." Then the Americans burned the bodies of the Filipinos on a funeral pyre.[33]

Likewise, during the Pacific War, "Burial of enemy dead in the South Pacific, as in the Southwest Pacific Area, was regarded as a problem of field sanitation," and the bodies of the Japanese were bulldozed into mass graves.[34] Those who are buried in this manner lose their identity as distinct human beings. Those who watch and participate in such anonymous mass burials come to regard the hundreds and thousands in the pit as little more than decaying flesh.

7.3　A U.S. infantryman douses a Japanese body with gasoline in preparation for burn-ing and burial. *U.S. Army Signal Corps. National Archives & Records Administration*

7.4   A Marine engineer uses a bulldozer to bury dozens of Japanese soldiers who were killed in a banzai counterattack at Tinian. *Kauffman. National Archives & Records Administration*

7.5   A U.S. military graves detail uses a bulldozer to bury the bodies of Iraqi soldiers killed along the Highway of Death in a mass grave. *Peter Turnley/Corbis*

But burning and burial in mass graves were far from the worst fate of enemy dead when racist attitudes prevailed. E. B. Sledge, a Marine who fought in the Pacific, witnessed many acts of desecration performed on enemy corpses. Teeth were gouged out, ears sliced off, and hands chopped off to keep as souvenirs. At Okinawa, one Marine lieutenant urinated into the mouth of a dead Japanese soldier whenever he had to relieve himself. Sledge wrote, "I was ashamed that he was a Marine officer." And, like some of the soldiers in the Plains fourscore years earlier, this same officer was known for trying to shoot the penises off of dead enemy soldiers.[35]

Of course, in a war of atrocities, each side says that the other "started it," as if the conflict were an escalated, grotesque schoolyard brawl. The Native Americans committed acts of outrage, as did the Filipinos, as did the Japanese. Sledge and a buddy were returning to a gun pit late one afternoon when they passed a shallow depression that they had not noticed previously. In it were three dead Marines who had been left there by their comrades during the battle—apparently the Marines had had to retreat temporarily without being able to bring the dead and wounded out. The dead Americans had been mutilated, their hands and heads cut off. And, in a recurring motif, the Japanese had cut the penises off of two men and had stuffed them in their mouths.[36]

While some behavior toward Japanese corpses perhaps bordered on criminality, other acts indicated indifference rather than savagery. Once, Sledge and his mortar crew came upon a Japanese machine-gun squad that had been killed. One corpse, still sitting upright, had the top of his head shot off. A Marine began throwing coral pebbles into the wound. "Each time his pitch was true I heard a little splash of rainwater in the ghastly receptacle."[37] Often, the enemy dead would simply be left to rot where they lay. On Okinawa, Sledge's patrol often passed by a Japanese corpse lying beside a stream. "He didn't appear to have been dead many days then, but we passed that same stream many times throughout April and watched the putrid remains decompose gradually into the soil of Okinawa."[38]

Such refusal to give the enemy a decent burial stands in stark contrast to the desire to recover and bury American dead as quickly as possible. John Bradley was one of the six Marines who raised the flag on Mount Suribachi at Iwo Jima. His son, James Bradley, later wrote *Flags Of Our Fathers*, an excellent account of the battle for Iwo Jima and the fate of the six men portrayed in perhaps the most famous war photograph ever. Describing the epic fight, he wrote, "In the midst of the battle the Marines buried their dead."[39]

Sledge said that in battles at Peleliu and Okinawa, "It was a strong Marine tradition to move our dead, sometimes even at considerable risk, to an

7.6   Grave of Marine who died taking a pillbox. Graves on beachheads were sometimes made by pulling the bank down on the remains, World War II. *Sgt. Stotz. National Archives & Records Administration*

area where they could be covered with a poncho and later collected by the graves registration people."[40] This solemn and devoted attention contrasted sharply with the treatment of the Japanese: "The enemy dead simply rotted where they had fallen. They lay all over the place in grotesque positions with puffy faces and grinning buck-toothed expressions."[41]

The United States has not escaped charges of cruelty in its actions toward its enemies. However, the resulting investigations have tended to be conducted like a political circus in which the authorities agree to hold hearings but do not seriously pursue any allegations of wrongdoing, or, if specific cases of barbarity are examined, further investigation is deemed unnecessary, regardless of the circumstances. During an examination of U.S. actions in the Philippine insurgency, Senator Tom Patterson of Colorado said, "When a war is conducted by a superior race against those whom they consider inferior in the scale of civilization, is it not the experience of the world that the superior race will almost involuntarily practice inhuman conduct?"[42] His words were an eerie preview of justifications used in World War II, in which all combatants fought "barbaric" enemies and ordered the systematic destruction of races considered to be "subhuman."

In an example of written instructions providing little care for the Japanese, "planning instructions" for an assault on Yap made no pretense that enemy dead would receive treatment equal to that accorded American dead:

> Enemy dead will be sprayed with sodium arsenite and buried as soon as possible by the most expeditious means. Burial sites should be so located that future construction or excavation will not expose the remains. No reports are desired except the numbers which are buried.[43]

At least in this case the United States could not be accused of hypocrisy.

In the European area of operations, German dead were treated differently, and it appears that mistreatment of enemy remains was the exception rather than the rule. Harry Mullendore, a member of the 607th Graves Registration Company, wrote: "German dead was [sic] processed and buried with the same concern as the American GI (including the German unidentified)."[44]

However, this is not to say that at all times soldiers have taken better care of enemy dead who were of similar racial and cultural background. In 1864, the Union retook Chancellorsville in northern Virginia, and veterans of the battle a year earlier "flocked in droves to see the old battle lines" but were horrified to find that the Confederates, while burying their own with care, were "satisfied with a perfunctory performance in disposing of the remains of their foe." One veteran was quoted as having said, "Our dead were but partially buried, and the skulls and bones lay about in great profusion." The dead Confederates fared much better, having "been decently buried" in neat and identified graves.[45]

Finally, lest it be thought racial and cultural prejudices toward enemy troops are a thing of the past, during the Gulf War a colonel strode upon a stage before his troops and, "like Wayne Newton doing Patton," said, "Sodom Insane is not going to back down, and neither are we. Why? 'Cause he's a crazy goddamn *Ay-rab* [italics added]."[46] And more recently, Louisiana Congressman John Cooksey, when being interviewed about airport security and racial profiling, said, "If I see someone comes in that's got a diaper on his head and a fan belt wrapped around the diaper on his head, that guy needs to be pulled over." Cooksey's statement and later half-hearted mea culpa, "My choice of words was not a good choice of words," are adequate evidence that racist attitudes continue to plague American mindsets.[47]

Combat Stress/Acclimation

A bad day for a civilian might start with the kids waking up sick, then continue with bad weather and a dead battery in the car. Then, the stock market is down and companies are announcing layoffs. Finally, the central air unit goes out. The civilian could legitimately claim to be "stressed out."

For Robert Graves, a captain in the British Royal Fusiliers in World War I, a bad day began the night before when he went on patrol in No Man's Land, where he crawled from shell hole to shell hole, accidentally stuck his hand in the decaying corpse of a soldier long dead, took the identification off of wounded Germans—slitting their throats in the process—and dodged machine-gun fire on the dash back to friendly trenches, all the while trying to avoid enemy soldiers doing the same.[48] There can be few situations more stressful than having to feel your way through pitch black, pistol and knife in hand, trying to silence a thudding heart and rasping breath, knowing not only that mere feet away someone else is doing the same but that they are trying to kill you, too.

Combat stress has been recognized as a legitimate cause of casualties, notwithstanding General George Patton's opinion that soldiers claiming to suffer from battle fatigue were nothing more than cowards. In World War II, Allied forces experienced "psychiatric casualties" at a rate ranging from 8 percent to 54 percent of all battle casualties, with the figure hovering around 23 percent for U.S. troops.[49] At its peak, the rate of discharges for psychiatric casualties was greater than the draft rate for new recruits.[50]

A civilian may do an excellent job for a company, yet still be laid off. A soldier similarly may do an excellent job, yet be horribly maimed or killed. As Dr. Michael Evan put it, "Soldiering is the only human profession in which success is shadowed by imminent physical destruction."[51] The stress that combat soldiers encounter is well documented, and it is accepted that a substantial percentage of those who fight will suffer psychiatric damage at least on a temporary basis. What is not obvious from the numbers of those who fall to combat fatigue is the percentage of soldiers affected to a degree that does not require their evacuation but that causes them to perform acts beyond the pale.

After capturing a Japanese pillbox, Sledge and his fellow Marines began taking souvenirs from the dead Japanese. While souvenir hunting has accompanied warfare since the beginning of mortal combat, what took place there deserves special note: Sledge saw soldiers extracting gold teeth, using a Ka-Bar knife. "It wasn't simply souvenir hunting or looting the enemy dead; it was more like Indian warriors taking scalps." And as if this weren't enough, one Marine began slicing through the cheeks of a Japanese soldier who was still alive.[52]

If such extreme acts as digging the teeth out of enemy dead become commonplace, the soldiers will get used to it. Realizing this, Sledge wrote:

> The corpses [Japanese] were sprawled where the veterans had dragged them around to get into their packs and pockets. Would I become this casual and calloused about enemy dead? I wondered. Would the war dehumanize me so that I, too, could "field strip" enemy dead with such nonchalance? The time soon came when it didn't bother me a bit.[53]

Another World War II veteran, Fussell, mentioned World War I poet Wilfred Owen's words, "My senses are charred. I don't take the cigarette out of my mouth when I write Deceased over their letters," when reflecting on how he didn't bother to wash the blood of a fallen soldier off his hands before sitting down to eat.[54] Vietnam vet Caputo said, "a callus began to grow

7.7   Marines searching for souvenirs surround a dead Japanese soldier at Tarawa. *National Archives & Records Administration*

around our hearts, a kind of emotional flak jacket that blunted the blows and stings of pity."[55] Indeed, as Michel de Montaigne said in his 1575 essay, *Of Custom, And That We Should Not Easily Change A Law Received*, "custom stupefies our senses."

Some soldiers return physically from the battlefield, but not emotionally from the "interior psychological world of terror, confusion and violence." Audie Murphy, the most decorated U.S. soldier in history, was originally turned down by the U.S. Marines and paratroops as "unsuitable for combat duty" because of his diminutive stature. After serving in the European Theater, he returned to the States and starred in Western B-movies. Those who worked with him noted his "dangerous intensity," and movie directors avoided camera close-ups of his face "for fear of frightening the audience."[56]

In combat, soldiers suffer from the ultimate "pursuit syndrome." Police officers attend courses on how to control their anger after apprehending fleeing suspects. Who can forget the video images, filmed by a KCAL Channel 9 television crew form a helicopter in April 1996, of California law enforcement agents clubbing immigrants who had fled from them in a disintegrating pickup truck? With pursuit anger, plus exposure to mortal danger, the death and/or dismemberment of buddies, days and nights under shelling, lack of sanitation, poor food, and living conditions so hellish no book or movie can accurately depict them, it is almost surprising that, once the fighting stops, only a few soldiers, not most, mutilate the bodies of enemy dead.

Pilot Charles Lindbergh was extremely critical of and greatly disturbed by the actions of Marines toward the Japanese dead. Yet Lindbergh himself maimed and killed when he strafed huts and dropped bombs, not knowing for sure if there were civilians present or not. He was removed from personal contact with the enemy, and knew it. After one mission, he wrote: "How can there be death down there? How can there be writhing, mangled bodies? . . . It is too far away, too separated to hold reality."[57] Lindbergh's observation that it is possible to dispense death from afar without a visceral recognition or understanding of the act of killing underscores unacknowledged problems with our current ability to throw down explosives from the sky and kill at a distance and at will.

During the Korean War, the vicious fighting was at and beyond the level of the Pacific conflict in World War II. The Chinese attacked in huge numbers, overrunning U.S. forces and wiping out whole companies and battalions. Isolated units often fought hand-to-hand at night and in subzero temperatures. Sergeant Sherman Richter said:

Once the battle begins you stop thinking, your mind goes berserk. For however long the battle goes on, you stay crazy. Why else would I have continuously pumped round after round in bodies that I knew were deader than a doornail? To me, they weren't dead. . . . Until the battle is over, until you stop pulling the trigger, you're crazy.[58]

Edgar L. Jones, in his oft-quoted article, "One War is Enough" in *The Atlantic Monthly*, wrote:

Not every American soldier, or even one per cent of our troops, deliberately committed unwarranted atrocities, and the same might be said for the Germans and Japanese. The exigencies of war necessitated many so-called crimes, and the bulk of the rest could be *blamed on the mental distortion* [italics added] which war produced.[59]

Those who do not actually participate in armed struggle may best understand battle stress by recalling the words of General Sherman, who is purported to have said during a graduation address at Michigan Military Academy on June 18, 1879: "War is at best barbarism. . . . Its glory is all moonshine. It is only those who have neither fired a shot nor heard the shrieks and groans of the wounded who cry aloud for blood, more vengeance, more desolation. War is hell."

Taunting

Victory in armed conflict is won by exerting tremendous amounts of energy and willpower against the energy and will of the enemy. After having achieved control of the battlefield, the soldiers, still on an adrenaline high, celebrate their victory. That triumph can be symbolically extended by desecrating remains. During the Trojan War in ancient times, Hector, a Trojan, wanted to behead Patroclus and feed his body to the dogs but was killed by the Greek hero Achilles. Achilles taunted Hector as he was dying, describing how he was going to feed *his* body to the dogs. Hector begged Achilles to ransom his body instead. However, death did not end the fight. After Hector's death, other Greek warriors came up and "not a man who collected there left him without wound. As each went in and struck the corpse, he looked at his friends, and the jest went round: 'Hector is easier to handle now than when he set the ships on fire.'"

Not satisfied, Achilles began to exact further vengeance, according to Homer's account. "The next thing that Achilles did was to subject the fallen prince to shameful outrage." He made a cut in the flesh between the Achilles tendon and heel, fastened leather straps through the slit, and proceeded to drag Hector's corpse behind his chariot around the city of Troy.[60]

An evil twin of taunting is boasting. Soldiers have mutilated enemy dead to obtain bragging rights. During World War II, collecting the heads of Japanese was, if not widespread, not an isolated incident. One popular practice was to put them on the front of tanks, like trophies. Lindbergh wrote down the story one Marine officer told him: "We found one Marine with a Japanese head. He was trying to get the ants to clean the flesh off the skull, but the odor got so bad we had to take it away from him."[61]

The Vietnam War, a messy conflict that was not little and never rose to the level of splendid, saw its share of desecration. Following the example of Australian soldiers, an American Marine attempted to cut off the ears of dead Viet Cong fighters. He was stopped by a sergeant who told Philip Caputo, "I caught the little sonuvabitch cutting the ears off one of those dead VC. He had a K-bar and was trying to slice the guy's ears off. The little jerk."[62] While the sergeant prevented this act of desecration, many other mutilations were not prevented.

Another emotion, not so evident even to soldiers themselves, may add to the desire for vengeance upon and desecration of enemy dead: to a certain extent, the taunting and contempt are coupled with unacknowledged envy. Swofford said,

> The dead men are envied their deaths, that perpetual state where they are required only to go on being dead. No other consequences exist for the corpse. The corpse suffers violence and contempt, the corpse is shot and knifed and cursed and burned, but the corpse will not suffer loneliness and despair and rage.[63]

Battlefield Justice

War is brutal by definition, and "battlefield justice" is frequently dispensed by those closest to and most familiar with the action. Take the case of killing surrendering enemy soldiers, a well-documented act of which a perfect example is the battle for Tarawa.

On November 20, 1943, the United States launched an amphibious landing on Tarawa, a small island in the Gilberts in the central Pacific (now part of the Republic of Kiribati). Tarawa was hardly more than an atoll, one mile long by a few hundred yards wide, and defended by approximately 3,000

Japanese Imperial troops. Sometimes it is clear from the outset, to both attackers and defenders, that an assault will be successful—or else that soon becomes apparent; there is no "if," only "when" it will be accomplished. The battle was over in four days, and only a little over a hundred Japanese survived.

Even though it was clear early on that the Marines would prevail, the Japanese continued fighting. Such efforts to stand to the end in the face of overwhelming superiority are poorly received by attackers, who may view the vain defense as nothing more than an attempt to drain them of manpower. When, in such circumstances, defenders eventually try to surrender, attackers often will not accept the offer and exact revenge.

Lindbergh, after arriving at Tarawa in August 1944, was told that surrenders during the assault were not allowed, and even when prisoners were taken, the only ones spared were those who could speak English. The Japanese dead were buried in mass graves that stood in stark contrast to the "lines of white crosses—row upon row making up a cemetery" for American dead there.[64] Lindbergh's observations are echoed by Andrew Jackson Wade, who served on an amphibian landing craft in World War II. He recalled how the Japanese dead were gathered together and "stacked up . . . like cordwood." Wade observed a frontloader dig a pit; then it "came on around there and shoved them all in, and covered them up, packed them down, put some dirt in there and shoved them down." When asked if this method was used due to a shortage of men, time, and/or equipment to do a proper burial, Wade replied, "They didn't care. They buried them all in them pits."[65]

Soldiers also perform acts of battlefield justice to avenge their dead, including executing live prisoners and mutilating remains. Dr. Joanna Bourke's *In the Presence of Mine Enemies: Face-to-Face Killing in Twentieth-Century Warfare* described the attitude of a soldier in Vietnam:

> Every time a friend was killed, he would personally take revenge, all the time talking to the ghosts of his comrades: "here's one for you baby. I'll take this motherfucker out and I'm going to cut his fucking heart out for you."[66]

The Marine who went out of his way to mutilate Iraqi dead during the Gulf War said to Swofford, "the man deserved to die and now that he's dead the man's corpse deserves to be fucked with."[67]

Sometimes battlefield justice takes the form of field soldiers conducting an ad hoc trial, passing judgment, and performing the execution. American soldiers in Europe near the end of World War II stood by or encouraged concentration camp victims to kill their German captors. Veteran Jack Hallett said, "Control was gone after the sights we saw, and the men were deliberately wounding guards that were available and then turning them over to the prisoners and allowing them to take their revenge."[68]

Undoubtedly, many stories of combat and its aftermath are embellished. Robert Graves said, "The memoirs of a man who went through some of the worst experiences of trench-warfare are not truthful if they do not contain a high proportion of falsities."[69] However, there is little doubt about the cruelty in armed conflict. All the rules of conduct are merely a very loose collar on the dogs of war, and often soldiers have given enemy dead little respect while going to great lengths to protect and honor their own.

The factors that work to create a warrior tend to create a person who cares little for the enemy when alive, much less when dead. As a Korean War veteran told Caputo, "Before you leave here [Vietnam], sir, you're going to learn that one of the most brutal things in the world is your average nineteen-year-old American boy."[70]

Perhaps when work continues on the relatively new and quickly growing study of the sociology of the body, we will better understand the causes of violence done to the bodies of enemy dead. In particular, Arthur W. Frank's identification of the "dominating body" as one of "four ideal types of body usage" holds promise. In Frank's view, the dominating body, whose action type is force, is

> constantly aware of its own contingency. Its world is warfare, and the dominating body is perpetually threatened by new situations and the unknown. . . . The dominating body's lack produces a fear which is turned outwards on others who are exterminated in order to combat that fear. In the context of war, others must die in order for the dominating body to live with itself. Finally, the dominating body must be dissociated from itself in order to punish and absorb punishment.[71]

Obviously, the soldier as the dominating body, as illustrated by the examples here, does not easily lay aside fear and force and reconfigure himself as an ordinary civilian immediately after life-threatening situations.

Swofford describes the treatment of enemy dead in layman's terms: "I understand what drives Crockett to desecrate the dead soldier—fear, anger, a sense of entitlement, cowardice, stupidity, ignorance."[72] Tom Gibson, infantryman serving with E Company featured in *Band of Brothers*, the book and the cable TV movie, said:

I firmly believe that only a combat soldier has the right to judge another combat soldier. Only a rifle company combat soldier knows how hard it is to retain his sanity, to do his duty and to survive with some semblance of honor. You have to learn to forgive others, and yourself, for some of the things that are done.[73]

Gibson's words are revealing not only for *what* he says but also for *how* he says it; the use of the passive voice—"things that are done"—is a form of disavowal that removes or displaces individual responsibility. Gibson's obvious, and understandable, bias points to the need for outside supervision and review of the actions of soldiers under stress. The recent maltreatment of Iraqi prisoners at Abu Ghraib by U.S. occupying forces is a vivid reminder that the military cannot be allowed to sit in sole judgment of its members' actions.

Ultimately, each man wages his own internal battle to maintain his dignity and that of the dead, and if he looks for help and support from his comrades, he will find it. During the battle at Peleliu, Sledge prepared to dig out some gold teeth from a Japanese corpse when Doc Caswell, a medic, talked him out of it, saying that he would expose himself to all kinds of germs. It wasn't until years later that Sledge realized Caswell was using the excuse of contamination by microbes only as a convenient argument to prevent him from contaminating himself in a moral fashion.[74]

Similarly, Swofford told his platoon member who was obsessed with the continual mutilation of an Iraqi body that he had "done everyone a favor by burying the corpse, even him, and that someday he'll be grateful I've stopped him."[75]

Another example of men rising above basic survival behavior is Lt. Waverly Wray, a Baptist country boy from Batesville, Mississippi, who parachuted into Normandy and forestalled a German counteroffensive at St. Mere-Eglise by attacking a German unit and killing eight officers and several infantrymen. The next day he insisted on burying the Germans, explaining that he had killed them and they deserved a decent burial.[76]

Traditionally, the soldiers in the field who fight swordpoint to swordpoint are the ones most insensitive to enemy remains. E. B. Sledge said, "Fighting was our duty, but burying enemy dead and cleaning up the battlefield wasn't for infantry troops, as we saw it."[77] Although their efforts fall short of the ideal, the quartermaster troops responsible for handling U.S. and enemy dead have tended to display the best behavior toward the bodies of the enemy. However, these specialized servicepersons are generally stationed at collection points and do not come into contact with enemy dead unless Americans bring them in.

Ultimately, despite allowances for behavior under stress, we are left with what John Donne's statement, "any man's death diminishes me." As Lindbergh said when he viewed a pit into which the Germans had thrown the cremated ashes of Jews:

> As Germans have defiled themselves by dumping the ashes of human beings into this pit, we have defiled ourselves by bulldozing bodies into shallow, unmarked tropical graves. What is barbaric on one side of the earth is still barbaric on the other. "Judge not that ye be not judged." It is not the Germans alone, or the Japs, but the men of all nations to whom this war has brought shame and degradation.[78]

Author's Notes

"I'm glad I made it. . . . In this case, it was not a close call for me."

So said Secretary of Defense Donald Rumsfeld, speaking to reporters about the decision to publicly display the bodies of Uday and Qusay Hussein. Had Rumsfeld called me before making this ill-fated decision—how was it that we also performed autopsies and showed the resulting incisions?—I would have told him that such actions would, from the Iraqi perspective, immediately transform the United States from the enemy of the Hussein oppressors to the enemy of Muslims.

When Charles V of Spain was advised to hang Martin Luther's corpse on the gallows, he replied, "I make war on the living, not the dead." Our handling of the remains of Hussein's sons was a way of attacking the living, albeit perhaps inadvertent, prompting the question, What was Rumsfeld thinking? And I wasn't the only one to ask it.

Peter Maguire, author of *Law and War: An American Story*, said, "If they [the insurgents or al Qaeda] had killed Bremer and put his body on Al-Jazeera to prove to us that he was dead, we'd have dropped the bomb on them." Maguire's thoughts are not unique, as evidenced by Edgar Jones's "One War is Enough" in the February 1946 *Atlantic Monthly*—quoted extensively over the years, even in making observations about the Iraq War:

> We Americans have the dangerous tendency in our international thinking to take a holier-than-thou attitude toward other nations. We consider ourselves to be more noble and decent than other peoples, and

7.8   Refrigerated trailer at the U.S. Army Morgue in Baghdad where combatant remains are kept (and presumably those of Uday and Qusay Hussein). *Michael Sledge*

consequently in a better position to decide what is right and wrong in the world. What kind of war do civilians suppose we fought, anyway? We shot prisoners in cold blood, wiped out hospitals, strafed lifeboats, killed or mistreated enemy civilians, finished off the enemy wounded, tossed the dying into a hole with the dead, and in the Pacific boiled the flesh off enemy skulls to make table ornaments for sweethearts, or carved their bones into letter openers. But we publicized every inhuman act of our opponents and censored any evidence of our own moral frailty in moments of desperation.[79]

To posit that combatant dead do not matter and there is no point in counting them, not even acknowledging the cost in lives on the other side, is to work half of an equation—and get equally unbalanced results—because somewhere, somebody else *is* counting and to them, their dead *do* matter. To the extent that we develop and refine our military might so that we can eliminate hundreds, thousands, or hundreds of thousands of combatants without losing a single American serviceperson, we will still miss the point that war kills, and when our enemies realize that they cannot kill us on a traditional field of battle, they will move—as they have already moved—to other fields, including those of civilians and ideologies.

My own transition from seeing the enemy, alive or dead, as little more than unnamed, faceless, soulless, and barely sentient beings to acknowledging them as actual people worthy of humane treatment after they no longer posed a threat began after the Gulf War. At that time, it was a family tradition for me to barbecue on Sunday night, and while I was running in and out of the kitchen I would usually have the evening news on. One Sunday night the news featured the "Highway of Death" that many Iraqis followed when fleeing Kuwait City, trying to return home. A few months earlier, the invading forces had followed this highway into Kuwait, meeting no meaningful resistance. Now on the run, these same troops were targeted by attack aircraft and the highway—there were actually two highways, but the one to Basra was the more noted—acquired its infamous moniker. Many Iraqis were burned to death in or alongside their vehicles. Since I very often burned the chicken when cooking it on the grill, blackening the skin, my kids began to ask if we were having "Iraqi chicken" for dinner.

What a difference ten years makes. My kids, now grown, still sometimes come by for dinner, and every now and then we talk in embarrassed terms about our insensitive naming of the burned chicken. Sadly, I have to admit that it was I who was insensitive: they were children and I was, supposedly, their role model.

The Highway of Death was major news for a short time period, and while researching reports of the coverage at the end of the Gulf War, I found that the major news networks asked very few questions about the necessity of the type and amount of killing, and none about what happened to the dead, who may have included Iraqi citizens and possibly even Kuwaiti citizens kidnapped by the Iraqis. Rather, the media readily accepted official military explanations that this was still a combat zone and that during such moments of chaos, armed forces must press their advantage. I admit that I am not a military person, and there are some accounts and reviews of this incident that say that the United States was using appropriate force for the circumstance.

But aside from the tactical and moral questions about this attack, what happened to the dead who were within land controlled by the United States? During my interviews for this book, I talked with "Nancy," a transportation company member during the Gulf War who wishes to remain anonymous. She described many of her experiences, and related to me a particularly regrettable, memorable task: she and others in her unit were ordered to round up charred Iraqi bodies and lay them out for subsequent burial by bulldozers in pits scooped out of the sand. She was told that this was done for "sanitation purposes," which of course brought to my mind the justification for mass

7.9   Burned corpse of an Iraqi caught on the Highway of Death. *Personal photo taken by Gulf War veteran who wishes to remain anonymous*

burial of the Japanese dead in World War II. But Iraq has a dry desert climate, and the bodies had already been incinerated. Where was the health hazard?

Obviously, in this and other instances, American leaders preferred quick burial to later scrutiny by servicepersons and media representatives. The lack of effort to uncover the graves of those we killed in the Gulf War stands in stark contrast to the assistance provided by the United States to disinter remains from the many mass graves of those murdered by the Saddam regime. Can we have it both ways?

I find myself once again acknowledging that part of the problem with combatant remains is that we are trying to establish order over madness. War, the killing of men, women, and children, is madness, yet we still resort to it.

Fortunately, we have made progress in the dual hate/respect relationship with enemy Soldier Dead, and the path for future development has a precedent of sorts in the 1990 passage of the Native American Graves Protection and Repatriation Act (NAGPRA). It provides for the return of Native American human remains and artifacts that are held by federally funded institutions. The act also protects unexploited graves on federal and tribal lands. This legislation is so far-reaching that the discovery of a single remains in 1996, the Kennewick Man, resulted in court battles that persist to this day.

Edgar Jones stated, "such flagrant violations of all moral codes reach into still-unexplored realms of battle psychology." He realized more than sixty years ago that there was much to be done in this field, and I hope that scholars and researchers with more education, experience, and resources than I possess will further develop the emergent theories of the body and their relationship to real world behavior, particularly during the use of force and aggression.

[8. Open Wounds]

I saw battle-corpses, myriads of them,
And the white skeletons of young men, I saw them,
I saw the debris and debris of all the slain soldiers of the war,
They themselves were fully at rest, they suffer'd not,
The living remain'd and suffer'd, the mother suffer'd,
And the wife and the child and the musing comrade suffer'd,
And the armies that remain'd suffer'd.
—WALT WHITMAN, "When Lilacs Last in the Dooryard Bloom'd"

IF ALL 88,000 PEOPLE in Tyler, Texas, suddenly disappeared, a national alarm would sound and we would devote unlimited resources to finding them. Any political leader who displayed less than complete support for the effort would feel the wrath of an enraged public. But if 88,000 Americans slipped away in ones, twos, and threes, over a period of years, their disappearance would generate much less news. Families of the missing, though, would be immediately and continually concerned, regardless of the lack of national attention, and unless their loved ones were found, their wounds would never fully heal.

There are approximately 78,000 Americans missing from World War II, 8,100 from the Korean War, and 1,900 from the Vietnam War, for a total of 88,000. They would fill the stands of a large football stadium. If they left the stands and stood in the field, one person per square yard, they would spill out into the parking lot, taking up the space of 15 more football fields. Lined up, one yard apart, they would stretch for almost 50 miles. It is only a guess as to how many family members are intimately involved with the 88,000 missing, but the number is certainly many times higher. Whatever the final numbers, as New York Mayor Rudolph Giuliani replied when asked how many people were killed in the attack on the World Trade Center, it is "more than we can bear."

And even when families have remains returned to them for final disposition, many find that "grief resolution" and "working through grief" are but words; the reality is that they have been permanently crippled—they carry the signs of a wound that only those similarly marked can recognize and understand.

Then, there are two other wounded parties who are not as readily apparent as grieving parents, spouses, and children. One is Armed Forces personnel—those who have seen too many dead in combat-related incidents and those who have worked intimately with remains in order to recover, identify, and return them to their loved ones. These service members often do not even know that they are injured. The other is our national sense of honor. Although hundreds of thousands of young people have been asked to lay down their lives, there is an unfulfilled obligation to tens of thousands to find them and bring them home. Since the wounds thus exacerbated are deep and extensive, many Americans search desperately for a healing treatment. But a complete cure is elusive because of many difficulties and challenges not fully understood by those unfamiliar with the problem.

Families of servicepersons who are reported killed find that they must rely on others to confirm death and identification. Like anyone else, they do not want to face the death, and their first job is "acknowledging and accepting the truth of the loss."[1]

Actually viewing a corpse helps the bereaved to accept both the reality and the finality of death. If, for example, a woman is informed that her husband has received a gunshot wound and is in a military hospital in Germany, she can travel there and observe the severity of the wound and, if the injury proves fatal, be present during the transition from life to death. But if her husband has been declared dead, yet there is no body to bury, she will naturally harbor some small doubt, which can take root, grow, and crumble the foundation of her belief in the words of U.S. military representatives.

A common statement made by women with husbands who have been declared dead in the Vietnam War but whose remains have not been returned—often called "Vietnam Widows" or "MIA Widows"—is that they "could not walk in a crowd without looking for a face."[2] This sentiment—or even longing—for a killed loved one is well understood by poet Sara Teasdale, whose "Dusk in War Time," 1922, vividly captures that sense of another's loss:

> A half-hour more and you will lean
> To gather me close in the old sweet way—
> But oh, to the woman over the sea
> Who will come at the close of the day?

A half-hour more and I will hear
The key in the latch and the strong quick tread—
But oh, the woman over the sea
Waiting at dusk for one who is dead!

Any brief perusal of the library, a bookstore, or the Internet will offer a glimpse of the vast doubt about the status of those presumably killed in previous wars, and it is easy to become completely lost in the information about what has or hasn't been done and, worse, what is or isn't true. Fixed landmarks that are accepted by all to be positions of certainty are difficult to find. To fully grasp the meanings of the terms that appear so frequently in military, historical, political, and community publications and on the Web, it is necessary to understand military lingo and service personnel status classifications. In particular, there are serious misconceptions and lack of knowledge about "Missing," "Accounted For," and "Unaccounted For."

Status Determination

"Accounted For" means:

(A) the person is returned to United States control alive;
(B) the remains of the person are recovered and, if not identifiable through visual means as those of the missing person, are identified as those of the missing person by a practitioner of an appropriate forensic science; or;
(C) credible evidence exists to support another determination of the person's status.[3]

Obviously, then, a soldier "Unaccounted For" is a missing person who has not returned alive, whose identifiable remains have not been found, or for whom there is no credible evidence to support a different interpretation. It is important to note that "unaccounted for" is not an official legal status but an interpretative term that covers several categories, including Missing, Missing in Action (MIA), and Killed in Action—Body Not Recovered (KIA-BNR).

A "missing person" is "a member of the armed forces on active duty who is in a missing status."[4] This includes:

Missing—The casualty is not present at his or her duty location due to apparent involuntary reasons and whose location is unknown,

Missing in Action (MIA)—The casualty is a hostile casualty, other than the victim of a terrorist activity, who is not present at his or her duty location due to apparent involuntary reasons and whose location is unknown.[5]

Killed in Action (KIA) denotes someone "who is killed outright or who dies as a result of wounds or other injuries before reaching a medical treatment facility" as a result of hostile activity.[6]

This seems straightforward, but the status classification of "Killed in Action—Body Not Recovered" (KIA-BNR) generates considerable controversy. It indicates a high level of confidence that the serviceperson was killed, but no remains could be found during recovery, no recovery effort can be mounted, or even if it could, the likelihood of recovering remains would be small. An example is when witnesses clearly see an airplane striking the ground at a high rate of speed and do not observe a deployed parachute. A later search of the crash site turns up the ejection seat and life-support items that would have been closely identified with the physical presence of the pilot, but not the pilot himself. Add fire to the impact at several hundred miles an hour and it becomes even more understandable why, in this case, few body elements still exist. Remains also may be carried off by animals as well as taken back by the earth.

The trouble with KIA-BNR classifications comes when the circumstances of the loss are not so clear as in the above example, as was the case with Michael Scott Speicher, a Navy pilot shot down at the opening of the air war against Iraq in the early morning of January 17, 1991. He and others in the Sunliner squadron from the aircraft carrier *Saratoga* were flying F/A-18 Hornets on a preemptive strike against radar installations. During the mission, an unknown aircraft, or "bogey," was picked up on radar but, because there was doubt as to whether it was friend or foe, permission was not given to engage it. By the time one of the Sunliner pilots finally made a visual confirmation that the bogey was a "bandit," a MiG 25, it had passed through most of the squadron, and they continued their bombing run against the radar installations.

Shortly after the MiG had supposedly hightailed it out of the area, a fireball lit the sky and an American crewman on an A-6E Intruder, flying nearby, saw a "flaming wreckage careening toward the desert below." When all the Sunliners save Speicher returned to the *Saratoga*, it became clear that a missile had struck his plane.[7]

What ensued after Speicher's failure to return can appropriately be described as a comedy of errors. Some of the foul-ups were failures to communicate on many levels, location mix-ups, uncertainty about whether he had been taken out by a ground-to-air or an air-to-air missile, and even the erroneous conclusion that the plane's airborne explosion was not survivable. The morning after Speicher's last mission, Secretary of Defense Dick Cheney and Chairman of the Joint Chiefs of Staff Colin Powell held a press conference during which Cheney stated that an aircraft had been lost. When asked by reporters if the loss was "a wounding or a death," Cheney hesitantly confirmed that the pilot had been killed.[8] His words, spoken under a perceived need to provide as much information as possible, no doubt hindered Speicher's potential rescue because there was now an "official line" rather than a open question as to the pilot's fate. In any event, no serious search-and-rescue missions were launched to find Speicher, though they could have been, and the fog of war settled on a bright young warrior, husband, and father.

Four months later, on May 22, 1991, after POWs from Iraq had returned and following a "Secretary of the Navy status review board that found 'no credible evidence' to suggest he had survived the shootdown," Speicher's status was changed from MIA to KIA-BNR.[9] However, there were still so many unanswered questions about the incident and the way events had unfolded afterward that some did not give up hope. Ten years later, on January 11, 2001, Secretary of the Navy Richard Danzig resurrected Scott Speicher by changing his status back from KIA-BNR to MIA, the first time such a reclassification had ever occurred. On October 11, 2002, Secretary of the Navy Gordon R. England further modified Speicher's status to Missing/Captured—or, to use a more familiar term, POW, presumably held by the Iraqis.

The reclassification, difficult to procure as it was, came about because of the dogged determination of a few individuals who refused to go along with the mindset of "he has to be dead because the paperwork says so" and who slowly and continually gathered assets and resources, much as a snowball rolling downhill picks up mass and momentum, until their case overcame inertia on the part of the Navy and other military organizations. Speicher's socially dead status, lasting "through three presidential administrations and innumerable opportunities to bring him home,"[10] provides a very recent and painful reminder that KIA-BNR is ultimately a matter of judgment, not factual certainty.

As of the time of final edits to this book, Captain Scott Speicher's status is still Missing/Captured, as determined by the Secretary of the Navy.[11]

There is an administrative action, a Presumptive Finding of Death (PFOD), that, like the KIA-BNR designation, is highly controversial and subjective. A PFOD is "a declaration by the Military Service Secretary or designee of the Military Service concerned, based upon a recommendation by a board or other official body that a person who was placed in a missing casualty status is dead."[12] This decision is rendered in cases in which it is believed that the serviceperson has been killed but the remains have not been found. As of this writing, all of the servicemen missing from World War II, the Korean War, and the Vietnam War have been classified as KIA-BNR or have had a PFOD decision rendered. In other words, in the records of the U.S. government, there are no living missing servicemen anywhere from these three wars.

In a strange twist involving status determination and the belief that classifications provide information about physical condition, Congressman Sonny Montgomery, a member of the Woodcock Commission that met with Vietnamese officials in 1977 to attempt to resolve issues regarding remains, urged that MIAs be reclassified as KIA-BNR because doing so "would relieve the servicemen's families of the anguish associated with their uncertain status."[13] Apparently, Montgomery believed that changing the name could change the characteristics of the actual object to which it related. One wonders what Colonel Harbold, known for insightful and sarcastic comments on shortsighted and insensitive actions regarding the dead, would have said about Montgomery's opinion.

Much of the controversy about the classification of the missing stems from their accompanying social death. Where, how, and when they died will never be known for sure since without remains, there is no absolute certainty of physical extinction.

The nature of military conflict is such that there will almost always be casualties for which remains will never be recovered, but the KIA-BNR status and PFOD findings are of such singular importance that they should be used very judiciously, and only after a case has cleared high hurdles of proof. That is often hard to do because of the circumstances of death in war.

Alive or Dead

Military deaths are much more complicated than civilian deaths. Hostile military forces, either overt or covert, often cause them; also, the actions of large numbers of people trying to capture and/or destroy one another do not result in complete and tidy record keeping or organized and efficient movement of bodies. How do you provide a full, fair, and complete account of the missing when the circumstances surrounding their loss are so chaotic and violent?

As of 1975, when the communist government in the north consolidated its hold on all of Vietnam, there were 2,585 Americans still unaccounted for in Southeast Asia. By February 2003, the number had declined to 1,902, as remains had been either returned by Vietnam and other countries or found by recovery teams. To be sure, many of the missing are known to be dead and their bodies have not been recovered—they are KIA-BNR. Consequently, 657 of the 1,902 are labeled "no further pursuit" and 200 are "deferred"; only 1,042 are classified as being subject to future recovery missions.[14] (No further pursuit cases are those in which "we have enough information to conclude that the individual perished, but all of the evidence indicates his or her remains are unrecoverable." Deferred cases are those in which "we have exhausted all current leads" and no further investigation will be conducted "until additional leads are developed.")[15]

Some of these KIA-BNR cases are fairly clear and uncontested, whereas some are subject to doubt, like that of Scott Speicher. To quote from the Joint Task Force Full Accounting (JTF-FA):

> Although the U.S. Government has thus far been unable to obtain definitive evidence that this number [unaccounted for] includes live Americans still being detained against their free will in Southeast Asia, the information available precludes ruling out that possibility.[16]

It is generally accepted that accounting for servicemen whose remains have not been returned or recovered is a difficult, slow process, but there is disagreement about the reasons. Indeed, the emergence of "activist" groups stems from family members of the missing who believe that the government has failed to address properly the issues surrounding those unaccounted for.

As a result of family activism and public attention, Congress was inexorably drawn into conducting investigations of the accounting for the Vietnam missing. The largest and most complete investigation of the POW/MIA matter took place during the tenure of the Senate Select Committee on POW/MIA Affairs from August 1991 to December 1992; its findings were that

> some POWs may not have returned at the end of the Vietnam War in 1973, although there was no credible evidence to suggest that any were still alive in captivity; that there was no "conspiracy" to cover up live POWs, but there was serious neglect and mismanagement of the issue; that about 100 POWs expected to be returned were not; and that de-

spite some dismissals of the possibility that some POWs were still alive, the committee could not make a similar firm dismissal.[17]

The Senate Select Committee cited several reasons a vigorous and effective investigation had not been undertaken, including differences about how to conduct such an investigation, the wish to put the whole unpleasant affair behind, and the lack of military leverage.[18]

Some, if not most, of the activists who still scrutinize the government's efforts to account for the missing feel that the Vietnam experience is simply another chapter in the book of betrayal begun almost 100 years ago. During World War I, the United States and Britain placed large amounts of ammunition at Archangel, Murmansk, and Vladivostok in northern Russia for use in the fight against Germany, along with troops to protect the stores. After the signing of the armistice, the western nations lent their support to the White Army of Russia and maintained a garrison to guard the supplies and prevent their falling into the hands of the Red Army. U.S. troops engaged in combat with the Bolsheviks before finally withdrawing from the area in 1920; the Americans had experienced extreme hardships and suffered from low morale, and political support for the mission had waned.

The United States refused to negotiate with a political entity it did not want to recognize, and it was not until the signing of the Rita Agreement on August 20, 1921, calling for U.S. relief work in the USSR, that 100 American POWs were turned over by the Soviets, on September 1. However, there were still 127 missing servicemen unaccounted for. After President Roosevelt recognized the Soviet government in 1933, 19 remains were released to the United States, but because forensic techniques were still relatively primitive, it was not possible to provide any credible level of assurance that all or any of them were American.

Of the 127 missing, 57 were classified at KIA-BNR and 70 as MIA. Later, the War Department made an "administrative determination" that the MIAs were KIA on the day they were reported as missing.[19] Thus, a bureaucratic decision—phrased in a way that evokes the image of a bureaucrat behind a desk, rubber-stamping every personnel folder in a huge stack with a big red KIA-BNR—condemned the soldiers to a social death from which any who might possibly be still alive would have little hope of escape.

The actions of the United States following the ill-fated Northern Russia expedition—the refusal to negotiate with supposedly politically unacceptable parties in power, the later agreement to supply aid, the subsequent return of remains, and the failure to obtain a final accounting—established a pattern that has been repeated. After the end of World War II, the United States suspected that its former ally, the Soviet Union, had prevented, or at least obstructed, the return of thousands of Americans in German POW camps that had fallen to the Red Army. While it is hardly likely that large numbers of Americans were forcibly detained by the Soviets—up to 25,000, by some allegations—Russian President Boris Yeltsin stated in 1992 that "about 450 Americans were not returned."[20] Reflecting the continuing concern that these citizens were unaccounted for, the United States and Russia established a joint commission in 1992 to "investigate the allegations of Soviet involvement with U.S. POWs in all wars since World War II."

Since then, although much information regarding the fate of the POWs has been found in Soviet archives and interviews, "there has been considerable obstruction of the Commission's work by officials still sympathetic to Communist ideology and the former Soviet regime." The Department of Defense Prisoner of War/Missing Personnel Office (DPMO) has an online list of alleged sightings of Americans in the Gulag and in concentration camps.[21]

Although the number of Americans held by the Soviets after World War II remains uncertain, the obstruction of Graves Registration Services searches for remains in Soviet-occupied areas is well documented. And, since the United States and the USSR became engaged in the Cold War shortly after the surrender of Germany and Japan, it is not unreasonable to suspect that the Soviets viewed Americans in their possession after World War II in the same way warring nations traditionally consider POWs—as the property of the nation that has custody, in a Machiavellian sense that "possession is nine-tenths of the law."

Regarding the Korean War, the "DPMO states that although there is no first-hand, direct evidence of Korean War POWs being transferred to the Soviet Union, the cumulative weight of circumstantial and secondary evidence is so compelling that they believe that at least small numbers of Americans were in fact so transferred."[22] As in the Archangel case, the United States did not wish to negotiate directly with North Korea about accounting for POW/MIAs and recovering remains. The North Koreans made overtures for direct talks with the United States only, but the Americans wanted the government of South Korea to participate in all discussions. North Korea's refusal to engage in discussions in an inclusive format made it obvious that, after the war and ever since, it intended to use the bodies of U.S. servicemen, dead or alive, as bargaining chips to obtain political legitimacy and aid.[23]

Doubtless, the U.S. government's negotiating position with North Korea was weakened by the desire to forget an unpleasant "police action," and because no "war" had been declared, the Army decided that the headstones on graves of soldiers killed in Korea would not be inscribed with "Korean War" but only with name, rank, and date killed. After criticism from both Congress and the public, the word "Korea" was added, but not "war."[24] Indeed, as Ted Barker, a Texas resident who maintains a Web site that lists those unaccounted for from the Korean War, said, "The sad thing about Korea is that it was not only a 'forgotten' war, it was an 'ignored' war."[25]

The Cold War also has its missing: 38 aircraft and 364 airmen. Eventually, 187 of the 364 crew members were returned to the United States; 34 remains were recovered; 11 men were, based on eyewitness reports, killed but no remains recovered; and 132 men are still unaccounted for and labeled "fate unknown." World War II German and Japanese POWs kept by the Soviets until 1954–55 reported seeing crew members of downed U.S. aircraft and, "In a 1992 letter to the U.S. Senate, Russian President Boris Yeltsin acknowledged the shooting down of some U.S. aircraft by the Soviets and the recovery of some surviving crewmen."[26] Since there is no reconciliation of returned aviators with those shot down, some U.S. POWs may still be held.

In part or wholly because of continuing activist interest in POWs from the Vietnam War, the U.S. government has renewed its search for World War II, Korean, and Cold War missing. In fact, Col. Paul Bethke, former Commander of CILHI, said, "You can't discount what our veterans' organizations and organizations like the National League of Families and all those organizations do to work the government, and also to keep that at the forefront and not let them forget."[27] The Joint POW/MIA Accounting Command (JPAC) mounts archival research investigations, necessary so that field missions know where to look. Then, when likely sites are chosen and permission is received from the countries where they are located, recovery missions are conducted. But even if remains are found from World War II and Korea, there may still be open wounds because the discovery of remains does not necessarily mean that they will be returned to their next of kin (NOK). Many records regarding personnel from these wars and their NOK have been lost or destroyed.

Fortunately for families, many nongovernmental groups and individuals, often using personal money, have conducted extensive searches for the NOK of missing servicemen. In particular, Hal Barker and his brother, Ted, established and maintain a Web site, www.koreanwar.org, that provides a list of Korean War missing for whom family DNA samples are needed. The Barkers, along with others such as Ed Moynagh, devote large amounts of time and resources to finding the next of kin. Moynagh will actually look up the hometowns of the missing and then either peruse the phone book or do an Internet search in those places for the phone numbers of people with the same last name as the missing. Singlehandedly, he has found the NOK of more than 400 Korean missing.

Moynagh's work is not that hard to duplicate. For instance, if you go to www.koreanwar.org and then go to the section "Search By State Or Territory For City and County DNA," you can look up the missing by county or parish within a state. Going to Dallas County will reveal that Donald Dean Tegt was a member of the Air Force 3rd Bomb Group and was shot down on July 4, 1951. His date of birth was February 23, 1921. How many Donald Dean Tegts can there be? How hard is it to search for this name to find the next of kin? Moynagh feels that the United States can, if it so chooses, assign this simple research job to a couple of file clerks or part-time college students and subsequently find the NOK for many of the missing.[28]

The Soldier Dead from World War II, though, do not have champions such as Moynagh or Hal and Ted Barker. And even if there were private groups to investigate on their own or to assist JPAC's research, the passage of time continues to erode the possibility of finding family members.[29]

Having knowledge of and DNA from NOK completes one side of the recovery/identification/return equation, but the other side is dependent upon forces beyond much of the control of JPAC. We need authorization from foreign governments to conduct search missions on their soil. And there is the distinct possibility that some remains are still being intentionally and surreptitiously held by Vietnam.

In 1979, a Vietnamese native of Chinese ancestry was expelled from Vietnam, along with many others of similar ethnicity. This man, Mr. Loc, testified on July 27, 1980 before the Subcommittee on Asian and Pacific Affairs of the Committee on Foreign Affairs, House of Representatives, 96th Congress. Mr. Loc, who later became known as "the mortician," revealed that from 1969 to 1973 he cleaned and treated the remains of American servicemen that were then stored in a "warehouse" in Hanoi. While the number of remains allegedly at the warehouse is uncertain, U.S. analysis put the figure at between 300 and 400.

From March 1974 through September 1990, Vietnam returned 442 remains that they claimed were American. These were parsimoniously turned over to American authorities in 31 separate instances, as the Vietnamese officials felt would best suit their political goals. Forensic examiners concluded that 270 to 280 were American. Assuming that all these remains came from the "inventory" at the warehouse, that would leave as few as 20 or as many as 130 remains unaccounted for.

Where are the rest of these remains that have not been repatriated? How many does Vietnam hold? To quote from the DPMO: "On two occasions, Vietnamese officials provided information to U.S. personnel indicating that Vietnam still had remains it had not repatriated. Although these statements are potentially equivocal, they warrant serious attention. We are continuing to follow up on both." Also, "The Vietnamese probably have records, however, that would answer this [possession of remains] question."[30]

The importance of repatriating these remains, whether the number is 20 or 130, is that doing so will resolve many questions for an even larger number of family members. However, repatriation may raise other questions, such as those asked about Navy Lieutenant Ron Dodge, shot down on May 17, 1967 over North Vietnam. Even though there were photographs and movies showing him alive after his capture, he was not returned with the other POWs during Operation Homecoming. Vietnam returned three remains in 1981, one of which was Dodge, and a subsequent U.S. demand for an explanation of the circumstances surrounding his death led the Vietnamese to declare that "it was a 'hostile act' to pose such a question."[31] While an anthropological exam by CILHI revealed "no evident trauma at the time of his death," the Vietnamese officials' defensive posture well illustrates their propensity for manipulating the remains issue.[32]

The mistreatment of U.S. POWs by North Korea, China, and North Vietnam is well documented, and the death of POWs in captivity is similarly well established. While North Vietnam's mistreatment of POWs is still vivid in memory, its actions pale in comparison to what happened during the Korean War. According to Paul M. Cole, in his RAND publication for the Under Secretary of Defense for Policy, "The gruesome nature of the POW camps administered by the North Koreans and Chinese resulted in the death of 2,730 U.S. POWs, 38 percent of all U.S. POWs in permanent camps [from July 1, 1951 through July 27, 1953]."[33] Since remains often bear evidence of mistreatment, and since current North Korean and Vietnamese officials are acutely aware of our highly advanced forensic abilities, their communist governments would logically be reluctant to release remains that would indict them—in the court of public opinion, at least. For this reason, it is possible that many remains will never be repatriated and their families will never be able to provide a final burial.

Finally, North Vietnamese officials have miscalculated the willingness of the U.S. government to trade aid for remains, much as President Lyndon Johnson miscalculated the willingness of the North Vietnamese communist government to sit down at a table and engage in political debate and compromise. Two days before a United Nations Security Council vote on UN membership for Vietnam, communist leaders let it be known that they were willing to repatriate the remains of three U.S. pilots shot down over North Vietnam. When the United States vetoed UN membership, the offer was withdrawn. During another vote to admit Vietnam, the United States abstained; ten days later, Vietnam repatriated the remains of twenty-two Americans.[34]

Secretary of State Henry Kissinger, while giving a speech to the Southern Governors Conference on September 16, 1975, said:

> I feel that they [the North Vietnamese] will use the missing in action for their political purposes, and we do not believe American foreign policy should be shaped by the holding of hostages—and even less by the remains of Americans who died in action.[35]

As shocking and horrible as bargaining for bones seems, using remains as currency is not new. Hector was scolded by Glaucus for giving up Patrocles' body so easily and for not bringing back the corpse of Sarpedon, an ally. Glaucus told Hector that if he had brought Patrocles' remains into Troy, they could have been used to bargain for Sarpedon's body.[36]

While communist governments have not been cooperative in either exchanging remains or providing access for Graves Registration personnel to retrieve American dead without some form of compensation, they have continued trying to link aid and remains. As recently as 1999, in a meeting in Berlin to discuss recovery missions to be conducted in 2000, North Korea insisted on "detailed requirements for humanitarian aid, which included materials for a clothing factory." In addition to allowing access to sites where remains might be located, the North Korean officials offered to "establish a nationwide bureaucracy from the central government down to county level to conduct remains searches." In response, the U.S. team said that only the Department of State had the authority to conduct such negotiations. No agreement was reached, but later meetings led to recovery missions and the recovery of remains. However, North Korea still attempts to "sell" its cooperation for financial aid while the United States continues to insist it cooperate purely on humanitarian grounds, without compensation other than to reimburse costs and to pay for damage to crops and land.[37] This refusal to pay "ransom" for remains is an extension of the U.S. refusal to pay ransom for "hostages, prisoners of war, or other individuals held against their will as a result of service to their country."[38] The government feels that any such payment could result in additional risk to Americans captured and held hostage.

Knowing that the United States is extremely desirous of recovering remains yet has an official policy of not paying ransom for them, enterprising individuals have contacted family members with requests for payments for search-and-recovery missions. Some of these entrepreneurs are, perhaps, genuine in their attempt to "trade bones," while others have more nefarious intentions. Their efforts are based purely on a profit motive, and while there is nothing wrong, per se, with a businessperson offering services for a profit, many claims of being able to obtain information about POWs and/or remains have proven to be bogus.[39] Without question, these "offers" have raised the hopes of next of kin that their loved one is still alive or that his remains can be found, while sowing doubt in their minds about the sincerity and ability of the United States to fulfill its commitment to account for the missing.

The problem of bargaining for bones or ransoming prisoners was exacerbated by the 1987 pledging of personal money by eight congressmen, a former congressman, and a former POW for the "return of a live prisoner from southeast Asia." The million-dollar pledge, later increased to $2.4 million by additional private pledges, was publicized worldwide, and was both praised and criticized.[40] At a minimum, this offer complicated the U.S. efforts to recover live prisoners or remains, but as in any case in which the public takes a course of action that seems counter to "official" actions, it begs the question about why private citizens often feel it necessary to pursue such an alternative.

It is very difficult to explain to families of the missing why we will not pay for the repatriation of remains. They often view the policy as a matter of money rather than strategic wisdom, saying, "If they can spend X amount for a cruise missile, then they can certainly spend Y to bring my husband's body back." Explaining the no-ransom policy is only one of many extremely sensitive subjects on which the military must communicate with the families of Soldier Dead.

And in all fairness to the countries in which our dead still lie, those nations' lives have moved on. They have built factories, roads, farms, and schools where battles took place and where the remains of our servicepersons may possibly rest. Washington, DC would probably not be too excited about the prospect of rerouting traffic on I-95 to make way for a search for remains, and the environmental impact study required to move large amounts of soil in California would probably be a major impediment to excavations of the type we have conducted in Vietnam and Laos. Certainly, large sums would be required to cover the costs.

The Worst News of My Life

The Army, Navy, Air Force, and Marines each have an office that provides assistance to family members when a serviceperson dies. There are slight variations in the names, but all incorporate "casualty" in some manner and all the offices have similar duties. Upon news of a soldier's death, regulations call for the primary next of kin (PNOK) and secondary next of kin (SNOK) to be personally notified by a uniformed representative of the relevant service branch.

The way the dreaded information is initially presented to families lays the foundation upon which the success of future communication between the NOK and armed services depends. The casualty notification officer needs to be sensitive and professional, but not aloof. During the initial notification, which is always done in person, the officer tells the PNOK whatever is currently known about the circumstances of the death and that a casualty assistance officer (CAO) will soon be in contact. The casualty notification officer must be of equal rank as or higher rank than the deceased person, while the CAO must be a captain or higher, a warrant officer, or a senior noncommissioned officer. Civilians may not be used. The CAO will the contact the PNOK and "will assist and counsel the PNOK on all matters pertaining to the deceased."[41]

Armed services regulations state that a CAO must have a moderate number of years of experience and be "knowledgeable, competent, dependable, sympathetic."[42] Nowhere, though, do the regulations require officers who deliver the news of the death of a loved one, or others who work with the NOK, to receive special mortuary, sociological, or counseling instruction. Without a doubt, this lack of training has sometimes led to personnel acting in a way that degrades the trust between the military and the next of kin and hinders the family's ability to work through the grief resolution process.

When Theresa (Terry) Buege opened her front door on the morning of January 31, 1991, to receive, in her words, "The worst news of my life," she saw a squadron commander, a flight surgeon, and a priest from the base in Florida where her husband had been stationed. The commander told her that her husband's plane had sent out a Mayday call and that his status was "Whereabouts Unknown." As she asked more questions, Terry learned that his gunship, *Spirit 03*, had probably been shot down behind enemy lines and that no searches would currently be mounted.

At this point, Terry did not know if her husband, Paul, was dead or alive. She said:

> I kept looking at this officer as he was reading me this message, and I kept looking up at him and asking, "Is my husband dead?" He would never answer me. He would just read the message over and over again. So I did not know what to think.

Later, when Terry asked the priest why the commander persisted in repeating the message she had already heard, he replied, "Sometimes it is very hard for these people. They are human beings, too, and it is very hard for them to watch people breaking apart."[43] Also, the priest told Terry that notification officers are instructed not to display much emotion because doing so just makes it worse for family members. Terry disagreed, saying that the officers need to establish an emotional rapport with the family.

Terry also objected to the formal Class A uniforms the notification officers wear. Class A is the full dress uniform for special and formal occasions; wearing it means putting on the spit and polish, which is a major part of military tradition. A serviceperson feels that to be addressed by someone in Class A is to be accorded the full dignity and respect of the military and the nation behind the uniform. Those who write the regulations believe that wearing Class A uniforms to convey bad news is a symbol of the care and concern of the government—it shows respect.

But the family may be more at ease and feel a stronger personal connection if addressed by someone in more "normal" attire—as Terry said in her particular case, in the flight suits that her husband usually wore. She said, "You [casualty notification officers] come in these blue uniforms, it is not friendly and you deliver this message, stiff and stern, and it is not very comforting at all."[44]

The day that began with a casualty notification officer bringing Terry Buege the terrible news only got worse. Her husband had asked her to communicate any bad news to his parents, but she was not able to reach them for a few hours. During that time, an Air Force representative kept calling her to find out if she had gotten in touch with them, because news of the identity of the missing crew could not be released until all next of kin had been notified; he told her that she was "holding things up."[45] While it is certainly commendable, and required by regulations, to delay public dissemination of casualty information until all family members have been contacted, such complaining to a distraught wife borders on cruelty.

All the wives of the *Spirit 03* dead faced other instances of insensitivity during the weeks and months after the initial casualty notification. Once the crew members were confirmed as KIA, each wife's status was changed to "unremarried widow," and they began a series of meetings to register for Social Security and Veterans Administration benefits. Unfortunately, these meetings were scheduled at the base recreation center, where homecoming celebrations were being held for returning aviators. One newly bereaved widow had her "appointment right when the majority of the guys [returning from the Gulf War] were coming into the recreation center."[46] Also, some of the women who were members of the officers' club began receiving monthly statements addressing them as "Widow ___." Terry Buege called the club manager and asked that her statements address her by her given name, or as "Mrs. Paul Buege," "Theresa Buege," or anything else but "Widow Buege." The manager at first said he could not accommodate her request, but he eventually did so.[47]

It seemed as if the *Spirit 03* widows' wounds would never be allowed to heal. Their husbands' personal effects were sidetracked and sat at Fort Dix in New Jersey for months when they should have been returned to the families much earlier. This mistake was discovered only when one of the widows asked a Mortuary Affairs officer how much longer they would have to wait. The horrified officer quickly remedied the matter. In yet another display of incredible insensitivity, when Terry Buege asked for her husband's POW bag—when Iraq announced that POWs were going to be released, fellow squadron members of the missing crew, not yet knowing if any were alive or dead, had pulled together some clothes for each of the men to wear upon release and put them into individual bags—she was told by the person in charge of Paul's particular area of specialization that the bag contained "only . . . clothes" and that it would be some time before it could be sent to her. Terry retorted that she "wouldn't [ever] receive anything more than clothes."[48]

While many of the oversights in Terry Buege's case were eventually resolved and many of the slights were all or partly offset by genuinely caring individuals, one arbitrary and irreversible action exacerbated her grief, hampered her recovery, and still pains her daily. As the men from Paul's squadron returned from the Persian Gulf, they kept telling her that they had seen his flight jacket on the beach near the crash site, but Terry had neither seen it nor been told of its recovery. Finally, after confirming that the jacket had definitely been found and placed in a body bag, she called an officer at Dover Air Force Base, where the remains had been sent. After he attempted to brush off her request for information about the jacket, she told him that he could either tell her what had happened to it or she would call her congressman and ask for an investigation. Two days later, the officer, without apology, explained that her husband's jacket had been incinerated and that she wouldn't have wanted to see it.

Terry was "furious" with the officer for making that decision for her and taking away the only real, tangible proof of Paul's death. She said:

> Every morning I have to get up and I have to tell myself that my husband is dead. All I have is a stranger come to my house and read a message from a general of the Air Force, and this total stranger told me that he was dead. I have no proof. . . . You took my opportunity away. If I would have seen that jacket, perhaps that would have made his death real to me. I could have buried something of my husband. That is what I would have done if I had the flight jacket. I would have put it in his casket, like I was really burying him.[49]

Regulations do call for the destruction of personal effects that may upset the next of kin, but the military must learn to look at these items from the perspective of a family member and to realize that the survivors of those killed in sudden, premature, and violent ways yearn for details. There is no reality worse than the scenario the imagination can conjure. Perhaps it would be best to save all personal effects and provide a written description of those that show the effects of the forces that killed the soldier; later, the NOK could review this list and make their wishes known as to future disposition.

Such a notification of all personal effects found with remains is also important in a way not apparent as first sight: the object may serve a different purpose than its obvious intent. In Terry's case, her husband put their wedding ring in a pocket of his jacket before flying. Yet, the ring was not returned to her.[50] It may have been lost during the crash or overlooked and burned along with the jacket. That jacket served as more than just an item of clothing; it was also a storage device. How many other servicepersons have sewn items with precious personal meaning into their clothing, slipped a "lucky coin" into a boot, or done something else of a similar nature? The military cannot possibly fathom all these possibilities, and when they take the object at face value they may overlook more subtle uses. Since the family has knowledge not shared by handlers of personal effects, it is important for them to be informed of all personal items recovered.

Paul Sledzik, former anthropologist at the National Museum of Health and Medicine at the Armed Forces Institute of Pathology (AFIP), says that in nonmilitary deaths, a complete list of all personal effects is made and pictures are taken. The family members then have the choice of reviewing the list and photos in full or not, and then of asking for the return of some, all, or no personal effects. In Sledzik's words, "When you take the choice away from the family, this is when your troubles begin."[51]

The burning of Paul Buege's jacket and the ensuing events exemplify the Penrosian Attitude of some military officials; they feel they know best and want to dispatch their duty quickly and with minimal effort. So they react to any form of questioning by obfuscating or trying to put the questioner on the defensive rather than taking the time and care to conduct an honest investigation, admit a mistake, or consider another point of view.

Insensitive military officials gouged Terry's wounds, but civilians did their share of damage too. Curiosity seekers drove by her house, and some people who objected to the U.S. actions in the Gulf War sent hate mail. One person wrote, "If your husband wouldn't have been a warmonger, then he might be home with you right now." Her children suffered too, through hurtful remarks made to them at school, as though they had had any say in determining their father's duty.[52]

And other people, though perhaps well-intentioned, keep reopening wounds that are slowly closing. Terry Buege has heard from more than one source that her husband might still be alive, captured, and held by Saddam Hussein. And during the recent Iraq War, twelve years after her husband was shot down, she was again plagued with uncertainty about his death—recalling questions that were not fully answered at the time, about whether he, and maybe others, could have made it out safely; questions that arose in part because of mistakes and, worse, perhaps even prevarications. Air force officials claimed that *Spirit 03* could not be found until a month after it was shot down, yet Terry said that she heard the father of one of the crew state that Colonel Jesse Johnson, a Special Forces commander, had told him that Navy SEALS were at the crash site within two days and had "secured" it.

While all plausible leads should be followed up, communications—from any source—to grieving family members should be based on the best information available, not on cover stories, whims, or fantasies. As Terry summed it up, "How many times am I going to have to bury my husband?"[53]

Unseen Casualties

The open wounds of Terry Buege and other next of kin with similar stories of the dead and presumed dead are visible for all to see. What is less apparent, though, is the damage to others that lies beneath the surface, often not acknowledged even by the wound carrier.

8.1   Wreckage of the *Spirit 03* being lifted onto a barge. Family members were first told that no pictures were taken and that no piece of remains was larger than three feet long. *Permission granted by Jennifer Lavery, who obtained photo through a Freedom of Information Act request*

The men and women in the U.S. Armed Forces have a bond that, while not based on blood, is so strong that it might well be considered familial; they are all members of an extended family who depend on one another for moral, spiritual, and physical support and comfort. It is not surprising, then, that service personnel feel a compelling need to find, identify, bury, and honor their comrades. Doing so is costly, though, for not all men and women are psychologically and emotionally suited for the task, and they do not always receive training that might help them cope.

While there are many anecdotal reports about the stress that accompanies handling remains, the Gulf War provided the opportunity for scientific psychological reviews. A study that compared Desert Storm troops performing Graves Registration duties to a similar group that remained stateside found that the former "endorsed a significantly higher number of PTSD [post-traumatic stress disorder] symptoms . . . than did those without war-zone exposure."[54] The study also reported that "Current and lifetime rates of PTSD were at 48% and 65%, respectively, for the Persian Gulf deployed sample, whereas no PTSD diagnoses were observed among troops not deployed to combat [handling human remains]."[55] Other studies showed that "inexperienced military mortuary workers . . . exhibited greater . . . psychological distress following actual recovery of war dead . . . than did their more experienced counterparts."[56]

Such findings are well supported by the workers' stories. Corporal Richard Oliver, who served in Korea from 1952 until 1954 with the 146th GRS Company, 2nd Platoon, said that you learned to "put a shield around yourself" while performing Graves Registration duties. One day, on the way to Wonju with a truck full of remains, he was stopped by mechanical trouble. Slowly, one after the other, he could hear the body bags unzip by themselves as the gases from the decomposing bodies expanded within the rubberized liners.[57] Even with an emotional shield, Oliver no doubt recalled that horrifying incident many times in later years.

There is stress, too, on the casualty notification and assistance officers who are not actually involved with physical remains but must handle the "remains" of families. The challenges faced by field and laboratory workers

8.2   Dead Marine on D-Day +5 at Iwo Jima. *Sgt. Mulstay. National Archives & Records Administration*

who recovered and identified bodies after the Gander, Newfoundland, crash of a transport plane carrying 248 soldiers were mirrored for the personnel who assisted the NOK. As recovery and identification dragged along—for completely understandable reasons—so did notification and assistance; there could be no funerals until remains were recovered and identified.

At that time, the Army's Survivor Assistance Officers (SAOs) helped "distraught relatives [to] negotiate the Army's often confusing administrative channels to obtain information and insurance benefits, and to assure that the remains, belongings, and personal affairs of the deceased [were] properly attended to." The SAOs were officially assigned administrative duties, but they often found themselves personally involved with the NOK for an extended period of time.[58]

A psychological study found that the nature and circumstances of the disaster caused the Gander SAOs to experience stress in four major areas. First, they "reported being unprepared to deal with the profound grief of widows and bereaved parents." Second, the "extreme confusion and disorder" that prevailed during the initial two weeks was "extremely trying." Third, the delay in identifying remains compounded the already excruciating grief of each family and complicated its relations with the Army representative. Fourth, the officers had trouble dissociating themselves from the deceased and family. Many had a "common experience . . . imagining oneself in the place of the deceased, often associated with a powerful desire *to relieve the pain of family survivors* [italics added]."[59]

The study concluded that the workers were "at risk for increased illness, psychiatric symptoms, and negative psychological well-being" and that because, unlike emergency rescue workers, they had to perform their duties over a lengthy period, they were even more at risk. The stress they experienced was "akin to the chronic stress of living near a nuclear or chemical disaster site," with subsequent psychological harm.[60]

Perhaps in recognition of the strain on personnel who must work closely with family members, Army regulations instruct casualty assistance officers to avoid stopping by "taverns or similar places before visiting with the NOK."[61] While the stated reason for this rule is to "avoid having 'liquor on your breath,'" it sidesteps the important issue of why a CAO would want, or need, to stop by a bar on the way to see a bereaved family.

Another group of service personnel also suffers, even in advance of handling remains. Dover Air Force Base, Delaware, is the military site to which most remains are flown for identification and preparation for return to the next of kin, and it was expanded before the Gulf War and equipped to handle the large number of expected deaths. To adequately staff the base, many Armed Forces personnel either volunteered for or were assigned duty there. Of those "likely to be exposed to the remains that would come to the mortuary for identification," 401 consented to a research project in which they answered questionnaires about personal data and psychosocial measures. The study found that women, people inexperienced in mortuary affairs, and nonvolunteers were at a higher risk and experienced symptoms that were associated with post-traumatic stress disorder, even before actually handling remains.[62]

Building on test results showing the negative impact of stress on mortuary workers at Dover Air Force Base and elsewhere, the Air Force issued instructions—AFRSSIR 44–153: Critical Incident Stress Management (CISM)—in 1999 to help its members handle traumatic events. Lieutenant Colonel Kevin Mulligan, Commander of the 436th Medical Operations Squadron at Dover, says CISM provides for pre-exposure training to help prepare workers for the stress they will experience from handling human remains.[63] AFRSSIR 44–153 also provides for postdeployment critical incident stress debriefings designed to "help prevent or mitigate long-term emotional problems after a traumatic event happens." These sessions are not meant as a substitute for therapy, but to "encourage people to understand the normal physical, emotional, cognitive, and behavioral reactions to traumatic events" so they can better cope with their experiences.[64]

AFRSSIR 44–153 was in force only two years when the Pentagon was attacked on September 11, 2001. Remains from the defense building were taken to the Dover morgue where workers, all volunteers this time, began the lengthy and painstakingly detailed task of identification and preparation. Afterward, an article describing the application of CISM at Dover appeared in the 2002 Supplement of *Military Medicine.* This article does an excellent job of presenting the background of stress factors and indicators in morgue workers and details how CISM was used in this particular situation to head off PTSD. Significantly, it emphasizes the fact that "There have been no controlled studies outlining psychological interventions to prevent or minimize the impact of being assigned to perform such duties [handling remains]" and that "the long-term impact on mortuary workers who participated in the handling of human remains from the September 11 attack on the Pentagon is not known."[65]

Given the well-documented fact that body and remains handlers *do* suffer stress, it is difficult to imagine future studies not being done in this field. Meticulous attention is given to bar-coding remains and personal effects. Communication with family members continues to improve. Yet, as the article says, "it may be difficult to obtain support from leadership or even receive

Institutional Review Board approval for a study involving the randomization to treatment vs. control groups during a critical incident."[66] The care of the living who care for the dead is certainly a topic worthy of more study, and political or administrative concerns about such research should be resolved.

There is still another group that incurs wounds: Armed Forces members who serve in combat and combat support. Rather than quote from psychological studies of the obvious, Ernie Pyle's words provide a poignant reminder of this damage. Pyle was called the GI's best friend; certainly, he lived as a soldier, often dirty and hungry, and always homesick, and he died as a soldier, from an enemy's bullet. After his death, Edwin Waltz, a Navy man, was sorting through Pyle's personal effects before sending them home. Among a few other items, he found a handwritten draft of a newspaper column, titled "And So It Is Over."

> And so it is over. The catastrophe on one side of the world has run its
> course . . . there are so many of the living who have burned into their
> brains forever the unnatural sight of cold dead men scattered over the

8.3   Remains of soldiers presumably killed by an Italian flamethrower. *U.S. Army Photo.
National Archives & Records Administration*

8.4   Dead Marines on Tarawa. *National Archives & Records Administration*

hillsides and in the ditches along the high rows of hedge throughout
the world. Dead men by mass production—in one country after another—month after month and year after year. Dead men in winter
and dead men in summer. Dead men in such familiar promiscuity that
they become monotonous. Dead men in such monstrous infinity that
you come almost to hate them.[67]

National Wounds

When family and military members are hurt by the death of a loved one or
their comrades, these wounds are not localized—they extend into the body
of the nation. Trust is lost because of the actions of modern-day Colonel
Penrose types who challenge the patriotism of those who pose irritating questions, and faith is lost when mishandling occurs and misinformation is disseminated. A nation can survive physical damage to its property and people;
much more damaging are the scars on its psyche that come from not honoring its obligations to the dead and their families. No one wants to accept a
check drawn on a morally bankrupt account.

The United States continues to be as divided about the POW/MIA/re-mains issues of Vietnam as it was about the war itself. These differences have been publicized in print and on television and posted on the Internet for all to see. Less obvious but no less painful are the wounds borne by the families of the 8,100 still missing from the Korean War and the 78,000 still missing from World War II. There are books that remain to be balanced with American families.

And we have accounts to settle with other countries, debts that affect the morale and health of American soldiers who realize the import of their actions—and thus our nation. Forty years after their service on Tarawa, a buddy of Andrew Jackson Wade recounted how Japanese dead were buried in mass graves. He said, "Andrew, do you remember that? That was sick, then, wasn't it?" Wade replied, "Yes, that whole thing was sick."[68]

When citizens die in service, the structure of our national sense of self is shifted. Balance is upset and equilibrium can only be reestablished by the movement of other members of the system. This rebalancing is not easy and, while the society as a whole may be relatively stable, some individuals find themselves at the extreme end of fulcrum points. In essence, the structure survives, but parts remain damaged. There is danger in that if too many

8.5   This grave marker at Punchbowl for an unknown does not even list the war in which he died. *Michael Sledge*

parts have to make major adjustments—as when there are large numbers of dead left unaccounted for—the entire system will be unsteady.

Unfortunately, it is almost, if not entirely, impossible to restore bereaved families to wholeness—we can only try to make their burden as bearable as possible. To a certain extent, those who work in Mortuary Affairs, in Casualty Assistance, or in any other capacity associated with the recovery, identification, return, and burial of Soldier Dead face challenges similar to what Kenneth Feinberg faced daily as Special Master of the Victim Compensation Fund for the families of those killed in the World Trade Center attack. His job was to set compensation amounts for relatives who accepted the government's payment in lieu of suing the airlines. When addressing complaints about delays in settling with victims, Feinberg said that "he could not bring people back" and that "he could not make them happy."[69] What he could do was act honestly and fairly, and treat the families with dignity and respect. Those who have lost their loved ones or comrades in military service deserve the same.

Author's Notes

"You had a situation where, rightly or wrongly, families were not told the truth. . . . Our families were lied to early on that we really weren't there [in Cambodia and Laos]," Johnie Webb, Deputy Director of JPAC, said during my interview with him and Col. Paul Bethke in November 2002. Both were with CILHI at that time. This frank admission of dishonesty continues to haunt the military-family relationship and has added immensely to the already considerable difficulties in recovering, identifying, and returning those killed in Southeast Asia.

As I continued my research into what happened to soldiers after their deaths, I was drawn inexorably into POW/MIA issues. I really didn't want to go there because so much work had already been done in this field, and it was fraught with inaccuracies, innuendoes, misinformation, disguised intentions, and politicized points of view. Besides, I was not an expert, and how could I expect to become one in the time I had available?

But this book had to include the Vietnam POW/MIA issues because, in a nutshell and as stated in the first chapter, "Why It Matters," one cannot be absolutely certain of death without concrete evidence: the cold, lifeless remains. I had to immerse myself in the miasma of myths and facts surrounding supposedly deceased U.S. servicemen.

A closer reading of Mr. Webb's words, "rightly or wrongly," further illustrates the complexity of the issue. How can it be "right" not to tell the truth?

Obviously, some loss situations may call for less than full disclosure: certain special operations probably fall into this category. But, unfortunately, having the ability and power to disseminate false information leads to the possibility of creating and perpetuating a cover-up. Timothy Castle's book, *One Day Too Long: Top Secret Site 85 and the Bombing of North Vietnam*, does an excellent job of depicting the extent to which national security concerns were used as a justification—illegitimately so, in the minds of many—for the extensive dissembling and even outright falsehoods that followed the capture of the radar site.

Military force has always called for covert and clandestine operations. Indeed, the Bible itself contains numerous examples of spies, operations behind enemy lines, and subterfuges. America's current operations in Afghanistan and Iraq also have employed Special Ops. In the case of death in these missions, it is hardly realistic to expect full details that could endanger those who are still, or will be, at risk. Yet the government's emphasis should be on providing more, rather than less, correct information and doing so sooner, rather than later.

Family members have told me that if they had been confident that whatever they had been told was true, they would have been cooperative and quiet. In other words, if they had been told that their serviceman was on a secret mission when his plane was shot down and that his remains could not be recovered without the loss of other lives, they would have reluctantly accepted the situation. However, if they subsequently learned that he had had a good chance of survival, that he might have been captured, and that the information they'd been given was a CYA (Cover Your Ass) statement to camouflage poor command decisions, they began to suspect anything and everything they were told and to ferociously fight for knowledge. Sadly and tragically, this is exactly what happened in many cases of soldiers lost in Southeast Asia and even in the Gulf War. The family's position can be summed up as, "Tell me what you can, but it has to be the truth."

In my interviews and talks with them, Armed Forces personnel who performed the "hands-on" work with remains were always serious about their work. I wondered, and even asked, if there were any moments of levity or attempts to dispel the morbidity of the situation by cracking jokes or other tension-relieving acts common in other professions. A good example of this stress relief is in chapter 6, "Burial," in which a soldier's "black book" was the source of some humorous speculation. I was assured that all handling was always done with due concern and care, without any horsing around.

I wondered how this business could be so different from any other and found somewhat of an answer during my trip to Baghdad. The noncommissioned officer in charge of the morgue there, Staff Sergeant Vincent, a dedicated professional, insisted on proper behavior by all those associated with handling remains. I personally witnessed his checking with the crew of a C-130 that was flying remains to Kuwait to be sure that they knew what their cargo was and what they were required to do. His men looked to him for guidance and instruction, and he provided it. He is a credit to the Army's Mortuary Affairs company. Yet Vincent is human, and beneath his calm, serious demeanor lies a sense of humor, albeit somewhat wry. In the morgue was a roughly built wooden rack that had a shelf holding exercise equipment: gloves, abdominal wheel, wrist tape, and weights. It was labeled, I HAVE YOUR COUNSELING RIGHT HERE.

During World War II, members of GRS units undergoing training were called "diggers," and two companies had pet mascots named Tombstone and Digger. In Vietnam, an unnamed—for obvious reasons—GREGG serviceman and his fellows used body bags to smuggle prostitutes into camp. When stopped at a checkpoint by a guard who, out of curiosity rather than concern for security, wanted to see the "body," he was persuaded to pass the vehicle through without unzipping the bag because he was told that the corpse had been out in the field and was full of maggots. William "Billy" Maloney, who served with the 114th GRS Company in Korea, told me that they had set up a tent called the "Rigor Mortis Inn." One can hardly fault these men for their attempts to relieve the emotional burden of their work, especially when they might—like Bob Vorisek, mentioned in chapter 6—find themselves at the bottom of a wet grave with remains floating to the surface of water-filled coffins, or, when lifting remains out overhead from graves dug 12 feet deep to keep polar bears from disinterring and eating the remains, have a coffin break open and spill decayed flesh and body fluids down on them.

Finding instances of lightness in a field that can be so dark further assured me that these are ordinary men and women who accomplish tasks that go unheralded, unnoticed, and mostly unappreciated. But, despite new attention paid to these workers, there are no selection processes in place to determine who is best equipped to take on what can be gruesome jobs, and there are no long-term studies on post-traumatic stress disorders associated with such duty. We can do better for these servicemen.

Finally, despite outreach programs by the DPMO and the various armed service branches, families are seldom asked what works best for them. The military still seems intent on deciding just what the next of kin need rather than instituting a feedback loop for their responses. We can do better for them, too.

[*Conclusion*]

Pile the bodies high at Austerlitz and Waterloo.
Shovel them under and let me work—
I am the grass; I cover all.
—CARL SANDBURG, "Grass"

FEW, IF ANY, endeavors match military service in terms of both potential rewards and potential losses. Political and military leaders have the burden of knowing that their decisions will often result in the certain death of men and women in their charge. Those who serve in the Armed Forces understand what duty means: they know that not only may they be harmed, but their lives may be forfeit, and they ask only that their efforts not be in vain and that they not be forgotten.

When soldiers die, our duty is to find them, give them a secure resting place and, when possible, identify them. In so doing, we preserve their place in history and assure our future. Winston Smith's job, in George Orwell's classic novel *1984*, was to eliminate written references to people who, for political reasons, had been eliminated in the flesh and were to be expunged from all texts; thus they were rendered "unpersons" and history was rewritten so that they never existed. By finding the mortal remains of those who have died in military service, we recognize their sacrifices and thereby keep them from becoming unpersons. They are our warriors, and they represent, on a national level, our belief system. On a personal level, they represent the willingness of individuals to support, protect, and even die for the values, ideals, and security of our nation-state. By bringing their remains home, we help bereaved families form a new social identity for them; by recognizing their contributions in our cemeteries and ceremonies, we attempt to give their sacrifice meaning.

When the United States first made the commitment to recover and return its military fallen, its ability to do so was not much more sophisticated than that of other countries. Battlefield interments were followed by large-scale sweeps after the Civil War, which gathered Union soldiers from their temporary burial locations and transferred them to permanent military graveyards. Later, as American involvement around the world grew, we learned how to bring our Soldier Dead back from foreign lands, even over the wishes of other countries, leaving only those who could not be found or those whose next of kin desired that they be buried where they fought and died.

After World War I and World War II, we searched for the fallen who were missing. These initial searches extended around the globe and lasted almost as long as the wars themselves. Eventually, the quest was officially ended, but the lost dead are not forgotten. When farmers, hunters, or others chance upon their remains, we still, when possible, identify and return them, thus providing a final disposition.

Searches for the dead after the Korean War were for many years hampered because of poor diplomatic relations—the communist government of North Korea severely limited and even prohibited access to territory it controlled. The fallen in these lands simply lay where they were while the natural actions of time and weather worked to reclaim their remains. After Vietnam, the U.S. public—and its political leaders—were so relieved to be no longer involved in that little-understood and misdirected war that they adopted an out of sight, out of mind attitude. The Missing and Presumed Dead got short shrift while the nation busied itself with forgetting—there was almost a collective amnesia about the war. Finally, after much political pressure was brought to bear, the government got around to old business, and attention was focused on those lost in Southeast Asia.

In Vietnam, Laos, and Cambodia, we developed new recovery and identification techniques to find and name remains of servicemen decades after their deaths. Eventually, and mostly because of the concern for soldiers unaccounted for from Vietnam, interest in World War II and Korean missing was renewed. There are more than seventy times as many missing from these conflicts as from Vietnam. The lessons learned in Southeast Asia were applied to battle and burial sites from World War II and the Korean War, and, as a result, relatives, often children of those long lost, are finally able to bury remains that have been returned to them.

As the acidic soil in Southeast Asia continues to eat away at bone fragments and as the "easy" cases—a relative term; none is really easy—are resolved, the focus may need to shift elsewhere. No political or military leader will go on record as saying, "There are only 100—or 200 or 300—soldiers left unaccounted for from Vietnam and we do not believe that we will ever be successful in recovering their remains," but improving relations with North Korea allows for more searches there, where remains are less fragmented and the soil less acidic. This change in emphasis on searching for unrecovered Soldier Dead has already been reflected in the merger of CILHI and JTF-FA into JPAC on October 1, 2003. Like many programs that have served their original purpose, the JTF-FA has quietly morphed into a new institution that will better reflect current realities.

During the Gulf War and the initial phase of the Iraq War, the numbers of American deaths were dramatically low—only slightly more than the number killed in just four days of battle in the Ia Drang Valley in Vietnam during the fall of 1965. And there is increased emphasis on accounting for all personnel. Still, two servicemen from the Gulf War were eventually determined to be KIA-BNR. Fortunately, and because of intensive search efforts, there are currently no unaccounted-for personnel from the Iraq War, although that situation could change as the "regime change" has not brought about the expected peace and U.S. soldiers are still dying.

Despite this progress, there are still families who carry open wounds. Some next of kin have found good reasons to doubt the veracity of government and military explanations about the fate of their loved ones. Others have found that the casualty reporting/communication methods and subsequent handling of personal effects and financial matters leave much to be desired. Many of the mishaps and insensitive actions they have experienced could be avoided, or at least alleviated, by more specialized training of personnel who have personal contact with the next of kin. This issue has yet to be fully addressed by Department of Defense officials.

Less obvious, but no less meaningful than the next-of-kin wounds are those carried by members of the Armed Forces who, in performing their duties, encounter death, whether on the battlefield or in support areas where Soldier Dead are identified and prepared for final disposition. The posttraumatic stress disorder (PTSD) they suffer is, like hypertension, a "silent killer." Soldiers with PTSD are walking wounded, carrying their burdens well into their subsequent civilian lives. Recent psychological work on the disorder, which began during World War I and expanded considerably during World War II, has shown the extent to which exposure to death and human remains adversely affects individuals. There is still much work to be done in refining methods of selecting, training, and supporting those who deal with the physical results of violence against human flesh and bone.

Since the Vietnam War, when body bags containing the remains of U.S. servicemen were displayed on television and in other media, our aversion to losing American lives has grown. Now, what has been called the "Dover Test," in which military gains are weighed against the vivid image of dead men and women being unloaded from air transports at Dover Air Force Base, has put political and military leaders in the unenviable position of trying to justify trading American lives for benefits that are intangible, questionable, or both.

In an effort to employ the use of force without sustaining large numbers of U.S. casualties, the military has developed new technologies that dispense death from unmanned Predator drones, aircraft remotely controlled by operators thousands of miles away. It is trying to develop similar technology for ground warfare. But even with advanced technology and tactics, such as in the Iraq War, the number of our dead—though small compared to those killed in previous wars and to enemy killed—still causes sufficient anguish among the public that leaders take steps to avoid the Dover Test. Banning the media from *all* places where the dead are transported is one such step.

It is not fair to saddle our government with the responsibility of protecting citizens by the use of force and at the same time hold it to an unattainable standard—doing so without losing lives. But, while our leaders must make tough decisions, they should not contrive to limit the visual impact of returning Soldier Dead so as to minimize discussion and dissent.

Finally, there is the issue of enemy dead. The United States has begun to cooperate with Japan and Vietnam on accounting for their missing. North Korea, which to date has not expressed much interest, may later become more concerned about recovering its huge numbers of missing soldiers. If it does, we will surely provide assistance, if for no other reason than to assure continued permission for American teams to search areas north of the 38th Parallel.

Iraq is another story entirely. In opposing Saddam Hussein, we did not enter into combat against machines only—we fought and killed other soldiers, and in large numbers. During and after the Gulf War, a bud of concern formed for the estimated 35,000 to 100,000 Iraqi dead. This bud of understanding, care, and compassion opened a little more during the Iraq War, when reporters wrote of quick and cursory burials on the battlefield and the many unburied dead along roadways, in bunkers, and in trenches.

But those stories are only the opening to a larger and more unpleasant dialogue. Since the military does not consider the information important, we do not know how many thousands—if not tens of thousands—of Iraqis have been killed during bombings and shelling and then buried, burned, or otherwise transformed to a state bearing little resemblance to the human beings they once were. At first, the military did not give body counts of enemy dead, saying that doing so in Vietnam had proved to be of questionable military value and that military gains in Iraq were not measured by the number of combatants killed. However, as public frustration and doubt about progress mounted, officials once again began to provide information on enemy fatalities in an attempt to show that America and its allies were "winning."

Fifteen months after the start of the Iraq War, and over a year after the end of "major combat operations," Arlington and private cemeteries across the United States continue to host solemn and tearful ceremonies in which a family openly grieves its loss, uniformed escorts and accompanying Armed Forces personnel say good-bye to a comrade-in-arms, and—though their attempts to digitize open psychic wounds usually fail—photographers struggle to capture the moment so the nation can know that another sacrifice has been made by one of its military members.

And across the world and in another land, these burials are echoed, in some form, a hundredfold. We seldom see those "other" images, though we would do well to be mindful of them. Despite the need to attain military objectives such as control over airspace and the subjugation of enemy forces, we must consider the consequences to our relations with a people who have also buried many of their own. If, as a warrior god, American military forces swoop down from the skies and smite our enemy without concern for loss of life or a reckoning of their dead, then—like Daniel Dravot in Kipling's "The Man Who Would Be King," who journeyed to a remote corner of Afghanistan to establish a kingdom for himself and who sought to impose a peace that he alone, wearing the trappings of a deity, could enforce—we will be unmasked for the men that we are and will pay a terrible price. If we do not ask or attempt to answer the question, "Was the cost in *all* lives worth it?" the unrecognized dead will haunt us forever.

Without doubt, it will be difficult to remove our battle dress and put on the garments of reconciliation, but we must resurrect the doctrine and policy that call for the honorable treatment of all enemy dead and follow the spirit, not just the letter, of regulations and agreements that call for the proper handling of those we kill. Officials and leaders who feel that devoting more resources to enemy dead either cannot or need not be done have only to study the past, when others holding similar positions initially opposed devoting more resources to our own dead. Ultimately, U.S. public spirit and desire will guide, if not dictate, the creation and subsequent implementation of a policy of more humane treatment and accounting for enemy dead.

Some believe that Armed Forces personnel, when they die, stand as silent sentinels over our freedom. As patriotic and moving as this seems, it is simply a fantasy. While the patriotic spirit that led our Soldier Dead to serve still exists and offers protection of our liberties, the dead have transcended the ordinary politics that resulted in their premature ends and claimed their futures; they have joined a society whose initiation rites are to die for others, and they are beyond our sensing and understanding. In forming of a postdeath identity for them that will carry us into a better future, we must face the humanity of our enemy as well. Then both American and enemy Soldier Dead may serve once again and help ensure that their ranks do not grow needlessly.

King George V, recognizing the cost of war in human lives, ended his tribute at Flanders thus:

> In the course of my pilgrimage, I have many times asked myself whether there can be more potent advocates of peace upon earth through the years to come, than this massed multitude of silent witnesses to the desolation of war.

Author's Notes

As I write this final paragraph in early summer 2004, American military personnel are engaged in an ongoing occupation of Iraq in which lives are lost daily. I subscribe to the DoD news e-mail list for updates of casualties, and every time my computer signals that I have a new message, I know that more often than not, it is a notice of another soldier killed. Is the cost worth it? This question is hotly debated on TV, in boardrooms, across bars and dinner tables, and, I hope, in White House and congressional offices. The United States and its coalition have attempted to establish a secular government in a region with a history of oppression by hereditary monarchs, religious fanatics, and simple thugs. No one will know the results for some time; the point is that our approach needs to be reexamined daily, and the scales of death should weigh *all* those killed, not just Americans, against what their deaths have accomplished.

The armed struggle in Iraq will not be our last. The ranks of Soldier Dead will continue to grow. In the meantime, I have done my best to tell about what happens to our soldiers after they die. I close with an account of a dream I had about three months after the first nighttime vision that launched me toward this book. I was in a junior high school, like one I attended: high ceilings, wide halls, red cement floor, putty-colored lockers, and windows across the top of the classroom walls. It was the period between classes; the students were out in the halls, and I floated above them, looking down at their preteen faces and bodies. All wore uniforms: white shirts, and khaki pants for boys and checked skirts for girls. A bell rang, and they all turned and walked toward one end of a hall and stood before a large black door. This door was different from the others in that it had no glass window or transom and no room number. The students all quieted down and stood attentively, waiting for it to open.

The meaning of the first vision was clear: "Go and find." The meaning of this dream still mostly eludes me. Even though there was no visual imagery obviously associated with my research at the time, I awoke with the feeling of connection to the story of Soldier Dead. My best interpretation now is that I, like the children who will be called upon to fight the next war, stood on a threshold, waiting for a door to open into a classroom unlike any I had been in before. When I first began this book, I thought that my fate was simply to tell of the heroic actions of others whose jobs begin when servicepersons die. Over time, I felt a slow and painful realization that my recounting of those details may have some small part to play in how well I, and the children in my dream, learn to face whatever is on the other side of that black door.

[Notes]

1. WHY IT MATTERS

1. Elizabeth Hallam, Jenny Hockey, and Glennys Howarth, *Beyond the Body: Death and Social Identity* (London: Routledge, 1999), 89.

2. Edward Steere, *The Graves Registration Service in World War II*, QMC Historical Studies, no. 21 (Washington, DC: U.S. Government Printing Office, 1951), 18.

3. Lt. Col. (then Sgt.) Charles D. Butte, *Graves Registration During World War II in Europe, 603rd Quartermaster Graves Registration Company*, 2. This document is held by the Quartermaster Museum in Fort Lee, Virginia.

4. Edward Steere and Thayer M. Boardman, *Final Disposition of World War II Dead: 1945–51*, QMC Historical Studies, series 2, no. 4 (Washington, DC: Historical Branch Office of the Quartermaster General, 1957), 185.

5. Maj. Scott T. Glass, "Mortuary Affairs Operations at Malmey—Lessons Learned from a Historic Tragedy," *Quartermaster Professional Bulletin—Autumn 1997*, http://www.qmfound.com/malmedy.htm (19 August 2001).

6. "U.S. fears soldiers executed: Blair also suspects Iraq killed two British POWs," http://www.msnbc.com/news/889604_asp.htm (27 March 2003).

7. "Pentagon: Bodies of missing soldiers found in raid," CNN.com/U.S. Special Report, 5 April 2003, http://www.cnn.com/2003/US/sprj.irq.soldiers.killed/ (4 September 2003). John W. Gonzales, "Last missing soldier found dead in Iraq," 29 April 2003, http://www.chron.com/cs/CDA/ssistory.mpl/metropolitan/1887820 (4 September 2003).

8. "U.S. military: Iraqis captured, murdered soldier in the 507th," *USA TODAY*, 28 May 2004, http://www.usatoday.com/news/world/iraq/2004-05-28-soldier-ambush_x.htm (29 May 2004).

9. J. M. Winter, *The Experience of World War I* (New York: Oxford University Press, 1995), 146.

10. Ibid.

11. John Ellis, *Eye-Deep in Hell: Trench Warfare in World War I* (1976; reprint, Baltimore: The Johns Hopkins University Press, 1989), 59.

12. E. B. Sledge, *With the Old Breed: At Peleliu and Okinawa* (1981; reprint, New York: Oxford University Press, 1990), 269.

13. Johnie Webb Jr., Deputy Director, U.S. Army Central Identification Laboratory Hawaii (CILHI), personal interview by author, Honolulu, Hawaii, 19 November 2002.

14. Marine Lt. Philip Caputo, *A Rumor of War* (1977; reprint, with a postscript by the author, New York: Henry Holt, 1996), xvii.

15. Ibid.

16. Sledge, *With the Old Breed*, 260.

17. Sledge, *With the Old Breed*, 269.

18. James Bradley with Ron Powers, *Flags of Our Fathers* (New York: Bantam, 2000), 175.

19. Richard Holmes, *Acts of War: Behavior of Men in Battle* (New York: The Free Press, 1985), 200.

20. Ibid.

21. Hallam, Hockey, and Howarth, *Beyond the Body*, 141.

22. James Tobin, *Ernie Pyle's War: America's Eyewitness to World War II* (New York: Free Press, 1997), 136.

23. Holmes, *Acts of War*, 202.

24. James Patrick Shenton, army medic, telephone interview by author, 21 June 2001.

25. Mark Bowden, *Black Hawk Down: A Story of Modern War* (New York: Penguin, 2000), 282.

26. Ibid., 338.

27. Shakespeare, *King Henry V*.

28. Homer, *The Iliad*, trans. E. V. Rieu (New York: Penguin, 1981), 313.

29. Ibid., 323.

30. Jance Lord, quoted in John D. Canine, Ed.D., Ph.D., *The Psychological Aspects of Death and Dying* (Stamford, CT: Appleton & Lange, 1996), 139.

31. Ibid., 110.

32. Hallam, Hockey, and Howarth, *Beyond the Body*, 4.

33. Paul Fussell, *Doing Battle: The Making of a Skeptic* (Boston: Little, Brown, 1996), 158.

34. Thucydides, *The Complete Writings of Thucydides, The Peloponnesian War*, trans. Richard Crawley, The Modern Library edition (New York: Random House, 1951), 108–109.

35. Wyoming Funeral Directors Association, *The Purpose of the Funeral*, http://www.wyfda.org/public/basics_5.html (3 August 2002).

36. John D. Canine, Ed.D., Ph.D., *The Psychological Aspects of Death and Dying* (Stamford, CT: Appleton & Lange, 1996), 100.

37. Hallam, Hockey, and Howarth, *Beyond the Body*, 62.

38. Associated Press, "WW-II MIA Buried at Arlington," *Canadian POW-MIA Information Newsletter*, vol. 2, April 1999, AP-Press Newswires Monday, 22 March 1999, http://www.ipsystems.com/powmia/New99/Arr1999.html (31 March 2001). (The U.S. government's use of classification sometimes has an important role in the efforts expended to acknowledge and/or retrieve the death of U.S. service personnel.)

39. Sheila Johnson, "Local Soldier's Grave Found after 54 Years," *The Times-Journal*, Fort Payne, Alabama, 29 May 1999, http://www.times-journal.com/archives/may9/5-29memorial.html (31 March 2001).

40. Associated Press, "Widow of Soldier to Spread Ashes off California Coast," *Four States—The Joplin Globe*, 27 August 1998, http://www.joplinglobe.com/1998/aug98/aug27/082798f5.html (31 March 2001).

41. Hallam, Hockey, and Howarth, *Beyond the Body*, 68.

42. Tom Morrow, "Old Marine Brings Closure for Japanese Family," *North County Times*, 20 August 2000, http://www.nctimes.com/news/082000/bbb.html (31 March 2001). (During World War II, the United States often buried Japanese dead in mass graves, if they buried them at all. Few resources were devoted to protecting the individual identities of Japanese casualties.)

43. Rick Hampson, "From Towers' Wreckage, Pieces of Lives Cut Short," *USA TODAY*, 15 July 2002, A1.

44. Chris Shilling, *The Body and Social Theory* (London: SAGE Publications, 1993), 73–74.

2. COMBAT RECOVERIES

1. Erna Risch, *Quartermaster Support of the Army: A History of the Corps 1775–1939* (Washington, DC: Center of Military History, U.S. Army, 1989), 463–64.

2. G. Kurt Piehler, *Remembering War the American Way* (Washington, DC: Smithsonian Institution Press, 1995), 41.

3. Edward Steere, *The Graves Registration Service in World War II*, QMC Historical Studies, no. 21 (Washington, DC: U.S. Government Printing Office, 1951), 4.

4. Ibid., 5.

5. Ibid., 7.

6. Ibid., 9.

7. Ibid.

8. Ibid., 10.

9. Ibid., 11.

10. Ibid., 12.

11. Ibid., 13.

12. Ibid., 13–14.

13. Ibid., 17.

14. Ibid., 18–19.

15. Ibid., 20.

16. Ibid., 90–92.

17. Lt. Col. John C. Cook, QMC, "Graves Registration in the Korean Conflict," *The Quartermaster Review*, March–April 1953, http://qmmuseum.lee.army.mil/korea/gr_korea.htm, 1–6 (2 February 2001).

18. Unpublished white paper, "Graves Registration Activities in The Korean War" (Quartermaster Historian's Office, Fort Lee, VA, 1954, photocopy), 79–80.

19. Tommy D. Bourlier, Director, and Douglas L. Howard, Deputy Director, U.S. Army Mortuary Affairs Center, personal interview by author, Fort Lee, VA, 25 June 2001.

20. Tommy D. Bourlier, "Graves Registration, Past, Present, Future," *Quartermaster Professional Bulletin* (September 1988):2.

21. Steere, *The Graves Registration Service in World War II*, , 22.

22. Jessica Mitford, *The American Way of Death Revisited* (New York: Vintage, 2000), 194.

23. Homer, *The Iliad*, trans. E. V. Rieu (New York: Penguin, 1981), 335.

24. http://www.defenselink.mil/news/Apr1999/m04161999_m057-99.html (2 February 2001).

25. Homer, *The Iliad*, 327.

26. *History of the American Graves Registration Service: QMC in Europe*, vol. 1 (Washington, DC: The Library Office of the Quartermaster General), 14–15. (This is a three-volume typescript, an official history prepared by the Cemeterial Division, OQMG.)

27. Letter from Charles J. Wynne, 2nd Lt. Inf. USA Commanding. Group #1 Unit, Unit 304 Graves Registration Service, J. Dell's Notes, *Graves Registration Service*, NARA, Record Group 92, 5–6.

28. James Tobin, *Ernie Pyle's War: America's Eyewitness to World War II* (New York: Free Press, 1997), 133–34.

29. The Virtual Wall is an impressive Web site honoring the fallen of Vietnam (http://www.thevirtualwall.org). Visitors can tour the Wall and search for the names of those who died. Clicking on the name provides a brief biography of the soldier and remembrances posted by friends and family.

30. Havery Sullivan, *Contact: Thirty Years Later: 1969*, http://www.lzsally.com/stories/contact30.html (September 2001).

31. Robert Black, "Closing the 'End of the Line,'" *Shipmate*, November 2000, http://usna.com/News_Pubs/Publications/Shipmate/2000/2000_11/closing.htm (22 July 2001).

32. Quoted in Steere, *The Graves Registration Service in World War II*, 76.

33. Steere, *The Graves Registration Service in World War II*, 105.

34. Lt. Ronald A. Milton, *Company History: 603 QM. GR. REG. CO., 1943–1945*, National Archives and Records Administration, College Park, MD, Record Group 92, 32.

35. Col. (then Sgt.) Elbert E. Legg, *Graves Registration in Normandie France, June 1944, 603 Quartermaster Graves Registration Company With The 82nd Airborne Division*, 7. This document is held by the Quartermaster Museum in Fort Lee, Virginia.

36. Ibid., 9.

37. Charles Phillips and Alan Axelrod, *Portraits of the Civil War: In Photographs, Diaries, and Letters* (New York: Barnes & Noble, 1993), 108.

38. *Personal Memoirs of U.S. Grant*, vol. 2 (New York: Charles L. Webster & Company, 1892), 275.

39. Joseph James Shomon, *Crosses in the Wind* (New York: Stratford House, 1947), 34.

40. Steere, *The Graves Registration Service in World War II*, 52.

41. Retired Lt. Col. (then Sgt.) Charles D. Butte, *Graves Registration During World War II in Europe, 603rd Quartermaster Graves Registration Company*, 8. This document is held by the Quartermaster Museum in Fort Lee, Virginia.

42. Ibid., 9.

43. *Unit History, 601st QM. CO.*, 3 May 1944, National Archives and Records Administration, College Park, MD, 601st diary Record Group 94.

44. Steere, *The Graves Registration Service in World War II*, 92.

45. Steere, *The Graves Registration Service in World War II*, 92.

46. Lt. Ronald A. Milton, *Company History: 603rd QM. GR. REG. CO., 1943–1945*, National Archives and Records Administration, College Park, MD, Record Group 92, 45.

47. Ibid., 45–46.

48. *Unit History, 601st QM. CO.*, 5 May 1944.

49. James Patrick Shenton, army medic, telephone interview by author, Shreveport, LA, 21 June 2001.

50. Pfc. Doug Michaud, interview by Donald Knox, *The Korean War: An Oral History, Pusan to Chosin* (New York: Harcourt Brace, 1985), 532.

51. Pfc. Robert E. Helman, telephone interview by author, 21 July 2001.

52. Unpublished white paper, "Graves Registration Activities in The Korean War," 82–83.

53. Al Santoli, *Everything We Had: An Oral History of the Vietnam War by Thirty-three American Soldiers Who Fought It* (New York: Ballantine, 1981), 3.

54. Ibid., 154.

55. James C. Harton Jr., "Water and Ammo in, Bodies Out," http://grunt.space.swri.edu/jhwatbod.htm (4 June 2002).

56. Lt. Gen. Harold G. Moore (retired) and Joseph L. Galloway, *We Were Soldiers Once . . . and Young* (New York: Harper Perennial, 1993), 126.

57. http://www.army.mil/usar/history/weekly/2001/week05.html.

58. *FM-1064 Mortuary Affairs Operations*, Headquarters, Department of the Army, Washington, DC, 16 February 1999, 2–1:2–2.

59. Tommy D. Bourlier, Director, U.S. Army Mortuary Affairs Center, personal interview by author, Fort Lee, VA, 25 June 2001.

60. Grant N. Marshall, Lois M. Davis, and Cathy D. Sherbourne, *A Review of the Scientific Literature as It Pertains to the Gulf War Illnesses*, vol. 4: "Stress," Rand Publication Database, http://www.rand.org/publications/MR/MR1018.4.1/, 59 (4 June 2002).

61. James E. McCarroll, Ph.D., et al., "Gruesomeness, Emotional Attachment, and Personal Threat: Dimensions of the Anticipated Stress of Body Recovery," *Journal of Traumatic Stress* 8 (2) (1995) (http://www.usuhs.mil/psy/gruesomeness.html), 3 (8 June 2002).

62. Patricia B. Sutker, et al., "Psychopathology in War-Zone Deployed and Nondeployed Operation Desert Storm Troops Assigned Graves Registration Duties," *Journal of Abnormal Psychology* 103 (2) (1994): 389.

3. NONCOMBAT RECOVERIES

1. Maj. William R. White, QMC, "Our Soldier Dead," *The Quartermaster Review*, May–June 1930, http://www.qmfound.com/soldier_dead.htm, 2 (4 March 2001).

2. http://usabmc.com/abmc44.htm (14 October 2001).

3. *History of the American Graves Registration Service: QMC in Europe*, vol. 1 (Washington, DC: The Library Office of the Quartermaster General), 29. This is a three-volume typescript, an official history prepared by the Cemeterial Division, OQMG.

4. J. Dell's notes, *Graves Registration Service*, National Archives and Records Administration, College Park, MD, Record Group 92, 10.

5. *Historical Report of the Chief Quartermaster, AEF, 1917–1919*, National Archives and Records Administration, College Park, VA, Record Group 92, 435. This report is a rough draft of the activities of the QMC in Europe during and after World War I.

6. J. Dell's notes, *Graves Registration Service*, 1.

7. *History of the American Graves Registration Service: QMC in Europe*, vol. 1, 36–37.

8. Edward Steere and Thayer M. Boardman, *Final Disposition of World War II Dead: 1945–51*, QMC Historical Studies, series 2, no. 4 (Washington, DC: Historical Branch Office of the Quartermaster General, 1957), 193–94.

9. Ibid., 186–88.

10. Ibid., 205.

11. Ibid., 208.

12. Ibid., 239–46.

13. Ibid., 254.

14. Ibid., 256.

15. Sgt. Herbert E. Hackett, telephone interview by author, 3 October 2002.

16. Steere and Boardman, *Final Disposition of World War II Dead: 1945–51*, 257–63.

17. Steere and Boardman, *Final Disposition of World War II Dead: 1945–51*,, 272.

18. Web site maintained by Sue Veldkamp, niece of 2nd Lt. John M. Buxton (deceased), http://www.matschca.com/jack/missing7.html (2 February 2002).

19. Steere and Boardman, *Final Disposition of World War II Dead: 1945–51*, , 594.

20. Quoted in Steere and Boardman, *Final Disposition of World War II Dead: 1945–51*, 596.

21. Steere and Boardman, *Final Disposition of World War II Dead: 1945–51*, 599.

22. Steere and Boardman, *Final Disposition of World War II Dead: 1945–51*, 551–54.

23. Steere and Boardman, *Final Disposition of World War II Dead: 1945–51*, 564.

24. Steere and Boardman, *Final Disposition of World War II Dead: 1945–51*, 566–67.

25. Steere and Boardman, *Final Disposition of World War II Dead: 1945–51*, 567.

26. Steere and Boardman, *Final Disposition of World War II Dead: 1945–51*, 610.

27. Edward Steere, *The Graves Registration Service in World War II*, QMC Historical Studies, no. 21 (Washington, DC: United States Government Printing Office, 1951), 156.

28. Steere and Boardman, *Final Disposition of World War II Dead: 1945–51*, 392.

29. Steere and Boardman, *Final Disposition of World War II Dead: 1945–51*, 395.

30. Steere and Boardman, *Final Disposition of World War II Dead: 1945–51*, 444.

31. Steere and Boardman, *Final Disposition of World War II Dead: 1945–51*, 457–62.

32. Steere and Boardman, *Final Disposition of World War II Dead: 1945–51*, 447.

33. Steere and Boardman, *Final Disposition of World War II Dead: 1945–51*, 468–70.

34. Steere and Boardman, *Final Disposition of World War II Dead: 1945–51*, 473–75.

35. Steere and Boardman, *Final Disposition of World War II Dead: 1945–51*, 480–82.

36. Lt. Col. John C. Cook, QMC, "Graves Registration in the Korean Conflict," *The Quartermaster Review*, March/April 1953, http://www.qmmuseum.lee.army.mil/korea/gr_korea.htm (9 February 2001).

37. "The Effort to Account for U.S. Servicemen Missing from the Korean War," http://www.aiipowmia.com/koreacw/kwrept1.html, 16 (15 February 2002).

38. "Operation Glory," condensed from Graves Registration Division, Korean Communications Zone (KCOMZ) *Historical Summary*, July–December 1954, http://www.qmmuseum.lee.army.mil/korea/op_glory.htm (19 February 2001).

39. "The Effort to Account for U.S. Servicemen Missing from the Korean War," http://www.aiipowmia.com/koreacw/kwrept1.html, 17 (15 February 2002).

40. "Search and Recovery," *The Quartermaster Review,* July/August 1954, http://www.qmfound.com/search_and_recovery_korea.htm (9 February 2001).

41. Pfc. Fred Fory, telephone interview by author, 2 February 2001.

42. "Memorial Affairs Activities—Republic of Vietnam," Mortuary Affairs Center (MAC), Fort Lee, VA, March 2000, http://www.qmmuseum.lee.army.mil/mortuary/MA-Vietnam.htm (16 February 2002).

43. Lt. Gen. Harold G. Moore (retired) and Joseph L. Galloway, *We Were Soldiers Once . . . and Young* (New York: Harper Perennial, 1993), 9.

44. Ibid., 230.

45. Ibid., 228.

46. Quoted in ibid., 337.

47. Ibid., 377–78.

48. Ibid., 378.

49. Ibid., 378.

50. Paul D. Mather, *M.I.A.: Accounting for the Missing in Southeast Asia* (Washington, DC: National Defense University Press, 1994), 10.

51. Ibid., 10–11.

52. Ibid., 15–16.

53. Ibid., 10–14.

54. David Lynch, "Entering War, U.S. Planners Made Two Key Assumptions," *USA TODAY,* 3 April 2003, 2A.

55. Steere and Boardman, *Final Disposition of World War II Dead: 1945–51,* 566.

56. Mather, *M.I.A.,* 20.

57. Mather, *M.I.A.,* 21–26.

58. Mather, *M.I.A.,* 26–29.

59. Mather, *M.I.A.,* 136–40.

60. "Remains of Korean War Soldier Return to U.S.," *Defense Link News,* Reference Number: No. 447–96, 26 July 1996, htp://defenselink.mil/news/Jul1996/b072696_bt447–96.html (15 August 2002).

61. Defense Prisoner of War/Missing Personnel Office (DPMO) and United States Army Central Identification Laboratory, Hawaii (CILHI), *Fiscal Year 2000 World War II Report to Congress,* 7.

62. Ibid., 17.

63. David Roath, Director, United States Army Memorial Affairs Activity Europe (USAMAA-E), personal interview by author, Landstuhl, Germany, 12 February 2003.

64. Darrin Peschka, "Burial to End Buddy's Long Search for Pilot," *Ottawa Herald,* Ottawa, Kansas, 16–17 September 2000, 1A. Also, Jack Curtis (formerly Lt.), telephone interview by author.

65. Letter from Robert L. Jones, Deputy Assistant Secretary of Defense, POW/Missing Personnel Affairs, to Jack T. Curtis, Rogers, AR, 13 October 2000.

66. *History of the American Graves Registration Service: QMC in Europe,* vol. 3, 76–77.

67. *History of the American Graves Registration Service: QMC in Europe,* vol. 3, 96–97.

68. It is common parlance to describe lives lost in an airplane crash as "souls."

69. Capt. Brooks Brenkus, "54th Quartermaster Company (Mortuary Affairs), 11 Sep. 2001–11 Nov. 2001, http://www.quartermaster.army.mil/oqmg/Professional_Bulletin/2002/Winter02/54th_QM_Co_MA.htm (7 April 2003).

70. Susan Sontag, "Looking at War: Photography's View of Devastation and Death," *The New Yorker*, 9 December 2002, 83, 90.

4. IDENTIFICATION

1. Capt. Richard W. Wooley, "History of the Dog Tag," http://www.173rdairborne.com/dogtag.htm (17 December 2002).

2. Edward Steere, *The Graves Registration Service in World War II*, QMC Historical Studies, no. 21 (Washington, DC: United States Government Printing Office, 1951), 6.

3. David Roath, Director, United States Army Memorial Affairs Activity Europe (USAMAA-E), "FM 10–286," e-mail to author, 23 December 2002.

4. *Welcome to . . . the Department of Defense DNA Registry*, http://www.afip.org/Departments.oafme.dna/history.htm (5 July 2001).

5. "Repository History," http://www.afip.org/Departments/oafme/dna/history.htm (4 January 2002); James J. Canik, Deputy Director, Armed Forces DNA Identification Laboratory (AFDIL), telephone interview by author, 7 January 2003.

6. Canik, telephone interview by author, 7 January 2003.

7. *History of the American Graves Registration Service: QMC. in Europe*, vol. 1 (Washington, DC: The Library Office of the Quartermaster General), 46. (This is a three-volume typescript, an official history prepared by the Cemeterial Division, OQMG.)

8. Ibid., 21.

9. *History of the American Graves Registration Service: QMC. in Europe*, vol. 3, 111.

10. *Graves Registration*, Technical Manual 10–630 (Washington, DC: War Department, 23 September 1941), sec. 4, par. 22.h–22.i, 16–17.

11. Ibid., sec. 5, par. 25.e, 24.

12. Edward Steere and Thayer M. Boardman, *Final Disposition of World War II Dead: 1945–51*, QMC Historical Studies, series 2, no. 4 (Washington, DC: Historical Branch Office of the Quartermaster General, 1957), 614–18.

13. Ibid., 631–32.

14. Ibid., 639.

15. The U.S. Army Central Identification Laboratory Hawaii (CILHI), "CILHI History," http://www.cilhi.army.mil/unithistory.htm (12 December 2002).

16. William R. Belcher, Ph.D., R.P.A., forensic anthropologist at the U.S. Army Central Identification Laboratory Hawaii (CILHI), personal interview by author, Honolulu, Hawaii, 19 November 2002.

17. *The Effort to Account for U.S. Servicemen Missing from the Korean War*, Defense Prisoner of War/Missing Personnel Office, 11 November 2000, 21; Ginger L. Couden, Public Affairs Spokeswoman, U.S. Army Central Identification Laboratory Hawaii (CILHI), "Question List for Dr. Holland," e-mail to author, 9 January 2003.

18. Col. Richard Dillon, Mortuary Affairs Officer, 377th Theater Support Command in Kuwait, telephone interview by author, 11 February 2003.

19. *Graves Registration*, Technical Manual 10–630, sec. 2, par. 6, 4.

20. *History of the American Graves Registration Service: QMC in Europe*, vol. 3, 65.

21. Unpublished white paper, "Graves Registration Activities in the Korean War" (Quartermaster Historian's Office, Fort Lee, VA, 1954, photocopy), 114.

22. Col. Thomas O. Rexrode (retired), telephone interview by author, 16 December 2002.

23. *History of the American Graves Registration Service: QMC in Europe*, vol. 3, 66.

24. *Historical Report of the Chief Quartermaster, AEF: 1917–1919*, National Archives and Records Administration, College Park, MD, Record Group 92, chap. 9, 439. (This report is a rough draft of the activities of the QMC in Europe during and after World War I.)

25. Steere and Boardman, *Final Disposition of World War II Dead: 1945–51*, 618.

26. *History of the American Graves Registration Service: QMC. in Europe*, vol. 1, 25.

27. *Graves Registration*, Technical Manual 10–630, sec. 3, par. 15, 9.

28. Senior Master Sergeant (now Chief Master Sergeant) Gina Nolan, Life Support Wreckage Analysis Branch, Joint Task Force Full Accounting (JTF-FA), personal interview by author, Honolulu, Hawaii, 19 November 2002.

29. *History of the American Graves Registration Service: QMC in Europe*, vol. 2, 46.

30. Steere and Boardman, *Final Disposition of World War II Dead: 1945–51*, 398.

31. Unpublished white paper, "Graves Registration Activities in the Korean War," 84.

32. Sgt. David Paul Gregg, 243rd Field Service Company, telephone interview by author, 17 November 2002.

33. The U.S. Army Central Identification Laboratory Hawaii (CILHI), "How Forensic Odontology Helps in the Identification Process," http://www.cilhi.army.mil/makinraidersforodon.htm (2 February 2001).

34. Robert W. Mann, Ph.D., forensic anthropologist at the U.S. Army Central Identification Laboratory Hawaii (CILHI), personal interview by author, Honolulu, Hawaii, 19 November 2002.

35. *Graves Registration*, Technical Manual 10–630, sec. 5, par. 25.e, 24.

36. *Identification of Deceased Personnel*, Field Manual 10–286, chap. 2 (Washington, DC: Headquarters, Department of the Army, 30 June 1976), sec. 2, par. 2–8.e–f, 5.

37. Ibid., app. G, 1–36.

38. Marine Lt. Philip Caputo, *A Rumor of War* (1977; reprint, with a postscript by the author, New York: Henry Holt, 1996), 169.

39. Steere, *The Graves Registration Service in World War II*, 5.

40. *History of the American Graves Registration Service: QMC. in Europe*, vol. 3, 65–66.

41. David D. Thompson, "Forensic Anthropology," *A History of American Physical Anthropology 1930–1980*, ed. Frank Spencer, chap. 15 (New York: Academic Press, 1982), 358–359.

42. *Army Regulations No. 30–1810*, originally issued 1 February 1924 and superseded on 8 December 1944, par. 7, 3.

43. Thompson, "Forensic Anthropology," 357–61.

44. Charles P. Warren, "Forensic Anthropology in a Military Setting," *Human Organization* 40 (2) (Summer 1981): 173.

45. Thompson, "Forensic Anthropology," 362.

46. Warren, "Forensic Anthropology in a Military Setting," 175.

47. Warren, "Forensic Anthropology in a Military Setting," 175.

48. Warren, "Forensic Anthropology in a Military Setting," 176.

49. Unpublished white paper, "Graves Registration Activities in the Korean War," 108–14.

50. *AFDIL . . . about us . . . mtDNA*, Armed Forces Institute of Pathology Web site, http://www.afip.org/Departments/oafme/dna/mtdna.htm (10 March 2001).

51. Robert W. Mann, Ph.D., personal interview by author, Honolulu, Hawaii, 19 November 2002.

52. Christopher C. Kelly, Public Affairs Officer, Armed Forces Institute of Pathology (AFIP), "Operation Noble Eagle: Forensic Dentistry Plays Essential Role Following Pentagon Terrorist Crash," *AFIP Letter* 159 (5) (October 2001): 7.

53. Michele Hammonds and Christopher C. Kelly, Public Affairs Officers, Armed Forces Institute of Pathology (AFIP), "Operation Noble Eagle: DNA Laboratory Plays Key Role in Pentagon, Somerset County Victim Identifications," *AFIP Letter* 159 (5) (October 2001): 4.

54. Army Regulation 638–2 (AR 638–2), *Deceased Personnel: Care and Disposition of Remains and Disposition of Personal Effects*, chap. 8, par. 8–14 (Washington, DC: Headquarters, Department of the Army, 22 December 2000), 46.

55. *Repository History*, http://www.afip.org/Departments/oafme/dna/history.htm (4 January 2003).

56. Unpublished white paper, "Graves Registration Activities in the Korean War," 118–19.

57. The U.S. Army Central Identification Laboratory Hawaii (CILHI), *Overview of the CILHI Laboratory*, http://www.cilhi.army.mil/laboratory.htm (16 January 2003).

58. Doug Arendt, "Operation Noble Eagle: Electronic Mass Disaster Dental Identification Triage Utilized Following Pentagon Attack," *AFIP Letter* 159 (5) (October 2001): 8.

59. James J. Canik, Deputy Director, Armed Forces DNA Identification Laboratory (AFDIL), "One Question . . . near the end, I think," e-mail to author, 13 January 2003.

60. Thomas D. Holland, Ph.D., Scientific Director, U.S. Army Central Identification Laboratory-Hawaii (CILHI), personal interview by author, Honolulu, Hawaii, 19 November 2002.

61. Johnie Webb, Deputy Director, U.S. Army Central Identification Laboratory Hawaii (CILHI), telephone conversation with author, May 2003; Ginger L. Couden, Public Affairs Spokeswoman, U.S. Army Central Identification Laboratory Hawaii (CILHI), "Scientific Breakthroughs Aid in Identifying Korean War Unknown," e-mail to author, 21 May 2003.

62. Steere, *The Graves Registration Service in World War II*, 208.

63. Quartermaster Foundation, "Tragedy at Gander," http://www.qmfound.com/gander.html, 2 (30 December 2002).

64. Karen Giles, Director of Mortuary Affairs, Dover Air Force Base, personal interview by author, 6 August 2003.

65. *POW/MIA AFFAIRS: Issues Related to the Identification of Human Remains From the Vietnam Conflict*, United States General Accounting Office Report to the Chairman and Vice Chairman, Select Committee on POW/MIA Affairs, U.S. Senate, October 1992, 40.

66. *History of the American Graves Registration Service: QMC in Europe*, vol. 1, 5.

67. *History of the American Graves Registration Service: QMC in Europe*, vol. 3, 83.

68. *History of the American Graves Registration Service: QMC in Europe*, vol. 3, 120–21.

69. Steere and Boardman, *Final Disposition of World War II Dead: 1945–51*, 66–67.

70. Unpublished white paper, "Graves Registration Activities in the Korean War," 75.

71. Donald M. Rothberg, "Assuming Nothing," *The VVA Veteran*, Vietnam Veterans of America, Inc., Web site, http://www.vva.org/TheVeteran/2001_09/mortuary.html, 2–3 (4 June 2002).

72. Sgt. David Paul Gregg, 243rd Field Service Company, telephone interview by author, 17 November 2002.

73. Nina Thomas, "Stranger's Grave," *The Online Gray Edition News*, 1 May 1998, http://www.graynews.maine.com/1998-05-01/stranger_s_grave.html (31 March 2001).

74. Letter from Alvin R. Sammon to Senator Richard B. Russell, 30 May 1944, Memorandum from R. P. Harbold, Memorial Division, OQMC, to Congressional Section, G.A.S., 5 June 1944, National Archives Record Group 92.

75. Steere and Boardman, *Final Disposition of World War II Dead: 1945–51*, 647.

76. *History of the American Graves Registration Service: QMC in Europe*, vol. 3, 57–71.

77. *History of the American Graves Registration Service: QMC in Europe*, vol. 3, 78–80.

78. *POW/MIA AFFAIRS: Issues Related to the Identification of Human Remains From the Vietnam Conflict*, 59.

79. "Tell Me About My Boy," compiled by the Quartermaster General under the supervision of the War Department Public Relations Division, 1 December 1946, 12.

80. Johnnie Parrish, brother of Sfc. Frank Parrish, telephone interview by author, 21 January 2003.

81. Ken Thorbourne, "He's 'AWOL' No Longer," *The Jersey Journal*, 6 March 2004, http://www.nj.com/news/jjournal/index.ssf?/base/news-2/107856785962741.xml (11 March 2004).

82. Harvey J. Andrews, Ph.D., Consultant, Senate Foreign Relations Committee, State of Oklahoma House Veterans Committee, http://www.aiipowmia.com/testimony/handrws.html (23 January 2003).

83. Dr. Steven Byers, Ph.D., "Morphological Approximation—CILHI," e-mail to author, 3 February 2003.

84. William R. Maples, Ph.D. and Michael Browning, *Dead Men Do Tell Tales* (New York: Doubleday, 1994), 200–201.

85. Dr. Madeleine J. Hinkes, Ph.D., "Ellis Kerley's Service to the Military," *Journal of Forensic Science* 46 (4) (2001): 782–783; Dr. Madeleine J. Hinkes, Ph.D., telephone interview by author, spring 2003.

86. Thomas D. Holland, Ph.D., personal interview by author, Honolulu, Hawaii, 19 November 2002.

87. *History of the American Graves Registration Service: QMC in Europe*, vol. 3, 82–85.

88. Steere and Boardman, *Final Disposition of World War II Dead: 1945–51*, 625–26.

89. Army Regulation 638–2 (AR 638–2), *Deceased Personnel: Care and Disposition of Remains and Disposition of Personal Effects*, chap. 8, par. 8–, 47.

90. Secretary of Defense William S. Cohen, DoD News Briefing, 30 June 1998, 1 p.m., http://www.defenselink.mil/news/Jul1998/t07011997_t0630cohen.html (2 February 2001).

91. *Background Paper on the Activities of the Department of Defense Senior Working Group on The Vietnam Unknown in the Tomb of the Unknown Soldiers*, http://www. defenselink.mil/news/fact_sheets/vubackgr.htm (2 February 2001).

92. Ibid.; DoD News Briefing, 27 April 1998, 12:40 p.m., Subject: Tomb of the Unknown Soldier, http://www.defenselink.mil/news/Apr1998/t04281998_tietunk_html (2 February 2001); Kenneth Bacon, ASD (PA), DoD News Briefing, 7 May 1998, 1:30 p.m., http://www.defenselink.mil/news/May1998/t05071998_t0507asd.html (2 February 2001).

93. Maples and Browning, *Dead Men Do Tell Tales*, 206.

94. *POW/MIA AFFAIRS: Issues Related to the Identification of Human Remains From the Vietnam Conflict*, 57–58.

95. *POW/MIA AFFAIRS: Issues Related to the Identification of Human Remains From the Vietnam Conflict*, 57.

96. J. Jarrett Clinton, M.D., M.P.H., Acting Assistant Secretary of Defense (Health Affairs), Memorandum for Assistant Secretary of the Army, Assistant Secretary of the Navy, and Assistant Secretary of the Air Force, 9 July 2001, posted at http://www.afip.org/Departments/oafme/dna/images/copyofafrssir3.gif (4 January 2003).

5. THE RETURN OF THE DEAD

1. G. Kurt Piehler, *Remembering War the American Way* (Washington, DC: Smithsonian Institution Press, 1995), 94.

2. *History of the American Graves Registration Service: QMC in Europe*, vol. 1 (Washington, DC: The Library Office of the Quartermaster General), 10. (This is a three-volume typescript, an official history prepared by the Cemeterial Division, OQMG.)

3. Ibid.

4. Ibid., 9.

5. Letter from Lt. Col. Charles C. Pierce, QMC, USA, to Chief, Quartermaster, AEF, 11 April 1919, National Archives and Records Administration, College Park, MD, Record Group 92, 3.

6. Piehler, *Remembering War the American Way*, 96.

7. Policy statement by Newton D. Baker, Secretary of War, 15 January 1920, National Archives and Records Administration, College Park, MD, Record Group 92.

8. "Plea for Our Dead in France," *The New York Times*, 15 April 1921, front page.

9. Letter from Rep. C. C. Dickinson to John W. Weeks, Secretary of War, 20 April 1921, National Archives and Records Administration, College Park, MD, Record Group 92.

10. Letter from William Henry Dennis to Col. Charles C. Pierce, Chief, Graves Registration Service, Washington, DC, 19 April 1921, containing a copy of letter by same to the editor, *The New York Times*, 18 April 1921, National Archives, Record Group 92.

11. Letter from John W. Weeks, Secretary of War, to Hon. C. C. Dickinson, 4 May 1921, National Archives and Records Administration, College Park, MD, Record Group 92.

12. Memorandum from Col. C. C.Reynolds, QMC, Assistant, to the Adjutant General, 9 December 1941, National Archives and Records Administration, College Park, MD, Record Group 92.

13. Memorandum by Maj. Gen. Emory S. Adams, the Adjutant General, War Department, 13 December 1941, National Archives and Records Administration, College Park, MD, Record Group 92.

14. Edward Steere, *The Graves Registration Service in World War II*, QMC Historical Studies, no. 21 (Washington, DC: United States Government Printing Office, 1951), 187.

15. Letter from Maj. Gen. J. A. Ulio, the Adjutant General, War Department, to Director, Military Personnel Division, 13 March 1943, National Archives and Records Administration, College Park, MD, Record Group 92.

16. Letter from J. M. Clack to Hon. Estes Kefauver, undated but just prior to 17 March 1943, National Archives and Records Administration, College Park, MD, Record Group 92.

17. Letter from Rep. Estes Kefauver to Maj. Gen. James A. Ulio, the Adjutant General, War Department, 24 February 1943, National Archives and Records Administration, College Park, MD, Record Group 92.

18. Memorandum by Maj. Gen. J. A. Ulio, the Adjutant General, War Department, 29 April 1943, National Archives and Records Administration, College Park, MD, Record Group 92.

19. Steere, *The Graves Registration Service in World War II*, 180.

20. Steere, *The Graves Registration Service in World War II*, 179.

21. Edward Steere and Thayer M. Boardman, *Final Disposition of World War II Dead: 1945–51*, QMC Historical Studies, series 2, no. 4 (Washington, DC: Historical Branch Office of the Quartermaster General, 1957), 15–16.

22. Ibid., 31.

23. Ibid., 39–40.

24. Unpublished white paper, "Graves Registration Activities in the Korean War" (Quartermaster Historian's Office, Fort Lee, VAa, 1954, photocopy), 34.

25. Dr. Steven E. Anders, "With All Due Honors: A History of the Quartermaster Graves Registration Mission," *Quartermaster Professional Bulletin* (September 1988): 25.

26. *Joint Pub 4–06: Joint Tactics, Techniques, and Procedures for Mortuary Affairs in Joint Operations* (no publisher listed; available on military Web sites), 28 August 1996, I-3.

27. *History of the American Graves Registration Service: QMC in Europe*, vol. 2, 52.

28. Memorandum from Lt. Col. Charles C. Pierce, U.S. Army, Chief, Cemeterial Division, to the Quartermaster General, U.S. Army, 14 December 1920, National Archives, Record Group 92.

29. *Joint Pub 4–06*, I-2.

30. "Tell Me About My Boy," compiled by the Quartermaster General under the supervision of the War Department Public Relations Division, 1 December 1946, 4–5.

31. WD AGO Form from Compton (first name not in document) at the General Counsel to Col. Zwicker of the Memorial Division, 19 December 1945, National Archives and Records Administration, College Park, MD, Record Group 92.

32. Memorandum from Capt. M. N. Greeley, QMC, Executive Officer, Cemeterial Division, to Chief, American GRS, QMC, in Europe, 25 January 1921, National Archives and Records Administration, College Park, MD, Record Group 92.

33. Letter from 1st Lt. C. M. Noetzel, QMC, to Col. Davis, 14 April 1920, National Archives and Records Administration, College Park, MD, Record Group 92.

34. Memorandum from Col. Charles C. , U.S. Army, Chief, Cemeterial Division, to 1st Lt. C. M. Noetzel, 20 April 1920, National Archives and Records Administration, College Park, MD, Record Group 92.

35. Report by the Quartermaster General of the Army, 1900, National Archives and Records Administration, College Park, MD, Record Group 92, 84.

36. Steere and Boardman, *Final Disposition of World War II Dead: 1945–51*, 345.

37. *History of the American Graves Registration Service: QMC. in Europe*, vol. 1, 6.

38. *History of the American Graves Registration Service: QMC in Europe*, vol. 1, 118.

39. *History of the American Graves Registration Service: QMC in Europe*, vol. 1, 119.

40. *History of the American Graves Registration Service: QMC in Europe*, vol. 1), 124–26.

41. *History of the American Graves Registration Service: QMC. in Europe*, vol. 1, 154.

42. *History of the American Graves Registration Service: QMC. in Europe*, vol. 1, 159–60.

43. Letter from Lt. Col. J. A. Moss, Infantry, Commanding, to Chief, AGRS, QMC in Europe, 12 October 1920, National Archives and Records Administration, College Park, MD, Record Group 92.

44. *History of the American Graves Registration Service: QMC in Europe*, vol. 1, 64.

45. *History of the American Graves Registration Service: QMC in Europe*, vol. 1, 184–85.

46. *History of the American Graves Registration Service: QMC in Europe*, vol. 3, 133–38.

47. James Paul and Martin Spirit, "The Falklands War Page of Remembrance," http://www.britains-smallwars.com/Falklands/roh.html, 28 July 2001.

48. *History of the American Graves Registration Service: QMC in Europe*, vol. 1, 156.

49. *History of the American Graves Registration Service: QMC in Europe*, vol. 1, 38.

50. *History of the American Graves Registration Service: QMC in Europe*, vol. 1, 196.

51. *History of the American Graves Registration Service: QMC in Europe*, vol. 1, 197–99.

52. *History of the American Graves Registration Service: QMC in Europe*, vol. 3, 44–45.

53. Steere and Boardman, *Final Disposition of World War II Dead: 1945–51*, 474.

54. Steere and Boardman, *Final Disposition of World War II Dead: 1945–51*, 251.

55. Paul D. Mather, *M.I.A.: Accounting for the Missing in Southeast Asia* (Washington, DC: National Defense University Press, 1994), 9.

56. Memorandum by Newton D. Baker, Secretary of War, 15 January 1920, National Archives and Records Administration, College Park, MD, Record Group 92.

57. Steere and Boardman, *Final Disposition of World War II Dead: 1945–51*, 521.

58. Steere, *The Graves Registration Service in World War II*, 179.

59. Steere and Boardman, *Final Disposition of World War II Dead: 1945–51*, v.

60. *History of the American Graves Registration Service: QMC in Europe*, vol. 2, 34.

61. GRS Form #120, Shipping Inquiry, from Chief, Graves Registration Service, QMC, to Elsie Michael, 7 June 1920, National Archives and Records Administration, College Park, MD, Record Group 92.

62. *History of the American Graves Registration Service: QMC in Europe*, vol. 2, 54.

63. Steere and Boardman, *Final Disposition of World War II Dead: 1945–51*, 41.

64. Steere and Boardman, *Final Disposition of World War II Dead: 1945–51*, 79–80.

65. *History of the American Graves Registration Service: QMC. in Europe*, vol. 1, 55–57.

66. Steere and Boardman, *Final Disposition of World War II Dead: 1945–51*, 93–117.

67. *History of the American Graves Registration Service: QMC in Europe*, vol. 1, 101.

68. *History of the American Graves Registration Service: QMC in Europe*, vol. 1, 103.

69. Steere and Boardman, *Final Disposition of World War II Dead: 1945–51*, 16.

70. *History of the American Graves Registration Service: QMC in Europe*, vol. 1, 145–46.

71. *History of the American Graves Registration Service: QMC in Europe*, vol. 1, 191.

72. *History of the American Graves Registration Service: QMC in Europe*, vol. 1, 71.

73. *History of the American Graves Registration Service: QMC in Europe*, vol. 1, 143–45.

74. Steere and Boardman, *Final Disposition of World War II Dead: 1945–51*, 344.

75. Steere and Boardman, *Final Disposition of World War II Dead: 1945–51*, 525.

76. This information has been obtained from the author's interviews with numerous officials at various locations: Landstuhl, Germany; Dover AFB, Delaware; and Baghdad, Iraq, to name a few, and is generally available to the public in a wide variety of sources. Thus, no specific cite to a written reference is given.

77. *History of the American Graves Registration Service: QMC in Europe*, vol. 3, 88.

78. *History of the American Graves Registration Service: QMC in Europe*, vol. 1, 205.

79. Steere and Boardman, *Final Disposition of World War II Dead: 1945–51*, 37–38.

80. Steere and Boardman, *Final Disposition of World War II Dead: 1945–51*, 523.

81. Steere and Boardman, *Final Disposition of World War II Dead: 1945–51*, 352–53.

82. Steere and Boardman, *Final Disposition of World War II Dead: 1945–51*, 303–304.

83. *History of the American Graves Registration Service: QMC in Europe*, vol. 1, 74–75.

84. *History of the American Graves Registration Service: QMC in Europe*, vol. 1, 161–80.

85. Steere and Boardman, *Final Disposition of World War II Dead: 1945–51*, 253.

86. *History of the American Graves Registration Service: QMC in Europe*, vol. 3, 17.

87. *History of the American Graves Registration Service: QMC in Europe*, vol. 1, 193.

88. *History of the American Graves Registration Service: QMC in Europe*, vol. 3, 103–108.

89. Steere and Boardman, *Final Disposition of World War II Dead: 1945–51*, 531.

90. *History of the American Graves Registration Service: QMC in Europe*, vol. 3, 111.

91. *History of the American Graves Registration Service: QMC in Europe*, vol. 2, 87–96.

92. Steere and Boardman, *Final Disposition of World War II Dead: 1945–51*, 212.

93. Steere and Boardman, *Final Disposition of World War II Dead: 1945–51*, 353.

94. "Transport Docks With 6,248 Coffins," *The New York Times*, 27 October 1947, front-page section, 3.

95. *History of the American Graves Registration Service: QMC in Europe*, vol. 1, 52–53.

96. Steere and Boardman, *Final Disposition of World War II Dead: 1945–51*, 658–59.

97. Statement by P. H. Hershey, Supervising Embalmer, 7 April 1920, National Archives and Records Administration, College Park, MD, Record Group 92.

98. Letter from Lt. Col. R. P. Harbold, Infantry, to Maj. L. A. Shipman, Zone Commander, 8 April 1920, National Archives and Records Administration, College Park, MD, Record Group 92.

99. Sworn statements taken by Col. H. K. Taylor, IGD, Assistant Port Inspector, 1 May–4 May 1920, National Archives and Records Administration, College Park, MD, Record Group 92.

100. Letter from Col. H. K. Taylor, IGD, Assistant Port Inspector, to the Port Commander, Port of Embarkation, Hoboken, New Jersey, 7 May 1920, National Archives and Records Administration, College Park, MD, Record Group 92.

101. Letter from Lt. Col. H. F. Rethers, QMC, to the Quartermaster General, Washington, DC, 7 June 1920, National Archives and Records Administration, College Park, MD, Record Group 92.

102. Emmitt S. "Bud" Minor, Technical Sergeant (retired), telephone interview by author, 24 September 2002.

103. Steere and Boardman, *Final Disposition of World War II Dead: 1945–51*, 663–68.

104. Letter from Frank J. Mitchell, Bridgeport, Connecticut, to the Adjutant General, U.S. Army, Washington, DC, 4 July 1921; letter from Col. George H. Penrose, U.S. Army, Chief, Cemeterial Division, to Frank J. Mitchell, 8 August 1921; letter from Frank J. Mitchell to Col. George H. Penrose, U.S. Army, Chief, Cemeterial Division, 10 August 1921; letter from Col. George H. Penrose, U.S. Army, Chief, Cemeterial Division, to Frank J. Mitchell, 12 August 1921. (All letters held at the National Archives and Records Administration, College Park, MD, Record Group 92.)

105. Letter from Harry B. Reid to Hon. John W. Weeks, Secretary of War, Washington, DC, 7 September 1921, National Archives and Records Administration, College Park, MD, Record Group 92.

106. Letter from Col. George H. Penrose, QMC, Chief, Cemeterial Division, to Harry B. Reid, 13 September 1921, National Archives and Records Administration, College Park, MD, Record Group 92.

107. Letter from Harry B. Reid to Col. George H. Penrose, QMC, Chief, Cemeterial Division, 16 September 1921, National Archives and Records Administration, College Park, MD, Record Group 92.

108. Letter from John W. Weeks, Secretary of War, to Harry B. Reid, undated but obviously shortly after 16 September 1921, National Archives and Records Administration, College Park, MD, Record Group 92.

109. Steere and Boardman, *Final Disposition of World War II Dead: 1945–51*, 673.

110. Steere and Boardman, *Final Disposition of World War II Dead: 1945–51*, 676–77.

111. Steere and Boardman, *Final Disposition of World War II Dead: 1945–51*, 680–81.

112. *Technical Instructions*, revised to include 11 November 1918, Graves Registration Service Quartermaster Corps U.S. Army, GRS Bulletin, no. 9-A, 27.

113. *History of the American Graves Registration Service: QMC in Europe*, vol. 1, 9.

114. *History of the American Graves Registration Service: QMC in Europe*, vol. 1, 111.

115. Memorandum from James H. Durbin, Office of the War Department, to Col. Charles C. Pierce, GRS, 19 April 1920, National Archives, Record Group 92.

116. Memorandum from Col. Charles C. Pierce, U.S. Army, Chief, Cemeterial Division, to James H. Durbin, Office of the Secretary of War, 20 April 1920, National Archives, Record Group 92.

117. Steere and Boardman, *Final Disposition of World War II Dead: 1945–51*, 58.

118. "Forty War Dead Are Sent to Homes," *The New York Times*, 23 October 1947, 28.

119. Steere, *The Graves Registration Service in World War II*, 64–66.

120. *History of the American Graves Registration Service: QMC in Europe*, vol. 1, 106–109.

121. *History of the American Graves Registration Service: QMC in Europe*, vol. 2, 26.

122. *History of the American Graves Registration Service: QMC in Europe*, vol. 1, 108.

123. "Tell Me About My Boy," Introduction.

124. Summary prepared by Lt. Gen. E. B. Gregory, Quartermaster General, "Procedures of World War I and II in Repatriating the Dead," 1 December 1945, National Archives and Records Administration, College Park, MD, Record Group 92, 3.

125. Steere and Boardman, *Final Disposition of World War II Dead: 1945–51*, 651.

126. Steere and Boardman, *Final Disposition of World War II Dead: 1945–51*, 690.

127. Larry Greer, Director of Public Affairs, Defense Prisoner of War/Missing Personnel Office (DPMO), personal interview by author, Washington, DC, 17 April 2002.

128. *History of the American Graves Registration Service: QMC in Europe*, vol. 1, 4.

129. *History of the American Graves Registration Service: QMC in Europe*, vol. 3, 14.

6. BURIAL

1. Edward Steere and Thayer M. Boardman, *Final Disposition of World War II Dead: 1945–51*, QMC Historical Studies, series 2, no. 4 (Washington, DC: Historical Branch Office of the Quartermaster General, 1957), 325–26.

2. *Historical Report of the Chief Quartermaster, AEF: 1917–1919*, National Archives and Records Administration, College Park, MD, Record Group 92, chap. 9, 422. (This report is a rough draft of the activities of the QMC in Europe during and after World War I.)

3. *History of the American Graves Registration Service: QMC in Europe*, vol. 1 (Washington, DC: The Library Office of the Quartermaster General), 5. (This is a three-volume typescript, an official history prepared by the Cemeterial Division, OQMG.)

4. Letter from Lt. Col. W. V. L. Applin, British Military Mission, to Capt. H. R. Lemly, USA, Cemeterial Branch, War Department, 10 December 1917, National Archives and Records Administration, College Park, MD, Record Group 92.

5. Edward Steere, *The Graves Registration Service in World War II*, QMC Historical Studies, no. 21 (Washington, DC: United States Government Printing Office, 1951), 17.

6. Ibid., 24.

7. Ibid., 20.

8. Ibid., 46.

9. Ibid., 53.

10. Ibid., 32–33.

11. Ibid., 45.

12. Cpl. Stanley Entman, telephone interview by author, 3 October 2002.

13. Steere, *The Graves Registration Service in World War II*, 161.

14. *Joint Pub 4–06: Joint Tactics, Techniques, and Procedure for Mortuary Affairs in Joint Operations* (no publisher listed; available on military Web sites), 28 August 1996, C-2.

15. Steere, *The Graves Registration Service in World War II*, 98–102.

16. Steere, *The Graves Registration Service in World War II*, 79.

17. Steere, *The Graves Registration Service in World War II*, 80–83.

18. Unpublished white paper, "Graves Registration Activities in the Korean War" (Quartermaster Historian's Office, Fort Lee, VA, 1954, photocopy), 61–62.

19. *Joint Pub 4–06*, C-1 and D-14.

20. Steere and Boardman, *Final Disposition of World War II Dead: 1945–51*, 280.

21. *History of the American Graves Registration Service: QMC in Europe*, vol. 1, 47.

22. *History of the American Graves Registration Service: QMC in Europe*, vol. 1, 26.

23. *History of the American Graves Registration Service: QMC in Europe*, vol. 1, 48.

24. *History of the American Graves Registration Service: QMC in Europe*, vol. 1, 138–51.

25. *History of the American Graves Registration Service: QMC in Europe*, vol. 2, 40–45.

26. *History of the American Graves Registration Service: QMC in Europe*, vol. 3, 102.

27. Steere and Boardman, *Final Disposition of World War II Dead: 1945–51*, 280.

28. Sgt. Robert Vorisek, telephone interview by author, 13 November 2002.

29. *History of the American Graves Registration Service: QMC in Europe*, vol. 1, 132.

30. *History of the American Graves Registration Service: QMC in Europe*, vol. 1, 27.

31. *History of the American Graves Registration Service: QMC in Europe*, vol. 1, 48–49.

32. Letter from C. W. Bailey to Lt. Col. Charles C. Pierce, QMC, American Expeditionary Forces, Graves Registration Service, Europe, 5 March 1919, National Archives and Records Administration, College Park, MD, Record Group 92.

33. Steere, *The Graves Registration Service in World War II*, 162.

34. Steere, *The Graves Registration Service in World War II*150–51.

35. Steere, *The Graves Registration Service in World War II*, 191.

36. Steere, *The Graves Registration Service in World War II*, 193.

37. Steere and Boardman, *Final Disposition of World War II Dead: 1945–51*, 395–401.

38. Steere and Boardman, *Final Disposition of World War II Dead: 1945–51*, 442.

39. Steere, *The Graves Registration Service in World War II*, 115.

40. Unpublished white paper, "Graves Registration Activities in the Korean War," 5–14.

41. Unpublished white paper, "Graves Registration Activities in the Korean War," 67–69.

42. Steere, *The Graves Registration Service in World War II*, 3.

43. Steere, *The Graves Registration Service in World War II*, 7.

44. Steere, *The Graves Registration Service in World War II*, 8.

45. Steere, *The Graves Registration Service in World War II*, 8.

46. G. Kurt Piehler, *Remembering War the American Way* (Washington, DC: Smithsonian Institution Press, 1995), 51.

47. Ibid., 50.

48. Ibid., 51.

49. Letter from Hanford MacNider, Assistant Secretary of War, to H. D. Wilson of Ruston, Louisiana, 20 January 1927, National Archives and Records Administration, College Park, MD, Record Group 92.

50. Letter from Sedgwick Women's Relief Corps No. 17, Department of California and Nevada, Santa Ana, California, to W. F. Kellogg, Secretary of State, 20 December 1928, National Archives and Records Administration, College Park, MD, Record Group 92.

51. Public law no. 810, 70th Congress, H. R. 10304, National Archives and Records Administration, College Park, MD, Record Group 92.

52. Piehler, *Remembering War the American Way*, 6.

53. Piehler, *Remembering War the American Way*, 130.

54. Piehler, *Remembering War the American Way*, 96.

55. *History of the American Graves Registration Service: QMC in Europe*, vol. 1, 114–15.

56. *History of the American Graves Registration Service: QMC in Europe*, vol. 1, 113.

57. Piehler, *Remembering War the American Way*, 132.

58. *History of the American Graves Registration Service: QMC in Europe*, vol. 2, 38–39.

59. *History of the American Graves Registration Service: QMC in Europe*, vol. 2, 35.

60. *History of the American Graves Registration Service: QMC in Europe*, vol. 2, 47–61.

61. Steere, *The Graves Registration Service in World War II*, , 9.

62. Letter from John W. Weeks, Secretary of War, to Mrs. John Francis Yawger, Recording Secretary General, NSDAR, Washington, DC, 23 June 1921, National Archives and Records Administration, College Park, MD, Record Group 92.

63. Letter from Mrs. Frederic W. Bentley, member of the American Battle Monuments Commission, to Dwight F. Davis, Secretary of War, 12 November 1925, National Archives and Records Administration, College Park, MD, Record Group 92.

64. Memorandum from R. P. Harbold, Cemeterial Division, to the Quartermaster General, 16 January 1925, National Archives, Record Group 92.

65. Steere and Boardman, *Final Disposition of World War II Dead: 1945–51*, 308.

66. Steere and Boardman, *Final Disposition of World War II Dead: 1945–51*, 307–19.

67. Steere and Boardman, *Final Disposition of World War II Dead: 1945–51*, 601.

68. Steere and Boardman, *Final Disposition of World War II Dead: 1945–51*, 569–72.

69. Steere and Boardman, *Final Disposition of World War II Dead: 1945–51*, 497–506.

70. Quartermaster Foundation, "Tomb of the Unknown Soldiers," *The Quartermaster Review*, January–February 1964, http://www.qmfound.com/tomb_of_the_unknown_soldiers_1964.htm, 3 (12 April 2001).

71. Steere and Boardman, *Final Disposition of World War II Dead: 1945–51*, 510–15.

72. American Battle Monuments Commission, World War II Casualties, http://www.abmc.gov/abmc45.htm (10 October 2002). Punchbowl figures derived from "Cemetery History & Map of Punchbowl," http://acresofhonor.com/history.html (27 October 2002).

73. *History of the American Graves Registration Service: QMC in Europe*, vol. 2, 117–18.

74. "This Week in Quartermaster History: 11–17 November," compiled by Dr. Steven Anders, U.S. Army Quartermaster Corps Historian, http://www.qmmuseum.lee.army.mil/historyweek/nov11–17.htm (2 February 2001).

75. *History of the American Graves Registration Service: QMC in Europe*, vol. 2, 121–27.

76. Quartermaster Foundation, "Tomb of the Unknown Soldiers," *The Quartermaster Review*, September–October 1963, http://www.qmfound.com/tomb_of_the_unknown_soldiers.htm (8 October 2002).

77. Piehler, *Remembering War the American Way*, 122.

78. Quartermaster Foundation, "Tomb of the Unknown Soldiers," *The Quartermaster Review*, January–February 1964, http://www.qmfound.com/tomb_of_the_unknown_soldiers_1964.htm, 2–8 (12 April 2001).

79. Department of the Navy, Naval Historical Center home page, "Frequently Asked Questions," http://www.history.navy.mil/faqs/faq85–1.htm.

80. *Joint Pub 4–06*, III-2.

81. U.S. Navy, "United States Navy Mortuary Affairs Burial at Sea Program," http://chinfo.navy.mil/navpalib/questions/burial.html (1 October 2002).

82. James P. Delgado, Maritime Preservation Program, "Chapter VI: Significance: Memorials, Myths and Symbols," *USS Arizona Memorial*, ed. Daniel J. Lenihan, Submerged Cultural Resources Unit, http://www.nps.gov/usar/scrs/scrs6c.htm, 3 (20 April 2003).

83. Dr. Valerie Curtis and Dr. Adam Biran, "Dirt, Disgust, and Disease: Is Hygiene in Our Genes?" *Perspective in Biology and Medicine*, http://muse.jhu.edu/journals/perspectives_in_biology_and_medicine/v044/44.1curtis.html, 1–3 (12 November 2002).

84. *History of the American Graves Registration Service: QMC in Europe*, vol. 2, 151.

85. *History of the American Graves Registration Service: QMC in Europe*, vol. 3, 113.

86. *History of the American Graves Registration Service: QMC in Europe*, vol. 1, 25.

87. Letter from Lt. Col. James V. Hunt, QMC, Assistant, to Hon. James M. Mead, U.S. Senate, 1 September 1945, National Archives and Records Administration, College Park, MD, Record Group 92.

88. *History of the American Graves Registration Service: QMC in Europe*, vol. 2, 152–53.

89. Steere, *The Graves Registration Service in World War II*, 185–86.

90. James C. Lee, "The Humble Undertaker Performed a Distasteful but All Too Necessary Role During the Civil War," *America's Civil War*, http://thehistorynet.com/AmericasCivilWar/articles/11962_text.htm.

91. Steere, *The Graves Registration Service in World War II*, 11.

92. *History of the American Graves Registration Service: QMC in Europe*, vol. 3, 104.

93. "Transport Docks with 6,248 Coffins," *The New York Times*, 27 October 1947, front-page section, 3.

94. Army Regulation 638–2, *Care and Disposition of Remains and Disposition of Personal Effects*, chap. 8, par. 8–12, 46.

95. Dr. Craig Mallak, CDR, MC, USN, Chairperson, Office of the Armed Forces Medical Examiner, telephone interview by author, 11 March 2004.

96. Unpublished white paper, "Graves Registration Activities in the Korean War,"123–25.

97. Tom Dowling, "The Graves We Dug," *Army* (January 1989): 39.

98. Gordon Johnson, "Their Duty to the Dead," *The Press-Enterprise*, San Diego, CA, 25 May 1997, 2D.

99. *History of the American Graves Registration Service: QMC in Europe*, vol. 1, 35.

100. Letter from Russell F. Enger, Sales Manager, Acacia Memorial Park, Mendota, Minnesota, to Sen. Henric[k] Shipstead, 23 March 1944; letter from Sen. Henrik Shipstead to Robert P. Patterson, Under Secretary of War, 27 March 1944; letter by R. P. Harbold, Memorial Division, OQMC, to Congressional Section, G.A.S. Division, 29 March 1944; letter from Robert P. Patterson to Sen. Henrik Shipstead, 4 April 1944. (All letters held at the National Archives and Records Administration, College Park, MD, Record Group 92.)

101. Karen Giles, Director of Mortuary Affairs, Dover Air Force Base, personal interview by author, 9 March 2004.

102. Steere, *The Graves Registration Service in World War II*, 28.

103. Sgt. Herbert E. Hackett, telephone interview by author, 3 October 2002.

104. Tommy D. Bourlier, Director of the U.S. Army Mortuary Affairs, personal interview by author, Fort Lee, VA, 25 June 2001.

105. Douglas L. Howard, Deputy Director of the U.S. Army Mortuary Affairs, personal interview by author, Fort Lee, VA, 25 June 2001.

106. Steere, *The Graves Registration Service in World War II*, 28.

107. Harry E. Mullendore, 3rd Platoon, Europe, 1944–1945, "The Way It Was: Memoirs of My Experiences in the 607th Graves Registration Company in the United States Army During World War II," unpublished, 4th edition, 174. (I owe many thanks to Lt. Col. Charles D. [Bud] Butte [retired] for providing me with reams of letters, journals, and photographs of Grave Registration Service personnel.)

108. Randy Wells, "Indiana Veteran Researches Lives of World War II Airmen," *Indiana Gazette*, Indiana, PA, 11 November 1996. (A copy of this article was furnished by Lt. Col. Charles D. [Bud] Butte [retired], personal collections, hereafter referred to as "Butte, Personal Collection." Butte has assembled a large volume of letters, reports, and pictures from Graves Registration Personnel who served in World War II and Korea.)

109. *Joint Pub 4–06*, B-8.

110. Letter from Paul Weiss to the Chief of Army Chaplains, Washington, DC, 15 May 1944, National Archives and Records Administration, College Park, MD, Record Group 92.

111. Unpublished white paper, "Graves Registration Activities in the Korean War," 80.

112. *History of the American Graves Registration Service: QMC in Europe*, vol. 3, photograph between 128 and 129.

113. *History of the American Graves Registration Service: QMC in Europe*, vol. 1, 50.

114. Steere, *The Graves Registration Service in World War II*, 168–70.

115. Steere, 171–77.

116. Steere, *The Graves Registration Service in World War II*, 178.

117. Steere, *The Graves Registration Service in World War II*, 67–71.

118. Thucydides, *The Complete Writings of Thucydides, The Peloponnesian War*, trans Richard Crawley, The Modern Library edition (New York: Random House, 1951), 102.

119. Piehler, *Remembering War the American Way*, 88.

120. *History of the American Graves Registration Service, QMC in Europe*, vol. 1, 127–31.

7. ALL BODIES ARE NOT THE SAME

1. *Joint Pub 4–06: Joint Tactics, Techniques, and Procedures for Mortuary Affairs in Joint Operations* (no publisher listed; available on military Web sites), Executive Summary, Theater Mortuary Affairs Support, vii.

2. *Technical Manual 10–630: Graves Registration* (Washington, DC: War Department, 23 September 1941), sec. 2, par. 12.b., 6–7.

3. Ibid., sec. 4, par. 21.b., 14.

4. *War Department Field Manual 10–63: Graves Registration* (Washington, DC: United States Government Printing Office, January 1945), sec. 3, par. 26, 28.

5. Edgar L. Jones, "One War is Enough," *TheAtlanticonline*, http://www.theatlantic.com/unbound/bookauth/battle/jones.htm (4 April 2004); originally published in the February 1946 issue of *The Atlantic Monthly*.

6. Roscoe C. Blunt Jr., *Foot Soldier: A Combat Infantryman's War in Europe* (Rockeville Center, NY: Sarpedon, 1994), 138, 85.

7. Pfc. Fred Fory, telephone interview by author, February 2002.

8. Marine Lt. Philip Caputo, *A Rumor of War* (1977; reprint, with a postscript by the author, New York: Henry Holt, 1996), 175–79.

9. Anthony Swofford, *Jarhead: A Marine's Chronicle of the Gulf War and Other Battles* (New York: Scribner, 2003), 238–39.

10. Ibid., 253.

11. William Tecumseh Sherman, Letter to James M. Calhoun, mayor of Atlanta and others, 12 September 1864, in *Bartlett's Familiar Quotations*, 16th ed. (Boston: Grolier Enterprises, Inc., by special arrangements with Little, Brown and Company, 1992), 492.

12. Dave Grossman, "Human Factors in War: The Psychology and Physiology of Close Combat," in *The Human Face of Warfare: Killing, Fear and Chaos in Battle*, ed. Michael Evans and Alan Ryan (St. Leonards, New South Wales, Australia: Allen & Unwin, 2000), 18.

13. Paul Fussell, *Doing Battle: The Making of a Skeptic* (Boston: Little, Brown, 1996), 124.

14. Caputo, *A Rumor of War*, 10, 12.

15. Robert Graves, *Good-bye to All That* (1957; reprint, revised with a prologue and an epilogue, New York: Anchor Books, 1998), 237.

16. Capt. Norman Allen, interview by Donald Knox, in *The Korean War: An Oral History, Pusan to Chosin* (New York: Harcourt Brace, 1985), 349.

17. Caputo, *A Rumor of War*, 36.

18. Greg Jaffe, "On a Remote Base, U.S. Drill Sergeants Train Iraqi Exiles," *Wall Street Journal*, 24 February 2003, front-page section, 1.

19. Stephen E. Ambrose, *Band of Brothers: E. Company, 506th Regiment, 101st Airborne from Normandy to Hitler's Eagle's Nest* (1992; reprint, with a foreword by the author, New York: Simon & Schuster, 2001), 27.

20. James Tobin, *Ernie Pyle's War: America's Eyewitness to World War II* (New York: Free Press, 1997), 100.

21. John W. Dower, *War Without Mercy: Race and Power in the Pacific War* (New York: Pantheon, 1986), 83.

22. Ibid., 55.

23. Quoted in ibid., 55.

24. Quoted in Peter Maguire, *Law and War: An American Story* (New York: Columbia University Press, 2000), 43.

25. Ibid., 44.

26. Ibid., 51.

27. Quoted in ibid., 56.

28. Quoted in ibid., 53.

29. Quoted in ibid., 60.

30. Dower, *War Without Mercy*, 10.

31. Caputo, *A Rumor of War*, xix.

32. Dower, *War Without Mercy*, 85.

33. Maguire, *Law and War*, 59.

34. Edward Steere, *The Graves Registration Service in World War II*, QMC Historical Studies, no. 21 (Washington, DC: U.S. Government Printing Office, 1951), 48.

35. E. B. Sledge, *With the Old Breed: At Peleliu and Okinawa* (1981; reprint, New York: Oxford University Press, 1990), 198–99.

36. Ibid., 148.

37. Ibid., 123.

38. Ibid., 196

39. James Bradley with Ron Powers, *Flags of Our Fathers* (New York: Bantam, 2000), 175.

40. Sledge, *With the Old Breed*, 249.

41. Sledge, *With the Old Breed*, 142.

42. Quoted in Maguire, *Law and War*, 61.

43. Steere, *The Graves Registration Service in World War II*, 142.

44. Harry E. Mullendore, 3rd Platoon, Europe, 1944–1945, "The Way It Was: Memoirs of My Experiences in the 607th Graves Registration Company of the United States Army During World War II," unpublished paper, 4th edition, 137.

45. Steere, *The Graves Registration Service in World War II*, 5.

46. Joel Turnipseed, *Baghdad Express: A Gulf War Memoir* (St. Paul, MN: Borealis Books, 2003), 6.

47. Clancy DuBos, "Politics," *Gambit Weekly*, 25 September 2001, http://www.bestofneworleans.com/dispatch/2001–09–25/politics.html (21 April 2004).

48. Graves, *Good-bye to All That*, 129–31.

49. Richard Holmes, *Acts of War: Behavior of Men in Battle* (New York: The Free Press, 1985), 259–60.

50. Grossman, "Human Factors in War," 7.

51. Michael Evans, "Close Combat: Lessons from the Cases of Albert Jacka and Audie Murphy," in *The Human Face of Warfare: Killing, Fear and Chaos in Battle*, ed. Michael Evans and Alan Ryan (St. Leonards, New South Wales, Australia: Allen & Unwin, 2000), 39.

52. Sledge, *With the Old Breed*, 120.

53. Sledge, *With the Old Breed*, 64.

54. Fussell, *Doing Battle*, 123.

55. Caputo, *A Rumor of War*, 96.

56. Evans, "Close Combat: Lessons from the Cases of Albert Jacka and Audie Murphy," 45–49.

57. Charles A. Lindbergh, *The Wartime Journals of Charles A. Lindbergh* (New York: Harcourt Brace Jovanovich, 1970), 834–35.

58. Sherman Richter, interview by Donald Knox, in *The Korean War: An Oral History, Pusan to Chosin* (New York: Harcourt Brace, 1985), 490–91.

59. Jones, "One War is Enough."

60. Homer, *The Iliad*, trans. E. V. Rieu (New York: Penguin, 1981), 407.

61. Lindbergh, *The Wartime Journals*, 919.

62. Caputo, *A Rumor of War*, 125.

63. Swofford, *Jarhead*, 243.

64. Lindbergh, *The Wartime Journals*, 914–15.

65. Andrew Jackson Wade, telephone interview by author, 14 September 2002.

66. Dr. Joanna Bourke, *In the Presence of Mine Enemies: Face-to-Face Killing in Twentieth-Century Warfare*, http://www.ihrinfo.ac.uk/projects/elec/sem21.html, 11 (8 June 2002).

67. Swofford, *Jarhead*, 239.

68. Quoted in Maguire, *Law and War*, 106.

69. Graves, *Good-bye to All That*, vi.

70. Caputo, *A Rumor of War*, 137.

71. Chris Shilling, *The Body and Social Theory* (London: SAGE Publications, 2000), 95–97.

72. Swofford, *Jarhead*, 239.

73. Ambrose, *Band of Brothers*, 206.

74. Sledge, *With the Old Breed*, 123.

75. Anthony Swofford, "Remember the Gulf: Scenes from the Last War with Iraq," *Harper's Magazine* (December 2002):55.

76. Stephen Ambrose, *Citizen Soldiers* (New York: Simon & Schuster, 1997), 21.

77. Sledge, *With the Old Breed*, 308.

78. Lindbergh, *The Wartime Journals*, 998.

79. Jones, "One War is Enough."

8. OPEN WOUNDS

1. John D. Canine, Ed.D., Ph.D., *The Psychosocial Aspects of Death and Dying* (Stamford, CT: Appleton & Lange, 1996), 100.

2. Sally Griffis, telephone interview by author, February 2002.

3. United States Code, Title 10, commonly referred to as "The Missing Persons Act," Department of Defense, Defense Prisoner of War/Missing Personnel Office Web site, §1513, http://www.dtic.mil/dpmo/family/mpa.htm (1 December 2002).

4. Ibid.

5. Department of Defense Instruction, no. 1300.18, Subject: Military Personnel Casualty Matters, Policies, and Procedures, 18 December 2000, sec. E2.1.1.24.

6. Ibid., sec. E2.1.1.22.

7. Amy Waters Yarsinske, *No One Left Behind: The Lieutenant Commander Michael Scott Speicher Story* (New York: Dutton, 2002), 25.

8. Ibid., 41.

9. "Navy Changes Status of Cmdr. Michael Scott Speicher," *Defense POW/MIA Weekly Update*, Department of Defense, Defense Prisoner of War/Missing Personnel Office Web site, 18 January 2001, http://www.dtic.mil/dpmo/wud/2001/010118.htm (5 March 2003).

10. Yarsinske, *No One Left Behind*, 2.

11. Larry Greer, Director of Public Affairs, Defense Prisoner of War/Missing Personnel Office (DPMO), e-mail to author, 14 August 2004.

12. Department of Defense Instruction, no. 1300.18, , sec. E2.1.1.30.

13. Paul D. Mather, *M.I.A.: Accounting for the Missing in Southeast Asia* (Washington, DC: National Defense University Press, 1994), 51–58.

14. "Vietnam-Era Unaccounted-For Statistical Reports," Department of Defense, Defense Prisoner of War/Missing Personnel Office Web site, http://www.dtic.mil/dpmo/pmsea/statistical_reports.htm (13 March 2003).

15. "DPMO FAQ Category: Family Liaison (What are the different pursuit status categories?)," Department of Defense, Defense Prisoner of War/Missing Personnel Office Web site, http://www.dtic.mil/dpmo/faq/faq_family11.htm (13 May 2003).

16. "Joint Task Force—Full Accounting," Joint Task Force—Full Accounting Web site, http://www.pacom.mil/JTFFA/about_JTFFA.htm (27 February 2003).

17. Robert L. Goldich, *POWs and MIAs: Status and Accounting Issues*, CRS Issue Brief for Congress, updated 20 December 2001, Congressional Research Service, The Library of Congress, received through the CRS Web, CRS-8, http://www.fas.org/man/crs/IB92101.pdf (1 March 2003).

18. Ibid.

19. Patricia Louise Wadley, "Even One Is Too Many: An Examination of the Soviet Refusal to Repatriate Liberated American World War II Prisoners of War," Ph.D. diss., Texas Christian University, 1993, chap. 1: Antecedents, http://aiipowmia.com/reports/wadley.html (9 April 2002).

20. Goldich, *POWs and MIAs*.

21. Goldich, *POWs and MIAs*.

22. Goldich, *POWs and MIAs*.

23. *The Effort to Account for U.S. Servicemen Missing from the Korean War* (Washington, DC: Defense Prisoner of War/Missing Personnel Office, 11 November 2000), 16.

24. G. Kurt Piehler, *Remembering War the American Way* (Washington, DC: Smithsonian Institution Press, 1995), 157.

25. Ted Barker, telephone interview by author, 5 May 2003.

26. Goldich, *POWs and MIAs*.

27. Col. Paul Bethke, Commander (former) U.S. Army Central Identification Laboratory Hawaii (CILHI), personal interview by author, Honolulu, Hawaii, 19 November 2002.

28. Ed Moynagh, USAF (retired), telephone interview by author, 3 March 2003.

29. Ginger Couden, Pubic Affairs Spokeswoman, U.S. Army Central Identification Laboratory Hawaii (CILHI), phone call to author, 6 March 2003.

30. *Vietnam's Collection and Repatriation of American Remains* (Washington, DC: Defense Prisoner of War/Missing Personnel Office, June 1999), 2, 3, 20, 27, 34.

31. Mather, *M.I.A*, 125–27.

32. S.Sgt. Sebastian Q. Harris, Public Affairs Officer, U.S. Army Central Identification Laboratory Hawaii (CILHI), e-mail to author, 28 April 2003.

33. Paul M. Cole, *POW/MIA Issues: Volume 1, The Korean War* (Santa Monica, CA: RAND, 1994), 34.

34. Mather, *M.I.A*, 60.

35. Henry Kissinger, quoted in Mather, *M.I.A*, 44–45.

36. Homer, *The Iliad*, trans. E. V. Rieu (New York: Penguin, 1981), 320.

37. *The Effort to Account for U.S. Servicemen Missing from the Korean War*, 31–32.

38. "Department of Defense Policy on Compensation for Return or Information Related to Unaccounted-For Personnel," Department of Defense, Defense Prisoner of War/Missing Personnel Office, 26 August 1999, http://www.dtic.mil/dpmo/faq/policy_09.htm (3 March 2003).

39. Mather, *M.I.A.*, 110–12.

40. Mather, *M.I.A.*, 118.

41. Army Regulation 600–8-1, *Army Casualty Operations/Assistance/Insurance*, chap. 6: "Casualty Assistance Program" (Washington, DC: Department of the Army, 20 October 1994), sec. 2, 6–11: Role of the casualty assistance officer, 48.

42. Ibid., sec. 4, 1–19: Casualty assistance policy, 4.

43. Theresa Buege, widow of Paul G. Buege, USAF (deceased), telephone interview by author, 30 January 2003.

44. Ibid.

45. Ibid.

46. Theresa Buege, unpublished manuscript.

47. Ibid.

48. Ibid.

49. Theresa Buege, telephone interview by author, 30 January 2003.

50. Theresa Buege, e-mail to author, 6 April 2004.

51. Paul D. Sledzik, Anthropologist and Curator of the National Museum of Health and Medicine Museum, Armed Forces Institute of Pathology, personal interview by author, 8 August 2003.

52. Theresa Buege, telephone interview by author, 30 January 2003.

53. Ibid.

54. Patricia B. Sutker, et al., "Psychopathology in War-Zone Deployed and Nondeployed Operation Desert Storm Troops Assigned Graves Registration Duties," *Journal of Abnormal Psychology* 103 (2) (1994): 387.

55. Ibid., 388.

56. Grant N. Marshall, Lois M. Davis, and Cathy D. Sherbourne, *A Review of the Scientific Literature as It Pertains to the Gulf War Illnesses*, vol. 4: "Stress," Rand Publication Database, chap. 5: "Gulf War Scientific Literature Linking Stress to Health Problems," http://www.rand.org/publications/MR/MR1018.4.1/, 63 (4 June 2002).

57. Cpl. Richard Oliver (discharged), telephone interview by author, 22 July 2001.

58. Paul T. Bartone, Ph.D., et al., "The Impact of a Military Air Disaster on the Health of Assistance Workers," *The Journals of Nervous and Mental Disease* 177 (6) (June 1989): 318.

59. Ibid., 320.

60. Ibid., 323–24.

61. Army Regulation 600–8-1, *Army Casualty Operations/Assistance/Insurance*, chap. 4: "Casualty Notification" (Washington, DC: Department of the Army, 20 October 1994), sec. 2, 4–13: Do's and don'ts for making personal notification, 35.

62. James E. McCarroll, Ph.D., et al., "Anticipatory Stress of Handling Human Remains from the Persian Gulf War," *The Journal of Nervous and Mental Disease* 183 (11): 700.

63. Lt. Colonel Kevin Mulligan, Commander, 436th Medical Operations Squadron, personal interview by author, Dover Air Force Base, 6 August 2003.

64. Air Force Instruction 44–153, 1 July 1999, Section 4. Critical Incident Stress Debriefings, Defusings, Demobilizations, 7.

65. Lt. Colonel Alan L. Peterson, Guarantor, "Psychological Intervention with Mortuary Workers after the September 11 Attack: The Dover Behavioral Health Consultant Model," *Military Medicine* 167, Supplement, 4 (83) (2002): 83, 85.

66. Ibid., 85.

67. James Tobin, *Ernie Pyle's War: America's Eyewitness to World War II* (New York: The Free Press, 1997), 4.

68. Andrew Jackson Wade, telephone interview by author, 14 September 2002.

69. Elizabeth Kolbert, "The Calculator: How Kenneth Feinberg Determines the Value of Three Thousand Lives," *The New Yorker* (25 November 2002):46.

[*Index*]

Note: Page numbers in **boldface** type indicate photographs in the text.

"Tell Me About My Boy" brochure, 132, 142, 174–75
and Tomb of the Unknowns controversy, 127–29
See also international relations
Poole, Charles, 177
Portugal, 162
possession of Soldier Dead, 29
authority over returns, 135–47, 172
conflicts among family members, 141–42
the dead as bargaining chips, 149, 159, 276–79
in *The Iliad*, 20–21, 30, 44–45
and Iraq War, 27
and Japanese control of the Philippines, 185–86
and media ban on access to the dead, 178
and seesaw battles of the Korean War, 40–41, 190, 199
and Somalia, 26
See also international relations; next of kin
postcombat recovery, 50–61
Civil War, 51
combat/postcombat recovery distinction blurred, 51, 57, 58
dangers of, 31
defined, 31
Gulf War, 60–61
Iraq War, 61
Korean War, 57
nighttime removal of the dead from medical units, 56
phases of, 51
soldiers assigned to collect remains from units other than their own, 38–39, 52–53
Vietnam War, 58–60
WWII, 51, 51–56
See also area clearance recovery; historical recovery; noncombat recovery; return of Soldier Dead
post-traumatic stress disorder (PTSD), 61, 223, 299
"psychiatric casualties" in WWII, 255
stress on mortuary workers in advance of casualties, 290
and unseen casualties, 287–88
POWs, 273–82
in China, 77
Cold War aviators, 277

and distrust of government, 294
in Korea, 276–77, 279
and MIA status, 272
and misidentification of remains, 125
and national wounds, 293
in the Philippines, 186
records kept by, 186
in Russia, 275–76
in Vietnam, 82, 274–75
In the Presence of Mine Enemies: Face-to-Face Killing in Twentieth-Century Warfare (Bourke), 260
Presumptive Finding of Death (PFOD), 272–73
Prevost, Habibah, 62–63, 94
Propaganda Team, 69–70, **70**
prostitutes, smuggled in body bags, 296
psychological issues
abuse of Iraqi prisoners, 243, 262
and casualty notification/assistance officers, 288–89
combat stress/acclimation, 255–58, 290–91
dehumanization of the enemy during training and combat, 244–46
and "dominating body" concept, 261
envy of the dead, 259
French woman's devoted care for American grave, 194–95
and missing dead, 269–70, 273
national wounds, 292–94
and notification of death, 282–86
objections to leaving the dead in foreign/hostile soil, 140–41, 176, 198–99
overseas graves as emissaries to host countries, 202–3, 298
and personal effects, 225, 228–30
post-traumatic stress disorder, 61, 223, 255, 287–88, 290, 299
pre-exposure training for mortuary workers, 290
"psychiatric casualties" in WWII, 255
psychological components of handling remains, 61, 215–17, 223, 228
"pursuit syndrome," 257
racial/cultural prejudice, 246–54
sanitization of death by killing at a distance, 257, 300
soldiers' difficulties in retrieving remains of their friends, 38, 51–52